The Protection of Religious Personnel in Armed Conflict

ADNOTATIONES IN IUS CANONICUM

Hrsg. von Elmar Güthoff und Karl-Heinz Selge

Band 32

PETER LANG

Frankfurt am Main · Berlin · Bern · Bruxelles · New York · Oxford · Wien

Stefan Lunze

THE PROTECTION OF RELIGIOUS PERSONNEL IN ARMED CONFLICT

PETER LANG
Europäischer Verlag der Wissenschaften

Bibliographic Information published by Die Deutsche Bibliothek
Die Deutsche Bibliothek lists this publication in the Deutsche Nationalbibliografie; detailed bibliographic data is available in the internet at <http://dnb.ddb.de>.

ISSN 0946-9176
ISBN 3-631-52272-X
US-ISBN 0-8204-6577-1

www.peterlang.de

In the evening of March 19th, 2003, my nephew and godson Niklas D. Lunze was born. In the following night that brought death and sorrow for many families in Iraq, his life brought light to our family. This book is dedicated to Niklas. The light of faith shines for many in moments of darkness and deserves the creation of a protected sphere – just as he does.

Acknowledgements

This book bases to a large extend on my licentiate thesis at the Faculty of Canon Law of the Catholic University Leuven. The three years of studies in Flanders were a formative influence and gave me the confidence to address questions in the context of war and peace. I owe my most sincere gratitude to the promoter of the original thesis, Prof. Dr. Silvio Ferrari from the Institute of International Law of the State University Milan (Italy) who granted me with the freedom that allowed me to explore own ideas on the issue while at the same time providing me with indispensable guidance in order to assure the quality of this project. I additionally thank Prof. Dr. Rik Torfs, Lic. not. and Reverend Prof. Dr. Luc De Fleurquin, S.T.L., Lic. not. for their valuable feedback as correctors of the thesis.

This book would not have been possible without the privilege to make use of very fine research facilities, namely the International Institute of Humanitarian Law (San Remo), the Institute for Theology and Peace (Barsbüttel), the library of the Catholic Military Bishop's Office (Berlin) and – last but not at all least – the Institute of Canon Law at Potsdam University. The humanitarian spirit of the building in which the latter Institute is housed goes back into the days of its construction as headquarters of the German Red Cross and proved to give helpful inspiration. I furthermore express my appreciation to those scholars who made themselves available and sacrificed time to discuss ideas and exchange views. I would like to particularly mention Comm. Prof. Dr. Giorgio Filibeck, Dr. Heinz-Gerhard Justenhoven, Prof. Dr. Eulogi Broto Alonso, J.C.L., Dr. Stefan Gatzhammer, M.A., Ass. iur. Peggy Wittke, LWissDir i. K. Harald Oberhem, Gregory Townsend, J.D., M.A., D.E.S., Ass. iur. Ralph Czarnecki, LL.M. and Dott. Annalisa Creta, E.MA.

I am thankful for the continuous interest in the development of this book and the tireless support they provided me with at all stages of the work: First and foremost to my family, the most important pillar of my life, specially to my brothers, my parents and my aunts, to the *commilitones* in Leuven and also to my friends. Among the latter, I particularly thank Dipl.-Jur. Hartmut Rank, Antoinette Pas, M.A., cand. iur. Holger Rentel, Antje Sydow, B.Eng., M.Sc., stud. theol. & phil. Elisa Mileta and Reverend Ewald Beha who each in his or her own way contributed to creating and maintaining what could be considered a constructive atmosphere of intellectual agility.

I am finally grateful to the editors of the series Adnotationes in ius canonicum, Prof. Dr. Dr. Elmar Güthoff and Dr. habil. Karl-Heinz Selge, for their mentoring and for offering me the opportunity to publish this monograph.

Foreword

Eichstätt, im August 2003

Wenn sich ein Berliner Student der Rechte mit dem Schutz von Seelsorgepersonal in bewaffneten Konflikten befasst, findet dies natürlich meine besondere Aufmerksamkeit als Katholischer Militärbischof für die Deutsche Bundeswehr mit Sitz seiner Kurie in Berlin. Mit dem Umzug meiner Kurie nach Berlin sind auch die jahrzehntelang unterbrochenen Verbindungen zwischen dieser Stadt und der Militärseelsorge wieder aufgenommen. Dies gilt im besonderen für die Beziehung der Militärseelsorge zum katholischen Leben in der Hauptstadt, die durch diese akademische Arbeit bereichert werden sollte.

Der Schutz von Seelsorgepersonal in bewaffneten Konflikten fällt in erster Linie in den Bereich von Abkommen zwischen Staaten, die die Bedeutung dieses Schutzes anerkannt haben. Durch die vielfältigen Aktivitäten des Heiligen Stuhls übernimmt aber auch die Katholische Kirche auf internationaler Ebene Verantwortung für den Schutz von Seelsorgepersonal. In Stellungnahmen haben die katholischen Bischöfe in Deutschland und ich immer wieder auf das sittliche Gebot des Respekts für das humanitäre Völkerrecht hingewiesen. All diese Anstrengungen sind in eine umfassende Friedenslehre der Kirche eingebettet, die in diesem Jahr besonders auf den 40. Jahrestag der Enzyklika „Pacem in Terris" von Papst Johannes XXIII. Bezug nimmt.

Die Umstrukturierung der Bundeswehr zu Streitkräften im Einsatz ist für die Militärseelsorge mit zahlreichen Veränderungen verbunden. Herausforderungen begegnen dabei insbesondere die Militärseelsorger, die deutsche Kontingente auf Auslandseinsätzen begleiten und dort eine besondere pastorale Situation vorfinden. Innerhalb der von der Religionsfreiheit eröffneten Freiräumen geben sie ein glaubwürdiges und aufrichtiges Zeugnis der christlichen Liebe ab. Bei dieser Entwicklung ist mir die Sicherheit der Militärseelsorger im Einsatz immer ein Anliegen von besonderer Bedeutung. Deshalb bin ich dankbar, dass diese Bemühungen auch von wissenschaftlicher Seite begleitet werden. Die vorliegende Arbeit verbindet die Interessen ihres Verfassers für das kanonische und das internationale Recht und vertieft bei ihren Untersuchungen auch die spezifische Situation der Katholischen Militärseelsorge in den Streitkräften der Bundesrepublik Deutschland. Insofern stellt diese Arbeit einen wichtigen Beitrag zur Sicherung der Rahmenbedingung für den Dienst der Kirche unter den Soldaten dar.

Die Genfer Konventionen lassen keinen Zweifel daran, dass die Verbreitung ihrer Inhalte unbedingte Voraussetzung für eine erfolgreiche Anwendung des humanitären Völkerrechts ist. Deshalb wünsche ich dem Thema des Schutzes von Seelsorgepersonal in bewaffneten Konflikten und der ihm gewidmeten Arbeit die Verbreitung und die Aufmerksamkeit, die sie verdienen.

+ Dr. Walter Mixa, Bischof von Eichstätt
Katholischer Militärbischof für die Deutsche Bundeswehr

Table of content

Acknowledgements	**VII**
Foreword	**IX**
List of Abbreviations	**XIV**
I. Introduction into the environment of the topic	**1**
II. Where does protection come from? - The History	**4**
1. Protection in ancient times	*4*
2. Protection of clergy in the era of classic canon law	*6*
a. The notion of just war and its practice	6
b. Clergy banned from war	8
c. The local and temporal Treuga Dei	10
3. At the threshold to modern times	*12*
4. On the path to the present order	*14*
a. The rise of the state in Europe	14
b. Protection for religious ministers by the state	16
III. Protection in early legal instrument	**18**
1. The Red Cross Convention (1864)	*20*
2. The Hague Conventions (1899/1907)	*21*
3. Revisions of the Red Cross Convention (1906/1929)	*23*
IV. Military chaplaincy and its protection in the catholic church	**25**
1. The Holy See and the Red Cross Movement	*25*
2. International Humanitarian Law and church doctrine	*30*
a. Bellum iustum revisited	30
b. Teaching of the church on international humanitarian law	33
c. Attempting an evaluation	37
3. Military chaplaincy and the church	*39*
a. The teaching office on military chaplaincy	39
b. Military chaplaincy in canon law	41

V. Military chaplaincy in Germany and the environment of foreign deployment **46**

1. A historic outline of military chaplaincy *47*

2 The legal regime for military chaplaincy *48*

3. Exemption of clergy from military service – another source of protection *55*

4. Company abroad - chaplains on missions *58*
a. Pastoral challenges during deployment 61
b. The role of chaplains in peace-keeping and humanitarian operations 65

VI. Protection of religious personnel - the contemporary legal regime **69**

1. The Geneva Conventions of 1949 *69*
a. Terminology 71
b. Stipulations in GC I of general nature 73
c. Means of protection 77
d. Retention of chaplains in GC I 81
e. Ministry to prisoners of war in GC III 86
f. Naval warfare regulations in GC II 93
g. Chaplains as protected persons 94

2. Additional Protocol I of 1977 *97*

3. Religious personnel in non-international armed conflict *102*

VII. The protection of civilian ministry **106**

1. Civilian ministry in armed conflicts *106*

2. Protection of civilian ministry in GC IV *110*

3. Protection of Places of worship *114*

4. Convergence of protection of religious personnel and civilian ministers *125*
a. The limits of the attachment criterion 127
b. Coherence from the facts in times of WMD 128
c. The option of a uniform level of protection 129

VIII. Protection of religious personnel – some problems in the German context **130**

1. The German national status of chaplains and protection in IHL *130*
a. Compatibility of the German model with IHL 130
b. Attachment and exclusivity in national law – a public law relationship? 132
c. Auxiliary religious personnel in Germany – the attachment criterion 135
d. Part-time religious personnel in Germany – the exclusivity criterion 140

2. The use of arms by chaplains *141*

3. Chaplaincy to atheists? *144*

IX. Spiritual assistance in the 21st century – Global challenges **153**

1. Religious personnel as IHL violators *153*

2. Ministry to Guantanamo detainees *157*

3. Religious ministers as instigators *165*

X. Conclusions **169**

Appendix **175**

I. Means of Protection *175*
a. Distinctive Emblems 175
b. Armlet of German Military chaplains 175

II. Identity Cards *176*

III. Shoulder boards used by Bundeswehr chaplaincy *178*

Bibliography **179**

Abstracts **205**

Index and Norms **211**

Footnotes in this monograph follow the Harvard Bluebook of Citation, 17th edition.

All internet references are as of February 21st, 2004.

List of Abbreviations

CHR	UN Commission on Human Rights
FAR	Rwandan Armed Forces
GC I	Convention (I) for the Amelioration of the Condition of the Wounded and Sick in Armed Forces in the Field. Geneva, August 12th, 1949.
GC II	Convention (II) for the Amelioration of the Condition of Wounded, Sick and Shipwrecked Members of Armed Forces at Sea. Geneva, August 12th, 1949.
GC III	Convention (III) relative to the Treatment of Prisoners of War. Geneva, August 12th, 1949.
GC IV	Convention (IV) relative to the Protection of Civilian Persons in Time of War. Geneva, August 12th, 1949.
HC	Convention for the Protection of Cultural Property in the Event of Armed Conflict. The Hague, May 14th, 1954.
ICC	International Criminal Court
ICCPR	International Covenant on Civil and Political Rights
ICRC	International Committee of the Red Cross
ICTR	International Criminal Tribunal for Rwanda
IDF	Israeli Defence Forces
JTF GTMO	Joint Task Force Guantanamo
KSK	Kommando Spezialkräfte (Special Forces Commando)
OEF	Operation Enduring Freedom
PA I	Protocol Additional to the Geneva Conventions of August 12th, 1949, and relating to the Protection of Victims of International Armed Conflicts (Protocol I), June 8th, 1977.
PA II	Protocol Additional to the Geneva Conventions of August 12th, 1949, and relating to the Protection of Victims of Non-International Armed Conflicts (Protocol II), June 8th, 1977.
POW	Prisoners of War
RPF	Rwandan Patriotic Front
SMC	Apostolic Constitution *Spirituali Militum Curae,* April 21st, 1986.
WMD	Weapons of Mass Destructions
UCMJ	Uniform Code of Military Justice

I. Introduction into the environment of the topic

Etsi deus non daretur[1] - a law valid "even if God does not exist": This is how the Dutchman HUGO GROTIUS envisions international law in the *prolegomena* to his groundbreaking work *De iure belli ac pacis.* He did so in the shine of enlightenment in order to accentuate the natural law aspect of his teachings without personally questioning the existence of a divine being. GROTIUS's thought might appear attractive to many contemporaries of our societies that some consider having reached a post-religious phase.[2] But even nowadays, there are attempts to reconcile religion with the *etsi deus non daretur*: In the context of his methodical atheism, the protestant theologian DIETRICH BONHOEFFER tried to interpret the suffering and seemingly powerless Christ on the cross with the hypothetical of a god-forsaken world as an expression of divine affection and presence.[3] The Christian then may not flight from but has to turn to the world.[4] Accordingly, the community of faithful is not freed from action but faced with responsibility to be with men even in times of darkness, of violence and of war.

Recurring to considerations as the aforementioned, the personnel of various religions try to meet the needs of those women and men living in the conflict zones of a world far from being peaceful. And yet, armed conflict as the environment for this service has an impact.[5] Still in our days, religious groups are not always allowed to practice their religion and therefore profoundly affected in their religious identity and in the physical integrity of their ministers: The latter are occasionally targeted on purpose[6] and exposed to special dangers even after the world saw the end of the cold war and after the threshold to the new millennium has been passed. But a state of war does not suspend all rules of

---

[1] *See* 2 HUGO GROTIUS, DE JURE BELLI AC PACIS, THE TRANSLATION, at 13 (photo. reprint Hein 1995) (1925).

[2] *See* Heinz Zahrnt, *Einführungs-Essay*, in 37 CHRISTLICHER GLAUBE IN MODERNER GESELLSCHAFT 15, 18-19 (Franz Böckle et al. eds. 1984).

[3] *See* DIETRICH BONHOEFFER, LETTERS AND PAPERS FROM PRISON 360 (1971), *see also* TRYGVE WYLLER, GLAUBE UND AUTONOME WELT 19-21 (1998) (for the devided discussion on Bonhoeffer's thought and about what he "really meant" in his approach to secularization that is ongoing and currently raises more questions than gives answers).

[4] Peter Selby, *Christianity in a World Come of Age, in* THE CAMBRIDGE COMPANION TO DIETRICH BONHOEFFER 226, 240 (John W. de Gruchy ed. 1999).

[5] *See* 'GULF SYNDROME' FORCES VICAR'S RETIREMENT (BBC news item October 30th, 2002), *available at* http://news.bbc.co.uk/1/hi/england/2374675.stm (for the prominent case of former British Chaplain Dave Peachell).

[6] *See* Protection of victims of armed conflict through respect of International Humanitarian Law, Reference Document 27th International Conference of the Red Cross and Red Crescent, § 1c, *available at* http://www.icrc.org/Web/eng/siteeng0.nsf/iwpList188/D1DBE52ED17E77DBC1256B66005D6CFF.

law and the moral order. Instead, a particular body of law, the law of armed conflict, is applied. This law grants to these personnel a special protection. On the background of other authors having already stated that academic research on the subject of protection of religious personnel has been rather limited,[7] it seems desirable to determine the *status quo* of that protection, to recall the evolutions that led to this status and to identify problems, if possible solutions, too. This is the task of this book that will not avoid to raise the question of the *raison d'être* of spiritual assistance in armed conflict and its protection. Such ontological reflections will in some aspects leave the domain of law and entertain interdisciplinary considerations. During my studies in canon law, I often perceived the canonistic discipline as an unloved child abandoned by both its parents, theology and law.[8] Though I strongly believe it should be different, it seems as if canon law is lost between law and theology. And nonetheless – or maybe even because of that – I decided to disembark into a research with strong interdisciplinary aspects: This protection of religious personnel is firmly rooted in canon law, has reasons in theological teachings on peace and in pastoral and ecclesiological considerations, is connected with current international policy affairs and sociological phenomena and is ruled by international humanitarian law (IHL). Protection of religious personnel in IHL is linked with the "special challenge" for public international law to also assure a minimum of civilization in armed conflict because this civilization includes religious practices.[9] In its attempt to provide a picture of the *status quaestionis*, this book will therefore also touch related academic fields without claiming full expertise therein. A particular emphasis has been laid on efforts to not get caught by the specific terminology of either one of these disciplines in order to compliment readers of different backgrounds.[10]

When this monograph takes historical developments as a basis for later results in a legal regime and examines them punctually, it will become clear that canon law in history dealt with matters that we nowadays would consider to fall into

---

[7] *See* GERALD I. DRAPER, REFLECTIONS ON LAW AND ARMED CONFLICTS 194 (1998), Wolf Werner Rausch, *Kirchliche Begleitung – wohin auch immer, Militärseelsorge im nationalen und internationalen Recht*, 1995 TRUPPENPRAXIS/WEHRAUSBILDUNG 379, 380 n.4, Jonathan G. Odom, *Beyond Arm Bands and Arms Banned, Chaplains, Armed Conflict, and the Law*, 49 NAVAL LAW REVIEW 1, 2 (2002), *available at* http://www.chaplain.navy.mil/Attachments/Chaplains_In_Armed_Conflict.pdf, *see also* Liselotte B. Watson, *Status of medical and religious personnel in international law*, JAG JOURNAL Sep-Oct-Nov 1965, at 41. ("a small aspect").

[8] *See* Stefan Lunze, *Der Apostolische Stuhl reformiert die Ausbildung im kanonischen Recht*, 2003 JURISTISCHE SCHULUNG 725.

[9] *See* Christian Tomuschat *Völkerrecht*, *in* 10 LEXIKON FÜR THEOLOGIE UND KIRCHE col. 854 (Walter Kasper ed., 3rd ed. 2001).

[10] However, the term "religious personnel" is used according to the definition of PA I throughout the text as religious ministers serving in a military environment. The common meaning of this term based on an understanding not narrowed by the PA I definition is taken into account when this monograph also examines the protection of civilian ministers, e.g. in chapter VII.

the domain of international law. Theological reflection on war and peace constructed the basis on which public international law was later built as an independent legal discipline in modern times.[11] Moral Theologians were the "fathers of public international law".[12] Even today, theology and public international law are still "cooperating to determine the fundamental structures of a global legal order".[13] As the great religions of the world share with international law the goal of an international society of peace and freedom, of harmonious dispute settlement without the resort to force, religion can be the source of idealism that fuels and fires international law.[14]

Presence of religions in armed conflict can only be understood as a "world service"[15]; thus protection can only be tackled from a global perspective.[16] Nonetheless, the particular set up in which protection is arranged on a national level plays an important part.[17] Some of the problems in the field could not be discussed without reference to national status of military chaplaincy. This is why at some points this book will make exemplary mention of national peculiarities and will in these cases use German ones.[18]

The Christian interpretation of international law in the light of the biblical image of man, as a creature that is able to enter into a personal, dialogical relation with his divine creator, a creature that is seen as a man in community with others and whose liberty is not an end in itself but ordered towards God's will, is one option with a long tradition[19] but cannot claim exclusivity. When this book takes recourse to Christian reasoning and particularly the teaching of the catholic church, this is to be understood as one contribution amongst others to a pluralistic discourse. This approach has been chosen since this book is published in a canon law series, the discipline that deals with the law of the catholic church and is thus influenced by the postulates of the teaching office of the church.

---

[11] *See* Otto Kimminich, *Theologie und Völkerrecht*, 1992 MILITÄRSEELSORGE 99, 101.

[12] *See* Otto Kimminich, *Der völkerrechtliche Gehalt der Enzyklika Pacem in Terris*, *in* ALFRED KLOSE, FRIEDEN UND GESELLSCHAFTSORDNUNG 67 (1988).

[13] *See* Kimminich, *supra* note 11, at 107.

[14] *See* Christopher G. Weeramantry, *Foreword to* RELIGION AND INTERNATIONAL LAW vii, vii-viii (Mark W. Janis & Carolyn Evans eds. 1999).

[15] Bernadin Gantin, *Discorso di apertura*, *in* DIECI ANNI DOPO 7, 39 (1996).

[16] *See* CLAUDE NICOLAS, L'ASSISTANCE SPRITUELLE DANS LE DROIT DE LA GUERRE 104 (1991).

[17] *See* Jean-Luc Hiebel, *Droit de l'Aumônerie, Droit de l'Assistance spirituelle*, 1 ANNUAIRE FRANÇAIS DES DROITS DE L'HOMME 531, 532 (1974).

[18] *See also* NICOLAS, *supra* note 16, *passim* (comparing different national models of chaplaincy instead).

[19] *See* MAX HUBER, DAS VÖLKERRECHT UND DER MENSCH 17 (1952).

II. Where does protection come from? - The History

This chapter follows the history of protection of religious personnel from ancient times until the first protection in the positive law of the 19th century.

1. Protection in ancient times

Spiritual assistance to the troops can already be found in the ancient Jewish scriptures. The priestly class of the Levites carried the ark of the commandments with the troops and provided assistance to them.[20] But Jewish priests also actively engaged in warfare.[21] The ancient Greeks considered temples and priests inviolable.[22] Roman priests were excluded from military service, for human blood should not stick to their hands when they immolated.[23]

Early Christianity condemned military service.[24] TERTULLIAN negated the question whether Christians may serve as soldiers at all.[25] This was not so much because of ethical considerations but because soldiers were continuously challenged by the pagan state religion and at risk of denying their faith in an environment where the cult of the emperor was at its strongest. In practice, however, the number of Christians even in the officer's ranks had grown by the third century.[26] MARCELLUS and MARINUS are examples for martyrs in the military of pre-constantinian times.[27]

Besides the pagan nature of the Roman Empire, there are other attempts to explain Christian objection to the waging of war. "We render aid to the emperor by means of our spiritual armament through our prayers".[28] The Alexandrian church father ORIGEN bases the aversion to the shedding of blood upon the need for purification of those who perform the divine sacrifices as priests.[29] "Even their [the Romans'] own priests are not placed among the soldiers, because God must be worshiped with pure hands".[30] This ancient Roman thought was upheld with

---

[20] *See Genesis* 14:18; *Numbers* 4:14; *Joshua* 6:1-20.

[21] *See* 2 *Samuel* 8:18.

[22] *See* COLEMAN PHILLIPSON, 2 THE INTERNATIONAL LAW AND CUSTOM OF ANCIENT GREECE AND ROME 2 (1911).

[23] *See* Bernhard Kötting, *Die Stellung der frühen Kirche zum Militärdienst*, 1981 MILITÄRSEELSORGE 183, 185.

[24] *See* Herbert Frohnhofen, *Zwischen Pazifismus und Heiligem Krieg*, 116 STIMMEN DER ZEIT 831, 832 (1991).

[25] *See* FRITZ DICKMANN, FRIEDENSRECHT UND FRIEDENSSICHERUNG 83 (1971), ADOLF HARNACK, MILITIA CHRISTI 76 (1981), CARL ERDMANN, DIE ENTSTEHUNG DES KREUZZUGSGEDANKENS 3 (1974).

[26] *See* HARNACK, *supra* note 25, at 84.

[27] *See* Kötting, *supra* note 23, at 184-186.

[28] Origen, *Against Celsus* VIII, 73, *cited in* HARNACK, *supra* note 25, at 86.

[29] *See* DICKMANN, *supra* note 25, at 84.

[30] *Supra* note 28.

regard to the new sacrifice of mass, instituted by Christ and offered in commemoration, and its scope of application broadened in the context of the priestly vocation of all Christians.[31] It is interesting to note that on the other hand Saint PAUL uses military terminology to illustrate his teachings.[32] Later, young Christianity speaks about martyrs, monks and clerics as *militia christi*.[33]

With the edict of Milan in 313 and Christian faith becoming state religion under CONSTANTINE, the dispute on Christians in the military became obsolete. The once persecuted religion was raised as state religion above the other religions.[34] A notion, which later developed into a full legal concept, was introduced by EUSEBIUS: The bishop and advisor to CONSTANTINE differentiated into two levels of Christian vocation. The laity had to shoulder the burdens of citizenship; its participation in Roman wars was approved. The clergy had to remain aloof from society in total dedication to God and was exempted from military service.[35] Recognizing that fighting under some circumstances was inevitable, the early church fathers still imposed some penance on anyone who shed blood. This practice was incorporated into the penitential canons which spread from the Celtic lands throughout Europe. The Penitential of the Venerable Bede established in the early 8th century that anyone who slays a monk or a cleric has to "lay aside his weapons and serve God or do penance for seven years".[36] The usual penance for killing a man in a public war was forty days.[37]

Even in these early times, a special pastoral care for soldiers was instituted: Priests and deacons were assigned for the ministry to the Roman legions.[38] Sources tell us about Bishop LAURENTIUS who assigned upon request in a decretal of Pope PELAGIUS in the year 560 some chaplains to Byzantine troops in Civitavecchia, but strictly prohibited them to engage in warfare.[39] From the earliest time of chaplaincy in the armed forces, this ministry was associated with the prohibition to actively engage in warfare.[40] CHARLEMAGNE determined in his *capitulare generale* of 769 that priests were to accompany the troops in the field

---

[31] *See* DRAPER, *supra* note 7, at 8, Frohnhofen, *supra* note 24, at 833.

[32] *See Roman* 13:12 (armor of light); *Ephesians* 6:13-17 (armor of God, righteousness as a breastplate, helmet of salvation, sword of the spirit).

[33] *See* Frohnhofen, *supra* note 24, at 833.

[34] *See* HARNACK, *supra* note 25, at 99.

[35] *See* FREDERICK H. RUSSELL, THE JUST WAR IN THE MIDDLE AGES 12 (1975).

[36] *cited in* 1 THE LAW OF WAR 8 (Leon Friedman ed. 1972).

[37] *See* Frohnhofen, *supra* note 24, at 838, DRAPER, *supra* note 7, at 22.

[38] *See* Anton Schlögel, *Schutz der Seelsorge im humanitären Völkerrecht*, *in* VÖLKERRECHT IM DIENSTE DES MENSCHEN 259 (Yvo Hangartner ed. 1996).

[39] *See id.*, JÖRN BLEESE, DIE MILITÄRSEELSORGE UND DIE TRENNUNG VON STAAT UND KIRCHE, 13, 435 (1969).

[40] *See also* BLEESE, *supra* note 39, at 13-14.

to celebrate mass and to administer the sacrament of penance.[41] This regulation originates in canon 2 of the first *Concilium Germanicum* (742/43) that had allowed only chaplains and no other clergy to join the armies on a military campaign. These regulations had effects on the non-permanent military chaplaincy in Europe throughout the Middle Ages.[42]

2. Protection of clergy in the era of classic canon law

a. The notion of just war and its practice

The origins of humanitarian law are closely linked with the idea of just war.[43] AUGUSTINUS AURELIUS (354-430) who on his part adopted the antique notion and particularly christianized CICERO's thoughts[44] was the starting point of the just war notion in Christian doctrine.[45] For him only wars undertaken for a just cause (*iusta causa*) were permissible. Since peace was a state of tranquility based upon a just order (*pax omnium rerum tranquillitas ordinis*), the wrongdoer breached the order and just war was a means to restore peace.[46] In this, just war avenged wrongs committed by the adversary.[47] If interpreted very narrowly, just war is the means to correct the wrongdoer motivated by internal charity through an external act of force.[48] Thus, just war in its pure sense does not even contradict the Christian commandment of charity but relates to it.[49] In most cases, though, the commandment of love will demand to refrain from using armed force.

The last of the church's fathers, ISIDOR OF SEVILLE (570 - 636), couched the idea of a just war into simpler formulations and the parallels to Cicero became even more evident through direct quotes.[50] Much of AUGUSTINE's and ISODOR's teachings became incorporated in GRATIAN'S decree. Through GRATIAN, the father of scientific canon law, the concept of just war was introduced into

---

[41] *See* 1 MONUMENTA GERMANIAE HISTORICA SRCIPTORES 32-34 (Georg Heinrich Pertz ed. 1835).

[42] *See* [Legum Sectio III, Concilia, Vol. II part. I : Concilia aevi Karolini, Vol. 1-1] MONUMENTA GERMANIAE HISTORICA, 44 (Albert Werminghoff ed. 1904), Schlögel, *supra* note 38, at 259.

[43] *See* Helmut Liedermann, *Das humanitäre Völkerrecht: von den Anfängen bis zur Gegenwart*, 1999 WIENER BLÄTTER ZUR FRIEDENSFORSCHUNG 1, 3.

[44] *See* DICKMANN, *supra* note 25, at 85, *see also* Cicero, III *Republic*, 23, 34-35, *in* 1 FONTES HISTORIAE IURIS GENTIUM 190 (Wilhelm G. Grewe ed. 1995).

[45] *See* WILHELM G. GREWE, THE EPOCHS OF INTERNATIONAL LAW 52, 54 (Michael Byers trans. 2000), KARL HEINZ ZIEGLER, VÖLKERRECHTSGESCHICHTE § 13 III 3 at 75 (1994).

[46] *See* GREWE, *supra* note 45, at 107.

[47] *See* [liber 6 q 10] Quaestiones in Heptateuchum, *in* 1 FONTES HISTORIAE IURIS GENTIUM, *supra* note 44, at 563.

[48] *See* 1 CHARLES JOURNET, L'ÉGLISE DU VERBE INCARNÉ 364 (1941).

[49] *See* Ernst-Wolfgang Böckenförde & Robert Spaemann, *Christliche Moral und atomare Kampfmittel*, 1960/61 MILITÄRSEELSORGE 267, 269.

[50] *See Etymologiae* XVIII, 1, 2-3, *in* 1 FONTES HISTORIAE IURIS GENTIUM, *supra* note 44, at 566.

modern international jurisprudence.[51] THOMAS AQUINAS did not add much to that concept in terms of substance but introduced a systematic clarity that identified three prerequisites for commencing a just war:[52]

- the authority of a ruler (*auctoritas principis*), who has no other means to restore order;
- the just cause (*iusta causa*) based on the wrong done by the adversary;
- the sincere intention (*recta intentio*) as a subjective element excluding impure motives.

Although the influence of Christian theologians on the evolution of just war doctrine is unquestionable, the contribution of canon law as a discipline "closer to the dirtiness and moral ambiguity of ordinary life than is theology"[53] was also significant. Canonists took up the matter of morality relating to warfare and thoroughly dealt with it.

In a time, when the international legal community was identical to the Christian community, united in the Roman Church, a supra-national consciousness of solidarity rooted in the clergy, the chivalry and the municipal communities strengthened the sense of a *populus christianus*, a community of the Christian people among and structured by the occidental nations[54] forming one *respublica christiana*. This solidarity found its strongest manifestation in the fight against those who did not share in the common, bond-building religion, against the infidels. Pope ALEXANDER II in an encyclical of 1063 called for a war against the Saracens and argued that in such a war, Christians were in a state of legitimate defense.[55] The Reformer PETER DAMIAN condemned the use of violence for the sake of faith and referred to the apostles who did not oppose violence with violent resistance but chose death over war.[56] Such positions did not prevail. Spiritual restraint in warfare matters ceased when the holy war idea unfolded and the first crusade was executed as a direct papal-ecclesiastical enterprise. The immediate ecclesiastical leadership even became an essential characteristic of the crusades.[57] Later, the power of the highest ecclesiastical authority to apply force against heretics became enshrined in the Fourth Lateran Council's resolutions in

---

[51] *See Decretum Gratiani* C.23 q.2,c.1+2, *in* 1 CORPUS IURIS CANONICI col. 894 (photo. Reprint Lawbook Exchange 2000) (Aemilius Ludwig Richter ed., Emil Friedberg rev. 1879).

[52] *See* Thomas de Aquino, *Summa Theologiae*, 2-2, qu. 40, in THOMAS DE AQUINO, 2 THOMAE AQUINATIS OPERA OMNIA ar. 1 at 579 (1980), 1 (for a just war test in 3 clear steps).

[53] JAMES TURNER JOHNSON, CAN MODERN WAR BE JUST? 13 (1984).

[54] *See* GREWE, *supra* note 45, at 51, 54.

[55] *See* 1 FONTES HISTORIAE IURIS GENTIUM, *supra* note 44, at 378, *Decretum Gratiani*, C. 23, qu. 8, c. 11, *in* 1 CORPUS IURIS CANONICI, supra note 51, col. 954.

[56] *See Letter of Petrus Damiani, in* 1 FONTES HISTORIAE IURIS GENTIUM, *supra* note 44, at 577, ERDMANN, *supra* note 25, at 131.

[57] *See* Frohnhofen, *supra* note 24, at 831, GREWE, *supra* note 45, at 111.

1215.[58] The practice of the exercise of this powerful tool in the hands of the popes only ended with the decline of papal power in the early 14th century.[59]

Just war doctrine and some of its narrower interpretations can be seen as a tool to limit warfare and its effects. In practice however, just war doctrine was very vulnerable to abuse and in many cases "did nothing than provide believers with a justification for war and all its infamy".[60]

b. Clergy banned from war

The emergence of two different spheres as the result of the investiture contest did not result in a strict separation of imperial and papal powers. In a changing political climate, the two spheres mixed up;[61] the pope claimed worldly *potestas* and at another time the emperor claimed spiritual *auctoritas*. The type of conflict was different though from what we know as difficulties in church-state-relations nowadays since both, the pope and the emperor, were organs of the one *res-publica christiana*. Their conflict took place in the same forum and was not yet a conflict between different *societates perfectae*. Thus, it is difficult to apply categories of a modern state to that type of conflict.[62]

In this political situation, a theoretical distinction existed: The spiritual power could order the temporal one to wage war, while the latter was obliged to punish the identified evil. But wars were to be fought by the temporal authority; the church and its priests were not permitted to participate directly.[63] The *Decretum Gratiani* took up AUGUSTINE's rule that "*ecclesia non sitit sanguinem*" and declared inadmissible the use of armed force by clerics. Bishops and any other cleric were not permitted to resort to arms. It stopped short of absolutely forbidding any clerical participation whatsoever because it allowed clergy to call other people to armed service for the protection of the oppressed and for the struggle against the enemies of God.[64] THOMAS AQUINAS mentions two reasons for that prohibition: The distraction of clergy from contemplation and the incompatibility of bloodshed and the ministry of the altar.[65] Some decretists then permitted

---

[58] *See* Concilium Lateranense IV, ch. 3, can. 3-5, *in* DOCUMENTS OF THE CHRISTIAN CHURCH 133 (Henry Bettenson ed., 2nd ed. 1963).

[59] *See* GREWE, *supra* note 45, at 113.

[60] JEAN PICTET, DEVELOPMENT AND PRINCIPLES OF INTERNATIONAL HUMANITARIAN LAW 13 (1985).

[61] *See* GERHARD CARL WILHELM GÖRRIS, DE DENKBEELDEN OVER OORLOG EN DE BEMOEIINGEN VOOR VREDE IN DE ELFDE EEUW 14 (1912).

[62] *See* CARL SCHMITT, DER NOMOS DER ERDE IM VÖLKERRECHT DES JUS PUBLICUM EUROPAEUM 30 (4th ed. 1997).

[63] *See* GÖRRIS, *supra* note 61, at 25, GREWE, *supra* note 45, at 110.

[64] *See Decretum Gratiani*, C. 23, qu. 8 *in* 1 CORPUS IURIS CANONICI, supra note 51, col. 853-54.

[65] *See supra* note 52, ar. 2 at 580.

clerical participation in the battles against pagans and infidels as well as in other cases of outmost necessity.[66]

RAIMUNDUS DE PENNAFORTE (1180-1275), a missionary to the Saracens who later became the Patron Saint of the canonistic discipline, drew the line from the existing prohibition to just war doctrine and formulated as one of five criteria required for a just war: The person has to be secular because shedding of blood is permitted only to him, not to an ecclesiastical person, to whom this is prohibited.[67] Thus, if clerics were involved, a war could not be justified. Then, a war was not just and therefore not permitted but forbidden. Similar formulations as with RAIMUNDUS may be found in the *Glossa ordinaria* to the *Decretum Gratiani* of TEUTONICUS (1170-1245) and a century later in BALDUS DE UBALDIS' *Consilia.*[68]

The biographer of Bishop BALDÉRIC DE LIÈGE illustrates how far away reality sometimes was from that normative ideal and specially how regalian bishops would act outside the dignity of their office:[69] Comte LAMBERT I. DE LOUVAIN (*le Petit, le Barbu*) felt threatened by a fortified castle that BALDÉRIC was building at the town of Hoegaerde. So he destroyed it and raided BALDÉRIC's lands. The political background of this conflict between Earl LAMBERT as a member of the self-confident local aristocracy and BALDÉRIC as the representative of an imperial church cannot be omitted.[70] After two rounds of negotiations and the excommunication of LAMBERT, BALDÉRIC joined his army with those of allied dukes and led them into the battle of Hoegaerde (October 10th or September 26th, 1013). The biographer at this point praises the bishop's fight against LAMBERT with strong words as service for the salvation of the people of God. However, after early gains of the party of Liège, one of BALDÉRIC's allies, ROBERT DE NAMUR, defected and sided with LAMBERT. The latter subsequently defeated BALDÉRIC. The biographer then comments this outcome with the remark that warfare conducted by a priest is a grave sin. As a clergyman, he was supposed to contribute to the fight with prayers, not with the sword.[71] It was left to a widow, Comtesse LUTGARDE DE LOOZ, to negotiate a reconciliation between BALDÉRIC and LAMBERT: BALDÉRIC lifted the excommunication and LAMBERT built a church at Hoegaerde to commemorate the three hundred victims of the

---

[66] *See* RUSSELL, *supra* note 35, at 105-11.

[67] *See Summa de paenitentia*, liber II, tit. V § 17, *in* 1 B UNIVERSA BIBLIOTHECA IURIS 485 (Javier Ochoa et al. eds. 1976).

[68] *See* Consilia V, *in* 1 FONTES HISTORIAE IURIS GENTIUM, *supra* note 44, at 576.

[69] *See* CHARLES LAYS, ÉTUDE CRITIQUE SUR LA VITA BALDERICI EPISCOPI LEODIENSIS 167 (1948), *see also* 4 MONUMENTA GERMANIAE HISTORICA SRCIPTORES 724 (Georg Heinrich Pertz ed. 1841) (for the Vita Balderici ep. Leodiensis).

[70] *See* LAYS, *supra* note 69, at 135.

[71] *See also* 4 MONUMENTA GERMANIAE HISTORICA SRCIPTORES, *supra* note 69, at 724, 728, 730.

battle. BALDÉRIC was said to have reproached himself for the loss of his men and for getting blood on his hands until the end of his days[72] and became an example for the fate of a regalian bishop who failed to live in the tension between his spiritual and his secular office.

The conclusion seems reasonable that the prohibition of clerical participation in warfare was clearly church doctrine. Violations of relevant stipulations exposed the problems of the church with its discipline.[73] However, these disciplinary difficulties did include the highest level of the ecclesiastical hierarchy.

But canon law influenced by just war theory did not limit its scope to the conditions for going to war (*iusta causa belli*) but also developed restrictions on the manner of conducting war (*iustus modus bellandi*). The Third Lateran Council in 1179 stated a level of protection in which "priests, monks, clerics ... should enjoy proper security".[74] Clergy was legally immune from the effects of warfare. This protection did not depart from humanitarian considerations but from the church's self-interest to protect the institution of Christianity.[75] Again, the denial of the right to participate in war to ecclesiastics extended to them at the same time the right of protection in wartime.[76] The exemption of clergy from warfare both as fighters and as targets in the context of just war is furthermore a clear example for the practical moral wisdom that may be derived from just war doctrine.[77] The achievement of canonists in containing the effects of warfare is intelligible in comparison with legists who still relied on JUSTINIAN's Code with the maxim *vae victis* and its hard stipulations of the ancient law of war especially with regard to the slavery treatment of captives.[78] It was canon law that improved not only protection for clergy but also relieved vanquished and prisoners and thus contributed to a humanization of warfare.[79]

c. *The local and temporal Treuga Dei*

Expeditions against the infidels as described above could only be undertaken if forces were not bound by conflicts within Christendom, namely by feudal hostilities. Drawing a clear distinction between war and feud turns out to be rather difficult: Unlike the holy war against infidels, feud was an internal con-

---

[72] *See* PIERRE-FRANÇOIS-XAVIER DE RAM, RECHERCHES SUR L'HISTOIRE DES COMTES DE LOUVAIN ET SUR LEURS SÉPULTURES A NIVELLES (976-1096) 19-20 (1851).

[73] *See* ERDMANN, *supra* note 25, at 13.

[74] *Concilium Lateranense III*, can. 22, *in* 1 DECREES OF THE ECUMENICAL COUNCILS 222 (Norman P. Tanner ed. 1990).

[75] *See* JUDITH GAIL GARDAM, NON-COMBATANT IMMUNITY AS A NORM OF INTERNATIONAL HUMANITARIAN LAW 12 n.21 (1993).

[76] *See* JAMES TURNER JOHNSON, JUST WAR TRADITION AND THE RESTRAINT OF WAR 131 (1981).

[77] *See also* JOHNSON, *supra* note 53, at 15 (showing that the effect of just war doctrine is not limited to remote ideas).

[78] *See* INGRID DETTER, THE LAW OF WAR 151 (2nd ed. 2000).

[79] *See* ZIEGLER, *supra* note 45, § 19 III 6, § 25 III 2, JOHNSON, *supra* note 76, at 122.

flict amongst powers within the *respublica christiana* and did not substantially question the unity of the *populus christianus*.[80] Lacking an effective superior acting as judiciary, feud was a form of self-help. Bearing in mind that modern states and thus the difference between inter-state and intra-state conflicts did not exist in medieval times, feud can be considered a type of warfare.[81] A detailed code of rules, which had originated in the ethos of occidental chivalry, governed the conduct in feud. This code contained stipulations on the exclusion of churches and certain persons – specially those unable to bear arms, amongst them clergy – from hostilities but was of course not always followed.[82] Unlike the protection of clergy under canon law that was a legal claim, the protection through the knightly code was more a gesture of condescension.[83] Nonetheless, feudal law and the chivalric code can be considered as sources of a medieval law of war.[84]

The church also realized that it had to provide protection against the cruelty of medieval warfare. A means of the church to contain the use of force became the institution of the *Treuga Dei*. The proclamation of a *Treuga Dei* could take different forms and brought about a discontinuation of hostilities. Though temporal and local in its nature, this break was more than an armistice and less then lasting peace, which is also underlined by the use of the term "*treuga*". It is the Latinized version of the Franconian term "*triuwa*" that names an end of hostilities regardless of its cause.[85]

Originating in France, the *Treuga Dei* movement soon spread throughout Europe and received its definitive canonical version in the Second Lateran Council (1139):[86] The *Treuga Dei* lasted from Wednesday night until Monday morning and continuously during Advent, Christmas, Lenten and Easter time. Priests, clerics and monks along with pilgrims, merchants and peasants were protected at all times. Breaches of the *Treuga Dei* were to be punished with excommunication.[87] These norms were incorporated in GREGORY IX'S *Decretalia*

---

[80] *See* SCHMITT, *supra* note 62, at 20.

[81] *See* DICKMANN, *supra* note 25, at 103, Paulus A. Hausmann, *Die Spuren der treuga dei im Völkerrecht oder Vom Wandel des Friedensverständnisses*, *in* FRIEDEN UND VÖLKERRECHT 235, 252 (Georg Picht et al. eds. 1973).

[82] *See* GEORG STADTMÜLLER, 1 GESCHICHTE DES VÖLKERRECHTS 69 (1951), ZIEGLER, *supra* note 45, § 19 IV 4 at 104, JOHNSON, *supra* note 76, at 132-135.

[83] *See* JOHNSON, *supra* note 76, at 139-141.

[84] *See* GREWE, *supra* note 45, at 105, 114.

[85] *See* Hausmann, *supra* note 81, at 248 sq.

[86] *See Concilium Lateranense II*, can. 11, *in* 1 DECREES OF THE ECUMENICAL COUNCILS, *supra* note 74, at 199.

[87] A typical *Treuga Dei* was proclaimed in 1082 by Bishop Henry of Liège and also included the county of Leuven. It became a bridge for the French Treuga Dei-movement to enter into the territories under the rule of the German Emperor. *See* GÖRRIS, *supra* note 61, at 196-198.

and became part of the Corpus Iuris Canonici.[88] Because of the social function of clergy that went – given e.g. the church's monopoly in education – far beyond a merely spiritual mission, they had nothing to do with war making and thus were not to be harmed.[89] Again, societal stability rather than humanitarian considerations were governing motives. The church's self-interest to protect its own personnel appears to be another obvious reason. Even these first structures of protection were shaken by abuse for instance by the common ruse in medieval combat to dress knights as monks and thus gain the element of surprise.[90] Other forms, like the first *Treuga Dei* proclaimed at the Synod of Charroux (989), exempted also religious places such as churches, cloisters and cemeteries from hostilities and imposed anathema against those who break into churches and those who injure clergymen.[91] This protection was imposed by canon lawand enforced with canonical sanctions. Papacy and episcopate became peace-enforcing powers.[92] In practice from the 11th century on, the *Treuga Dei* gained modest success in the following century but was hardly ever applied after the 12th century. Instead, it was eventually transformed into secular forms like the *Landfriede* or *Trève*.[93]

3. At the threshold to modern times

From the 13th century on, the unity of the *respublica christiana* was challenged by the emergence of stronger political entities: Partitions of the *populus christianus* started to form their own structures. Unlike the crusades that were a common enterprise of the *populus christianus*, the era of discoveries starting in the late 15th century brought about friction within the European family of Christian nations.[94] The pope and his missionary bulls still provided the legal title for the Spaniards to seize land oversees in the run of their *conquista*.[95] This practice, however, did not concern an international legislative power of the pope but was tied to the ancient papal claim to govern all parts of the world not inhabited by Christians.[96]

---

88 *See Decretales Gregorii IX*, X 1.34.1+2, *in* 2 CORPUS IURIS CANONICI col. 203 (photo. Reprint Lawbook Exchange 2000) (Aemilius Ludwig Richter ed., Emil Friedberg rev. 1879).

89 *See* JOHNSON, *supra* note 76, at 127 (using the term "Peace of God" for this categorical protection).

90 *See* JOHNSON, *supra* note 76, at 133.

91 *See* BRIAN TIERNEY, [1 Souces of Medieval History] THE MIDDLE AGES 135 (4th ed. 1983), STADTMÜLLER, *supra* note 82, at 68.

92 *See* GÖRRIS, *supra* note 61, at 240 sq.

93 *See* GREWE, *supra* note 45, at 115.

94 *See id.* at 142.

95 *See* MATTHIAS GILNER, BARTOLOMÉ DE LAS CASAS UND DIE EROBERUNG DES INDIANISCHEN KONTINENTS 71 (1997).

96 *See* GREWE, *supra* note 45, at 196.

FRANCISCO DE VITORIA enumerates in his writings a number of legal titles the Spaniards may dispose of to gain rule over Indians.[97] Thus, they were legally entitled to move freely and to preach the gospel. And if resistance was met, this legal title provided a *iusta causa* for a just war. But it again becomes clear that spiritual and temporal powers were *diversi ordines*: The relations between the conquering armies and the missionary orders were not free of tension. VITORIA was rather reluctant in mandating Spanish wars for the sake of conversion and also determined a number of illegitimate legal titles to wage war against Indians.[98] LAS CASAS, the Dominican whose rules on the treatment of Indians were designed to relief them from Spanish exploitation, is another example of clergy eager to protect the indigenous population from the brutality of the conquerors.[99] He particularly criticized the indiscriminate warfare of the *conquistadores* who did not attempt to spare the innocent but deliberately targeted all classes of protected persons.[100] Even in these times, clergy exposed themselves in advocating the rights of the weak and oppressed.

Canonical protection for clergy lasted throughout the Middle Ages and eventually merged with chivalric custom. In the late 14th century, HONORÉ BONET enumerates among those to be granted exemption from warfare: bishops, abbots, monks and "all other men of the Church not named earlier".[101] FRANCISCO DE VITORIA upheld the prohibition to kill clergy even in just warfare unless they were found to be fighting since they belonged to the class of innocents.[102] Nonetheless, he held that unintended killing of innocents was justified as a means of last resort if the killing is the lesser of two evils.[103] VITORIA thus introduced an aspect of proportionality.

The synthesis of canonical protection and chivalric custom formed a single doctrine of protection and resulted in a status of immune non-combatants that was no longer based on the protection of certain social functions but on the altruistic notion of Christian charity.[104] Clergymen now were protected not because they were a stabilizing factor in medieval society but because their priestly mission was understood as a service to public welfare. It was charity that "compelled the monk to raise and pray for all men in the cold hours of morn-

---

[97] *See* FRANCISCO DE VITORIA, 2 VORLESUNGEN 456-57 (Ulrich Horst et al. eds. 1997).
[98] *See id.* at 407-09.
[99] *See* A. H. BÖHM, HET RECHT VAN KOLONISATIE 34, 36 (1936), SCHMITT, *supra* note 62, at 82
[100] *See* GILNER, *supra* note 95, at 213.
[101] *Cited in* GILBERT HAY, 1 THE BUKE OF THE LAW OF ARMYS 237 (1901).
[102] *See* FRANCISCO DE VITORIA, *supra* note 97, at 582, JAMES BROWN SCOTT, THE SPANISH ORIGIN OF INTERNATIONAL LAW 230 (1934).
[103] *See* HEINZ-GERHARD JUSTENHOVEN, FRANCISCO DE VITORIA ZU KRIEG UND FRIEDEN 138-39 (1991).
[104] *See* JOHNSON, *supra* note 76, at 145-46.

ing".[105] This evolution also reflected the development in the ideals and interests of the church, not merely as the source for a transcendent moral judgement in times of war but also as a "human institution deeply engaged with the world".[106] In the late 17th century, with the formation of the first standing armies, particular orders were entrusted with the pastoral care of these armies, for instance the Jesuits in Spain and the Habsburg Empire.[107]

4. On the path to the present order

a. The rise of the state in Europe

Reformation did not condemn service as soldiers[108] but destroyed the unity of faith under the ecclesiastical discipline of pope and emperor. The structure of a state emerged that was sovereign to pope and emperor. The state - a juridical person often ruled by an absolute natural person - produced a secular public law separate from the spiritual authority of the church. Administered by a central government and situated in fixed borders, it entered into relations with other states.[109] Linked by treaties and by traditional bonds, states became the subjects of a new *ius gentium*. Two developments contributed to that outcome: the seizure of land outside of Europe and the denominational wars in Europe in the 16th and 17th century. These post-reformation wars had shown the devastating effects of waging just war within what had been the *respublica christiana*. The war of suppression conducted by the catholic Spanish military power against the rebellion of the protestant Dutch, the Thirty Years War between the Emperor and his catholic partisans and the Swedish King and his protestant partisans revived the holy war ideology.[110] These conflicts had frontlines without regard to existing structures. This made the scene look like an internecine civil war of the *populus christianus* with only one possible result: extermination. Religious-confessional motives blocked attempts to limit the effects of warfare. Furthermore, denominational wars made clear that the decision for one religious faith over another in terms of its justness was impossible.[111] After the peace of Westphalia (1648), war was taken away from the theological arena. ALBERICO GENTILI requests theologians to be silent when it comes to the law of war. "*Silete Theologi in*

---

[105] *Id.* at 150.

[106] *Id.*

[107] *See* Schlögel, *supra* note 38, at 261, ARTURO MARCHEGGIANO, DIRITTI E DOVERI DEL CAPPELLANO MILITARE IN TEMPO DI GUERRA 40 (Rivista Militare ed. 1992).

[108] *See* Confession of Augsburg (1530), part XVI, English translation *available at* http://www.ctsfw.edu/etext/boc/ac/augustana16.asc.

[109] *See* SCHMITT, *supra* note 62, at 36, 112.

[110] *See* GREWE, *supra* note 45, at 219.

[111] *See* JOHNSON, note 53, at 61.

munere alieno".[112] The inter-state war of the new order looked different and allowed for a rationalized war, *une guerre en forme*. Like ROUSSEAU puts it: *La guerre est une relation d'État à État*.[113] Two state parties - public persons of equal moral rank - meet to distribute the territory of Europe through land warfare amongst themselves.[114] It was this understanding of states and their wars that allowed to fully develop the category of non-combatants.[115]

Yet, the just war notion had to go through significant changes: Just war was not abandoned, but the place of the substantive *iusta causa* was taken by the formal-legal category of the *iustus hostis* quality that could be applied to both parties.[116] As a consequence, just war changed from a substantive to a procedural notion. The substantive notion of just war determined the right to make war and thus fell into the domain of the *ius ad bellum*. The procedural notion then focused on how to make war and thus lied in the field of the *ius in bello*. A *bellum iustum* is given if a certain requirement of form is fulfilled. War results in a decision through a certain procedure, not extermination at any prize. War is not outlawed, but contained or "hedged".[117] It must not be omitted that the field of application of early modern war was primarily land warfare in Europe. Warfare at sea with its strong property aspect in making prize of a ship and colonial wars with the superiority of the colonial power were yet different. The question for verification of the *iusta causa* became irrelevant because the sovereign decided in his national domain. Thus, this formerly objective criterion looses its significance and turns into a subjective aspect that lies totally in the judgement of the sovereign state.[118] The mutual assumption of a *iusta causa*, the *bellum utrimque iustum* – totally excluded in earlier times – became possible.[119] "Regular war, as regards its effects, must be accounted just on both sides".[120] The way was paved to the non-discriminatory concept of war in the classical law of war. The 19th century could harvest the fruits of the new understanding of just war, of the

---

[112] ALBERICO GENTILI, 1 DE IURE BELLI LIBRI TRES bk 1, ch. 12 at 92 (photo. reprint 1995) (Oxford ed. 1933).

[113] *See* JEAN-JACQUES ROUSSEAU, GESELLSCHAFTSVERTRAG bk. 1, ch. 4 at 12 (Alexander Heine ed. 1977).

[114] *See* SCHMITT, *supra* note 62, at 114.

[115] *See* Liedermann, *supra* note 43, at 4.

[116] *See* Böckenförde/Spaemann, *supra* note 49, at 273, GREWE, *supra* note 45, at 208.

[117] SCHMITT, *supra* note 62, at 69, *see also* GREWE, *supra* note 45, at 209 n.34 (on possible misunderstandings regarding the term "hedging").

[118] *See* GREWE, *supra* note 45, at 204.

[119] *See* FRANCISCO DE VITORIA, *supra* note 97, at 576-78.

[120] EMER DE VATTEL, 3 THE LAW OF NATIONS OR THE PRINCIPLES OF NATURAL LAW bk. III, ch. 12, § 190 at 305 (photo. reprint 1995) (Charles G. Fenwick trans. 1916) (La guerre en forme, quant à ses effets, doit être regardée comme juste de part et d' autre.).

possibility of a *bellum utrimque iustum* and the mutual respect of the state parties when codifying the law of war in Geneva and The Hague.[121]

As international law was taken away from theology, it now had to exist without recourse to a common ideology or morality provided by the universal church – *etsi deus non daretur*. The role of the pope as adjudicator and distributor of colonial territories failed after the 16th century.[122] The capability of the church to moderate warfare, to contribute to the "hedging" of war had perished in the religious wars. Its ability to influence structural orders became indirect.[123] The formation of an international legal order was left to the members of the new State system. Limitations of war then based on the attempts of the writers of the 16th and 17th century to ground these limits on a universal natural law.[124] The concept of a limited war in the 18th century also resulted in efforts to restrict the theater of military operations and thus in relief for the inhabitants of belligerent nations.[125]

b. Protection for religious ministers by the state

Canon law influenced by just war theory protected clergy for some time. When underlying doctrine went through changes, this also affected the protection once granted. GROTIUS considered clergy to be generally exempt from the natural law postulate that no one is enjoined from waging war.[126] To him, this stipulation was the result of a special enactment (*lex specialis*). He thus put it on a level distinct from the supreme natural law and allowed for exceptions in cases of extreme necessity. This view may be interpreted as a first secularization and rationalization of protection. Quoting ancient sources, GROTIUS thought that in a lawful war those who perform religious duties had to be spared.[127] With him, we again find the dualism that their abstention from the use of arms is to be answered with restricting violence toward them. GENTILI followed a similar reasoning and – quoting ERASMUS - called the disregard of the rule to spare clergymen from war "a cruel slaughter".[128]

And just as international law and the law of war become emancipated from canon law and theology, the task of protection was shifted from the church to the state. The different way to wage war was also reflected in legal instruments designed by the belligerents to ease the effects of war. Cartels to relieve the

---

[121] *See* GREWE, *supra* note 45, at 534.
[122] *See id.* at 196.
[123] *See* SCHMITT, *supra* note 62, at 120.
[124] *See* JOHNSON, *supra* note 76, at 149.
[125] *See id.* at 27.
[126] *See* 2 GROTIUS, *supra* note 1, at 165-166.
[127] *See id.* at 736.
[128] ALBERICO GENTILI, 2 DE IURE BELLI LIBRI TRES 261 (photo. reprint 1995) (trans. Oxford ed. 1933).

wounded and prisoners of war (POW), treaties of capitulation for single garrisons and ceasefires were concluded. Many of these instruments of local and temporary scope also contained stipulations on clergy ministering to armed forces.[129] If captured they had to be released by all parties without having to pay *Rançon* (ransom). They were allowed to continue their ministry – especially to the wounded and the sick. At this point, similarities of religious and medical personnel become evident. Their property had to remain untouched and was not considered prize. By the end of the 17th century, these regulations were rather detailed.[130] It was recognized that clergymen as non-combatants were subject to a specific protection in times of war.[131]

SCHLÖGEL argues that the protection of clergy was not only older than this of medical personnel but goes further and concludes that the legal protection of medical personnel was derived from the protection of religious ministers as both groups non-combatants.[132] The best explanation of the historic relations between protection of medical and religious personnel is found with GREEN: By the 16th century, writers began to assert that doctors enjoyed a special immunity in warfare. Often, these doctors happened to be in clerical orders.[133]

With the consent of states becoming a source of international law, the protection fell into the domain of international conferences and their outcomes as positive law. What started out as a protection of certain groups in the times of classical canon law gradually developed into the protection of the innocent and in modern international law into the category of non-combatants. Military chaplains fell into this category. Their immunity is linked with the principle of discrimination meaning that there must be no direct intentional attacks on non-combatants or non-military targets.[134] Together with the principle of proportionality – the means of war must be proportionate with their military ends – the principle of discrimination does not only form an integral part of the law of war but stands

---

[129] *See* NICOLAS, *supra* note 16, at 10-11, *see also* ERNST JULIUS GURLT, ZUR GESCHICHTE DER INTERNATIONALEN UND FREIWILLIGEN KRANKENPFLEGE IM KRIEGE *passim* (photo. reprint 1972) (1873) (a comprehensive compilation of these treaties).

[130] *See* Schlögel, *supra* note 38, at 262.

[131] *See* GURLT, *supra* note 129, at 8.

[132] *See* Schlögel, *supra* note 38, at 264, Rausch, *supra* note 7, at 380, *see also* JEAN PICTET, HUMANITARIAN LAW AND THE PROTECTION OF WAR VICTIMS 79 (1975) [herinafter: PICTET, VICTIMS] (custom of respect for priests preceded that of respect for doctors), JEAN S. PICTET, THE GENEVA CONVENTIONS OF 12 AUGUST 1949, COMMENTARY, I GENEVA CONVENTION 219 (1952) (chaplains and medical personnel placed on the same footing since the 17th century), OTTO KIMMINICH, SCHUTZ DER MENSCHEN IN BEWAFFNETEN KONFLIKTEN 184 (1979) (protection of religious personnel as old as that of medical personnel).

[133] *See* LESLIE C. GREEN, THE CONTEMPORARY LAW OF ARMED CONFLICT 25-26 (2nd ed. 2000).

[134] *See* WILLIAM O'BRIEN, THE CONDUCT OF JUST AND LIMITED WAR 342 (1981).

as the *ius in bello* portion of the just war doctrine.[135] O'BRIEN here also applies the term of "limited war" when he refers to this *ius in bello* aspect.[136]

HENRY WAGER HALLECK who was together with FRANCIS LIEBER responsible for the "Instructions for the Army of the United States in the Field" – better known as the Lieber-Code of 1863 – differentiates the enemies in combatants and non-combatants and names "ministers of religion" to fall into the latter category.[137] He gives two reasons: the lack of resistance on their part and the demand of humanity. Art. 53 of the Lieber-Code then states that "the enemy's chaplains, officers of the medical staff, ... if they fall into the hands of the American Army, are not prisoners of war, unless the commander has reasons to retain them. In this latter case, or if, at their own desire, they are allowed to remain with their captured companions, they are treated as prisoners of war, and may be exchanged if the commander sees fit".[138] Note that the status of retained chaplains here is that of POW.

III. Protection in early legal instrument

International humanitarian law knows numerous stipulations that are concerned with the protection of the exercise of religion, of the exercise of pastoral care and of the right for pastoral care. The Lieber Code as a national legal instrument has already been mentioned. The most important sources of protection are without doubt the Red Cross Conventions concluded in Geneva. Examining these conventions chronologically as they go through various revisions helps to understand what problems evolved in this development and what attempts later were undertaken to solve these problems in the legal norms currently in force.

Modern international humanitarian law is essentially connected with the person of HENRY DUNANT and the book on his "Memory of Solférino" that describes the terrifying impressions that DUNANT found himself exposed to on June 24th, 1859 during the second major battle in the French-Austrian war.[139] In this book, he also mentions emperor Napoleon's chaplain, the Abbé LAINE, who "in the thickest of the fight ... went from one field hospital to the next bringing consolation and sympathy to the dying".[140] The development on the justification

---

[135] *See id.* at 338.
[136] *Id.* at 40.
[137] HENRY WAGER HALLEK, ELEMENTS OF INTERNATIONAL LAW AND LAWS OF WAR 191 (1866), *but see* Watson, *supra* note 7, at 44 (incorrectly attributing protection not to the non-combatant characteristic but to the exclusive engagement criterion of positive law).
[138] THE LAW OF WAR, *supra* note 36, at 168-69.
[139] *See* Wolf Werner Rausch, *Seelsorge im humanitären Völkerrecht*, BEITRÄGE AUS DER EV. MILITÄRSEELSORGE 4/1992, at 24, 26.
[140] *See* HENRY DUNANT, EINE ERINNERUNG AN SOLFERINO 18 (1979).

and limitation of war in theory and practice crystallized in the positive law of the 19th and 20th century in response to DUNANT's impressions.[141] So it was the great humanitarian surge of the second half of the 19th century that produced the Red Cross Movement and the Red Cross Conventions for the better treatment of the sick and wounded in wars. It cannot be denied that many of the distinguished persons who guided this humanitarian movement were Christian in their way of life.[142] DUNANT, for instance, in a letter of 1896 addressed to Mons. EGGER, the Bishop of St. Gallen, wanted the pope to know that the work that he conceived and that he was granted to accomplish was "uniquely inspired by the spirit of Christ, by the most sincere catholic sentiment that exists in the world, pure charity".[143] KUSSBACH considers IHL together with human rights law the field of public international law that is marked by Christian charity most.[144] It has become clearly, however, that the Movement is humanitarian and not religious in essence.[145] In this context, it is significant to note that the red cross is not the cross of the Christian faith.[146]

In 1864, the Swiss government extended an invitation to all European states and to some countries in the Americas to send delegates to an international congress in Geneva to discuss an international treaty relating to the wounded. This invitation was also a result of efforts by a group of dignitaries including DUNANT who in 1880 founded the International Committee of the Red Cross (ICRC).[147] The delegates attending the 1864 congress passed the first Red Cross Convention. This instrument marks the penetration of a purely ethical principle designed to directly protect the individual into international law. Man in need for help notwithstanding his enemy character is in the center of attention.[148] With the ratification of this treaty by the U.S.A. on July 26th, 1882, this instrument became the first to have a rudimentary universal character.[149]

---

[141] *See* James Turner Johnson, *Historical Roots and Sources of the Just War Tradition in Western Culture, in* Just War and Jihad 3, 20 (John Kelsay et al. 1991).

[142] *See* Jean-Luc Hiebel, ASSISTANCE SPIRITUELLE ET CONFLITS ARMÉS 26 (1980), Giorgio Filibeck, *The Force of Law Against the Law of Force*, L'OSSERVATORE ROMANO [english], August 11th/18th, 1999, at 6, *available at* http://www.petersnet.net/research/retrieve.cfm?recnum=1190.

[143] *Cited in* HERIBERT FRANZ KÖCK, DIE VÖLKERRECHTLICHE STELLUNG DES HEILIGEN STUHLS 612 (1975).

[144] *See* Erich Kussbach, *Schutz der Religionsfreiheit und des geistlichen Beistands in bewaffneten Konflikten*, 21 ÖSTERREICHISCHE MILITÄRISCHE ZEITSCHRIFT 385 (1983).

[145] *See also* PICTET, *supra* note 132, at 305, NICOLAS, *supra* note 16, at 86 n.1, Maurice Schubiger, *Die geistige Betreuung gestern, heute und morgen in den Genfer Abkommen*, DER FELDPREDIGER No. 71 (August 1991), at 2.

[146] *See infra* 78, DRAPER, *supra* note 7, at 18, *see also* Schubiger, *supra* note 145, at 4.

[147] *See* Liedermann, *supra* note 43, at 4.

[148] *See* HUBER, *supra* note 19, at 31-32.

[149] *But see* DRAPER, *supra* note 7, at 57 (who speaks of a truly universal character), *see also* HIEBEL, *supra* note 142, at 28 (speaking of a universal character).

1. The Red Cross Convention (1864)

The initial Red Cross Convention, the Convention for the Amelioration of the Condition of the Wounded in Armies in the Fields concluded in Geneva on August 22nd, 1864 stipulated in its Art. II[150] that "persons employed in hospitals ... as well as chaplains" participated "in the benefit of neutrality, whilst so employed, as so long as there remain any wounded to bring in or to succor". In the framework of the ten articles of the convention, the interpretation of neutrality must be broad and take into account two main aspects: Neutrality is composed of protection as an outside aspect and respect meaning a recognition as a internal aspect.[151] Only if protection and respect are combined, human dignity is fully protected.[152] The term neutrality also underlines that even though the countries are belligerents, certain groups of its military do not contribute to combat action.[153] Although this convention was directed primarily at medical relief, the need for spiritual aid was also included.[154] However, the protection of Art. II only applied for chaplains working in hospitals and not generally to all chaplains attached to armed forces.[155] This is indicated in the wording of Art. II that limits the protection to the time of employment ("whilst so employed") and the presence of wounded ("as long as...").

The most significant prerogative[156] of chaplains unfolds under the power of the adversary party. They have the right to chose: They may even after capture or occupation by the enemy continue to fulfill their duties or may withdraw in order to rejoin the corps to which they belong. Then, when they chose to cease from their functions, the occupying army must deliver them to the outposts of the enemy.[157] This very favorable right to choose is later not taken up again.[158] Chaplains also have the right to keep their private property.[159] As a sign of their neutrality, they are allowed to wear an armlet that bears the red cross on white ground and is to be delivered by the military authority.[160]

---

[150] THE LAW OF WAR, *supra* note 36, at 189.
[151] *See* Rausch, *supra* note 139, at 26.
[152] *See* Schlögel, *supra* note 38, at 265.
[153] *But see* Watson, *supra* note 7, at 42 (emphasizing that members of armed forces of a belligerent cannot be neutrals).
[154] RODERICK O'BRIEN, A MANUAL OF INTERNATIONAL HUMANITARIAN LAW FOR RELIGIOUS PERSONNEL 11 (1993).
[155] *See* Sigmar Stadlmeier, *Die Stellung des Militärseelsorgers im humanitären Völkerrecht, in* PAX ET IUSTITIA 521, 522 (Hans Walter Kaluza et al. eds 1990), Kussbach, *supra* note 144, at 386, *but see* NICOLAS, *supra* note 16, at 91 (for a broader interpretation).
[156] *See* Watson, *supra* note 7, at 44.
[157] *See supra* note 150, Art. III.
[158] *See* Schlögel, *supra* note 38, at 265.
[159] *See supra* note 150, Art. IV.
[160] *See id.* Art. VII.

2. The Hague Conventions (1899/1907)

A Russian initiative invited in August 1898 for an international conference to consider ways to limit world armaments and secure peace that took place in The Hague from May to July 1899.

The Adaptation to Maritime Warfare of Principles of the Geneva Convention of 1864 (Hague, III of July 29th, 1899) read in its Art. VII[161] that "[t]he religious, medical, or hospital staff of any captured ship is inviolable, and its members cannot be made prisoners of war. On leaving the ship they take with them the objects and surgical instruments which are of their own private property." The inviolability that is instituted here is in its nature similar to the neutrality of the 1864 Red Cross Convention. The term "religious staff" could allow to cover auxiliary religious personnel as well.[162] They are allowed to continue their activities "while necessary, and can afterwards leave when the Commander-in-Chief considers it possible." The necessity requirement for pastoral activities and the discretion of the commanding officer are new aspects different from the right to choose of the 1864 Red Cross Convention. A novelty is also the obligation of the belligerents to guarantee to the staff that has fallen into their hands the enjoyment of their salaries intact. This privilege is due to the fact that chaplains are expected to render their services without respect for nationality.[163]

The Adaptation to maritime warfare of Principles of the Geneva Convention (Hague, X of October 18th, 1907) stipulates the same in its Art. X[164] as the Hague Convention III had, but alters the salary clause to guarantee "the same allowances and the same salary as to the staff of the same grades of their own navy".

Art. 4 of The Convention relative to certain restrictions with regard to the exercise of the right of capture in naval war (Hague XI, October 18th, 1907)[165] exempts naval vessels charged with religious missions from capture. The wording of this stipulation – that is considered to be still valid – appears to give an absolute immunity from capture – and *a fortiori* from attack – to these vessels without them having to ask for a safe conduct. However, state practice seems to have followed a procedure in which these missions are notified to the opposing state and the latter grants safe conducts indicating the conditions of

[161] THE LAW OF WAR, *supra* note 36, at 241.

[162] *See* Schlögel, *supra* note 38, at 266, Rausch, *supra* note 139, at 27, Rausch, *supra* note 7, at 380.

[163] *See* JAMES BROWN SCOTT, [1 Conferences] THE HAGUE PEACE CONFERENCES OF 1899 AND 1907 at 609 (1909).

[164] THE LAW OF WAR, *supra* note 36, at 357.

[165] *See* JAMES BROWN SCOTT, [2 Documents] THE HAGUE PEACE CONFERENCES OF 1899 AND 1907 at 467 (1909).

exemption.[166] The exemption from capture cannot be claimed if there be the slightest participation in warfare.[167] For "a higher reason", ships from belligerent countries on religious missions are also not affected by the requirement to depart from a neutral port within 24 hours after a declaration of war.[168]

The San Remo Manual, a current work on the state of law of naval warfare, refers to the Hague Convention XI of 1907 when it exempts naval vessels "charged with religious, ... or philanthropic missions" from attack and capture.[169] The commentary concedes that the interpretation of the term "religious missions" creates difficulty for there is a lack of state practice in this regard. The commentators presume that it covers voyages undertaken for missionary and "perhaps" humanitarian work organized by religious orders. They explicitly exclude missions using force or advocating the use of force for religious ends.[170]

The Hague Regulations Respecting the Laws and Customs of War on Land annexed to the Convention Respecting the Laws and Customs of War on Land (Hague IV of October 18th, 1807) deal with the prohibition to use certain weapons, the treatment of prisoners of war and the protection of civilians from military fighting.[171] Limitations on the use of certain weapons certainly also have protective effects on religious personnel, e.g. as they are protected from indiscriminating weapons. But while the question for weapons available for use would lead us into a broad field, these effects on the protection that this monograph deals with are rather indirect and thus will not be examined further.

One of the most fundamental principles of the law of armed conflict is the distinction of combatants and non-combatants[172] that is reflected in Art. 3 of the Hague Regulations. The norms of this document also hold religious convictions and practice of civilians to be respected.[173] A similar clause had already been included in Art. 38 of the 1874 Brussels project of an International Declaration concerning the Laws and Customs of War. Furthermore, the property of religious institutions is of equal status as private property. Its seizure is prohibited

---

[166] *See* INTERNATIONAL INSTITUTE OF HUMANITARIAN LAW, SAN REMO MANUAL ON INTERNATIONAL LAW APPLICABLE TO ARMED CONFLICTS AT SEA 133, 207 (1995).

[167] *See* SCOTT, *supra* note 163, at 618.

[168] *See* Art. 14 of the Convention concerning the rights and duties of Neutral Powers in naval war, *in* SCOTT, *supra* note 165, at 513.

[169] INTERNATIONAL INSTITUTE OF HUMANITARIAN LAW, *supra* note 166, No. 47 f at 17, No. 136 e at 35.

[170] *See id.* at 133.

[171] *See also infra* at 114 (for protection of religious buildings in the Hague Regulations).

[172] *See* Otto Kimminich, *Die friedenstiftende Kraft des Völkerrechts, in* 17 DOKUMENTATION ZUR KATHOLISCHEN MILITÄRSEELSORGE 115, 169 (Katholisches Militärbischofsamt ed. 1991), *but see* Watson, *supra* note 7, at 44 (incorrectly considering unprotected non-combatants legitimate targets).

[173] *See* THE LAW OF WAR, *supra* note 36, Art. 46 of the Hague Regulations at 322.

and has to be persecuted.[174] POW enjoy complete liberty in the exercise of their religion including attendance at the services of whatever church they may belong to.[175] Condition is that they comply with the measures of order and police issued by the military authorities of the Occupying Power. This stipulation underlines that the main reason for protection of chaplains in armed conflicts is not found in the privileged person of the chaplain but in the needs of those who are involved in the plight and dangers of warfare and captivity.[176]

3. Revisions of the Red Cross Convention (1906/1929)

The First Hague Conference of 1899 also offered an opportunity to approach the Swiss government for a revision of the 1864 Red Cross Convention. A conference for this purpose met in 1906 and on July 6th produced a new revised Convention relating to the wounded and the sick. In Art. IX[177] the modern formulation appears that "chaplains attached to armies shall be respected and protected under all circumstances". Respect means "to spare, not to attack".[178] The emphasis is on a passive conduct. To protect means "to come to someone's defense, to lend help and support".[179] An active and positive duty is demanded here.[180] Translated into military action, protection and respect means that chaplains "must not knowingly be attacked, fired upon or unnecessarily prevented from discharging their proper functions".[181] Chaplains "become casualties by accident, not by design".[182] This clause from the manuals only comprises certain prohibitions constituted by respect.

It is then Art. XII of the same legal instrument that brings about significant changes: Chaplains continue to exercise their functions "under the direction of the enemy" if they have fallen into the hands of the adversary. A tendency that was started in the Hague Convention III is now fully developed and incorporated into the Red Cross Convention. Spiritual affairs may be subject to interference from occupying forces.[183] The right to chose a return to own troops is restricted: Chaplains' repatriation may only happen when their assistance is no longer indispensable and within such a period and by such a route as may accord with military necessity. The right to private property is maintained. If chaplains do

---

[174] *See id.* Art. 56 of the Hague Regulations at 323.
[175] *See id.* Art. 17 of the Hague Regulations at 317.
[176] *See* Rausch, *supra* note 139, at 28.
[177] THE LAW OF WAR, *supra* note 36, at 262.
[178] COMMENTARY ON THE ADDITIONAL PROTOCOLS (Yves Sandoz et al. eds. 1978), No. 446 at 146.
[179] *Id.*
[180] *See* Jean-Luc Hiebel, *Human rights relating to spiritual assistance as embodied in the Geneva Conventions of 1949*, 1980 INTERNATIONAL REVIEW OF THE RED CROSS 3, 17.
[181] DEPARTMENT OF THE ARMY, THE LAW OF LAND WARFARE NO. 225 at 89 (1956).
[182] U.S. MARINE CORPS, FLEET MARINE FORCE MANUAL (FMFM) 3-61, MINISTRY IN COMBAT NO. 1004 e (June 22nd, 1992).
[183] *See* Schlögel, *supra* note 38, at 266; Rausch, *supra* note 139, at 26.

not have a military uniform, they may be issued a certificate of identity to prove their status in addition to the armlet with the distinctive emblem.[184] SCHLÖGEL concludes that the 1906 Red Cross Convention only brings change for the worse with regard to protection of chaplains.[185]

In World War I, the Occupying Power's right of direction and the formulation that return is conditioned by the fact that assistance is no longer indispensable had been interpreted without taking into account the historical right to chose. Repatriation was practically excluded.[186] In 1929, under the impression of World War I, the Red Cross Convention was revised again. The interrelation of war impressions and convention revisions in general is striking. The Convention for the Amelioration of the condition of the Wounded and Sick of the Armies in the Field adopted on July 27th, 1929 left the stipulations concerning chaplains unchanged with one significant exception: their return. It is stated in Art. XII[187] that chaplains may not be detained after they have fallen into the power of the adversary. They have to be sent back to the belligerent to whose service they were attached. This has to happen as soon as a way is open for their repatriation and military exigencies permit so. The return of chaplains to their own party takes priority.[188] Only in the meantime, while waiting to be returned, they continue to exercise their functions as earlier under the direction of the adversary and are preferably assigned to minister to their own troops. Longer retention is possible only by a special agreement between the belligerents.[189] Stipulations on the use of the armlet with the distinctive emblem and the identity card are specified in detail.

The Convention Relative to the Treatment of Prisoners of War also of July 27th, 1929 takes up the stipulations of the Hague Regulations of 1907 with regard to the right of free exercise of religion for POW in its Art. XVI.[190] In addition to the Hague Regulations, the norm now also turns its attention to the ministers of a religion when it states that they are allowed to fully minister to the members of their religion.

Another revision conference scheduled for 1940 and also entrusted with the task to work out a convention for the protection of civilians in war was delayed due to World War II.[191]

---

[184] *See* Art. XX Geneva Convention 1906. The Armlet is sometimes also terminologically referred to as armband or brassard, *see* Odom, *supra* note 7, at 14.

[185] *See* Schlögel, *supra* note 38, at 267.

[186] *See id.* at 268.

[187] *See* THE LAW OF WAR, *supra* note 36, at 479.

[188] *See* Stadlmeier, *supra* note 155, at 523.

[189] *See also* PICTET, *supra* note 132, at 236, 241.

[190] *See* THE LAW OF WAR, *supra* note 36, at 497-98.

[191] *See* Hugo Schwendenwein, *Der Schutz der religiösen Sphäre in den Genfer Konventionen vom Roten Kreuz*, *in* PAX ET IUSTITIA 509, 510 (Hans Walter Kaluza et al. eds. 1990).

IV. Military chaplaincy and its protection in the catholic church

The status of chaplains is reflected on three levels, namely canon law as internal regulations of a religious community, public law of the state as the equivalent in a national jurisdiction and the level in which both levels relate to each other in agreements between church and state.[192] This book continues in the succeeding two chapters with an examination of these levels and will address the environment of military chaplaincy in the universal church and the German state. This is done for two motives: Firstly, chaplaincy and more than that the protection of spiritual assistance is not an end in itself but has an independent *raison d'être*. This reason for being is very well reflected in canonical and national norms. Secondly, some problems can only be discussed if the status of chaplaincy has been explained. The national legal status of chaplaincy is linked with the question for the protection of religious personnel in IHL.[193] Particularly in Germany, issues relating to protection of religious personnel in the past decade have been raised in the context of a national status debate. The controversies in this debate should not be omitted here and will be taken up in chapter VIII.

1. The Holy See and the Red Cross Movement

Even though the catholic church approached the evolution of IHL with some hesitance, it never rested inactive.[194] This is clearly reflected in the attitude of the Holy See which as representative of the church in the international arena takes up the causes of the catholic church doctrine. In these activities, the significance of the contribution by the Holy See for the conditions of military chaplaincy[195] becomes evident.

The invitation to attend the first conference to adopt the first Red Cross Convention in 1864 was also extended to the Holy See by the President of the Swiss Confederation. Cardinal GIACOMO ANTONELLI, the Secretary of State, answered in a reply that the Holy See was peace loving by nature and alien to warlike enterprises. Thus, it could not contribute to the discussions of that conference. However, the Holy See appreciated the efforts undertaken and did not fail to contribute to the implementation of the outcome of the conference because religious assistance to suffering people was considered to be of highest value.[196] It seems that already at this early stage, a misunderstanding existed with regard to

---

[192] *See also* Hiebel, *supra* note 17, at 532.
[193] *See* Rausch, *supra* note 139, at 24.
[194] *See* NICOLAS, *supra* note 16, at 114.
[195] *See* DORBJØRN OLSEN, DIE NATUR DES MILITÄRORDINARIATS 438 (1998).
[196] *See* KÖCK, *supra* note 143, at 596, Joseph Joblin, *At the Origins of Humanitarian Law: the Attitude of the Holy See*, L'OSSERVATORE ROMANO [english], August 11th/18th, 1999, at 3, 6, *available at* http://www.petersnet.net/research/retrieve.cfm?recnum=1187.

the role the Holy See expected to play at the conference envisaged in Geneva. While many European nations – particularly France and its King NAPOLEON III – were interested in an increased moral value of the adopted convention by the participation of a papal delegation, the Holy See was preoccupied with considerations regarding the secular signal that would come from its presence. Such considerations are clearly underlying the first reply of the Holy See to the invitation to join the adopted convention. The *charge d'affaires* in Switzerland informed the Swiss government in 1867 that the Holy See did not intend to wage war against anybody and in case it had to defend itself would care for the wounded of the aggressor with the same Christian love as it would care for its own wounded.[197] As the pressure increased, the *Saint-Siège* ratified the Red Cross Convention on May 9th, 1868[198] and considered this a particular gesture that "spiritual assistance may be brought more easily and more regularly".[199]

The initiative of Czar NICHOLAS II for the Hague Conference in 1899 was also addressed to the Holy See and received its favorable attention.[200] Valuable input from a Holy See delegation was expected particularly with regard to the good services that the pope had provided as a recognized institution of arbitration and mediation.[201] While the Holy See after its accession to the Red Cross Convention was regularly invited to the Conferences of Parties – the Red Cross Conferences –,[202] both, the first (1899) and the second (1907) Hague Peace Conference took place after the Italian unification and when the pope was *prigioniero in Vaticano*. Still, some diplomats had seen the possibility to use the Hague conference to resolve the Roman question. The link to the initiative of the Czar was seen in the fact that just and stable peace was impossible as long as Catholics were disturbed by the "intolerable situation of the pope".[203] However, these efforts failed. The great powers were not interested in raising highly politicized questions at the proposed conference. Even a participation of the Holy See without reference to the Roman question but as traditional mediator among nations[204]

---

[197] *See* KÖCK, *supra* note 143, at 596.

[198] *See* Schlögel, *supra* note 38, at 269, *see also* KÖCK, *supra* note 143, at 597 n.9 (for the text of the instrument of accession), at 604 n.32 (for the fact that the papal delegation at some Red Cross Conferences even after the Lateran treaties appeared as Etats Pontificaux), Joseph Joblin, *Le Saint-Siège et la Vie Internationale Contemporaine*, 31 ARCHIVUM HISTORIAE PONTIFICIAE 225-253 (1993) (for an in-depth study on the attitude of the Holy See to ratification of the Red Cross Convention).

[199] *See* Joblin, *supra* note 196.

[200] *See* David Alvarez, *The Holy See and the first Hague Peace Conference (1899)*, 26 ARCHIVUM HISTORIAE PONTIFICIAE 431 (1988).

[201] *See* KÖCK, *supra* note 143, at 617, *see also* at 785-86.

[202] *See id.* at 598.

[203] Alvarez, *supra* note 200 at 431, 432.

[204] *See also* Josef L. Kunz, *The Status of the Holy See in International Law*, 46 AMERICAN JOURNAL OF INTERNATIONAL LAW 312 (1952) (for examples during the Vatican Captivity).

was not feasible. Opposed to the wishes of the Secretary of State, Cardinal MARIANO RAMPOLLA, relayed to the Dutch government via its internuncio in The Hague, the Holy See was not given an opportunity to demonstrate the moral and humanitarian contributions that it could make to the resolution of serious world problems.[205] The papacy was not admitted to the first Hague Conference in 1899 because "influential quarters" had prevented it – namely Italy that had threatened to boycott any conference to which the Holy See was a party and was supported by its ally Germany.[206] As a protest, the internuncio in The Hague was recalled to Rome and did not return until 1911. Pope LEO XIII publicly blamed Italy in a speech in December 1899 as "the single voice" that kept the Holy See from exercising its mission of peace.[207] Nonetheless, a compromise was reached between the Dutch government and the Holy See. Guided by placatory motives in its national policy towards Catholics, the Dutch government came forward with a seemingly surprising request: At the final session of the Hague conference, on July 27th, 1899, a correspondence between Queen WILHELMA of the Netherlands and LEO XIII was read to the delegates. In this exchange of letters shortly prior to the beginning of the conference on May 18th, 1899, the Dutch government pointed out that it had wished that a delegation of the Holy See had participated in the conference. The "masterly reply"[208] of the pope dwelled strongly on what he called his natural position as a peacemaker on earth. For similar reasons, the Holy See was not invited to the second Hague Conference in 1907[209] and, all in all, did not play a prominent role in The Hague.[210]

After its accession to the 1864 Red Cross Convention, the Holy See continued to have a sceptical view on the Red Cross Movement and its seemingly liberal thought, suspected the influence of freemasonry and disapproved what it considered the sectarian spirit within the ICRC.[211] This attitude changed in the wake of World War I. The Holy See and the ICRC cooperated constructively in initiatives regarding the protection of POW and opposition to the use of chemical weapons. From 1921 on, the Holy See also participated in the Red Cross Conferences and for instance promoted in 1922 the universality of the International League of Red Cross Societies[212] when an accession of the German Red Cross

---

205 *See* Alvarez, *supra* note 200 at 431, 433.
206 *See* Schlögel, *supra* note 38, at 270, Alvarez, *supra* note 200 at 433-34.
207 *Cited in* KÖCK, *supra* note 143, at 619.
208 SCOTT, *supra* note 163, at 84-85.
209 *See* KÖCK, *supra* note 143, at 620 n.28.
210 *See* DRAPER, *supra* note 7, at 18.
211 *See* KÖCK, *supra* note 143, at 599 n.14.
212 The League of Red Cross Societies was renamed in October 1983 to the Leage of Red Cross and Red Crescent Societies and in November 1991 became the International Federation of Red Cross and Red Crescent Societies.

Society was disputed.[213] The changed attitude is well reflected in a letter of the Secretary of State, Cardinal PIETRO GASPARRI in January 1923 to the Secretary General of the League of Red Cross Societies. In this letter, it is stressed that the pope saw with favor the spreading and the development of works that, like the Red Cross, were designed to develop a spirit of human solidarity in the world. But the letter also pointed out that this solidarity in order to be effective and really felt had to be stimulated by the divine principles of the Christian religion.[214]

Article 24 of the Vatican Concordat with Italy, which is a component of the 1929 Lateran Pacts, obliged the Holy See to take no part in any international congresses called to settle temporal rivalries between other states. The Holy See, however, reserved the right of exercising its moral and spiritual power in any case. The provision makes another exception for the event that other parties make a mutual appeal to the pacific mission of the Holy See. A conference convened to revise the Red Cross Convention is certainly not designed to deal with temporal rivalries but more an occasion that calls for the moral and spiritual input on the part of the Holy See. Accordingly, after the Roman question had been settled in the Lateran Pacts, it was no question that the Holy See could participate in revision conferences. And so the diplomatic conference to revise the Red Cross Convention in 1949 was the first that papal representatives attended.[215] By that time, the interest of the Holy See into the issue of humanitarian law and the protection of the victims of war had grown to an extend that a papal delegation did not only participate on the expert level of a study commission of religious organizations[216] and the governmental level of the diplomatic conference but also as a member *sui generis* on the level of the national Red Cross Societies. Another result of that grown interest were improved relationships with the ICRC that were aided by the perception of the Holy See that the ICRC endeavored "to facilitate the work of chaplains"[217] and coordinated its work with other agencies carrying out humanitarian activities.[218] The special

---

[213] *See* KÖCK, *supra* note 143, at 599-601.

[214] *See* KÖCK, *supra* note 143, at 613.

[215] *See* Schlögel, *supra* note 38, at 270.

[216] *See infra* 69.

[217] *See* FEDERAL POLITICAL DEPARTMENT, 2-A FINAL RECORD OF THE DIPLOMATIC CONFERENCE FOR THE ESTABLISHMENT OF INTENATIONAL CONVENTIONS FOR THE PROTECTION OF WAR VICTIMS AND HELD AT GENEVA ON APRIL 21ST, TO AUGUST 12TH, 1949, at 261 (1950), KÖCK, *supra* note 143, at 603, 606.

[218] *See* FEDERAL POLITICAL DEPARTMENT, 2-B FINAL RECORD OF THE DIPLOMATIC CONFERENCE FOR THE ESTABLISHMENT OF INTENATIONAL CONVENTIONS FOR THE PROTECTION OF WAR VICTIMS AND HELD AT GENEVA ON APRIL 21ST, TO AUGUST 12TH, 1949, at 21, 323 (1950), *see also* Thomas G. J. Kerstiens, *Philosophy and practical possibilities of church organizations, in* ASSISTING THE VICTIMS OF ARMED CONFLICT AND OTHER DISASTERS 61, 65 (Frits Kalshoven ed, 1989) (for a critical view on the cooperation of the ICRC and church organizations).

character of religious organizations in armed conflict as being distinct from relief organizations was a topic of particular attention for the Holy See's delegation to the 1949 diplomatic conference.[219] The Holy See ratified the Geneva Conventions on February 2nd, 1951[220] and the 1954 Hague Convention on the Protection of Cultural Property in the Event of Armed Conflict and its Protocol on February 24th, 1958.

The Holy See was again party to the diplomatic conference 1974-1977 that adopted the PAs, contributed constructively and won many other delegations for the sake of protection of religious freedom due to its recognized expertise in the field.[221] The Holy See nonetheless delayed the ratification of the PAs as it deemed PA II unsatisfactory. But Papal diplomats could eventually be convinced of the intrinsic value of PA II that admittedly weak in substance is important as a symbol. The ICRC also considered the Holy See's ratification important as it undoubtedly had a favorable effect in a number of capital cities, particularly in Latin America.[222] The Holy See ratified both PAs on November 21st, 1985.[223]

The Holy See enjoys continuously good and lively relations with the ICRC both in Geneva and in the field.[224] They cooperate in particular cases that as a result of the nature of both institutions' diplomacy often remain discrete.[225] The ICRC remains religiously neutral but seeks cooperation with contemporary spiritual and moral authorities. As IHL, of which the ICRC considers itself the custodian, and the majority of the great religions are built to a large extend on the same values, both unite their efforts in dialogue for the promotion of these values.[226] At the same time, the Holy See holds collaboration with the ICRC in high esteem.[227] Since 1967, the Holy See's representative to the UN and to the other international organizations in Geneva was also entrusted with the contacts to the ICRC.[228] JOHN PAUL II acknowledged the ICRC's contribution to "instill-

---

[219] *See id.* at 322.
[220] *See* KÖCK, *supra* note 143, at 606.
[221] *See* Kussbach, *supra* note 144, at 391.
[222] *See* HANS PETER GASSER, PERSUADING STATES TO ACCEPT HUMANITARIAN TREATIES, *available at* http://www.icrc.org/Web/eng/siteeng0.nsf/iwpList74/49849BB8753552BCC1256B66005B05D1.
[223] *See* HUMAN RIGHTS IN THE TEACHING OF THE CHURCH 181 n.* (Giorgio Filibeck ed. 1994).
[224] *See also* TOMASI, *infra* note 268, No. 6 (describing the catholic church as a partner and supporter of the Movement of the Red Cross and the Red Crescent).
[225] *See* KÖCK, *supra* note 143, at 608-611.
[226] *See* Yves Sandoz, *This Is Not a Celebration But a Reflection on Common Values*, L'OSSERVATORE ROMANO[english], August 11th/18th, 1999, at 5, *available at* http://www.petersnet.net/research/retrieve.cfm?recnum=1189.
[227] *See* GIOVANNI PAOLO II, DISCORSO AL COMITATO INTERNAZIONALE DELLA CROCE ROSSA No. 6 (June 15th, 1982), *available at* http://www.vaticanradio.org/ArchivioViaggi/OrganjsmiInternazionali/CRI15_06_82.htm.
[228] *See* KÖCK, *supra* note 143, at 607.

ing respect for the basic rights of man and his dignity".[229] The ICRC received in irregular intervals financial contributions from the Holy See.[230] The cooperation is also reflected in the plan of Action of the 1999 International Red Cross Conference. The final goal 1.4 (Action proposed No. 18) projects that the ICRC develops innovative ways in collaboration with religious and other comparable institutions to promote the acceptance of IHL and Red Cross and Red Crescent principles by all relevant actors in armed conflict situations.[231]

2. International Humanitarian Law and church doctrine

a. Bellum iustum revisited

In the first chapter, we have followed the evolution of the *bellum iustum* doctrine from the Middle Ages to the rise of the modern state, from a substantive to a procedural notion. It was argued that with this evolution, the authorship of legal acts designed to protect religious personnel shifted from the church to the state. Even though it did not influence the level of protection any longer, the just war doctrine lived on in the teachings of the catholic church on peace.

What theoretically had been imagined in the 19th century as a seemingly clean duel among European states unmasked in two disastrous world wars. Totalitarian ideology became the cause to justify total warfare waged with the weaponry of the 20th century, cost the lives of millions and resulted in the loss of the most valuable achievement of the classical law of nations, the containment or "hedging" of war.[232] The international community met this development with the establishment of the United Nations (UN) that represent the obligatory way of modern civilization and of world peace.[233] Its basic principles – amongst them the comprehensive ban of a resort to force or threat therewith – are enshrined in the UN-Charter that forms as a *ius contra bellum* the corner stone of our present day international legal order. The UN's system of collective security opted for a discriminatory approach in *ius ad bellum* and allowed the application of armed force only in two exceptional cases: in self-defense[234] and when mandated in accordance with chapter VII of the UN-Charter. As a result, a discriminatory *ius*

---

[229] John Paul II, *Address to the International Committee of the Red Cross* (June 15th, 1982), *in* HUMAN RIGHTS IN THE TEACHING OF THE CHURCH, *supra* note 223, B.198.4 at 274.

[230] *See* KÖCK, *supra* note 143, at 612, *see also* Vatican Information Service Daily Bulletin of December 5th, 1997 (US-$ 100.000 from the Holy See for the ICRC).

[231] *See Plan of Action for the years 2000-2003*, INTERNATIONAL REVIEW OF THE RED CROSS 880-895 (1999), *available at* http://www.icrc.org/Web/eng/siteeng0.nsf/iwpList188/E5749851E7D0231BC1256B66005DE9C1.

[232] *See* GREWE, *supra* note 45, at 622.

[233] *See* PAUL VI, DISCOURS À L'ORGANISATION DES NATION UNIES À L'OCCASION DU 20ÈME ANNIVERSAIRE DE L'ORGANISATION No. 1 (October 4th, 1965), *available at* www.vatican.va/holy_father/paul_vi/speeches/1965/documents/hf_p-vi_spe_19651004_united-nations_fr.html.

[234] *See* Art. 51 UN-Charter.

ad (vel contra) bellum was combined with a non-discriminatory *ius in bello*. The outlawry of war as such even went as far as to positively approach unjust causes in a criminal arena. The discussion about the penalization of the act of aggression reached a peak through the incorporation of aggression in the list of crimes of the Statute of the International Criminal Court (ICC). However, the ongoing discussion about the definition of the crime and the uncertainty of the ICC's future given the resistance of a number of states indicate that the development in this regard is yet unfinished. On the part of the church, the creation of the ICC was welcomed as a contribution "to assuring on the world scale the efficient protection of human rights".[235]

As often in history, theory and practice follow parted paths: The prohibition of the use of force faces a reality where the application of armed force outside the UN-Charter framework takes place, where recourse to institutions of the classical law of nations such as reprisals or interventions happen.[236] With view on this doctrinal evolution, THOMAS AQUINAS' just war requirements may be recalled and applied to this setting. Then it seems highly questionable how a war can possibly be just in practice or if a war of the past has been just.[237] In this sense, just war doctrine in misleading. The practical implementation of the just war doctrine in a war theater is also what underlied FRANCISCO DI VITORIA's doubts about just war.[238] Some writers go as far as to attribute the ability to combine internal love with external battle only to Saints. War still exists as a reality, in most cases is not justified by the UN-Charter causes and even then might only be in accordance with a procedural understanding of just war. Nonetheless, there are voices that compare the standard of the Charter with the ongoing reality and consider it too reductionistic.[239]

Different from this rather formal view is the claim of the church for a moral judgment according to its substantive understanding of just war that it never gave up when the doctrine developed into a different direction in international law. Though there are singular voices that come to the conclusion that war in modern times is to be prohibited as such[240] the teaching office does not consider

---

[235] *See* Giovanni Paolo II, *Messagio per la Giornata Mondiale della pace 1999* (December 8th, 1998), *in* I DIRITTI DELL'UOMO NELL'INSEGNAMENTO DELLA CHIESA B.314 at 456 (Giorgio Filibeck ed. 2001).

[236] *See* GREWE, *supra* note 45, at 682-84.

[237] *See* JOURNET, *supra* note 48, at 364, *see also* O'BRIEN, *supra* note 134, at 44 (regarding difficulties in fully implementing the principle of discrimination), Heinz Karst, *Stellungnahme eines Soldaten*, 1961/62 MILITÄRSEELSORGE 126, 134 (elaborating the dilemma of judgement for a soldier).

[238] *See* FRANCISCO DE VITORIA, *supra* note 97, at 566-78.

[239] *See* JOHNSON, note 53, at 21.

[240] *See* ALFREDO OTTAVIANI, 1 INSTITUTIONES IURIS PUBLICI ECCLESIASTICI 153 (3rd ed. 1947).

modern warfare *per se* as prohibited,[241] neither did *Vaticanum II*[242] nor did the Catechism for the Catholic Church.[243]

But significant changes in the past 30 years must be noted. JOHN XXIII explained his conviction for peaceful conflict resolution with the destructive force of modern weapons.[244] Just war arguments were raised when authors discussed in the 1980s the possibility to apply the known principles of proportionality and discrimination to nuclear warfare. Neither the church nor for instance the International Court of Justice in its nuclear arms opinion clearly condemned all use of nuclear weaponry. It evolved as common Christian doctrine that the use of armed force alone could never solve conflicts and create peace in the sense that peace is "not merely the absence of war … [but] the fruit of love"[245] On the background of this substantive understanding of peace, the catholic church leaves behind just war doctrine and instead embraces the notion of a just international order.[246] Even though this change in the Holy See's policy is also noted with reservation or even with opposition,[247] it is also reflected in the local churches, for instance, by the German episcopate that declared "Just Peace" a role model for the church and named its latest document on peace ethics accordingly. This development does not totally deny a justification of armed conflict, but it builds up a strong pressure to first exhaust all alternative options of conflict resolutions before resorting to armed force. An illustrative example in this regard was the Holy See's forceful diplomatic initiative prior to U.S. led Operation Iraqi Liberty in 2003, the third Gulf War.

This shift towards the notion of a just international order - if understood correctly - can only be effective vis-à-vis the *ius ad bellum* aspect of the just war doctrine. There are no indicators that principles as discrimination – linked with non-combatants' immunity – and proportionality that are *ius in bello* outflows of

---

[241] *See* Böckenförde/Spaemann, *supra* note 49, at 274.

[242] *See* PASTORAL CONSTITUTION ON THE CHURCH IN THE MODERN WORLD "GAUDIUM ET SPES" No. 79 (December 7th, 1965), *available at* http://www.vatican.va/archive/hist_councils/ii_vatican_council/documents/vat-ii_cons_19651207_gaudium-et-spes_en.html.

[243] *See* CATECHISM OF THE CATHOLIC CHURCH No. 2309 (October 11th, 1992), *available at* www.vatican.va/archive/ccc_css/archive/catechism/p3s2c2a5.htm.

[244] *See* JOHN XXIII, PACEM IN TERRIS No. 126, 127 (April 11th, 1963), *available at* http://www.vatican.va/holy_father/john_xxiii/encyclicals/documents/hf_j-xxiii_enc_11041963_pacem_en.html.

[245] PASTORAL CONSTITUTION ON THE CHURCH IN THE MODERN WORLD "GAUDIUM ET SPES", *supra* note 242, No. 78.

[246] *See* Heinz-Joachim Fischer, *Der Vatikan entdeckt die gerechte internationale Ordnung*, FRANKFURTER ALLGEMEINE ZEITUNG, February 26th, 2003, at 5.

[247] *See* Regina Einig, *Die Achse der Unzufriedenheit*, DIE TAGESPOST, April 5th, 2003, at 3, *see also* JOHNSON, *supra* note 76, at 343.

the just war doctrine[248] are questioned. War as such is opposed, but if this opposition does not succeed, subsidiary mechanisms still come into play.

b. Teaching of the church on international humanitarian law

The Holy See's efforts in the international arena are designed to strengthen a wider role of the judicial element in international relations[249] in order to create in the place of a law of war a "law of peace, conceived in justice and solidarity".[250] The law is considered "the best guarantee of respect for persons".[251] In line of these efforts, the Message for the World Day of Peace 2004 was planned to be devoted to the topic of "International law – a way to peace".[252] After a shift in the Holy See's international policy, the original topic of international law was addressed in the greater context of teaching peace.[253] The message acknowledged difficulties of the present international legal order to deal with conflicts involving non-state terrorist groups, but insists on the primate of the law.[254]

Of particular interest is also the link between peace and justice. Peace can never be without justice under the law. Justice and charity that along with truth and liberty form the pillars of peace[255] stand in the center of humanitarian law.[256] IHL is under the primate of charity and justice is a first act of charity.[257] In humanitarian law, charity is not limited to mere expressions of favor at the

---

[248] *See supra* at 18.

[249] *See* John Paul II, *Address to the International Court of Justice* (May 13th, 1985), *in* HUMAN RIGHTS IN THE TEACHING OF THE CHURCH, *supra* note 223, B.184 at 254.

[250] JOHN PAUL II AND THE FAMILY OF PEOPLES 222, 259 (Ponifical Council for Justice and Peace ed. 2002).

[251] John Paul II, *Apostolic Letter on the occasion of the 50th anniversary of the outbreak of the Secon World War* (August 27th, 1989), *in* HUMAN RIGHTS IN THE TEACHING OF THE CHURCH, *supra* note 223, A.116.4 at 184.

[252] *See* Communication 370/2003 of the Vatican Press Office (July 17th, 2003), *available at* http://www.vatican.va/news_services/bulletin/news/13595.php?index=13595.

[253] *See* Heinz-Joachim Fischer, *Erziehung zum Frieden*, FRANKFURTER ALLGEMEINE ZEITUNG, December 16th, 2003, at 5 (attributing the change of focus to the change in the office of Secretary for Relations with States: Archbishop Jean-Louis Tauran, responsible for the strong opposition against the war in Iraq was elevated to the dignity of Cardinal but replaced in his former office by Archbishop Giovanni Lajolo who was expected to follow a more moderate course), *see also* ADDRESS OF HIS HOLINESS POPE JOHN PAUL II TO THE DIPLOMATIC CORPS ACCREDITED TO THE HOLY SEE (January 12th, 2004), *available at* http://www.vatican.va/holy_father/john_paul_ii/speeches/2004/january/documents/hf_jp-ii_spe_20040112_diplomatic-corps_en.html (for a similarly cautious tone).

[254] See JOHN PAUL II., AN EVER TIMELY COMMITMENT: TEACHING PEACE, Message of His Holiness Pope John Paul II for the Celebration of the World Day of Peace, No. 8 (January 1st, 2004), *available at* http://www.vatican.va/holy_father/john_paul_ii/messages/peace/documents/hf_jp-ii_mes_20031216_xxxvii-world-day-for-peace_en.html.

[255] *See* JOHN XXIII, *supra* note 244, subitle of the encyclical.

[256] *See* Kimminich, *supra* note 12, at 73.

[257] *See* Pictet, Jean, *The Principles of International Humanitarian Law*, 1966 INTERNATIONAL REVIEW OF THE RED CROSS 455, 469.

disposal of the one who grants it but is established as a matter of right. The weak, the victim and those who come to his help can claim respect and protection under the law. Even though the relevant norms are still undermined by violation, the creative force of the law cannot but be acknowledged.[258] As IHL protects human dignity by protecting man's freedom it fulfills the call to create an "order that is in accordance with the dictates of freedom".[259]

In view of the church, its own teaching as well as human reason both assert the permanent validity of the moral law during armed conflict.[260] But it is precisely when armed conflict erupts that "the need for regulations to curb the brutality of the warfare becomes urgent".[261] The church strongly rejects an absolute right to defense with regard to the *ius in bello*:[262] Certain means of warfare cannot not be justified. Because of their disproportionality their use would be an injustice that could not remedy the original injustice. Thus, catholic doctrine recognizes the IHL principle of proportionality.[263]

The church considers as ends for humanitarian law: rendering warfare less cruel, helping the victims of war in the name of the charity of Christ and educating the conscience with respect to human dignity.[264] The Second Vatican Council in its Pastoral Constitution on the Church in the modern world expressly referred to "international agreements aimed at making military activity and its consequences less inhuman".[265] It stated that IHL "must be honored" and improved so that "the frightfulness of war can be better and more workably held in check".[266]

The Holy See attaches importance to IHL "as a protection of the dignity of the human person even in the tragic context of war"[267] and looks at IHL as an

---

[258] *See* Kimminich, *supra* note 12, at 75.

[259] JOHN XXIII, *supra* note 244, No. 80.

[260] *See* CATECHISM OF THE CATHOLIC CHURCH, *supra* note 243, No. 2312.

[261] JOHN PAUL II, MESSAGE TO THE MILITARY CHAPLAINS (March 24th, 2003), *available at* http://www.vatican.va/holy_father/john_paul_ii/speeches/2003/march/documents/hf_jp-ii_spe_20030325_cappellani-militari_en.html.

[262] *See* Böckenförde/Spaemann, *supra* note 49, at 278, *see also* JOHN PAUL II., *supra* note 254, No. 6 (mentioning the principles of necessity and proportionality as limits to the natural right to legitimate defense).

[263] *See* ERNST JOSEF NAGEL, DIE FRIEDENSLEHRE DER KATHOLISCHEN KIRCHE 159-61 (1997).

[264] *See* GIORGIO FILIBECK, LA CHIESA E IL DIRITTO UMANITARIO 4 (unpublished paper presented at the International Course for the formation of catholic military chaplains in humanitarian law, Rome, March 25th, 2003).

[265] PASTORAL CONSTITUTION ON THE CHURCH IN THE MODERN WORLD "GAUDIUM ET SPES", *supra* note 242.

[266] *Id.*

[267] JOHN PAUL II, *supra* note 261.

"important, invaluable, non-negotiable and still relevant instrument".[268] No clearer statement can be imagined than JOHN PAUL II's proclamation that "[i]nternational humanitarian law must be imposed in ... conflicts. ... [T]hese rules must be observed".[269] He rates IHL as "a laborious achievement" of the 20th century[270] and as a guarantee for a minimal protection of human dignity.[271]

The Holy See expressively called for the development of humanitarian law in order to respond to new human development paradigms and progress in human rights reflection.[272] It expressed its appreciation for the role of the ICRC in this development.[273] The Holy See already discerns elements of such a development "particularly in aiding the victims of war".[274] The German bishops even dealt with the efficiency of IHL at a practicable level and called for superiors and subordinates to be well informed on the norms governing IHL.[275] The work of religious personnel present in the armed forces in this regard is also understood as a "significant although limited" contribution to the building of the conscience on which respect for normative structures like humanitarian law can be based.[276] The formation of the conscience in order to foster an authentic desire for peace is an important duty of military chaplains.[277] They convey values in order to make IHL "not merely a juridical code, but first and foremost an ethical code".[278] The catholic church here is also willing to make use of the network of catholic educational institutions to increase respect for humanitarian law.[279]

---

[268] SILVANO M. TOMASI, INTERVENTION BY THE HOLY SEE AT THE 28TH INTERNATIONAL CONFERENCE OF THE RED CROSS AND RED CRESCENT SOCIETIES (December 2003), *available at* http://www.vatican.va/roman_curia/secretariat_state/2003/documents/rc_seg-st_20031209_red-cross_en.html, No. 3.

[269] INTERNATIONAL INSTITUTE OF HUMANITARIAN LAW, POPE JOHN PAUL II TO THE INTERNATIONAL INSTITUTE OF HUMANITARIAN LAW 9 (1982).

[270] JOHN PAUL II AND THE FAMILY OF PEOPLES, *supra* note 250, at 216.

[271] *See* GIOVANNI PAULO II, LA VITA CHRISTIANA COME CAMMINO VERSO LA PIENA COMUNIONE CON DIO (General Audience, August 11th, 1999), *available at* http://www.vatican.va/holy_father/john_paul_ii/audiences/1999/documents/hf_jp-ii_aud_11081999_it.html.

[272] *See* DIARMUID MARTIN, INTERVENTION AT THE MEETING OF THE CCW GROUP OF GOVERNMENTAL EXPERTS (July 23rd, 2002), *available at* http://www.vatican.va/roman_curia/secretariat_state/documents/rc_seg-st_doc_20020723_martin-geneve_en.html.

[273] *See* GIOVANNI PAOLO II, *supra* note 261, No. 3.

[274] John Paul II, *supra* note 249.

[275] *See* GERECHTER FRIEDE No. 141 at 80 (Sekretariat der Deutschen Bischofskonferenz ed. 2000).

[276] *See* Filibeck, *supra* note 142 (for the example South Africa).

[277] *See* JOHN PAUL II, ADDRESS TO THE THIRD INTERNATIONAL AND INTERDENOMINATIONAL CONFERENCE OF CHIEF MILITARY CHAPLAINS OF EUROPE AND NORTH AMERICA (February 6th, 1992), *available at* http://www.vatican.va/holy_father/john_paul_ii/speeches/1992/documents/hf_jp-ii_spe_19920206_military-chaplains_en.html.

[278] JOHN PAUL II, *supra* note 261.

[279] *See* TOMASI, *supra* note 268.

On many occasions, catholic representatives stood up against violations of humanitarian law. "To flout law and humanitarian conventions" was condemned as "a step backwards".[280] Disrespect for and violations of humanitarian law were denounced. Instead of a public opinion becoming accustomed to IHL violations, a firm and united reaction on the part of the international community were demanded.[281] Indiscriminate destruction was considered by *Vaticanum II* "a crime against God and man himself" to merit "unequivocal and unhesitating condemnation".[282] The destruction of places of worship and the mistreatment and murder of religious personnel were mentioned.[283] In some numbers the Catechism of the Catholic Church even reads like an IHL manual: "Non-combatants, wounded soldiers, and prisoners must be respected and treated humanely".[284] The demand to protect religious personnel as non-combatants is thus also a demand of catholic faith. "Actions deliberately contrary to the law of nations" are considered crimes.[285]

JOHN PAUL II particularly stressed the view on the individual as the basis of humanitarian law.[286] The human person as subject of rights stood in the center of attention. In this, the interest of the person that transcended the interests of the states was underlined. It is a concern of the church to point out the link between religion and IHL. The "tendency to mitigate the traditional ferocity of war, so as to ensure more humane treatment for those involved in the hostilities" is seen in line with the Christian view of man.[287] Religious affirmation of man's autonomous value and pre-eminent dignity as person may even offer a basis for developments in IHL.[288] The church also draws attention on a coherent understanding of IHL. The link between human rights and humanitarian law had already been stressed in the debate regarding a preamble to the convention during the 1949 diplomatic conference by the Holy See's representative.[289] The growing body of IHL "finds solid foundation and true value only in connection with human rights".[290] Both fields have universal character as they base on the human person as the original and autonomous subject.

---

[280] JOHN PAUL II AND THE FAMILY OF PEOPLES, *supra* note 250, at 202.

[281] *See* TOMASI, *supra* note 268, No. 2, JOHN PAUL II AND THE FAMILY OF PEOPLES, *supra* note 250, at 216, 239, GIOVANNI PAULO II, note 271.

[282] PASTORAL CONSTITUTION ON THE CHURCH IN THE MODERN WORLD "GAUDIUM ET SPES", *supra* note 242, No. 80.

[283] *See* JOHN PAUL II AND THE FAMILY OF PEOPLES, *supra* note 250, at 216, 274.

[284] *See* CATECHISM OF THE CATHOLIC CHURCH, *supra* note 243, No. 2313.

[285] *Id.*

[286] *See* JOHN PAUL II AND THE FAMILY OF PEOPLES, *supra* note 250, at 222, 258.

[287] INTERNATIONAL INSTITUTE OF HUMANITARIAN LAW, *supra* note 269, at 8.

[288] *See id.*

[289] *See supra* at 70.

[290] INTERNATIONAL INSTITUTE OF HUMANITARIAN LAW, *supra* note 269, at 7.

During a conference on the protection of victims of war, the head of the Holy See's delegation, Archbishop TABET, underlined the transcendent roots of IHL:[291] Without the conviction that human dignity had a transcendent source, man would hardly refrain from using all available means of combat that assure victory at any price. As the international order is a man-made structure, like man it cannot rest on a purely material and worldly fundament. It must also be rested on conscience because conversion to peaceful ends is first and foremost a personal transformation. Thus, the building of the modern civilization must be based on spiritual principles because these principles do not only provide support but also shed light upon this world and stimulate men.[292]

c. Attempting an evaluation

A monograph on protection of religious personnel cannot leave open the question whether the goals of humanitarian law, to establish a minimum of humanity in warfare, can be reached.[293] It is true: Whatever legal protection there is, it might provide relief only to a relatively small part of the miseries of war. Whatever is undertaken to humanize warfare can never be used not to consider the preservation and safeguarding of peace the highest goal of all activities in international politics.[294] Public awareness in many cases prefers not to deal with humanitarian law because it sees its weaknesses and is focused on peace as a total abstention from force.[295] But the prohibition to use armed force in international disputes as recognized in international law does not contradict efforts to frame a law that is applicable in armed conflict. The Holy See even gave an example for connecting a humanitarian law pledge with the call for peace when its declaration on the ratification of the PAs affirmed the abolition of war as the ultimate goal of all efforts in view of the vocation of man and human civilization.[296] In addition, the attempt to regulate for the case of a violation of the prohibition to use armed force must not be interpreted as a legitimizing a possibly illegitimate use of force.[297] IHL takes no stance on the morality of a conflict. Furthermore: The invention of weapons of mass destruction (WMD) in modern

---

[291] *See* Paul F. Tabet, *Humanitarian Assistance is equivalent with a moral imperative*, *cited in* NAGEL, *supra* note 263, at 231, *see also* Filibeck, *supra* note 142 (for the transcendent foundation of human dignity as center of humanitarian law), Michel Veuthey, *International Humanitarian Law and Spirituality*, 21 REFUGEE SURVEY QUARTERLY No. 3, at 45 (2002) (for a comprehensive overview on the broader link of IHL with spirituality).

[292] *See* PAUL VI, *supra* note 233, No. 7.

[293] *But see* Rausch, *supra* note 139, at 36.

[294] *See* O'BRIEN, *supra* note 134, at 329.

[295] *See* ANDREAS VON BLOCK-SCHLESIER, DIE FRAGE DER AKZEPTANZ DES HUMANITÄREN VÖLKERRECHTS AM ENDE DES 20. JAHRHUNDERTS 121 (1999).

[296] *See* FILIBECK, *supra* note 264, at 5.

[297] *See* O'BRIEN, *supra* note 154, at 12, Stadlmeier, *supra* note 155, at 521, Kimminich, *supra* note 172, at 160, OTTO KIMMINICH, RELIGIONSFREIHEIT ALS MENSCHENRECHT 122 (1990).

warfare does not make impossible their use in practice. In this case, war is not impossible but survival afterwards. Thus, it should be recognized that IHL does not consider war as unavoidable or even desirable, just as law of armed conflict and law to prevent conflict do not contradict each other but go hand in hand.[298]

Then it is necessary and ethical to prepare for the eventuality of war when efforts to avoid it have failed in order to contain the misery of war.[299] The quest to put a just international world order into place does not necessarily succeed. The realization of the limited effects of legal protection in warfare compared to the miseries and destructions does not give the slightest right to refrain from raising these legal claims or the call for their implementation. Human life, human dignity are neither quantitatively measurable nor statistically comparable values. And it is this very human dignity that is at stake.[300] The idea of humanity must be upheld in order to not pull down the bridge to a better future. The worst there could be is a cynical nihilism, skepticism towards human rights and humanity born in defeatism.[301]

The author of a theological thesis on the legal basis of catholic military chaplaincy in the *Bundeswehr* concludes his passage on protection in humanitarian law with the remark that "international law agreements ... are certainly very good, but I would prefer to refrain from testing their efficiency in practice".[302] This evaluation falls certainly short. It suffices insofar as it expresses the hope that war is not inevitable and not a perennial fact of human life in view of man's imperfect nature and history.[303] For some, this hope is fueled by the "inexhaustible optimism" of the Christian notion of peace.[304] Until this point of history, war has been a human reality but there has been progress in the development of means that can guarantee the security of international life without any recourse to arms.[305] The international community has developed substantive legal instruments that can serve as such means. It is true that "[t]he world will never be the dwellingplace of peace, till peace has found a home in the heart of each and

---

[298] *See* Kussbach, *supra* note 144, at 385, Kimminich, *supra* note 172, at 161.

[299] *See* Karl Hörmann, *Krieg (ethisch)*, *in* KATHOLISCHES SOZIALLEXIKON 1556 (2nd ed. 1980), O'BRIEN, *supra* note 134, at 329.

[300] *See* Filibeck, *supra* note 142.

[301] *See* HUBER, *supra* note 19, at 54-55

[302] REINHOLD BARTMANN, DIE RECHTLICHEN GRUNDLAGEN DER KATHOLISCHEN SEELSORGE IN DER BUNDESWEHR 97 (unpublished „Diplom" thesis, University of Regensburg produced after 1986).

[303] *See* GIUSEPPE BERTELLO, INTERVENTION OF THE HOLY SEE AT THE 27TH INTERNATIONAL CONFERENCE OF THE RED CROSS AND RED CRESCENT SOCIETIES (November 2nd, 1999), *available at* http://www.vatican.va/roman_curia/secretariat_state/documents/rc_seg-st_doc_19991102_croix-rouge_fr.html, *but see* O'BRIEN, *supra* note 134, at 329.

[304] Paul VI, *Message for the 1969 World Day of Peace* (December 8th, 1968), *in* HUMAN RIGHTS IN THE TEACHING OF THE CHURCH, *supra* note 223, A.118 at 186.

[305] *See* PAUL VI, *supra* note 233, No. 5.

every man".[306] In the meantime, men will have to undertake all efforts to establish new relationships in human society, under the mastery and guidance of truth, justice, charity and freedom. Religions and their ministers are expected to contribute spiritual assistance as mankind shoulders this immense task. And this meantime, until this world is a dwellingplace of peace, it is the appropriate field of application for humanitarian law in armed conflict not only because also religious ministers need legal protection in armed conflict.

3. Military chaplaincy and the church

a. The teaching office on military chaplaincy

Statements of popes on the activities of military chaplains were often related to wars. On October 8th, 1914, for instance, BENEDICT XV urged his priests in the belligerent countries to remain impartial and not to animate the faithful against the enemy countries.[307] His call remained unheard. Bavaria is an example: Upon request of the ministry of war, chaplains and even the Archbishop of Munich readily expressed their willingness to lift the spirits of the troops and the population as preachers and to support the government against the emerging pessimism.[308] History has shown, that a number of chaplains tried to compensate their non-combatant status by becoming more bellicose and patriotic than the fighting troops. In some instances, chaplains resigned to become combatants to express their patriotism more unequivocally.[309] PIUS XII admonished the universal clergy in his Apostolic Exhortation *Asperis Commoti Anxietatibus* after the outbreak of World War II on December 8th, 1939.[310] Military service inconsistent with priestly vocation caused a crisis that should not be underestimated. The pope pointed out pastoral challenges and chances of the adverse circumstances. He recalled piety and spirituality as sources of strength to resist the evil in times of war. The difficulties of war crimes and clerical vocation are evident in the DEFREGGER-Case. MATTHIAS DEFREGGER was drafted by the German *Wehrmacht* after concluding his philosophical studies as a seminarian, was eventually promoted to the rank of a captain and became the commander of a communications unit. In this capacity, he was involved in the illegal execution of 17 male inhabitants in the Italian village Filetto in June 1944.[311] The campaign was in retaliation against a partisan attack that killed four German soldiers. In 1949, DEFREGGER was ordained as a priest and in 1968 – while the public

[306] JOHN XXIII, *supra* note 244, No. 165.

[307] *See* Georg Moser, *Friedensbemühungen der Päpste in unserem Jahrhundert*, 1973 MILITÄRSEELSORGE 161, 162.

[308] *See* Arnold Vogt, *Militärseelsorge in den königlich bayerischen Streitkräften bis 1918*, 1986 MILITÄRSEELSORGE 126, 160.

[309] *See* Alan Wilkinson, *The paradox of the military chaplain*, 84 THEOLOGY 249, 253 (1981).

[310] *See* 31 AAS 696-701 (1939).

[311] *See Der Fall Defregger*, 23 Herderkorrespondenz 393, 394 (1969).

prosecutor was already conducting investigations against him – consecrated as auxiliary bishop of Munich. His ordinary knew about the incident, but neither the nuntiature nor the Roman dicastries were informed. The affair became public in 1969 and produced numerous media reports. An article in the *L'Osservatore Romano* made clear that his appointment would not have occurred if the authorities of the Roman Curia had known his background. DEFREGGER resigned from his office the same year for "reasons of his health".[312] Criminal charges were dropped the following year since the prosecution considered DEFREGGER'S conduct a reprisal not prohibited at that time.[313] A similar position had earlier been taken by DEFREGGER'S ordinary. Besides the tragic figure of Bishop DEFREGGER, who did not dissociate from his actions, the role of his ordinary is particularly disconcerting as his management of the affair obscured credible testimony for the sake of victims of war on the part of the church.

The teaching office of the church does not expressively refer to the protection of military chaplains. Instead, the link to religious freedom must be seen here. *Vaticanum II* declared that "the human person has a right to religious freedom" and saw it founded "in the very dignity of the human person".[314] In its description of the effects of religious freedom, the Council outlines the shapes of a right to spiritual assistance in practice.[315] The Council also underlined the responsibility of the governments to "assume the safeguard of the freedom of religion of all its citizens, in an effective manner, by just laws and by other appropriate means".[316] These formulations apply obviously also to the protection of a religious sphere for members of the armed forces ("all its citizens") through international treaties ("by other appropriate means"). Accordingly, the states and the church grant themselves mutual help in order to remain faithful to their particular tasks.[317]

Vaticanum II also asked for special concern for faithful who are not adequately catered for by the ordinary pastoral ministry of the parochial clergy.[318] It took the policy decision to establish military vicariates - if possible - in every

---

[312] GÜNTER ASSENMACHER, DIE WEHRPFLICHTBEFREIUNG DER GEISTLICHEN 134-135, 135 n.270 (1987).

[313] *See* Gisela Friedrichsen, *Krieg ist nicht human*, DER SPIEGEL, No. 23, March 3rd, 2002, at 58.

[314] DECLARATION ON RELIGIOUS FREEDOM "DIGNITATIS HUMANAE" ON THE RIGHT OF THE PERSON AND OF COMMUNITIES TO SOCIAL AND CIVIL FREEDOM IN MATTERS RELIGIOUS No. 2 (December 7th, 1965), *available at* http://www.vatican.va/archive/hist_councils/ii_vatican_council/documents/vat-ii_decl_19651207_dignitatis-humanae_en.html.

[315] *See* Hiebel, *supra* note 17, at 537.

[316] DECLARATION ON RELIGIOUS FREEDOM, *supra* note 314, No. 6.

[317] *See* OLSEN, *supra* note 195, at 425.

[318] *See* DECREE CONCERNING THE PASTORAL OFFICE OF BISHOPS IN THE CHURCH "CHRISTUS DOMINUS" No. 18 (October 28th, 1965), *available at* http://www.vatican.va/archive/hist_councils/ii_vatican_council/documents/vat-ii_decree_19651028_christus-dominus_en.html.

country. The Council held spiritual care of military personnel to require special consideration "because of the unique conditions of their way of life".[319] The appreciation of the church for military chaplaincy is also reflected in statements of JOHN PAUL II who valued their "irreplaceable spiritual and human role, sharing the life and problems of the armed forces".[320] The role of the armed forces as defenders of inalienable human values such as life, freedom, law and justice offered many pastoral opportunities for the church.[321] Even a reference of military chaplaincy and respect for rights is drawn because it was a task of chaplaincy to encourage soldiers to act in a way which "reflects deep reverence for God and, consequently, unfailing respect for the dignity and rights of other persons".[322] However, in the understanding of the church, the role of chaplains both in war and in peace may always and only be that of pastors of souls.[323]

The approaches to demand protection of freedom of religion by the state and to offer spiritual assistance to members of the armed forces are combined in practice in the letter to the participants of the Helsinki Conference for Security and Cooperation in Europe: JOHN PAUL II specified the tasks of the state in this regard and underlined the understanding of the church that freedom of religion meant the liberty also for individuals in military establishments to receive religious assistance.[324] In protecting a religious sphere and in providing spiritual assistance in armed conflict, both partners fulfill their respective tasks.

b. Military chaplaincy in canon law

The Code of Canon Law of 1917 dealt with military chaplaincy only in can. 451 § 3 CIC/1917 and put the regulation of military chaplaincy into the competence of special norms by the Apostolic See. These norms were usually either statutes regulating the status of military vicars and their jurisdiction or norms on the obligations common to military vicars, e.g. with regard to their visits *ad limina*.

But we will later see that protection for clergy in armed conflict may come from another source because the 1917 Code still knew ecclesiastical privileges, namely the *privilegium immunitatis*: Can. 121 CIC/1917 held clergy to be exempt from military service. Who violated this right of the church as author of a law, decree or other order could be punished with excommunication reserved to

---

[319] *Id.* No. 43.

[320] John Paul II, *Witnesses to Christ in Military Life*, L'OSSERVATORE ROMANO [english], June 2nd, 1999, at 4, *available at* http://www.petersnet.net/research/retrieve.cfm?RecNum=1081.

[321] *See id.*

[322] JOHN PAUL II, *supra* note 277.

[323] *Id.*

[324] *See* John Paul II, *Letter to the Heads of State who signed the Helsinki Act* (September 1st, 1980), *in* HUMAN RIGHTS IN THE TEACHING OF THE CHURCH, *supra* note 223, B.248.4 at 331.

the Holy See.[325] A clergy could not individually waive a privilege of his state.[326] Accordingly, volunteering for the armed forces was prohibited[327] and was considered an implicit resignation from ecclesiastical offices.[328] The prohibition of voluntary military service also forbid participation in civil war and internal disturbances.[329] Seminarians had to serve their obligatory military service prior to their ordinations.[330] Like the prohibitions of earlier times, the *privilegium immunitatis* was rooted in the traditional understanding of a practical and spiritual incompatibility of the religious ministry and the service at arms.[331]

After World War I, the Sacred Consistorial Congregation issued the Decree "*De clericis et militia redeuntibus*".[332] The introductory note complains that military draft had taken "spiritual means" (clergy) from the parishes and seminarians from the institutes of formation. The decree continues to regulate canonical proceedings for clergy, religious and seminarians returning from war. It prescribed spiritual exercises for the returnees and allowed the local ordinary to dispense from irregularities while the dispensation of clergy who carried arms and may have wounded or killed others deliberately or who volunteered for military service was reserved to the Apostolic See.[333]

The Code of Canon Law of 1983 – like its precursor - assigns military chaplaincy to the domain of special legislation in can. 569 CIC.[334] In many cases, stipulations on military chaplaincy are also contained in concordats that form a part of the law according to can. 3 CIC. Difficulties concerning the theological and juridical nature of the ecclesiastical jurisdictions for military ordinariates led to the absence of more precise regulations on a military pastoral structure in the 1983 code.[335]

The catalogue of prohibitions and privileges of the 1917 Code is not carried over into the new Code. Can. 285 § 1 CIC obliges clergy to refrain from things

---

[325] *See* can. 2334 No. 1 CIC/1917.

[326] *See* can. 123, can. 72 § 3, 4 CIC/1917, *see also* HERIBERT JONE, 1 GESETZBUCH DER LATEINISCHEN KIRCHE 153 (1950).

[327] *See* can. 141 § 1 CIC/1917, *see also* ASSENMACHER, *supra* note 312, at 209, 213 (for the possibility of dispensation).

[328] *See* can. 188 No. 6 CIC/1917, *see also* can. 141 § 2 CIC/1917 (for seminarians to be laicized).

[329] *See* JONE, *supra* note 326, at 169.

[330] *See* can. 987 No. 5 CIC/1917.

[331] *See* ASSENMACHER, *supra* note 312, at 212.

[332] *See* 10 AAS 481-86 (1918).

[333] *See also* ASSENMACHER, *supra* note 312, at 217-221 (for other details of the decree).

[334] *See* ERWIN SIMON, DIE KATHOLISCHE MILITÄRSEELSORGE NACH DEM CODEX IURIS CANONICI UND DEN DAZU ERGANGENEN SONDERBSTIMMUNGEN UNTER BERÜCKSICHTIGUNG DER MILITÄRSEELSORGE IN DER BUNDESWEHR *passim* (1962) (for different models to organize military chaplaincy in canon law prior to the 1983 Code).

[335] *See* Eduardo Baura, *The Military Ordinariates from the perspective "Communio Ecclesiarum"*, *in* DIECI ANNI DOPO 55, 98 (1996).

that are unbecoming of their state and leaves detailed rules to particular law. Nonetheless, this norm is understood in the light of the old code to forbid carrying weapons "unless there was just reason for taking such precaution".[336] Unlike the 1917 Code, the Code of 1983 does not contain a *privilegium immunitatis* since *Vaticanum II* renounced such privileges claimed from the state to grant privileges to the church.[337] This renouncement was taken into account by the Pontifical Commission for the Reform of the CIC. But military service is considered to be hardly in keeping with the clerical state in can. 289. This is why the norm forbids clerics and candidates for sacred orders from the time of their *admissio* to volunteer for military service without the permission of their ordinary. "Military service" in this norm includes medical and other auxiliary services.[338] The preceding norm of can. 287 § 1 CIC that obliges clerics to foster peace and harmony among the people was originally meant as a commandment to justify the later prohibition of voluntary military service.[339] Such an understanding would have been inconsistent with the view of *Vaticanum II* on the service of military personnel as "agents of security and freedom of peoples ... making a genuine contribution to the establishment of peace."[340]

As members of the *communio* of the church, military personnel have the right to receive assistance from the sacred pastors out of the spiritual goods of the church according to can. 213 CIC. This right is another basis for military chaplaincy[341] and must be understood to apply also to extreme situation such as armed conflict. This right is also recognized as a moral right in other churches since ecclesiastical company in armed conflict does not mean a justification for that conflict but reflects the care for human lives involved in warfare.[342] In how far sacred ministers can be obliged to expose themselves to the increased risk could be subject of further inquiries.

On April 21st, 1986, JOHN PAUL II promulgated the Apostolic Constitution *Spirituali Militum Curae* (SMC).[343] Without prejudice to concordatarian provisions, SMC – together with national statutes – provides the specific legislation

---

[336] JOHN P. BEAL ET AL., NEW COMMENTARY OF THE CODE OF CANON LAW 374 (2000).

[337] *See* PASTORAL CONSTITUTION ON THE CHURCH IN THE MODERN WORLD "GAUDIUM ET SPES", *supra* note 242, No. 76, Heinrich J. F. Reinhardt, *can. 289*, No. 1, 2, *in* 2 MÜNSTERISCHER KOMMENTAR ZUM CODEX IURIS CANONICI (Klaus Lüdicke ed., 36th delivery December 2002), OLSEN, *supra* note 195, at 425.

[338] *See* Heinrich J. F. Reinhardt, *supra* note 337, No. 3.

[339] *See* Heinrich J. F. Reinhardt, *can. 287*, No. 1, *in* 2 MÜNSTERISCHER KOMMENTAR ZUM CODEX IURIS CANONICI (Klaus Lüdicke ed., 36th delivery December 2002).

[340] PASTORAL CONSTITUTION ON THE CHURCH IN THE MODERN WORLD "GAUDIUM ET SPES", *supra* note 242.

[341] OLSEN, *supra* note 195, at 418.

[342] *See* Rausch, *supra* note 139, at 35.

[343] 78 AAS 481-86 (1986) [herinafter: SMC].

that can. 569 CIC speaks about. SMC is framework legislation[344] because circumstances differ from place to place. These "general norms" are to be supplemented by statutes approved by the Holy See for each country.[345] BAURA considers SMC not to be special, but specific legislation fulfilling the legislative mandate by the *Vaticanum II.*[346]

SMC determines that military ordinariates are special ecclesiastical territories and legally comparable to dioceses.[347] The *Annuario Pontificio* of 2003 enumerated 34 military ordinariates.[348] Even though military ordinariates are supra-diocesan entities, they have a similar structure like dioceses regarding ordinary, presbytery and people.[349] Academia is still divided over the question whether the military ordinariates are particular churches or not – even though this problem "is more academic than practical".[350] While *Vaticanum II* stressed the character of military chaplaincy as interdiocesan task, SMC underlines similarities and comparability to a particular church.[351] The responsibility for the erection of military ordinariates rests with the Holy See[352] and according to Art. 76 of the Apostolic Constitution *Pastor Bonus*[353] is exercised by the Congregation for Bishops. The Central Office for pastoral coordination of the military ordinariates founded in 1985 is attached to this dicastry.

The jurisdiction of the military ordinary is proper and ordinary.[354] It is not delegated - like prior to SMC when military vicars were considered to be vicars of the Roman Pontiff[355] - but attached to his office. It is, however, only personal and cumulative to the ordinary jurisdiction of the territorial ordinary.[356] In this, SMC takes up the notion of cumulative jurisdiction – opposed to exemption - that was already followed in Art. 2 (2) of the Instructions *Sollemne Semper* of

---

344 *See* EDUARDO BAURA, LEGISLAZIONE SUGLI ORDINARIATI CASTRENSI 17 n.7 (1992) (for the term "legge-quadro").

345 *See* SMC, *supra* note 343, preamble, Art. 1 § 1, Art. 13.

346 *See supra* note 318, BAURA, *supra* note 344, at 7, *see also* critically OLSEN, *supra* note 195, at 281, 313.

347 *See* SMC, *supra* note 343, Art. 1 § 1.

348 *See* ANNUARIO PONTIFICIO PER L'ANNO 2003 (Direzione dell'Annuario Pontificio presso la Segreteria di Stato ed. 2003).

349 *See* Baura, *supra* note 335, at 129.

350 Baura, *supra* note 335, at 126, *see* Michel Dubost, *Spirituali Militum Curae and evangelium vitae*, *in* DIECI ANNI DOPO 161, 172 (1996), Gantin, *supra* note 15, at 27, *see also* Jean Beyer, *Die Apostolische Konstitution Spirituali Militum Curae über die Militärordinariate*, 1990 MILITÄRSEELSORGE 235, 247 (for it is a particular church), OLSEN, *supra* note 195, at 379 (for it is not a particular church).

351 OLSEN, *supra* note 195, at 313.

352 *See* SMC, *supra* note 343, Art. 1 § 2.

353 80 AAS 879 (1988).

354 *See* SMC, *supra* note 343, Art. 4.

355 *See* Beyer, *supra* note 350, at 240, OLSEN, *supra* note 195, at 292.

356 *See* Beyer, *supra* note 350, at 240.

the Consistorial Congregation[357] that in 1951 established universal rules for military chaplaincy. The personal and cumulative jurisdiction of the military ordinary constitutes a specialization of the jurisdiction[358] and reflects the joint responsibility of the College of Bishops.[359] Military personnel fall firstly and chiefly under the jurisdiction of the military ordinary and in a secondary way under that of the diocesan bishop.[360] If there is no military chaplain to minister to the needs of military personnel, the proper pastor of the territory where the military base is located has pastoral responsibility for military personnel in his parish – by own right.[361] This concept may cause problems of competence that ought to be solved from the perspective of the church as a *communio*.[362] The jurisdiction of the military ordinary is effective even in times when the subjects are beyond national boundaries, e.g. when military personnel is operating on mission abroad. On such missions, the ratio of special structures for military chaplaincy as a pastoral of mobility[363] becomes especially evident.[364]

In 1997, JOHN PAUL II decided that military ordinaries would no longer be assigned titular sees but would have the episcopal title of a bishop or archbishop for the military ordinariate of their respective country.[365] This measure is also in line with the Apostolic See's policy to limit the use of titular sees in the universal church as it is expressed in no longer assigning a titular see to bishops emeriti, to coadjutor bishops or heads of territorial prelatures.[366]

Military chaplains are not pastors in the canonical sense. Their community is not a parish in the canonical sense though they possess the rights and obligations like a pastor to his parish.[367] Thus, military chaplains are the equivalent of pastors of personal parishes. Besides the faculties mentioned in can. 566 CIC (hearing confession, preaching, administration of the Viaticum, anointing of the sick, confirmation of those in danger of death), he must be provided with all faculties which proper pastoral care requires. Military chaplains are usually granted pas-

---

357 43 AAS 562-65 (1951).

358 *See* BAURA, *supra* note 344, at 17, 21.

359 *See* Baura, *supra* note 335, at 113.

360 *See* SMC, *supra* note 343, Art. 5.

361 *See* JOHN P. BEAL ET AL., *supra* note 336, at 739.

362 *See* Baura, *supra* note 335, at 107, *see also* Pontifical Statutes, *infra* note 394, Art. 32 (for a conflict resolution mechanism in practice), OLSEN, *supra* note 195, at 378 (for examples of such conflicting competences).

363 *See* Beyer, *supra* note 350, at 239.

364 *See* Baura, *supra* note 335, at 101, Beyer, *supra* note 350, at 240-41.

365 *See Letter of the Congregation for the Bishops, Prot. N. 552/97*, 1997 PASTORALIS MILITUM CURA No. 2, at 3.

366 *See* Eduardo Baura, *The Episcopal Title of the Military Ordinary*, 1997 PASTORALIS MILITUM CURA No. 2, at 15.

367 *See* SMC, *supra* note 343, Art. 7.

toral faculties for solemn baptism, assisting marriages and conducting funerals.[368]

Under the 1983 Code of Canon Law, only priests can be chaplains in the canonical sense.[369] Nonetheless, there is no reason why deacons and laypersons could not participate in the exercise of pastoral care in analogy to can. 517 § 2 CIC and other relevant norms.[370] This view is supported by SMC that in Art. 6 § 2 expressively refers to "priests and deacons" and envisions a partnership of priests and deacons.[371] However, only priests may officiate as chaplains enjoying the rights and bound by the duties of pastors.[372] Concordatarian frameworks even allow for further going rules.

Canon law because of its nature contributes very little to the protection of religious personnel. SMC does not deal with protection of clergy in any aspect. Furthermore, the protection under humanitarian law does not refer to internal religious norms.[373] The CIC only indirectly provides protection that is yet to be examined.[374] But canonical norms establish the environment in which catholic military chaplaincy takes place in the various nations and are thus relevant.

V. Military chaplaincy in Germany and the environment of foreign deployment

This chapter will turn its attention to the legal status of military chaplaincy in Germany, national norms governing this status and the role of chaplains on deployment abroad. In order to make the current legal regime understandable, the history of this status will be briefly outlined.

---

[368] *See* JOHN P. BEAL ET AL., *supra* note 336, at 739.

[369] *See* can. 564 CIC, *but see* William T. Diteweg, *The permanent deacon as military chaplain*, 51 THE JURIST 340, 361 (1991) (considering this norm a description, not a definition).

[370] *See* e.g. the Instruction on Certain Questions Regarding the Collaboration of the Non-Ordained Faithful in the Sacred Ministry of Priests, 89 AAS 852-77 (1997), *see* Beyer, *supra* note 350, at 255 *see also* Art. 12 (1) of the Statutes of the military ordinariate of the Netherlands, *in* BAURA, *supra* note 344, 280 (including deacons in the clergy of the Dutch military ordinariate), Diteweg, *supra* note 369, at 360 (for permanent deacons in the practice of the U.S. Archdiocese for Military Service), Alfred E. Hierold, *Die Statuten für den Jurisdiktionsbereich des Katholischen Militärbischofs für die Deutsche Bundeswehr*, 1990 ARCHIV FÜR KATHOLISCHES KIRCHENRECHT 94 (1990) (for the reluctant formulations in the norms for Germany), ASSENMACHER, *supra* note 312, at 146-49 (for the restrictions for permanent deacons regarding military service). In Germany, permanent deacons like Karsten Erdmann are only in exceptional cases employed but not as chaplains but as as pastoral assistants, *see* NEUEINSTELLUNGEN IN DIE KATHOLISCHE MILITÄRSEELSORGE IM JULI UND AUGUST, *available at* http://www.kmba.de/aktuell/internas/060803/060803.htm.

[371] *See also* Diteweg, *supra* note 369, at 359.

[372] *See* SMC, *supra* note 343, Art. 7.

[373] *See* MARCHEGGIANO, *supra* note 107, at 13.

[374] *See supra* V.3.

1. A historic outline of military chaplaincy

The regulations of the decree of the *Concilium Germanicum* and of CHARLEMAGNE's *capitulare generale* expired not until the 16th century when a military chaplaincy was structured according to a model of the Swedish King GUSTAV ADOLF II in the *Geistliche Kriegsz-Ordnung* of 1564.[375] Later, with the development of standing armies, two different approaches emerged in Germany:

In Brandenburg/Prussia that favored the Lutheran confession, chaplaincy was integrated into the armed forces already in the 17th century. In 1717 the military parish became exempt. The chaplaincy in the Prussian army was headed by an army provost and was part of the military chain of command. This attempt to protect the military chaplaincy from influences by the civilian churches was consistent with the societal position of the military in Prussia and the instrumental role that Prussian monarchs and officers attributed to religion. FREDERICK II – the Great – stated in his military regulations of the year 1743:[376] A soldier who would not fear God would neither fear his military superiors. Religion was seen as formal obligation of duty, as a means to maintain discipline. Chaplaincy was structured accordingly.[377]

Bavaria, which was in favor of Catholicism, had a civilly structured chaplaincy only effective in times of war.[378] Chaplains were civilians and did not have a military rank. The experiences of the German-Austrian war 1866 resulted in the demand of the clergy to get the officer rank, to wear a uniform and to be better equipped. Only one thing in fact changed: Field chaplains now had to wear a white-violet armlet because Bavaria had acceded to the 1864 Red Cross Convention.[379] It was only the direct comparison of the two structures in the German-French war of 1870/71, in which Prussian and Bavarian troops fought side by side, that resulted in a favor for the Prussian model by the catholic church in Bavaria. In practice, nothing changed since Art. 61 of the Imperial Constitution held the federal states responsible for ecclesiastical matters in the military. And Bavaria was reluctant to take over the Prussian model mainly for financial reasons while most of the other federal states in fact copied the Prussian structures.[380]

---

[375] *See* MONICA SINDERHAUF, HISTORISCHE ENTWICKLUNG DER MILITÄRSEELSORGE 2 (unpublished paper dated February 13th, 2003), *see also* BLEESE, *supra* note 39, at 23.

[376] *See* BLEESE, *supra* note 39, at 25-143, 435.

[377] *See* JENS MÜLLER-KENT, MILITÄRSEELSORGE IM SPANNUNGSFELD ZWISCHEN KIRCHLICHEM AUFTRAG UND MILITÄRISCHER EINBINDUNG 8 (1990).

[378] *See* Vogt, *supra* note 308, at 127-28, BLEESE, *supra* note 39, at 124.

[379] *See* Vogt, *supra* note 308, at 133.

[380] *See id.* at 135-36.

The Prussian model was exposed to severe interferences of military policy and ideology in World War I.[381] Nonetheless, it survived the revolution and was taken over as the uniform model for the *Reichswehr* of the Weimar Republic. The *Reichskonkordat*[382] ended difficulties regarding the canonical jurisdiction of catholic chaplains. The Nazis generally opposed denominational religiosity but acknowledged the military use of chaplaincy as a tool in combat.[383] With the increased degree of ideologization of the *Wehrmacht*, chaplaincy activities became more difficult, but never ceased.

2 The legal regime for military chaplaincy

After World War II, a chaplaincy existed from 1951 for the 28.000 German paramilitary troops with the labor service units that assisted allied forces, e.g. in minesweeping. The question for a legal regulation of military chaplaincy became a topic again in the early 1950s. After the Berlin blockade and the Korean War and with the growing confrontation between the eastern and the western blocks it became increasingly clear that the division of Germany with two German states since 1949 was a more permanent state of affairs than had been believed earlier. With this development, a policy of re-armament in the context of a collective security endeavor came in reach. The first approach in the framework of the European Defense Community failed, but instead, Germany was invited to accede to the North Atlantic Alliance founded 1949 in Washington and in May 1955 became the 15th member of NATO. The formation of German Federal Armed Forces, the *Bundeswehr,* also included the development of a comprehensive concept for military chaplaincy, which took into account the experiences of German military chaplaincy in two world wars. Negotiations of the Federal Ministry of Defense with the protestant and the catholic churches then had the outcome that chaplaincy in the *Bundeswehr* should be as independent and at the same time as close to the troops as possible. Military chaplaincy was considered to be a task in the responsibility of the churches. This understanding for the role of chaplains in the *Bundeswehr* influenced the legal arrangements between the churches and the state regarding military chaplaincy. The result was a disintegrated and civilian status of military chaplains in Germany that is very different from the status in most other countries.

The Basic Law – the German equivalent of a constitution – guarantees freedom of religion in its Art. 4 and guarantees access of churches to the armed forces in Art. 140 by way of incorporating Art. 141 of the Weimar Constitution of 1919. These provisions are the constitutional basis for military chaplaincy in

---

[381] *See* SINDERHAUF, *supra* note 375, at 5.
[382] *See infra* note 388.
[383] *See* MÜLLER-KENT, *supra* note 377, at 22.

Germany and are statutorily developed in § 36 Military Service Act:[384] The soldier has a right to spiritual assistance and undisturbed exercise of religion. Participation in religious services is voluntary. The Joint Service Regulation on military chaplaincy sees it as a "contribution to assure the free exercise of religion in the armed forces supervised by the churches and appreciated and supported by the state".[385] Deriving military chaplaincy from freedom of religion[386] also makes clear that chaplaincy may only serve the individual who is situated in a particular group – the armed forces – and must not serve a military purpose. Chaplaincy is not designed to uphold morale or justify the use of armed force. The chaplain is a pastoral worker in a specific military setting, but not a religious officer or a military priest.[387]

Three other legal documents are important with regard to chaplaincy in Germany:

(i) The concordat between the German *Reich* and the Holy See[388] of 1933 that both, church and state, consider to be still in force. This international treaty guarantees in Art. 27 a catholic military chaplaincy. The four paragraphs of the norm contain furthermore general stipulations on the appointment of the military ordinary by the Holy See with the consent of the German government and on the appointment of his clergy. The regulation of the details is left to Pontifical Statutes for the catholic military chaplaincy that are promulgated by the pope in agreement with the German government.[389]

(ii) The Military Chaplaincy Agreement[390] of February 1957 between the Federal Republic of Germany and the Evangelical Church in Germany (EKD) that provides the details of the status of chaplains as discussed *infra*.

(iii) The Military Chaplaincy Act of 1957[391] ratifying the Military Chaplaincy Agreement regulating that the status of the Military Chaplaincy Agreement is to be applied also for catholic chaplains.

On the canonical level, Pontifical Statutes promulgated by the Holy See for the various countries supplement nationally the framework legislation of

---

384 1975 BGBl. I at 2273.

385 *See ZDv 66/1*, in DOKUMENTATION ZUR KATHOLISCHEN UND EVANGELISCHEN MILITÄRSEELSORGE 63, No. 1 at 63 (7th ed. 2002).

386 *See also* OLSEN, *supra* note 195, at 426-28 (on difficulties of upholding religious freedom in the environment of armed forces)

387 *See* Hiebel, *supra* note 17, at 532.

388 1933 RGBl. II at 679, 25 AAS 389 (1933).

389 *See also id.* (for the stipulations on Art. 27 § 4 of the final protocol to the *Reichskonkordat*).

390 1957 BGBl. II at 702 [herinafter: Military Chaplaincy Agreement].

391 1957 BGBl. II at 701.

SMC.[392] These norms apply universal legislation on a national setting and adapt them accordingly. The *Reichskonkordat* makes reference to such statutes and assigns to them to regulate the organization of catholic military chaplaincy. With the Apostolic Brief *Moventibus Quidem*,[393] Pope JOHN PAUL II promulgated new "*Statuten für den Jurisdiktionsbereich des Katholischen Militärbischofs für die Bundeswehr*"[394] in order to take into account the novelties of SMC. Prior to this promulgation dated November 23rd, 1989, the draft produced by the German military ordinary had been reviewed by the Congregation for the Bishops and agreement with the German Federal Government had been reached. This procedure is unique for the promulgation of pontifical law.[395] The new statutes entered into force on January 1st, 1990 and underline the ecclesiastical character of military chaplaincy and the freedom and independence of religious activities.[396]

Military chaplaincy is an "important part of pastoral care as a whole".[397] As a "church amongst soldiers" it is in its nature identical with the "church in the dioceses".[398] The impression of chaplaincy as a separate and exempt entity is avoided. The statutes follow the model of a cumulative jurisdiction already established by universal norms:[399] The military ordinary possesses all rights and obligations of a diocesan bishop for the internal and external forum. He possesses ordinary, personal and proper jurisdiction that is not dependent from the jurisdiction of any other bishop. However, this jurisdiction is not exclusive but cumulative to a secondary jurisdiction of the territorial ordinary and the territorial parish priest. The latter pastors will always act from own rights but only as secondary instances. The area of jurisdiction of the German military ordinary is not considered a particular church in full legal form like a diocese, but an organizational form of a particular church.[400] Pastoral districts are the sub-divisions.[401] In the exercise of their ministry, military chaplains enjoy the rights and obligations like pastors of a parish.[402] The statutes furthermore circumscribe the exact personal scope of the military ordinary's jurisdiction as encompassing

---

392 *See* SMC, *supra* note 343, Art. 1.

393 81 AAS 1284 (1989).

394 Pontifical Statutes for the Area of Jurisdiction of the Catholic Military Bishop for the German Bundeswehr, 81 AAS 1284 (1989) [herinafter: Pontifical Statutes].

395 *See* BAURA, *supra* note 344, at 223 n.*.

396 *See* Kredel, Elmar Maria, *Anprache bei der Übergabe des Apostolischen Breves, in* PÄPSTLICHE DOKUMENTE FÜR DIE MILITÄRSEELSORGE IN DER DEUTSCHEN BUNDESWEHR 42, 43 (1990).

397 *See* Pontifical Statutes, *supra* note 394, Art. 27.

398 *Pastorale Leitlinien der Katholischen Militärseelsorge*, 2001 MILITÄRSEELSORGE 5, ch. I, No. 1.8 [herinafter: Pastoral Guidelines].

399 *See* Pontifical Statutes, *supra* note 394, Art. 3.

400 *See* Alfred E. Hierold, *§ 54 Militärseelsorge, in* HANDBUCH DES KATHOLISCHEN KIRCHENRECHTS 555, 558 (Joseph Listl et al. eds., 2nd ed. 1999), Hierold, *supra* note 370, at 97.

401 *See* Pontifical Statutes, *supra* note 394, Art. 7.

402 *See id.* Art. 23.

catholic soldiers, catholic civilians integrated in the armed foces and their family members.

The office of the military vicar general, who by analogy possesses all powers accorded to a vicar general by canon law, does not cease with the vacancy of the Episcopal See even though the military vicar general may not introduce substantive changes.[403] Given the temporary assignment of clergy to the pastoral care of military chaplaincy,[404] the German military ordinariate does not incardinate and does not maintain its own seminary.[405]

In Germany, chaplaincy to the armed forces is integrated in the defense community but like the other two civilian branches of the military community (military justice,[406] military administration[407]) is not part of the armed forces (*Streitkräfte*) as such.[408] Pastoral care to servicemen and -women is organized under the responsibility of the respective church.[409] The catholic and the protestant military chaplaincies are similarly structured. Their cooperation with the military branches works alike.[410] The state is obliged to respect the independence of the pastoral care of the chaplains, to organize the chaplaincy and to bear the costs. The budget of the Federal government for military chaplaincy in the fiscal year 2004 amounts to a total of EUR 27.9 Million.[411] Both branches of military chaplaincy have a total of 573 employees – including administrative and technical staff - in the fiscal year 2004.[412] The catholic chaplaincy has 97 service posts for chaplains, but only 92 budgetary posts which results in 5 structural vacancies. The catholic church contributes additionally EUR 8,5 Million from its church tax funds to military chaplaincy related purposes.

---

[403] *See id.* Art. 6, 10.

[404] *See* Hierold, *supra* note 370, at 110.

[405] *See* Pontifical Statutes, *supra* note 394, Art. 17, *see also* SMC, *supra* note 343, Art. 6 § 3, 4 (for the option to incardinate and erect seminaries), Gantin, *supra* note 15, at 42 (favoring seminaries and incardination to allow a specialized ministry adapted to the social environment and specific nature of service in the armed forces).

[406] *See* Art. 96 (4) GG .

[407] *See* Art. 87 b GG.

[408] *See* Knut Ipsen, *§ 87 a*, No. 13, *in* 7 KOMMENTAR ZUM BONNER GRUNDGESETZ (Rudolf Dolzer et al. eds, 22nd delivery January 1969), *see also* Ulrich Tammler, *Das Katholische Militärbischofsamt als selbständige Bundesoberbehörde*, 1988 NEUE ZEITSCHRIFT FÜR WEHRRECHT 106, 107 n.5 (for the four pillar model: armed forces, military administration, military justice, military chaplaincy).

[409] *See* Military Chaplaincy Agreement, *supra* note 390, Art. 2 (1).

[410] *See* ZDv 66/1, *supra* note 385, No. 2 at 64.

[411] *See* Entwurf zum Bundeshaushaltsplan 2004 : Einzelplan 14 *in* ENTWURF EINES GESETZES ÜBER DIE FESTSTELLUNG DES BUNDESHAUSHALTSPLANS FÜR DAS HAUSHALTSJAHR 2004 (HAUSHALTSGESETZ 2004), Drucksache 15/1500, at 66 (Deutscher Bundestag ed. August 15th, 2003), *available at* http://dip.bundestag.de/btd/15/015/1501500.pdf.

[412] *See id.* at 141.

The military ordinary is a residing bishop of a German diocese[413] and – like his protestant counterpart – does not hold a civil office.[414] This is to ensure the independence from state influence and the cooperation with the other ordinaries in Germany. The temporary assignment of clergy to the military ordinariate is also designed to assure the rooting of chaplaincy in the German ecclesiastical life.[415]

The chaplain is independent in handling his affairs and with regard to his pastoral care activities only bound by the norms of his church[416] – even if he is deployed on mission abroad.[417] For the time of their service with the chaplaincy, chaplains are civil servants *pro tempore* (*Beamte auf Zeit*).[418] The reference to this status in Art. 27 *Reichskonkordat* constitutes an exception to can. 285 § 3 CIC that forbids clergy to assume public offices because in Germany, civil servantship is associated with the exercise of executive power.[419] Military chaplains particularly deal with the administrative affairs of the state related to military chaplaincy, e.g. the administration of the federal budget for military chaplaincy.[420] The civil servant status also takes into account the security demands of the environment of armed forces.[421] The *Reichkonkordat* leaves the details of this status to state regulations. The German legislator has fulfilled this task in applying the status of chaplains under the Military Chaplaincy Agreement on catholic chaplains as well.[422] Only the senior chaplains – military deans – are civil servants appointed for life tenure. The loss of the ecclesiastical faculties to the minister leads to a loss of the civil servant status.[423] Even though civil servants serve the state in a public law relationship, it is only the military ordinary who decides what clergy is assigned in what position to military chaplaincy.[424] This responsibility is also reflected by the fact that a senior chaplain is assigned

---

413 Pontifical Statutes, *supra* note 394, Art. 2, *but see* SMC, *supra* note 343, Art. 2 § 3 (the military ordinary is free of other duties which involve care of souls), *see critically* Beyer, *supra* note 350, at 242.

414 *See* ZDv 66/1, *supra* note 385, No. 10 at 65.

415 *See id.* No. 14 at 67.

416 *See* Pontifical Statutes, *supra* note 394, Art. 13, ZDv 66/1, *supra* note 385, No. 13 at 66.

417 *See* ZDv 66/1, *supra* note 385, No. 13 at 66, *see also* Udo Loest, *"Unabhängig von staatlicher Weisung"*, *in* FÜR RUHE IN DER SEELE SORGEN 48, 50 (2003).

418 *See* Military Chaplaincy Agreement, *supra* note 390, Art. 19.

419 *See* Beamtenrechtsrahmengesetz [Framework Act on Civil Servantship], 1999 BGBl. I at 654, § 2, Bundesbeamtengesetz [Federal Civil Servants Act], 1999 BGBl. I at 675, § 4.

420 *See* Tammler, *supra* note 408, at 108, 114, 117, Hierold, *supra* note 370, at 105.

421 *See* Jörg Ennuschat, *Sollen Militärgeistliche Staats- oder Kirchenbeamte sein? : Verfassungs-, völker- und beamtenrechtliche Aspekte*, 1996 ZEITSCHRIFT FÜR EVANGELISCHES KIRCHENRECHT 419, 428-29.

422 *See* Military Chaplaincy Act, *supra* note 391, Art. 2.

423 *See* Military Chaplaincy Agreement, *supra* note 390, Art. 23.

424 *See* Pontifical Statutes, *supra* note 394, Art. 15, 16.

to manage deployment affairs at the Armed Forces Joint Operations Command Center.[425]

Chaplains do not have a military rank and are not part of the military chain of command although they have the right to directly address the commanding officer or the highest-ranking German officer in a multinational contingent.[426] The chaplain is a civilian since in the German understanding it does not take a good soldier to be a good pastor to soldiers. Nonetheless, the chaplain has to be able to understand military structures and procedures even though he himself might not have received any military training.[427] Chaplains, however, enjoy the privileges of senior officers for instance with regard to board, lodging and transportation. Furthermore, they are invited to staff meetings and must be informed about cases of death, serious disease or injuries, suicide attempts, self-mutilation and crimes committed by soldiers. Chaplains are never subordinate to military personnel. The catholic vicar general or the protestant general dean is both ecclesiastical and civil superior. Their twin nature[428] is also reflected in their administrations: The respective ecclesiastical authority for military chaplaincy – the catholic military bishop's office or the protestant church office[429] - is also a federal office under the authority of the Federal Minister of Defense.[430] Both authorities are not integrated into the military administration.[431]

During military exercise and on mission, chaplains wear protective clothing and gear. This gear is not considered a uniform, but since it looks very similar often mistaken for a uniform.[432] It is worn with a cross on the shoulder boards.[433] Especially on missions in non-Christian environments, the use these insignia re-

---

[425] *See* Joachim Robrahn, *Der Militärpfarrer im Auslandseinsatz*, 2003 MILITÄRSEELSORGE 12-17.

[426] *See* ZDv 66/1, *supra* note 385, No. 15 at 67, No. 34 at 69.

[427] *See* Rausch, *supra* note 7, at 383.

[428] *See* Volkmar Kruk, *Die rechtlichen Probleme der Militärseelsorge*, 1997 NEUE ZEITSCHRIFT FÜR WEHRRECHT 1, 4.

[429] The catholic military ordinariate is located at the seat of the federal government, thus Berlin, *see* Pontifical Statutes, *supra* note 394, Art. 6, while the protestant church office is located at the seat of the Ministry of Defense, thus Bonn, *see* Military Chaplaincy Agreement, *supra* note 390, Art. 14.

[430] *See* ZDv 66/1, *supra* note 385, No. 17, 18 at 67.

[431] *See* Tammler, *supra* note 408, at 108, 112, 121, *but see* ALBERT BALL, DIE ERRICHTUNG VON BUNDESOBERBEHÖRDEN 90-91 (1964).

[432] *See* Andreas Stooss, *Die Armeeseelsorge gestern – heute – morgen*, TRUPPENINFORMATIONSDIENST, Bulletin 4/99, at 11, 12 (mistaking protective gear for a uniform), *see also* Pontifical Statutes, *supra* note 394, Art. 14, GUSTAV ADOLF RIEHM, LES PROBLÈMES D'UNE PROTECTION PARTICULIÈRE DU PERSONNEL AUXILIAIRE ET DU MATÉRIEL DES AUMÔNIERS MILITAIRES ET DES MINISTRES CIVILS D'UN CULTE 2 (paper submitted to the Colloquium on spiritual and intellectual assistance in the time of armed conflicts and civil disturbances, Milan, September 21st-23rd, 1973).

[433] *See infra* Appendix III (for a sample).

quires sensibility.[434] Before deployment abroad, chaplains participate in the preparatory exercises of their unit insofar as safeguarding their personal security on mission demands so.

Chaplains also teach *Lebenskundlichen Unterricht*, a non-obligatory subject that deals with moral and ethical questions, both to recruits and officers.

Chaplains are assigned to a unit and have to cooperate with the commander of that unit (*Zuordnung auf Zusammenarbeit*[435]). The chaplain is not member of a hierarchy parallel to the military hierarchy[436] but partner of the commander in the sense of a critical solidarity.[437] The *Zuordnung auf Zusammenarbeit* model reflects on the grassroots level the mutual perception of partnership and cooperative understanding that are the basis for church and state relations in Germany.[438] Church and state are separated but do not exist without relations or even in opposition to each other. This concept was designed to combine the independence of chaplaincy with its integration into military life. The result is a balance of ecclesiastical independence in a state institution paired at the same time with cooperation to be close to the troops.[439]

The disintegrated and civilian status of military chaplaincy in Germany is very different from the status of chaplaincy in most other countries – even different from the status of chaplaincy of most allies. The German status, however, turns out to be helpful particularly on missions because servicemen and -women see chaplains first and foremost as pastors rather than as soldiers.[440] In this, the status of German chaplaincy assures its acceptance in the armed forces.[441]

The two existing branches of military chaplaincy, the catholic and the protestant, are well established and commonly recognized – both by the church and the state. In 2000, the German bishops expressed their gratitude especially to chaplains accompanying soldiers during operations in areas of crisis.[442] A similar

---

[434] *See* Jürgen Walter, *Als Seelsorger in Afghanistan*, *in* FÜR RUHE IN DER SEELE SORGEN 68, 72 (2003) (it is interesting to note that the author does not speak of the armlet with the red cross), *see also* Dale R. Herspring, SOLDIERS, COMMISSARS AND CHAPLAINS 46 (2001) (for the same problem during Operation Desert Storm).

[435] *See* ZDv 66/1, *supra* note 385, No. 13 at 66.

[436] *See also* Hiebel, *supra* note 17, at 534.

[437] *See* Peter Michaelis, *Unabhängig und solidarisch zugleich*, *in* FÜR RUHE IN DER SEELE SORGEN, 156, 158 (2003), Reinhard Gramm, *Den Standort geistig bestimmen*, 1990 INFORMATIONEN FÜR DIE TRUPPE 78, 83, *see also* Bruno Falk, *Militärseelsorge: Rechtliche Stellung und Verhältnis zur militärischen Führung*, 1973 TRUPPENPRAXIS 818, 820 (expressing approval for the current legal status in the 1970s).

[438] *See also* Military Chaplaincy Agreement, *supra* note 390, Art. 27 (for the "friendship clause").

[439] *See* Pastoral Guidelines, *supra* note 398, No. 1.14.

[440] *See* Dirck Ackermann, *Das deutsche evangelische Militärseelsorgemodell im internationalen Praxistest*, *in* FÜR RUHE IN DER SEELE SORGEN 116, 121 (2003).

[441] *See* Roland Löffler, *Seelsorge im Ernstfall*, ZEITZEICHEN 11/2000, at 54.

[442] *See* GERECHTER FRIEDE, *supra* note 275, No. 143 at 81.

expression of gratefulness was included in the 2002 report of the Defense Commissioner of the German Parliament and particularly acknowledged their dedication also to non-confessional soldiers.[443] Fears that the debate on the status of chaplains initiated by the eastern protestant churches could have damaged the reputation and acceptance of military chaplaincy in society seem to have not been justified.[444] Questions rising in the future will most likely derive from the higher level of church-state-relations. An example is the built up of response forces by the European Union (EU).[445] Church-state-relations in the EU are questions of heated controversy as various countries follow rather different approaches, from a strict separation of church and state in France to a state church in Greece. This diversity is also well reflected in the discussion on a reference to religion in the preamble of a constitution for the European Union. Challenges in the context of structural military reform will then most likely be dealt with along established lines. For the case of EU military forces that would mean that each contingent follows its national approach. The level of European integration in defense matters – a core issue of sovereignty – is still significantly lower than for instance that of NATO. In the European context, the question of military chaplaincy to joint EU forces does not seem to be a question of the foreseeable future. The emergence of new structures is more likely on a national level. An awareness of an ethic and ethnic pluralism is spreading in German society and brings questions of cultural identity into public discussions. Sooner or later, this development will also effect church-state relations as it already has in neighboring countries. There are few reasons why the field of military chaplaincy would be excluded.[446]

<u>3. Exemption of clergy from military service – another source of protection</u>

§ 11 of the German Conscription Act[447] exempts from military conscription those who have been ordained as pastors in a protestant confession, who have received the consecration as deacon or have been entrusted with a similar office in another religious community. This stipulation makes no distinction between military chaplains or civilian ministers. In the catholic reading it follows up on

---

[443] *See* UNTERRICHTUNG DURCH DEN WEHRBEAUFTRAGTEN - JAHRESBERICHT 2002 (44. BERICHT), Drucksache 15/500, at 32 (Deutscher Bundestag ed. November 3rd, 2003), *available at* http://dip.bundestag.de/btd/15/005/1500500.pdf, *see also* Speech of the Minister of Defense at the inauguration of the new protestant military bishop (September 23rd, 2003) *available at* http://www.kmba.de/aktuell/internas/230903/230903_struck.htm (for the appreciation on the part of the Minister).

[444] *See also infra* 133-135 (for an analysis of the discussion in the eastern protestant churches).

[445] *See also* Beyer, *supra* note 350, at 241 (for problems of ecclesiastical jurisdiction in multinational operations).

[446] *See also infra* at 150 (for the establishment of chaplaincies other than the existing).

[447] *See* 2002 BGBl. I at 954.

Art. 6 of the *Reichskonkordat*[448] that assures clergy an exemption from obligations incompatible with their state according to the norms of canon law. But military service is not enumerated in the catalogue of examples (jury and lay judge duties). Relevant here is the *privilegium immunitatis* of the 1917 Code of Canon Law. The German Federal Administrative Court also sees the roots of § 11 in the concordatarian norm.[449] Thus, the concordat incorporates a canonical norm that – as has been seen above – has a long-standing tradition in the law of the catholic church. This incorporation is reflected in § 11, it is the *ratio legis* of this norm.[450] Its extension on protestant and other religious ministers is a dictate of religious parity and equal treatment. Other religious communities thus profit indirectly and by "coincidence"[451] from a norm of canon law.

The exemption exceeds the scope of a protection of spiritual assistance – though this consideration of course plays a role[452] – as it is not linked with a specific function. § 11 is oriented towards a vertical model of religion with privileges only for a ministerial office that by the internal order of the religious community has an elevated position.[453] Exempted ministers must be received "firmly and on principle irrevocably" into the clerical state.[454] Point of reference is the spiritual office. This is difficult for religions that do not know such an office for their ministers or presume it for all their members. The Federal Administrative Court developed the criterion of a full-time occupation in this regard.[455] The clerical state and its equivalents in other religions are exempted as such. However, a functional link is constructed between the existence of a clerical state and the viability of a religious community.[456]

---

[448] *See supra* note 388.

[449] *See No. 60, in* 34 ENTSCHEIDUNGEN DES BUNDESVERWALTUNGSGERICHTES (BVERWGE) 291, 296-97 (1970).

[450] *See* Rudolf Kreutzer, *Der Begriff des Geistlichen im Wehrpflichtgesetz*, 11 DIE ÖFFENTLICHE VERWALTUNG 151 (1958), *but see* Dietrich Pirson, *§ 64 Das Dienstrecht der Geistlichen und Kirchenbeamten, in* 2 HANDBUCH DES STAATSKIRCHENRECHTS DER BUNDESREPUBLIK DEUTSCHLAND 845, 856 (Joseph Listl ed. 1995), (considering the exemption of clergy to be an instrument to assure spiritual assistance in times of war).

[451] *See Bundesverwaltungsgericht, in* 1988 NEUE JURISTISCHE WOCHENSCHRIFT 393, 396.

[452] *See No. 60, supra* note 449, at 295, *but see* Harald Bogs, *Probleme des Geistlichenprivilegs im Wehrrecht*, 9 DER STAAT 43, 53-54 (1970) (criticizing the general exemption of religious ministers regardless of their function).

[453] *See Art. 11, in* Dieter Walz, Wehrpflichtgesetz 218, No. 33 at 229 (2002), *see also § 11, No. 4a, in* Wolfgang Boehm-Tettelbach (ed.), WEHRPLICHTGESETZ (3rd ed., continued looseleaf collection as of 2003) (a Jewish rabbiwould qualify).

[454] *See* No. 41, 6 ENTSCHEIDUNGEN IN KIRCHENSACHEN (KirchE) 217, 219 (1969) („fest und grundsätzlich unabänderlich").

[455] *See No. 60, supra* note 449, at 299.

[456] *See Bundesverwaltungsgericht*, 1963 NEUE JURISTISCHE WOCHENSCHRIFT 1169, 1170 ("kultisch nicht existenzfähig" without state devoted to spiritual tasks).

The norms on exemption of clergy have caused considerable disputes in the legal discipline, particularly in the application of the equivalence clause on personnel of religions communities other than the protestant and catholic churches. The cases of Jehovah's witnesses[457] and the Scientology Church[458] also reached the Federal Administrative Court and produced the views mentioned.[459] Basis was always the view of the Court that a religion could not be determined subjectively.[460] It would be interesting to see how the Court would decide similar cases nowadays as the Federal Constitutional Court has recently decided that some subjective aspects have to be taken into account in defining a religion.[461]

Already VATTEL in 1758 polemicized against the exemption of clergy from military service because "[t]o defend one's country is duty not unworthy of the most sacred hands".[462] For him, exemption could only come from service in an indispensable function. Still, the German norms were subject of discussion in the protestant churches because military service was considered an integral part of societal life and should not be withhold from religious ministers. It was, however, accepted with view on assuring civilian ministry even in times of war with the clear awareness that military chaplaincy – a ministry without arms – would be maintained and properly be taken care of even in times of war.[463]

According to § 12 (2) of the German Conscription Act,[464] those in preparation for a spiritual office mentioned in § 11 are deferred from military service if they apply for. In the state of defense, those deferred candidates serve in the medical corps.[465]

It is disputed whether § 11 fulfills the requirements of the *privilegium immunitatis* that demands also the exemption of members of religious orders – cleric and lay alike.[466] The practice of the *Wehrmacht* in World War II was different and based on a secret annex to the *Reichskonkordat*. Those who were in preparation for priesthood were excused from military service and all exercises.

---

457 *See id.* at 1169; *No. 60, supra* note 449.
458 *See Bundesverwaltungsgericht, supra* note 451.
459 *See also* ASSENMACHER, *supra* note 312, at 90-117.
460 *See* Bundesverwaltungsgericht, 34 NEUE JURISTISCHE WOCHENSCHRIFT 1460, 1461 (1981), ASSENMACHER, *supra* note 312, at 111.
461 *See* Bundesverfassungsgericht, case 1 BvR 1783/99, § 55 (January 15th, 2002), *available at* http://www.bverfg.de/entscheidungen/frames/2002/1/15.
462 VATTEL, *supra* note 120, bk. III, ch. 2, § 10 at 238.
463 *See* No. 60, *supra* note 449, at 297, ASSENMACHER, *supra* note 312, at 77-84, 121.
464 *See supra* note 447.
465 *See id.* § 48 [2] Nr. 4.
466 *See* can. 121 CIC/1917 (the norm form all clergy), can. 614 CIC/1917 (the norm for all religious), can. 680 CIC/1917 (the norm for members of order-like communities), can. 672 CIC/1983 (canons on clergy applicable for religious), can. 285, 289 CIC/1983, *see also* Ulrich Tammler, *Die Stellung der Ordensleute im Wehrrecht der Bundesrepublik Deutschland*, 1983 MILITÄRSEELSORGE 165, 179, ASSENMACHER, *supra* note 312, at 86.

For a general mobilization, clergymen were only draft-exempt if they were pastors of a parish or fulfilled enumerated functions. Other clergy had to serve with the military chaplaincy or the medical corps while seminarians and religious only served with the medical corps.[467] Today, the administrative practice of the German conscription authorities exempts members of religious orders who have taken a religious vow or novices who are in preparation thereof on the basis of equality considerations.[468]

4. Company abroad - chaplains on missions

The most decisive change for the *Bundeswehr* in the past decade – as for many armed forces in Europe – has been the transformation from a military designed for territorial defense to a military designed for global deployment. "Germany's security and freedom is defended at the Hindukush" as a common expression phrases it these days. Mobility and rapid deployment stand in the center of attention in military policy. And yet, this change to a military on mission is not complete. A landmark in this development has been the 1994 decision of the German Constitutional Court on the legality of *Bundeswehr* out of area-missions.[469] In its ruling, the court determined that the *Bundeswehr* could be deployed worldwide in the context of a system of collective security that serves the preservation of peace and with the approval of the German Federal Legislature. Prior to this decision, the German constitution was interpreted as to allow a deployment outside the NATO area only for humanitarian purposes. Assistance to victims of an earthquake 1960 in Agadir/Morocco was one of the first examples for such a mission. In 2002, on average 9000 soldiers were deployed on missions abroad.[470] On July 31st, 2003, about 8160 soldiers were deployed abroad.[471]

Deployment abroad had not been unknown to German chaplains. They accompanied their troops during multi-national exercises and served on posts abroad with German troops stationed in allied countries but these were not operational missions. On the basis of their status, *Bundeswehr* chaplains accompanied navy minesweep vessels to the Persian Gulf after the second Gulf War and the first German UN Blue Helmet contingent 1991 to Cambodia. Thereafter they provided spiritual assistance to German forces in Somalia, in the Balkans and in the

---

467 *See* Tammler, *supra* note 466, at 181.

468 *See id.* at 186, *§ 11, No. 3, in* Boehm-Tettelbach, *supra* note 453, *see also* ASSENMACHER, *supra* note 312, at 27 n.4.

469 *See* 90 BVerfGE 286.

470 *See* UNTERRICHTUNG DURCH DEN WEHRBEAUFTRAGTEN, *supra* note 443, at 16.

471 *See* AUSLANDSEINSÄTZE - AKTUELLE ZAHLEN DER IM AUSLAND EINGESETZTEN DEUTSCHEN SOLDATEN, http://www.bundeswehr.de/forces/print/einsatzzahlen.php (variable page as of August 8th, 2003).

post-September 11th, 2001 operations.[472] Chaplains have grown into their new role and adapted conceptually. Their presence proved to be indispensable.[473]

Most of these missions were not armed conflicts though. The air campaign in the Kosovo was an exception but did not involve chaplains in the combat environment. Some elements of armed hostilities are found in the context of anti-terrorist campaigns of Operation Enduring Freedom (OEF). The mandate for the deployment of German forces in OEF was passed by the German Federal Legislature on November 16th, 2001 and prolonged respectively for twelve months on November 15th, 2002 and November 14th, 2003. With OEF, German nuclear, biological and chemical defense elements were stationed in Kuwait and accompanied by chaplains. Even though these elements were not involved in the hostilities of the third Gulf War, they were positioned in a target area of Iraqi missiles. Under the parliamentary OEF mandate that is based on the right of individual and collective self-defense under Art. 51 UN-Charter and relevant UN Security Council resolutions, up to 100 special forces may be deployed.[474] A protocol statement of the Minister of Foreign Affairs described the task of these special forces to be police-military and mentioned as examples hostage rescue and arrests.[475] The German Special Forces Commando (*Kommando Spezialkräfte* - KSK) was set up in September 1996 as part of the Division Special Operations for hostage rescue, evacuation or other operations demanding special capabilities. From 1998 on, KSK forces arrested war criminals in Bosnia. Four commando companies and a long-range reconnaissance company together with supportive units have about 960 soldiers.[476] KSK forces were operating in the context of OEF in Afghanistan on request by U.S. forces. From November 2002,

---

[472] *See* Loest, *supra* note 417, *passim*.

[473] *See* Peter Baader, *Schutz religiöser Freiheitsrechte in den Streitkräften*, 2000 TRUPPENPRAXIS/ WEHRAUSBILDUNG 744, 745.

[474] *See* ANTRAG DER BUNDESREGIERUNG, EINSATZ BEWAFFNETER DEUTSCHER STREITKRÄFTE BEI DER UNTERSTÜTZUNG DER GEMEINSAMEN REAKTION AUF TERRORISTISCHE ANGRIFFE GEGEN DIE USA AUF GRUNDLAGE DES ARTIKELS 51 DER SATZUNG DER VEREINTEN NATIONEN UND DES ARTIKELS 5 DES NORDATLANTIKVERTRAGS SOWIE DER RESOLUTION 1368 (2001) UND 1373 (2001) DES SICHERHEITSRATS DER VEREINTEN NATIONEN, Drucksache 14/7296, at 3 (Deutscher Bundestag ed. November 7th, 2001), *available at* http://dip.bundestag.de/btd/14/072/1407296.pdf, *see also* FAQ on special forces on OEF mission *available at* http://www.einsatz.bundeswehr.de/ einsatz_aktuell/oef_spezial/faq/faq_spez.php.

[475] *See* BESCHLUSSEMPFEHLUNG UND BERICHT DES AUSWÄRTIGEN AUSSCHUSSES (3. AUSSCHUSS) ZU DEM ANTRAG DER BUNDESREGIERUNG – DRUCKSACHE 14/7296 –, Drucksache 14/7447, at 4 (Deutscher Bundestag ed. November 14th, 2001), *available at* http://dip.bundestag.de/btd/ 14/074/1407447.pdf.

[476] *See* MICHAEL MARTIN, ENTEHUNG, GLIEDERUNG UND RECHTSLAGE DEUTSCHER SPEZIALEINHEITEN AM BEISPIEL DER EINSATZEINHEITEN DES KOMMANDO SPEZIALKRÄFTE UND DER GRENZSCHUTZGRUPPE 9, at 4-7 (unpublished seminar paper, University of the Armed Forces, February 17th, 2000), *see also* website of the KSK on its structure, http://www.deutschesheer.de/ C1256B6C002D670C/vwContentByKey/N25GJCN3505SWINDE.

after the withdrawal of Canadian special forces, German KSK forces were conducting operations independently. Chaplains accompanied these forces, too. Given the nature of these operations, their impressions hardly become public.[477]

The German Ministry of Defense does not qualify any of the missions the *Bundeswehr* is currently involved in as armed conflict even though humanitarian law is applied in hostilities. For the case of commando operations, this is reasoned with the police-military task of the forces, the asymmetry to the Al Qaida enemy who is not qualified as combatant and the relevant rules of engagement. Even if operations in the framework of OEF are not considered to amount to an armed conflict, they nonetheless produce another quality of conflict. Deployed chaplains are faced with this new quality of conflict and also a new level of threat. But not many months ago, questions regarding German chaplains in armed conflict as the ones raised in this book would have been rejected as irrelevant.

It has never been a question, either on the part of the churches or on that of society, whether chaplains would accompany the troops on their new missions.[478] Though the missions of the *Bundeswehr* abroad where in some cases subject to heavy societal dispute, the question of legitimacy of military chaplaincy was never seriously raised in the context of the legitimacy of the mission itself.

Deployment abroad and company of forces on missions has become one of the most important aspects in the ministry to the armed forces. By the year 2000, 30 % of the protestant chaplains had been deployed on missions abroad.[479] During Easter 2003, 9 catholic chaplains served on missions abroad. It goes without saying that the international engagement of military chaplaincy also causes shortages in chaplaincy at home.

The Joint Service Regulation on military chaplaincy[480] and the German Field Manual for operations in times of peace[481] regulate that chaplains advise the commander in ecclesiastical matters and questions of military chaplaincy. Chaplains have to follow the security rules of their contingent and the general service routine abroad. They advise the commander furthermore in religious and ethical questions and are mediators to the religious communities of the deployment country.

---

[477] *But see* Alfred Gronbach, *Auf Leben und Tod*, *in* FÜR RUHE IN DER SEELE SORGEN 102-104 (2002), *see also* Robrahn, *supra* 425, at 17 (for periodical visits of chaplains to KSK forces).

[478] *See* Wolf Werner Rausch, *Seelsorge – ganz konkret*, 1994 WEHRAUSBILDUNG 310, 310.

[479] *See* Löffler, *supra* note 441, at 53.

[480] *See* ZDv 66/1, *supra* note 385, No. 13 at 66, No. 34 at 69.

[481] *See Handbuch für Auslandseinsätze im Frieden*, *in* DOKUMENTATION ZUR KATHOLISCHEN UND EVANGELISCHEN MILITÄRSEELSORGE 123, No. 2705 at 125 (7th ed. 2002).

a. Pastoral challenges during deployment

From a pastoral point of view, chaplaincy in the armed forces offers the opportunity for credible Christian testimony. It is remarkable to note that the interest in chaplaincy work has increased as the *Bundeswehr* was restructured to an army on mission while in society as a whole secularization is progressing. Ministry in the camp during missions abroad is quantitatively increased and qualitatively different from ministry in barracks at home. The demand for the services that military chaplaincy provides is significantly higher than at home.[482] Chaplains accompany the armed forces on missions because their presence during field missions gains emotional weigh:[483] Taking soldiers serious, approaching them and their sometimes hidden longing for spiritual stability, collecting them where they are, this is the task of chaplaincy in a modern army.[484] The chaplain and his presence in operations express human solidarity to those in hardship.[485] A special gesture of solidarity by spiritual company was a letter by Pope JOHN PAUL II to the German service personnel deployed abroad in April 2003.[486]

From an outside view, the accompanying chaplain brings the own culture into the unknown and in some cases hostile environment of the mission. While at home, services are usually held during the week since most soldiers return to their families during the weekends, services on missions abroad take place on Sunday.[487] Sunday service helps to structure a week of duty with its ever-recurring events and is considered an alternative to the daily grind. The offer is important for the camp routine and even for those soldiers who do not actively participate at services.[488] Ecumenical efforts in military chaplaincy are in a field of tension between narrow denominationalism and shapeless religiosity. This tension is often increased by a lack of qualified religious personnel.[489] Sunday service is an evident example that a balance between denominational identity and achieved ecumenism must be reached.[490]

---

[482] *See* Dirck Ackermann, *Einsatz – Auf der Suche nach der Religion?*, *in* FÜR RUHE IN DER SEELE SORGEN 51 (2003).

[483] *See* Pastoral Guidelines, *supra* note 398, ch.I § 4.2.2.

[484] *See* Christoph Stucki, *Die Armeeseelsorge vor neuen Herausforderungen*, 166 ALLGEMEINE SCHWEIZERISCHE MILITÄRZEITSCHRIFT 23 (5/2000).

[485] *See* Hiebel, *supra* note 17, at 535.

[486] *See* SOLDATEN ALS DIENER DER SICHERHEIT UND DER FREIHEIT DER VÖLKER (April 20th, 2003), *available at* http://www.kmba.de/aktuell/internas/200403/200403.html.

[487] *see also* Dubost, *supra* note 350, at 173-74 (for a similar situation in France).

[488] *See* Gotthold Patberg, *Nicht jeder Tag ist Mittwoch*, *in* FÜR RUHE IN DER SEELE SORGEN 81, 81 (2003).

[489] *See* Stooss, *supra* note 432, at 12.

[490] *See* Peter Michaelis & Walter Theis, *Seelsorgerische Begleitung bei Auslandseinsätzen deutscher Soldaten*, 2001 MILITÄRSEELSORGE 67, 75.

Soldiers on missions abroad – many of them do not have religious ties at all – expect and make use of the assistance offered as they see that chaplains share their situation and live under the same circumstances but are devoted to their spiritual well-being.[491] The chaplain is close to the troops and present in their daily duty. He spends time with them on duty - e.g. goes on patrol with them - and joins them as they spend the little time they have off duty. His presence in the field is only to serve the servicemen and -women he accompanies and who live under special physical and psychological strain. He joins them as they cover some distance on their path through life. In many instances, he is just there for others. He is available to the military personnel without regard of their confession, their religious affiliation or non-affiliation. His presence – unlike that of military psychologists and psychiatrists – does not serve a military related purpose. This closeness paired with extreme exposure to enmity, sorrow, injury, crisis, and also threat of death results in questions that servicemen and -women would not ask themselves with the same urgency in ordinary circumstances at home. Crisis, war and "metaphysical homelessness" induce a remarkable and sometimes dramatic renaissance of the *Gretchenfrage*, the question question as to one's own position *vis-à-vis* religion.[492] According to chaplains on missions, these questions very often leave the area of military mission and its purpose and reach a level that deals with the meaning of human activity and human existence. In many cases, soldiers react to their own questions with surprise and sometimes even with fear of the depth into which they are venturing. Chaplains can provide in conversations valuable assistance if they offer answers and interpretations from a religious horizon.[493] They interpret guilt and suffering as fundamentally given aspects of the finite and transitory nature of man.[494] In the face of spiritual reactions in conflict stemming from fear, uncertainty, demoralization and helplessness, chaplains address spiritual healing to restore hope, trust and community.[495] They offer assistance in borderline situations that is different from an indifferent approach to live on as if nothing had happened. In some cases they provide guidance to the "ultimate recourse of religion".[496]

---

[491] *See* GARY R. COUNCELL, CHAPLAIN ROLES IN HUMANITARIAN AND CIVIC ASSISTANCE OPERATIONS 52 (unpublished Directed Study, U.S. Army War College 1994) (for examples of U.S. chaplains in the context of the Somalia mission).

[492] Jochen Hörisch, *Gegenfragen an Gretchen*, DER TAGESSPIEGEL, April 20th/21st, 2003, at 25.

[493] *See* Georg Kestel & Walter Theis, *Pastorale Gegebenheiten und Schwerpunkte der katholischen Militärseelsorge*, 2001 MILITÄRSEELSORGE 50, 55, *see also* Ackermann, *supra* note 482.

[494] *See* Stucki, *supra* note 484.

[495] *See* Karen H. Stocks, *Understanding The Chaplain's Role in an Age of Weapons of Mass Destruction*, 166 MILITARY MEDICINE Suppl. 2, at 55 (2001).

[496] *See* Jean-Luc Hiebel, CONTENU DE L'ASSISTANCE SPIRITUELLE POUR LES DIFFERENTS CROUANTS RELIGIEUX 21 (paper submitted to the Colloquium on spiritual and intellectual assistance in the time of armed conflicts and civil disturbances, Milan, September 21st-23rd, 1973).

The impact of chaplaincy is also dependent on the individual chaplain and his personality because the organization brings the chaplain to the troops, but he has to find his way to their hearts himself. The chaplain is supported by a religious spirituality, the reference to the transcendent. Chaplains speak about the prayer of the hours and bible study as sources of their own strength and endurance.[497]

His role as advisor to the commander allows the chaplain to share impressions on developments within the troops with the commander – keeping, of course, his professional confidentiality. In many cases, chaplains have been like an early warning system, a seismograph, and foresaw or suspected developments and gave their counsel in good time. The resort to chaplains' services increases with the precariousness and awkwardness of a situation.[498] And yet, as the demand for chaplaincy services increases in operation, this rise is temporary: It decreases again as troops are repatriated and return home.

As the chaplain walks around the camp, he is faced with many opportunities to interact with the troops and to talk to them. He reacts to identified needs in a sensible and credible manner.[499] He develops initiatives for spiritual assistance according to the needs he discovers: services, choir, bible groups, off duty time activities... Discussions on biblical and religious topics are organized as well as retreats that allow reflection on the changes in personality that come along on mission abroad and that may have effects on life at home. In other cases, an immediate spiritual assistance in response to traumata is needed. On missions abroad, in the cramped conditions of a camp, death is a special challenge to the chaplain. A comrade killed in action, by an accident or by suicide leaves the survivors helpless behind. Training usually deals with caring for wounded comrades and only in few instances takes up the possibility of death. In such hard times – the killing of four soldiers in Kabul in the bombing of a German military transport in early June 2003 is a recent example – chaplains comfort those who survived since they carry the message of hope of their community in a very profound manner.[500] They attempt to find words in a speechless situation. Another example is reported in Bosnia when the accident of an armored vehicle left one dead and three comrades wounded. In collaboration with the military psychologist and the psychiatrist, counseling for the casualties and their fellow soldiers was organized. Even though the dead soldier was not a member of a denomination, a memorial service was held in the camp.[501] German chaplains on missions can furthermore take advantage of education they received in critical incident

---

[497] *See also* Hiebel, *supra* note 17, at 535.
[498] *See* Michaelis/Theis, *supra* note 490, at 72-73.
[499] *See id.* at 74.
[500] *See* Hiebel, *supra* note 17, at 535.
[501] *See* MARTIN BOCK, DIE EINSTELLUNG ZUR MILITÄRSEELSORGE IN DER BEVÖLKERUNG UND BEI SOLDATEN IM BOSNIENEINSATZ DER BUNDESWEHR 10 (2001).

stress management. Chaplains cooperate with the professional services of the military psychologists, social workers and legal advisors. This cooperation bases on mutual respect and recognizes the distinct competency of each service.[502] A "joint cell for the soul" in the organizational charts of the staff would not only undermine the quality of each competency but also the special status of chaplaincy.

And while the individual soldier makes his own experiences in the environment of the mission, the life of those who are dear to him goes on at home. He lives in the tension of the reality of those he left that he experiences only indirectly and selectively in communications from home and of the reality of the operation. In some instances, people break down under the burden of this tension. The German Armed Forces Association estimates that every third soldier deployed abroad has to deal with failed social relationships. Providing assistance in dealing with the helplessness to respond to developments at home from the distance is also a task for chaplaincy. The severe effects of deployment especially on family life encouraged the catholic military ordinary to ask the Institute for Marriage and Family of the Catholic University Eichstätt for a systematic scientific study of these effects.[503] Already now, military chaplains assist families in the process of repatriation with specifically designed weeks of retreat.

Important components of spiritual assistance to German soldiers on missions are religious teams (KAS, EAS) that operate recreational facilities often named "oasis". In the multinational operations in the Balkans, these teams cooperate in the European Christian Home Organizations for the Services (ECHOS) that provide welfare services and run soldiers' homes in Croatia, Bosnia and the Kosovo.

Given this pastoral reality in mission where sometimes more than 50 % of the deployed soldiers are non-confessional, is there room for evangelization as an aspect of the *ministerium pacis inter arma*? Certainly yes, if evangelization is understood in the beginning as a very basic familiarization with values. If "the glory of god is the living man"[504] and military chaplaincy puts this man into the center of its attention, then such evangelization takes place. Religion provides the spirit for answers to questions from the military personnel deployed on mission. This work in many cases can only follow a very existential approach and

---

[502] *See* Pastoral Guidelines, *supra* note 398, ch.I § 4.3.1, Michaelis/Theis, *supra* note 490, at 76, *see also* NICOLAS, *supra* note 16, at 285 (for an international comparison of cooperation with professional services).

[503] *See* Joachim Simon, *Achterbahn der Emotionen*, 2003 AUFTRAG No. 250, at 32, Peter Wendl, *Initiativen zur Besserung der Bedingungen von Soldatenpaaren in „Fern-Beziehungen"*, 2003 MILITÄRSEELSORGE 44-51.

[504] IRENAEUS OF LYON, ADVERSUS HAERESES [Against the Heresies], IV, 20, 7.

seems to be distant from elaborate pastoral concepts.[505] If a pastoral approach comprises and is demanded by non-denominational military personnel as well, the legitimacy of the presence of religious personnel on mission seems difficult to question. This will have to be taken into account when determining their legal protection.

Chaplaincy in the armed forces is not an end in itself. The need for protection is not the invocation of a privilege for clergy, not the attempt of religion that in ordinary society is increasingly marginalized to at least defend a fortress of protection in extreme situations such as armed conflict. The reasoning for protection is different now than it was for instance for the *Treuga Dei* when a church that had lost its influence in worldly matters tried to mobilize its spiritual authority and canonical penal instruments to protect its clergy. Religion does not try to invoke a personal privilege for itself but for the work it is undertaking. It is this purpose as defined by the pastoral mission of chaplains that justifies protection. Within this context, it seems then rather appropriate to perceive protection of spiritual assistance as a condition or in remuneration for that same assistance.[506]

b. The role of chaplains in peace-keeping and humanitarian operations

The tasks of chaplains in mission are not restricted to spiritual assistance to own troops and allied forces. Post-cold-war conflicts are manifold and military operations as well. Humanitarian, peace-keeping, peace-enforcing or quasi-policing missions bring along various demands for chaplains – depending highly on the specific context of the mission. Many of these missions do not take place in the environment of armed conflict. But as the example of Operation Enduring Freedom mentioned above illustrates, have parallels to the factual situation of an armed conflict.[507]

During missions abroad, it is essential for military chaplaincy as an ecclesiastical service to establish contacts with religious institutions of the host country and to act as a contact between local culture and population to the foreign mili-

---

505 *See also* Petra Henn, *Im Kontext der Neuevangelisierung – Theologische, pastorale und praktische Überlegungen zur „neuen" Bischöflichen Ordnung für die Fort-, Aus- und Weiterbildung der hauptamtlichen katholischen Militärgeistlichen und Pastoralreferenten*, 2002 MILITÄRSEELSORGE 96-102 (on the necessary training and education for chaplains as a prerequisite for all chaplaincy activities that are finally ordered towards evangelization), *but see* Gantin, *supra* note 15, at 43, Baura, *supra* note 335, at 103 (on the role of chaplaincy in the "new evangelization").

506 *See* Hiebel, *supra* note 496, at 25.

507 *See also* COUNCELL, *supra* note 491, at 13, 70 (for the potential of a humanitarian or civic assistance operation to turn into a low-intensity conflict).

tary.[508] During UNOSOM II in Somalia, for instance, the local Mullah contacted the chaplains of the German camp Belet Huen on a regular basis.[509] Attempts to use religious contacts of the chaplain militarily for instance in the context of an intelligence assessment in a conflict with ethno-religious background must be met with restraint.[510] In history, there are examples of chaplains who used their chaplain status as a cover for carrying or seeking military information. Buying bibles literally was used as a pretext for spying and running contraband goods.[511] That the issue is still debated in intelligence circles became public in 1996, when the U.S. Senate Intelligence Committee addressed the topic. The Committee restated the ban to use U.S. American clergy for intelligence purposes by the Central Intelligence Agency. This prohibition, however, may be waived by the director of the agency and does not effect a possible recruitment of foreign religious personnel.[512]

The church has a dual function in the international community: a critical to name injustice and to mobilize remedying forces, and a prophetical as an advocate for peace and non-violent conflict resolution. In order to fulfill this dual function, the church must be present for the individual, within the society and within the international community. Horizontal communication and solidarity among the particular churches also prove to be a helpful tool in this regard since they allow for a broad view when determining interests.[513] This is the ecclesiological context in which a Christian military chaplaincy works. The chaplain should thus try to establish contact to the local church – if there is one. Coordinated with the military leadership, the chaplain also establishes bonds with the aid agencies of his church and local initiatives. The catholic caritas that provides relief to the population in need regardless to religion is a commonly known example.[514] His pastoral activities may include the staff of these agencies and initiatives.[515] An example regarding cooperation between local church and chaplaincy was a refugee camp in the Balkans: After an inquiry of the catholic

---

[508] *See* Pastoral Guidelines, *supra* note 398, ch.I § 4.4.4, Michaelis/Theis, *supra* note 490, at 76, Baader, *supra* note 473, *see also* MARCHEGGIANO, *supra* note 107, at 158 (for an Italian perspective in this regard), William Merrifield, *The Unit Ministry Team in Military Operations Other Than War*, THE ARMY CHAPLAINCY, Summer-Fall 1997, *available at* http://www.usachcs.army.mil/TACarchive/ACTNG/merrifield.htm (for the American approach of contacts of Unit Ministry Teams to their "civilian counterparts").

[509] *See* Rausch, *supra* note 478, at 312.

[510] *See* Ackermann, *supra* note 440, at 119.

[511] *See* RICHARD M. BUDD, SERVING TWO MASTERS 54-55 (2002) (for examples of the American Civil War).

[512] *See* UNITED STATES SENATE, SPECIAL REPORT OF THE SELECT COMMITTEE ON INTELLIGENCE, JANUARY 4, 1995 TO OCTOBER 3, 1996, 104th Cong. 24 (January 22nd, 1997).

[513] *See* Julius Döpfner, *Die Friedensfunktion der Kirche*, 1971 MILITÄRSEELSORGE 4, 9.

[514] *See* Kerstiens, *supra* note 218, at 62 (for more examples of caritas activities).

[515] *See* Walter, *supra* note 434, at 73.

movement Pax Christi and arranged by the chaplain of the German contingent, *Bundeswehr* troops contributed to improve living conditions in the camp. A pragmatic cooperation of the civilian peace movement and the military could be observed.[516]

A tension is felt in military chaplaincy, a tension between the restraint of one's own activities and the needs on the spot. This tension is very tangible with LOEST who succinctly states that spiritual assistance for third persons – e.g. the civilian population of the country of deployment – is not given.[517] But then the chaplain would act like the priest in the parable of the Good Samaritan who passes by on the opposite site when he sees the half-dead victim of the robbery.[518] And the practice shows a different picture – especially with regard to various forms of relief. LOEST is without doubt right as far as proselytism or missionary activities in the country of deployment are concerned. But a view like his cannot lead to withhold spiritual assistance from everyone who is not member of the own forces. Spiritual needs go beyond the fence of the camp.

One of the chaplain's "substantial tasks" is furthermore the assistance in organizing humanitarian aid to civilian population in need.[519] Relief as an end of spiritual assistance covers material help of any kind.[520] While relief is not always direct spiritual assistance, it nevertheless often represents its means. It links the person in need with the rest of the world and thus has an eminent spiritual sense that transcends its function of responding to an urgent need. The right to receive relief, moreover, affects the right to spiritual assistance inasmuch as such assistance cannot ignore the material distress of victims of war.[521] The chaplain thus contributes to the humanitarian activities his troops are involved with. For instance during the SFOR mission in Bosnia, chaplains had numerous contacts to international aid organizations and social and religious institutions in Bosnia - in addition to a high presence in camp. German chaplains at Camp Rajlovac arranged support of the soup kitchen of Caritas Social Service in Sarajevo by the kitchen of the field hospital. Their "laughing helps" campaign raised more than EUR 260.000 and collected toys, wear and other goods for children who suf-

---

516 *See* Peter Michaelis, *Die Militärseelsorge im Auslandseinsatz*, *in* BEITRÄGE ZUR EVANGELISCHEN MILITÄRSEELSORGE, I/97, 60, 68.

517 *See* Loest, *supra* note 417, at 50, *see also* ANDREW J. BULLARD, THE ROLE OF ARMY CHAPLAINS IN HUMANITARIAN RELIEF OPERATIONS 14-16 (unpublished Directed Study, U.S. Army War College 2001) (calling for freedom and flexibility to perform ministerial duties beyond the confines of the military on the background of constitutional restraints for military chaplains in the U.S.A.).

518 *See Luke* 10:31.

519 Pastoral Guidelines, *supra* note 398, ch.I § 4.4.3.

520 *See* Hiebel, *supra* note 180, at 8.

521 *See id.* at 9.

fered from the effects of war.[522] Furthermore, projects in the field of civilian-military-cooperation (CIMIC) have become key components of post-conflict missions. In Bosnia, chaplaincy supported the CIMIC group assigned with the task to assist in building up civilian structures and organizations by mediating with the catholic priest in the town of Filippovici.[523] With the International Security Assistance Force (ISAF) in Afghanistan, to mention another example, the reconstruction of kindergartens, schools, hospitals and police stations plays an important role and also contributed to the motivation of the soldiers deployed in mission.[524] In some cases, soldiers on mission raised funds and organized aid from their own initiative.[525] So the helping aspect of a mission even gets a spiritual dimension for the forces deployed.

The German Field Manual for operations in times of peace obliges chaplains to cooperate with the chaplain of the other denomination , with the chaplains of other nations and – conditioned by the situation on the spot – with the religious institutions of the country of deployment. Such cooperation was practiced in Bosnia during the SFOR mission: Chaplains had numerous contacts to other nations' chaplaincies. Once a month, the commanding U.S. chaplain invited all chaplains of the various contingents for a chaplains' lunch at headquarters in Ilidza. As Camp Rajlovac was also the locality of a *Bundeswehr* field hospital servicing to SFOR troops from other posts, chaplains from other contingents came to visit hospitalized members of their flock and on this occasion also paid a visit to the German chaplain. A mutual provision of pastoral care of chaplains to each other was a result of these meetings.[526]

In many cases, German operations for humanitarian are executed by civilian aid agencies of which some have a religious background. If for instance a chaplain was attached to the German catholic relief agency of the Order of Malta "Malteser" operating under a UN mandate, the protection of the Convention on the Safety of United Nations and associated Personnel would apply.[527]

---

[522] *See* Wolfgang Schmidt, *Helfen und wieder loslassen*, *in* FÜR RUHE IN DER SEELE SORGEN 174, 175 (2003).

[523] *See* BOCK, *supra* note 501, at 12.

[524] *See* Carl Hubertus von Butler & Jürgen Walter, *Schritte auf dem Weg des Friedens*, *in* FÜR RUHE IN DER SEELE SORGEN 25, 29(2003).

[525] *See* Schmidt, *supra* note 522, at 175.

[526] *See* BOCK, *supra* note 501, at 9.

[527] *See* Horst Fischer, *Humanitäre Hilfe im Ausland*, 1996 HUMANITÄRES VÖLKERRECHT 198, 203 (for this case), *see also* Convention on the Safety of United Nations and associated Personnel, U.N. Doc. A/49/59 (December 9th, 1994), *available at* http://www.un.org/law/cod/safety.htm.

VI. Protection of religious personnel - the contemporary legal regime

1. The Geneva Conventions of 1949

This monograph continues with the examination of the 1949 Geneva Conventions. As their norms are currently in force, they form the core of the protection for religious personnel.[528]

World War II can be considered a fundamental challenge to humanitarian law and the law of armed conflict. After 1945, the question was raised whether efforts should be focused and limited on banning war as such or whether these efforts should be complimented by new rules.[529] Opting for the latter, efforts were undertaken to revise the Red Cross Conventions soon after the end of the war. It speaks for the importance that the ICRC contributed to the question of religious assistance that it instituted a commission for the study of the conventional dispositions with regard to the religious and intellectual needs of POW and civilian internees.[530] A number of religious organizations, amongst them the Jewish World Congress, the World Council of Churches and the Holy See,[531] contributed to the work of this commission and its proposals were remarkably well received in the later diplomatic conference.[532] It was then only the Holy See as a permanent subject of general international law[533] who was among the 69 delegations that took part in the diplomatic conference taking place from April 21st through August 12th, 1949 in Geneva.[534] This time, the presence of the Holy See's delegation did not meet objections.[535] The GCs are meanwhile ratified by almost all nations in the world and are considered customary international law.

The uprooting of contemporary men from religious traditions and the closer relations of states that underline their peculiarities make it difficult to determine a spiritual basis and objective for international agreements.[536] The diplomatic conference in 1949 was an example in this regard as it turned out to be impossible to agree on a preamble to the conventions passed.[537] The draft preamble proposed by a Working Party set up for this purpose referred to religion pro-

---

[528] *See infra* V.1 (for a historic outline of chaplaincy in Germany).
[529] *See* Rausch, *supra* note 139, at 28.
[530] *See also* JEAN S. PICTET, THE GENEVA CONVENTIONS OF 12 AUGUST 1949, COMMENTARY, III GENEVA CONVENTION 226 (1960), FEDERAL POLITICAL DEPARTMENT, *supra* note 217, at 260-61.
[531] *See also* HIEBEL, *supra* note 142, at 118 (for a complete list of participating religious organizations).
[532] *See* KÖCK, *supra* note 143, at 603 n.31.
[533] *See* Kunz, *supra* note 204, at 310.
[534] *See* Schlögel, *supra* note 38, at 268, Schwendenwein, *supra* note 191, at 510.
[535] *See* Kunz, *supra* note 204, at 313.
[536] *See* HUBER, *supra* note 19, at 15-16.
[537] *See* NICOLAS, *supra* note 16, at 100.

claiming the "divine origin" of respect for the personality and dignity of the human being. This formulation was considered a compromise between those who wished the convention to allude to a divine principle and those who did not deem that it should include a profession of faith.[538] The Holy See's representative, Mons. COMPTE pleaded strongly for a reference in the preamble to human rights and the mentioning of the "divine principle" on which the rights and duties of man were based - without a statement of dogma.[539] As the great majority of nations believed in a Supreme Being, "it should be possible to find a formula to express that belief in the Preamble".[540] In this line of argumentation, a preamble with reference to the deity would also "increase the confidence of the peoples" in the later conventions.[541] But even the compromise formula of the Working Party was unacceptable for the parties of the conference under communist governments and the project of a preamble failed completely.[542] The missing preamble, however, does not take away the fact that the whole international community went beyond ideological controversies and agreed upon a set of conventions that express the demand for the protection of the human person in a legal fashion.

The drafts of four conventions were presented to the conference held in Geneva. In practice, the protection of religious personnel is now very similar to the protection of medical staff.[543] Historically, it had been the other way around: Modern protection of medical personnel developed from a tradition that protected clergymen.[544] However, aggregating religious personnel with medical personnel seems justified also from a pastoral point of view in which the activities of religious personnel during crisis situations on missions often appear as "first aid for the soul".[545] The joint mentioning of chaplains and medical personnel in the protection clauses of the GCs constitutes the parallels in the protection of the two groups. Religious personnel to a large extend enjoy the same protection and treatment as medical personnel.[546] SCHOLLMEYER even goes as far as to

---

[538] *See* FEDERAL POLITICAL DEPARTMENT, *supra* note 217, at 164.
[539] *See id.*, *see also id.* at 692-93, Schubiger, *supra* note 145, at 3.
[540] FEDERAL POLITICAL DEPARTMENT, *supra* note 217, at 323.
[541] *Id.* at 113.
[542] *See* FEDERAL POLITICAL DEPARTMENT, *supra* note 218, at 522-23 (for the expression of "deep regret" made by the Holy See delegation at the final vote), *see also* FEDERAL POLITICAL DEPARTMENT, *supra* note 217, at 393 (for the Holy See's efforts to push for a preamble with precedural motions), Frits Kalshoven, *The Undertaking to Respect and Ensure Respect in All Circumstances*, 2 YEARBOOK OF INTERNATIONAL HUMANITARIAN LAW 3, 25 (1999) (for the drafting history of the preamble as a whole).
[543] *See* U.S. MARINE CORPS, *supra* note 182, No. 1004 e, HANS-PETER GASSER, EINFÜHRUNG IN DAS HUMANITÄRE VÖLKERRECHT 39 (1995).
[544] *See supra* at 17.
[545] *See* Michaelis/Theis, *supra* note 490, at 71.
[546] *See* PIETRO VERRI, DICTIONARY OF THE INTERNATIONAL LAW OF ARMED CONFLICT 97 (1992).

say that "a number of stipulations concerning medical personnel are applicable for chaplains without special reference".[547] At some points, however, the 1949 diplomatic conference invested more efforts for clarity in the status of medical personnel than it did for the clarity in religious personnel's status.[548]

The Conventions first and foremost protect the rights of individuals, amongst them religious liberty. This becomes evident when discrimination for religious motives is prohibited in all relevant legal instruments.[549] Freedom of religion and conscience is a fundamental requirement on which the right for spiritual assistance as enshrined in the GCs is based upon.[550] It is for this reason that any encroachment of freedom of religion compromises spiritual assistance and its ministers.[551] It has been regretted that the GCs do not explicitly refer to freedom of religion.[552] This would have certainly underlined the origin of chaplains' protection but also given a level of attention that in the early times of human rights popularity might have turned out to be disadvantageous.

This book will examine the legal instruments not only with regard to the personal protection of chaplains – SEIBT calls it active protection[553] – but also with regard to the passive protection of their ministry. Another appropriate system stresses the legal approach: HIEBEL differentiates between the right to give and the right to receive spiritual assistance.[554] This scheme takes into account the two perspectives the GCs have, the outlook on the minister and on the recipient of spiritual assistance.

a. Terminology

The Geneva Conventions do not protect ministers of religion as such but only a certain group of them. Terminology with regard to this protected group is not uniform. An abstract definition is lacking.[555] GC I uses both terms, "chaplains"[556] and "religious personnel".[557] As "chaplain" seems to be the term of art, it is unclear whether the use of the term "religious personnel" – e.g. in Art. 15 that speaks of free passage of religious personnel on their way to a besieged or encircled area – means something else. GC II – like some of the Hague conven-

---

[547] *See* Karl-Josef Schollmeyer, *Die völkerrechtliche Stellung des Militärgeistlichen*, 1966 NEUE ZEITSCHRIFT FÜR WEHRRECHT 59, 60.

[548] *See* Hiebel, *supra* note 180, at 13-14.

[549] *See* common Art. 3 to the GCs, Art. 9, 75 PA I, Art. 2 PA II.

[550] *See* Kussbach, *supra* note 144, at 388.

[551] *See* Hiebel, *supra* note 180, at 7.

[552] *See id.* at 4, 7.

[553] *See* HORST SEIBT, COMPENDIUM OF CASE STUDIES OF INTERNATIONAL HUMANITARIAN LAW 98 (1994).

[554] *See* Hiebel, *supra* note 180, at 3.

[555] *See* Kimminich, *supra* note 132, at 184-85.

[556] *See* Art. 4, 6, 7, 9 GC I.

[557] *See* Art. 15 GC I, Annex II.

tions – also uses the term "religious personnel" but without the restrictive definition that PA I introduced later. This could be interpreted as very far-reaching, to cover auxiliary personnel as well as not exclusively devoted personnel like lay preachers.[558] In practice, "religious personnel" in GC II is interpreted like "chaplains" in GC I.[559] In this interpretation, insufficiencies remain with regard to auxiliary religious personnel that are commonly not considered to be covered by protection according to present day terminology. RIEHM criticized that a possible inclusion of these personnel was not granted enough attention in GC I-III. Instead, he suggests conceiving the chaplain as the head of a mobile and independent religious unit and *de lege ferenda* also extend protection to auxiliary personnel.[560]

The English term "chaplains" is not always translated as *aumôniers* in the equally authentic French language version,[561] but also as *personnel religieux.*[562] In other instances, *personnel religieux* is translated into "religious personnel".[563] The terminology used is not uniform in the documents themselves and in the different language versions. This does not make it easier to determine the scope of protection.[564]

KOERBER defines military chaplains in international law as persons who by an act of installation according to the rules of their respective confession – be it consecration, ordination or another type of appointment – have been invested with a spiritual function and have been designated as members of the armed forces exclusively to the pastoral care of the persons entrusted to them.[565] Religious personnel (*personnel religieux*) is nowadays defined as "military or civilian persons such as chaplains who are exclusively engaged either temporarily or permanently in the work of their ministry (spiritual assistance) and attached to the armed forces or to medical units, medical transports, or civil defense organizations".[566] This definition is clearly worded after the PA I has entered into

---

[558] *See* Stadlmeier, *supra* note 155, at 531, *see also infra* at 77 (broad interpretation of the term "religious personnel" is irrelevant as Art. 17 GC IV allows access of civilian ministers of religion to besieged areas).

[559] *See* JEAN S. PICTET, THE GENEVA CONVENTIONS OF 12 AUGUST 1949, COMMENTARY, II GENEVA CONVENTION 199, 201 (1960).

[560] *See* RIEHM, *supra* note 432, at 3-4, *see also infra* VIII 2 c (for question of auxiliary personnel in Germany).

[561] *See* Art. 24 (1) GC I, Art. 35 GC III.

[562] *See* Art. 33 GC III.

[563] *See* Art. 36 GC II.

[564] *See* Stadlmeier, *supra* note 155, at 523.

[565] *See* H. E.Koerber, *Probleme der Bestimmungen über die Militärgeistlichen in den Genfer Abkommen vom 12. August 1949*, 1966 REVUE DE DROIT PÉNAL MILITAIRE ET DE DROIT DE LA GUERRE 417, 418.

[566] VERRI, *supra* note 546, at 97.

force[567] and technically speaking only valid for PA I, but should be kept in mind also as a tool to interpret the GCs.[568]

It is also only GC IV that uses the term "spiritual assistance".[569] The other GCs use different terms with regard to the work of chaplains: spiritual needs, religious ministration, religious character, religious needs. The term "spiritual assistance" of GC IV prevailed in the legal discipline as a description of religious activities in armed conflict situation. It implies a character of assistance that – taking into account the modern thought of the 19th century – follows a comprehensive approach towards human nature going beyond its mere religious aspect. The use of this term also underlines that assistance is not only a responsibility of the religious communities but also of the national states and of the international community.[570] Christian churches have accepted the term spiritual assistance as well.[571] HIEBEL finds that the reluctant use of the term spiritual assistance in the GCs stresses humanitarian necessity and obscures the nature of spiritual assistance as an outflow of human rights.[572]

b. Stipulations in GC I of general nature

Art. 24 GC I repeats the known principle of inviolability: "[C]haplains attached to the armed forces shall be respected and protected in all circumstances." This is "old law".[573] They may not be made the subject of military attack. They are not legitimate military targets. Also with the principle of necessity, no reasonable basis exists for allowing enemy forces to target a chaplain who finds himself on the battlefield for the sole purpose of providing spiritual comfort.[574] The protection applies at any place and at any time throughout the duration of an armed conflict: on the battlefield and behind the lines.[575]

The personnel of military chaplaincy are protected because their service to assist individuals in their religious effort is a highly valued task that deserves the support of the states. They themselves and their activities appear to be "supranational and quasi-neutral".[576] This demands and justifies international protec-

---

567 *See* MARCHEGGIANO, *supra* note 107, at 16.

568 *See* Peter Rößler, *Rechtsstellung der Geistlichen nach dem IV. Genfer Abkommen und den Zusatzprotokollen*, 1989 MILITÄRSEELSORGE 304, 307. The Annex II to GC I makes use of the term "religious personnel".

569 *See* Art. 38 No. 3 GC IV, Art. 58 (1) GC IV.

570 *See* NICOLAS, *supra* note 16, at 2-6.

571 *See* Hiebel, *supra* note 17, at 541, HIEBEL, *supra* note 142, at 2 *see also* OLSEN, *supra* note 195, at 414-18 (for the terminology in documents of the teaching office).

572 *See* Hiebel, *supra* note 180, at 4.

573 *See* Schlögel, *supra* note 38, at 270.

574 *See* Odom, *supra* note 7, at 10.

575 *See* PICTET, *supra* note 132, at 220, Walter Rabus, *Religious personnel, in* THE HANDBOOK OF HUMANITARIAN LAW IN ARMED CONFLICTS 369, No. 811 at 371 (Dieter Fleck ed. 1995).

576 PICTET, *supra* note 132, at 244, PICTET, *supra* note 530, at 218.

tion.[577] It is difficult to qualify protection of religious personnel as a condition or a return for their presence.[578] The rights of chaplains are not mere personal privileges but adjusted to the collective measure of spiritual assistance and linked with this function.[579] The good of the combatants who need chaplains' assistance is the "ultimate justification of their privileged status".[580]

Chaplains are protected if they are attached to the armed forces. The two criteria for protection of chaplain are established here: attachment and – since attachment is only unequivocal if it is undivided – exclusivity. But to what groups may chaplains be attached to? KOERBER advocates a narrow interpretation of the term "armed forces" meaning only regular forces, troops whose task is to safeguard the security and existence of a country.[581] He rejects the notion to consider all combatants as armed forces and distinguishes accordingly into military chaplains ministering to regular armed forces and ministers ministering to other groups of combatants. All the same, he allows military chaplains attached to regular armed forces to minister to all combatants and to the civilian entourage of armed forces.

Each of the conventions cannot be seen separate from the others because some issues are dealt with in more than one convention and other issues have to be judged in the context of the conventions as a whole. Accordingly, KOERBER uses the argument that Art. 37 GC II for naval warfare speaks of religious personnel assigned to the spiritual care of the persons protected by the convention. With reference to Art. 13 GC II, chaplains under GC II are then entitled for protection if they provide spiritual assistance to one of the following groups:[582]

- To the armed forces or militias and members of other volunteer corps if they form part of the armed forces or otherwise have combatant status,
- To persons who accompany the armed forces without actually being members thereof. If chaplains minister to this entourage, they need the authorization from the armed forces that these persons are accompanying.
- To members of crews of the merchant marine[583] and the crews of civil aircrafts;

---

[577] *See* Schollmeyer, *supra* note 547, at 60.

[578] *See* Hiebel, *supra* note 17, at 542.

[579] *See* Hiebel, *supra* note 180, at 22, *see also* Schubiger, *supra* note 145, at 5, MARCHEGGIANO, *supra* note 107, at 161 (for clearly privilegious conditions).

[580] PICTET, *supra* note 132, at 248, PICTET, *supra* note 530, at 220, *see also* DRAPER, *supra* note 7, at 274 (drawing the link from protection to the religious needs of military personnel including those hors de combat with view on the humane treatment requirement reflected in the GCs).

[581] *See* Koerber, *supra* note 565, at 418-19.

[582] *But see also* HIEBEL, *supra* note 142, at 140-141 (disregarding this reference and thus concluding that GC I-II ignore chaplains attached to non-regular armed forces).

[583] *See also* PICTET, *supra* note 559, at 211.

- To inhabitants of a non-occupied territory, who on the approach of the enemy, spontaneously take up arms to resist the invading forces, but did not have time to form themselves into regular armed units. This so called "levée en masse" must carry arms openly and respect the laws and customs of war.

The groups of protected persons are the same in GC I as Art. 13 GC I is identically worded, but the stipulations on chaplaincy make no reference to it. KOERBER excludes a direct application of Art. 37, 13 GC II on GC I, but concedes that his postulate to allow an attachment only to regular armed forces comes to the intolerable result that religious ministers to militias at sea are protected under GC II but are not protected once they have landed and GC I is applied.[584] He concludes that GC I leaves a gap that is filled by applying the legal concept of GC II as framed in Art. 37, 13 GC II unto GC I.[585] KOERBER's result by devious means would have been avoided if a broader interpretation of the term "armed forces" in Art. 24 GC I was not excluded in the first place. Given the practice of GC II and its legal concept, the interpretation of "armed forces" should take into account the groups of protected persons in Art. 13 GC I and thus imply a protection of chaplains servicing the groups enumerated there. KOERBER's inconsistent position has become finally obsolete as the PAs have explicitly opted for the understanding of armed forces in such a broader interpretation including militias and voluntary corps.[586]

The attachment must be original in a spiritual function. The draft of a clergyperson does not constitute a protection by itself.[587] This becomes also clear in Art. 36 GC III that speaks of ministers of religion not officiating as chaplains to their own forces.[588] Thus, a minister of religion can be drafted as a soldier and becomes a combatant[589] – though he receives certain prerogatives as POW. The attachment of chaplains is an act of the state. The decision rests "with the competent military authorities" and the relationship between chaplain and armed forces "must be an official one".[590] In the case of chaplains ministering to groups other than regular armed forces as listed in Art. 13 GC I, the attachment is car-

---

[584] *But see* HIEBEL, *supra* note 142, at 141 (who instead reduces the level of protection of GC II in view of GC I).

[585] *See* Koerber, *supra* note 565, at 420, *but see* Stadlmeier, *supra* note 155, at 525 (who takes the applicability of Art. 13 GC I for granted).

[586] *See* Knut Ipsen, *Combatants and Non-Combatants, in* THE HANDBOOK OF HUMANITARIAN LAW IN ARMED CONFLICTS 65, No. 304 at 70 (Dieter Fleck ed. 1995).

[587] *See* Koerber, *supra* note 565, at 419.

[588] *See* PICTET, *supra* note 530, at 230, *see also* FEDERAL POLITICAL DEPARTMENT, *supra* note 217, at 332.

[589] *See* Stadlmeier, *supra* note 155, at 525, *see also* FEDERAL POLITICAL DEPARTMENT, *supra* note 217, at 440 (about confusions of chaplains and ministers of religion).

[590] PICTET, *supra* note 132, at 219, *but see* HIEBEL, *supra* note 142, at 199-200 (critizing this understanding as too narrow).

ried out by the consent of the responsible leader.[591] Chaplains cannot attach themselves.[592] A unilateral declaration of the religious minister himself or his religious community is insufficient to constitute chaplains' status.[593] Instead, he must be received into the group he is attached to, designated or at least accepted.[594] A minister serving to warriors without combatant status or serving without attachment does not receive the protection of a chaplain.[595] The responsibility of the belligerents for the attachment must be seen in the context of the states who as parties to the GCs are responsible for the application of the norms and in particular for ensuring that no abuses will be committed by protected persons.[596] The Armed Forces of the Philippines know "civilian priests who serve as volunteer chaplains".[597] It should be examined further whether these personnel can be considered being attached to the armed forces.

A direct participation of chaplains in rendering assistance to the victims of war such as wounded, sick, shipwrecked or POW is not required for them in order to be entitled to the protection of the GCs as they are protected by reason of their spiritual office.[598] The GCs understand pastoral assistance wider than merely as an aspect of medical care[599] though this aspect plays an important part in practice.[600] On the other hand, carrying out medical tasks does not infringe the exclusivity criterion.[601]

Special agreements between the parties to the GCs must not affect the situation of chaplains as defined by GC I or restrict their conventional rights.[602] Art. 15 (3) GC I proposes local arrangements between Parties to the conflict to allow for the passage of religious personnel to a besieged or encircled area. This norm takes into account that religious personnel should "always be allowed free

---

591 *See* Koerber, *supra* note 565, at 421.

592 *See* PICTET, *supra* note 132, at 220.

593 *See* Barthold C. Witte, *Völkerrechtliche Aspekte der Militärseelsorge*, *in* EKD-INFORMATIONEN MILITÄRSEELSORGE doc. 12 at 2 (Kirchenamt der Evangelischen Kirche in Deutschland ed. 1993).

594 *See* COMMENTARY ON THE ADDITIONAL PROTOCOLS, *supra* note 178, No. 637 at 195; the problem regarding chaplaincy to the levée en masse is discussed *infra* at 127.

595 *See* PICTET, *supra* note 132, at 220, *but see* O'BRIEN, *supra* note 154, at D2 (excluding protection for chaplains of certain combatant groups as well).

596 *See* COMMENTARY ON THE ADDITIONAL PROTOCOLS, *supra* note 178, No. 637 at 195.

597 Art. VI, Sec. 1 (3) of the Statutes Military Ordinariate of the Philippines, *in* BAURA, *supra* note 344, at 207.

598 *See* Rabus, *supra* note 575, No. 812 at 371, PICTET, VICTIMS, *supra* note 132, at 79, *but see also* Watson, *supra* note 7, at 41 (giving the impression that chaplains serve only the wounded and the sick).

599 *See* O'BRIEN, *supra* note 154, at D1.

600 *See* PICTET, *supra* note 132, at 219.

601 *See* COMMENTARY ON THE ADDITIONAL PROTOCOLS, *supra* note 178, No. 362 at 127.

602 *See* Art. 6 GC I, *see also* MARCHEGGIANO, *supra* note 107, at 96 (for a list of possibile agreements effecting chaplains).

access when their presence is required, in order that they may bring consolidations of religion to all, whether wounded or fit".[603] It is unclear, whether the use of the term "religious personnel" in this norm widens the scope of protected personnel and also implies civilian personnel. The ratio of the norm would justify such a wide interpretation. The use of the term religious personnel in the heading of Annex II to GC I that obviously refers to religious ministers in a military setting, however, contradicts such an interpretation. In conclusion, it does not matter whether civilian ministers are covered by Art. 15 (3) GC I because the access of civilian "ministers of all religions" to besieged locations is similarly regulated in Art. 17 GC IV.

Only two norms of GC I deal with the recipients of religious ministry. Firstly, the Occupying Power is under an obligation to give "moral care" to the wounded and sick.[604] Thus, spiritual assistance may be provided from a chaplain of the Occupying Power to those in need, to wounded, sick and shipwrecked even if they are members of enemy armed forces.[605] The term "moral care" here appears as a *lapsus linguae*, an editorial mistake. Secondly, the parties to the conflict have to ensure that the dead are interred honorably and if possible according to the rites of the religion to which they belonged.[606] The reference to a religious burial is a novelty of the 1949 GC I and is still not contained in the parallel stipulation to burials at sea in GC II.[607] The German Humanitarian Law in Armed Conflicts Manual interprets the GC I stipulation as a duty of the parties to assist the chaplains within the means available to them.[608] There is, however, not an absolute right to a religious burial.[609] Moreover, cremation may only occur for imperative reasons of hygiene or for motives based on the religion of the deceased.[610]

c. Means of protection

Art. 40 GC I and the similarly worded Art. 42 GC II regulate the exterior signs of protection of chaplains: armlet and identity card. The distinctive emblem itself does not constitute a protection but is an exterior sign thereof. A person fulfilling the respective requirements is entitled for protection even without displaying the distinctive emblem. Nonetheless, the use of the armlet is advisable because it signalizes the entitlement of protection to the belligerents and avoids mistaking chaplains – especially those in uniform – as combatants. To bar the right to bear

---

603 PICTET, *supra* note 132, at 157.
604 Art. 18 (4) GC I.
605 *See* Rabus, *supra* note 575, No. 805 at 370.
606 *See* Art. 17 (3) GC I.
607 *See* Art. 20 GC II.
608 *See* Rabus, *supra* note 575, No. 807 at 370.
609 *See* PICTET, *supra* note 132, at 179, Hiebel, *supra* note 180, at 4.
610 *See* Art. 17 (1) GC I, *see also* FEDERAL POLITICAL DEPARTMENT, *supra* note 217, at 297.

the armlet to chaplains attached to civilian institutions such as civil aviation as PICTET does[611] is not supported by the GCs because chaplains may be attached to the crews of civilian aircrafts.[612]

The armlet (water-resistant![613]) bearing the distinctive emblem is to be affixed to the left arm, issued and stamped by the military authority. "Affixed" means that it should not be taken off and put on again at will.[614] The issuance and provision of these signs is in the responsibility of the party to the conflict, not of the minister's religious community.[615] The distinctive emblem is described in Art. 38 GC I as the red cross on a white ground, formed by reversing the Swiss Federal colors, and intended "to be without any religious significance" and "to be employed by persons of all beliefs".[616] Even the Holy See in the statement of the head of its delegation to the 1949 diplomatic conference, Archbishop PAUL BERNADINI, considered the red cross to be "devoid of all religious significance".[617] Initiatives during the diplomatic conference to have a more neutral emblem to take the place of the red cross or to have other symbols added met opposition and failed.[618] However, the 1949 conventions - as the 1929 conventions - also recognized as distinctive emblem the red crescent or the red lion and sun on a white ground as in use at that time. The red Shield of David that is used in Israel is not recognized by the convention as the danger was felt to establish national symbols instead of signs of neutrality.[619] Difficulties remained and initiatives by the ICRC were taken to create an additional protective emblem to stand alongside the red cross and the red crescent. This additional emblem would particularly serve those countries that would not want to use the two existing. The diplomatic conference of states called by the Swiss government in its capacity as depositary for the GCs to adopt the additional emblem[620] was postponed in October 2000 and early 2001 because of the events in the Middle East region.

---

[611] *See* PICTET, *supra* note 559, at 209 (particularly with an inconsistent view on attachment to civil aviation compared to attachment to merchant marine).

[612] *See supra* at 74.

[613] *See* PICTET, *supra* note 132, at 310 (lack of water resistance obviously cannot held to deprive of protection).

[614] *See id.*

[615] *See* O'BRIEN, *supra* note 154, at O2. In Germany, the armlet is issued by the Military ordinariate that is both a military and a state authority.

[616] PICTET, *supra* note 132, at 303.

[617] FEDERAL POLITICAL DEPARTMENT, *supra* note 217, at 150, *see also* note 146 (for the non-religious character of the Red Cross Movement).

[618] *See* FEDERAL POLITICAL DEPARTMENT, *supra* note 217, at 151.

[619] *See* PICTET, VICTIMS, *supra* note 132, at 93, HILAIRE MCCOUBREY & NIGEL D. WHITE, INTERNATIONAL LAW AND ARMED CONFLICT 259 (1992), *but see also* Odom, *supra* note 7, at 13 (about a customary recognition of the Red Shield of David).

[620] *See infra* Appendix I a (for the latest proposal for an additional distinctive emblem as published on the ICRC webpage).

The 28th International Conference of the Red Cross and Red Crescent scheduled for November 2000 to adapt the Movement's statutes so that societies and countries using the additional emblem could be admitted was also postponed. However, the revised draft of a 3rd additional protocol had been sent to the parties of the GCs.

The identity card is the proof of the right to wear the armlet and also necessary as a proof of the chaplain status.[621] It is of pocket size and also bears the distinctive emblem. Worded in the national language, it mentions at least the surname and first names, the date of birth, the rank and the service number of the bearer. It states in what capacity the bearer is entitled to the protection of the Geneva Conventions. It has to show the holder's photograph and also either his signature or his fingerprint or both. It also must be embossed with the stamp of the military authority.[622]

The norm recommends a uniform identity card throughout the same armed forces and a similar type for all parties of the GCs. For this purpose, a model is annexed to GC I.[623] At the outbreak of hostilities, the parties to a conflict inform each other of the form they are using. GC I also recommends to keep a duplicate of the card with the home country.[624]

Compliance with the details on the issue of armlet and identity card becomes difficult when chaplains are attached to forces other than regular armed forces according to Art. 13 GC I. In these cases, armlets and identity cards issued by the responsible commander or leader have to be sufficient. Protection must not be refused because an armlet or identity card lacks the necessary stamp of a state authority.[625] Other authors see the stamp as a sign of the official accountability of a state for the issuance of the armlet and identity card and consider them to have "no protective value"[626] without the stamp.[627]

Chaplains must not be deprived of their identity cards or of the right to wear the armlet. In case of loss, they are entitled to receive duplicates of the cards and to have the armlet replaced. It is furthermore commonly accepted that chaplains should wear the identity disk worn by all members of the armed forces.[628]

Even though the stipulations on the use of the distinctive emblem are clear from a legal point of view, practical problems persist: The use of the armlet is

---

621 *See* PICTET, *supra* note 132, at 312.
622 *See* Art. 40 (2) GC II.
623 *See infra* Appendix II a.
624 *See* Art. 40 (3) GC II.
625 *See* Koerber, *supra* note 565, at 422.
626 PICTET, *supra* note 132, at 311.
627 *See also* Odom, *supra* note 7, at 12.
628 *See* O'BRIEN, *supra* note 154, at O2, Schollmeyer, *supra* note 547, at 62, Rabus, *supra* note 575, No. 808 at 371, PICTET, *supra* note 132, at 315.

met with reservations on the part of the medical military staff who do not see the link between the emblem, the medical care they provide and the activities of the chaplain that entitle him to the use of the emblem. The armlet may also create distance between the chaplain and the troops as it represents a privilege of the chaplain that the troops do not enjoy. In this way, the armlet interferes with the pastoral approach of the chaplain being amongst and with his troops.

The use of the distinctive emblem of the red cross by military chaplaincy in the German *Bundeswehr* is regulated by decree of the Ministry of Defense.[629] The decree's definition of the protected group covers military chaplains but not auxiliary religious personnel unless they are at the same time members of the medical corps. If deployed in armed conflict, German religious personnel wear around the left arm an armlet[630] that shows the red cross on white ground on one side and on the other side the red cross on a white disk and on olive-green ground.[631] Unlike the armlet of medical personnel, chaplains wear an armlet that additionally has a violet middle stripe. The armlet is issued and stamped by the catholic military bishop's office or the protestant church office by order of the Ministry of Defense. In issuing and stamping the armlet, these authorities act as state organs. The bearer of the armlet must also be in possession of the identity card for medical and religious personnel according to the GCs. Eligible personnel may wear the distinctive emblem also in times of peace. Generally, the armlet is worn with only the white side visible. In extraordinary circumstances, the commander of a division or a higher ranking officer may order to turn the armlet to the olive-green side if military necessity demands so and after having consulted the competent senior medical officer and the legal advisor - not the chaplain. Such a camouflage order would concern the safety of the troops and the chaplain would have to respect it.

In Germany, chaplaincy does not have the right to mark its vehicles with the distinctive emblem. RAUSCH considered such a marking to be helpful given the importance of transportation in modern times.[632] Under IHL, however, the conveyance of religious personnel may be considered a medical transportation and a vehicle therefore exclusively assigned may be considered a medical trans-

---

[629] *See* 1960 MINISTERIALBLATT DES BUNDESMINISTERIUMS DER VERTEIDIGUNG (VMBl.) 288 changed by 1968 VMBl. 85 and 1981 VMBl. 103.

[630] *See also* Odom, *supra* note 7, at 15 (for the incorrect implementation of the left arm requirement of Art. 40 GC I, Art. 42 GC II into national U.S. Navy Uniform Regulations as right arm), PICTET, *supra* note 132, at 310 (protection should not be denied if the armlet is worn on the right arm).

[631] *See infra* Appendix I b (for a sample).

[632] *See* Rausch, *supra* note 139, at 35, see also Jim Edwards, *Lesson from the dirt*, THE NAVY CHAPLAIN, No. 4, Fall 2003, at 8, 9 (particularly on the role of chaplain's transportation during operation).

port under PA I.[633] The transportation of religious personnel here establishes an indirect link to the wounded, sick and shipwrecked.[634] Thus, transportation of religious personnel in vehicles identified as medical transports does not compromise the status of these vehicles.[635] Chaplaincy vehicles are already marked with the distinctive emblem e.g. by the U.S. Armed Forces.[636] German reluctance regarding this question might be caused by the fact that German chaplains usually have enlisted personnel as drivers. Subjects of improved could also be the other materials of chaplaincy.[637] Unlike medical supplies, the articles used for religious purposes are not explicitly protected under humanitarian law unless they are meant for POW or civilian populations.[638] These examples underline the cultural context in which spiritual assistance is often understood.[639] In the understanding of the German IHL Manual, it would be in keeping with the spirit of the GCs to respect the material required for religious purposes and not to use it for alien ends.[640]

d. Retention of chaplains in GC I

As a result of their protection "in all circumstances",[641] chaplains are also protected in captivity, be it temporarily or for a lengthy period.[642] The GCs again had to address the question of chaplains' return or a possible continuation of their activities when being held captive. This question was among "the most important" issues resolved by GC I.[643] As elucidated *supra*, different approaches in this regard were followed in the history of revisions of the Red Cross Convention. After some discussion,[644] the 1949 revision introduced yet another approach that reflects itself both in GC I and in GC III. Sometimes, the two conventions even have overlapping provisions what caused controversies in the plenary of the Geneva diplomatic conference. These editorial weaknesses, in SCHLÖGEL's opinion, do not question the appropriate results that are "admirable" and deserve "full appreciation".[645]

---

[633] *See* Art. 8 f, g PA I *see also* GREEN, *supra* note 133, at 330 (for an indistinct application of provisions for medical personnel).
[634] *See* COMMENTARY ON THE ADDITIONAL PROTOCOLS, *supra* note 178, No. 382 at 130.
[635] *See* O'BRIEN, *supra* note 154, at O2, HIEBEL, *supra* note 142, at 370.
[636] *See* U.S. MARINE CORPS, *supra* note 182, No. 3003 d.
[637] *See* Rausch, *supra* note 139, at 35.
[638] *See* Art. 23 GC IV, Art. 69 No. 1 PA I, Rabus, *supra* note 575, No. 813 at 371, *see also supra* at 92, 88 and *infra* 111, 111, 111.
[639] *See* Hiebel, *supra* note 180, at 5.
[640] *See* Rabus, *supra* note 575, No. 813 at 371.
[641] Art. 24 GC I.
[642] *See* PICTET, *supra* note 132, at 220.
[643] *Id.* at 235.
[644] *See* PICTET, VICTIMS, *supra* note 132, at 80-83, PICTET, *supra* note 132, at 238.
[645] *See* Schlögel, *supra* note 38, at 272.

According to Art. 28 GC I, chaplains who fall into the hands of the adverse party, can be retained only for a factual cause, a "real and pressing need",[646] namely the spiritual demands and the number of prisoners of war. Retention as a "secondary possibility",[647] an "exceptional measure"[648] can only occur to serve POW.[649] Though retention will in most cases be the rule in practice, repatriation as the dominant principle has priority.[650] This priority, however, is from a legal point of view not as strong as in the 1929 Red Cross Convention.[651] Also in contrast to the 1929 Convention that permitted retention only by special agreement,[652] the decision is now in the hands of the Detaining Power. The U.S.A., for instance, retain chaplains in the ratio of one chaplain per 1000 POW, the ICRC recommends one for 1000 to 2000 POW.[653] If the Power of origin considers the number of retained chaplains excessive, it may open negotiations with the Detaining Power and call upon the good services of either the Protecting Power or the ICRC.[654] MARCHEGGIANO concludes that in view of the variety of tasks related to spiritual assistance, the case that it is no longer necessary to retain chaplains will hardly occur and repatriation is thus more a theoretical than a real option.[655]

The formulation of chaplains "who fall into the hands of the adverse party" of the norm implies that capture is a mater of chance. Deliberate attempts to take chaplains captive, a "hunt" on chaplains would be "completely contrary to the spirit" of the GCs.[656] If there is doubt about the chaplain quality of a person, a competent tribunal in accordance to Art. 5 (2) GC III decides on the matter.[657]

Retained chaplains are not considered prisoners of war.[658] This provision is the consequence of the right to respect that chaplains enjoy.[659] Instead, they at least

---

[646] PICTET, *supra* note 132, at 241.
[647] *Id.* at 261.
[648] PICTET, *supra* note 530, at 218.
[649] *See* Schwendenwein, *supra* note 191, at 510 514.
[650] *See* PICTET, VICTIMS, *supra* note 132, at 81, PICTET, *supra* note 132, at 240, Schollmeyer, *supra* note 547, at 63.
[651] *See* Schlögel, *supra* note 38, at 270.
[652] *See* Watson, *supra* note 7, at 44.
[653] *See* U.S. ARMY, ARMY REGULATION 190–8, ENEMY PRISONERS OF WAR, RETAINED PERSONNEL, CIVILIAN INTERNEES AND OTHER DETAINEES § 3-15 k (October 1st, 1997), http://www.au.af.mil/au/awc/awcgate/law/ar190-8.pdf, ICRC, *La Rétention et la relève du personnel sanitaire, Accords-types e commentaire*, 1955 REVUE INTERNATIONAL DE LA CROIX-ROUGE 7, 10.
[654] *See* PICTET, *supra* note 132, at 242.
[655] *See* MARCHEGGIANO, *supra* note 107, at 99.
[656] *See* PICTET, *supra* note 132, at 242.
[657] *See* Ipsen, *supra* note 586, No. 316 at 92.
[658] *See* Art. 28 GC I, *see also infra* at 87 (for the status of chaplains voluntarily remaining for POW ministry).
[659] *See* Hiebel, *supra* note 180, at 16, HIEBEL, *supra* note 142, at 199-200.

benefit from the provisions of GC III for POW. These norms form a minimum of their status.[660] Norms of GC III that are not of advantage for chaplains are not to be applied.[661] They thus enjoy a specific status that combines the protection POW receive and the exercise of religious functions. This status may be called the stability of religious personnel.[662] It is e.g. part of this minimal protection that chaplains – like prisoners of war – have to be released and repatriated without delay after the cessation of hostilities.[663] The detainee status of chaplains in captivity with the bottom line of the GC III regulations results in a status "not absolutely clear",[664] but was devised as a compromise formula on the 1949 diplomatic conference.

Detained chaplains are subject to the military laws and regulations of the Detaining Power and under the authority of its competent service.[665] Thus, they are subordinated to the general orders of the camp commander because it is the Detaining Power and not the individual chaplain that is responsible for the spiritual welfare of the POW.[666] Even though chaplains' liberty is restricted in this way, they are allowed to continue to carry out their spiritual duties addressed to the POW. The continuation of their activities is the basis for all other rights of chaplains.[667] The "continue" implies a straight line from activities in combat and to those in captivity practically without break.[668] Protection of religious personnel follows this line. Continuation happens in accordance with their professional ethics and preferably to those armed forces to which they themselves belong. The "preferably" implies that a ministry to allied forces of the same religion is possible, too.[669] In any case, exceptions may be made "where circumstances so demand".[670]

SEIBT considers this obligation to observe disciplinary regulations and professional responsibility as conduct to establish relations of trust. Chaplains' prerogatives are then granted in return.[671] This explanation may be true with regard to the *mens legislatoris*. It must be clear, however, that the status of detained

---

[660] *See* Art. 33 GC III, *see also* PICTET, *supra* note 530, at 218.
[661] *See* PICTET, *supra* note 132, at 243, 253-56.
[662] *See* ERIC DAVID, PRINCIPES DE DROIT DES CONFLITS ARMÉS No. 2.200 (2nd ed. 1999).
[663] *See* Art. 118 (1) GC III, *see also* O'BRIEN, *supra* note 154, at R.5.
[664] PICTET, VICTIMS, *supra* note 132, at 81.
[665] *See infra* 91 (for the interpretation of the military laws and regulations requirement or Art. 33 GC III in the light of the disciplinary routine requirement for religious exercise in Art. 34 GC III).
[666] *See* PICTET, *supra* note 530, at 219.
[667] *See* HIEBEL, *supra* note 142, at 192.
[668] *See* PICTET, *supra* note 530, at 219.
[669] *See* Rabus, *supra* note 575, No. 805 at 370, *see also* MARCHEGGIANO, *supra* note 107, at 99 (interpreting "forces to which they themselves belong" with regard to the military branch [army, navy, air force]).
[670] PICTET, *supra* note 132, at 247, PICTET, *supra* note 530, at 220.
[671] *See* SEIBT, *supra* note 553.

chaplains is not conditioned by a previous conduct in favor of the Detaining Power.

For carrying out their spiritual duties, thus for their ministry and not as personal privileges,[672] chaplains further enjoy the following facilities:[673]

(a) They are authorized to visit periodically – a frequency is not specified – the prisoners of war in labor units or hospitals outside the camp. Visits of POW in penitentiaries or those living in private families would also be authorized.[674] The Detaining Power must provide them with the required means of transportation. Nonetheless, the camp authorities can exercise the supervision "it considers necessary" over these journeys.[675] They may, for instance, designate an escort to accompany the visiting chaplain on such trips.[676] Furthermore, chaplains on visits must not abuse their right to visit but may leave camp only for the purpose of visiting prisoners "entrusted to their care".[677] Otherwise, this right of visitation may be restricted to some extend.[678]

(b) Like the highest-ranking senior medical officer, all chaplains have direct access to the military and medical authorities of the POW camp in all questions arising out of their duties. They do not have to take the course via the prisoners' representative when addressing the detaining authorities even though they could do so and also take part in the election of the prisoners' representative.[679] HIEBEL sees in the right of direct access an orientation of the GCs towards a vertical understanding of religion in which the minister is a leader of his community.[680] The camp administration grants to chaplains the facilities they may require for correspondence relating to these questions. This provision undoubtedly strengthens the chaplains' position. It is in individualized since chaplains "do not form a separate corps, are few in number, and are often of different denominations".[681]

(c) Retained chaplains in a POW camp are subject to its internal discipline but must not be required to perform any work outside their religious duties.[682]

During hostilities, the parties to the conflict are encouraged to find arrangements for relieving retained personnel and to settle the procedure of such relief. As opposed to the 1929 Red Cross Convention that considered such agreements

---

[672] *See* PICTET, *supra* note 132, at 248, *see also* Schubiger, *supra* note 145, at 5.
[673] *See* Art. 28 (2) GC I.
[674] *See* PICTET, *supra* note 132, at 248, *see also* PICTET, *supra* note 530, at 221.
[675] PICTET, *supra* note 132, at 248, PICTET, *supra* note 530, at 221.
[676] *See* Odom, *supra* note 7, at 37.
[677] PICTET, *supra* note 132, at 248, PICTET, *supra* note 530, at 221.
[678] *See* PICTET, *supra* note 530, at 218.
[679] *Id.* at 222.
[680] *See* HIEBEL, *supra* note 142, at 209.
[681] PICTET, *supra* note 132, at 251, PICTET, *supra* note 530, at 222.
[682] *But see* O'BRIEN, *supra* note 154, at R.4 (chaplains could chose to apply for suitable work).

to be obligatory, they are now only facultative.[683] They could include agreements of replacement of chaplains directly from the enemy party.[684] On request by the 1949 diplomatic conference, the ICRC prepared model agreements for retention and relief of religious personnel.[685]

The 1949 diplomatic conference also rejected a proposal to exclude chaplains from the group of retained personnel eligible for repatriation.[686] Accordingly, Art. 30 GC I then regulates the return of chaplains to their party if retention is not indispensable. The selection of personnel to be repatriated – and therefore also of the personnel to be retained[687] – may not discriminate for reasons of religion but is to be made preferably according to the chronological order of capture and the state of health.[688] Return takes place as soon as a road is open and military requirements permit so. STADLMEIER mentions militarily important knowledge that has to be kept secret from the enemy party as a military requirement that would bar repatriation.[689] The release of a chaplain into the territory of his home state that the former Detaining Power still occupies does not fulfill the duty to return this chaplain.[690] Pending their repatriation, captured chaplains enjoy a detainee status in accordance with Art. 28 GC I. On their departure, they may take with them the effects, personal belongings, valuables and instruments belonging to them.

If a chaplain is attached to the medical units or medical transports of a recognized and authorized aid society from a neutral country,[691] he must not be detained. According to Art. 32 GC I he may return to his country and if this is not possible to the territory of the party he was servicing. Until route for his repatriation is open and until military considerations permit so, he enjoys a status similar to this of detained chaplains. He is privileged in that he is to be provided the same food, lodging, allowances and pay as are granted to the corresponding personnel in the armed forces of the Detaining Power.

The question of escape of detained chaplains from detention is of little practical relevance.[692] On the other hand, chaplains - unlike other POW - in some

---

[683] *See* Schlögel, *supra* note 38, at 270.

[684] *See* O'BRIEN, *supra* note 154, at R.5.

[685] *See* ICRC, *supra* note 653, at 7-31, *see also* Eduardo de Nó Louis Magalhaes, *Los acuerdos-tipo sobre retención y relevo del personal sanitario y religioso*, 1958 REVISTA ESPAÑOLA DE DERECHO MILITAR, No. 5, at 135-148 (1958).

[686] *See* PICTET, *supra* note 132, at 261 n.1.

[687] *Id.* at 265.

[688] *See* Art. 31 GC I.

[689] *See* Stadlmeier, *supra* note 155, at 526 n.27, *see also* PICTET, *supra* note 132, at 245, 262 (for the risk of espionage by retained personnel).

[690] *See* PICTET, *supra* note 132, at 262, Rabus, *supra* note 575, No. 827 at 373.

[691] *See* meanwhile defined in Art. 8 d iii PA I, *see also* Art. 27 GC I.

[692] *See* Hiebel, *supra* note 180, at 25-26.

countries are not under an obligation to escape as long as their status as detainees is respected.[693] As chaplains are not POW but retained personnel, they remain with their ministry to some extend in the service of their country of origin. A flight may then violate their service obligations or even constitute desertion and be punished by their home country. In any case, a flight can be considered a breach of the camp discipline and punished by disciplinary measures of the Detaining Power.[694]

e. Ministry to prisoners of war in GC III

The norms of GC III contain a number of provisions concerning spiritual assistance to POW, which is a result of the intensive efforts of the Holy See during the 1949 conference in this regard.[695]

Chapter IV of GC III deals with chaplains retained to assist POW. Art. 33 GC III stipulates that chaplains may be retained to assist prisoners of war. Even though they are not considered POW,[696] they receive as a minimum the benefits and protection of GC III. Chaplains must be granted all facilities necessary to provide for religious ministration to POW. Within the scope of the military laws and regulations of the Detaining Power and under the control of its competent services, they may continue to exercise their spiritual functions for the benefit of POW, preferably those belonging to the armed forces upon which they depend, in accordance with their professional etiquette. Chaplains are not subject to the camp commander's authority with regard to the exercise of their ministry.[697] Compulsion comes to an end when chaplain's activities enter the field of the "professional conscience or of the sacerdotal mission".[698] Art. 33 GC III also restates the access to POW outside the camp and the chaplains' right to directly address the camp administration. Though excluded from labor duties, chaplains along with medical personnel are the only officers to continue to work in captivity since commissioned officers are usually excluded from any labor duty.[699] Nonetheless, the exclusion from labor duty is no justification for giving chaplains the same rations as prisoners receive who do not work.[700] Chaplains also receive working pay in accordance with Art. 62 (2) GC III.[701]

---

[693] *See* DEPARTMENT OF DEFENSE, INSTRUCTION 1300.21, CODE OF CONDUCT TRAINING AND EDUCATION, Enclosure 2 E2.3.3.3 at 24-25 (January 8th, 2001), *available at* http://www.dtic.mil/whs/directives/corres/pdf/i130021_010801/i130021p.pdf (for U.S. Armed Forces).

[694] *See* PICTET, *supra* note 132, at 255-56, *see also* PICTET, *supra* note 530, at 218.

[695] *See* Schlögel, *supra* note 38, at 272, *see also* PICTET, *supra* note 530, at 226-27.

[696] *See also* Art. 4 c GC III.

[697] *See* Schollmeyer, *supra* note 547, at 64, Rabus, *supra* note 575, No. 835 at 374.

[698] PICTET, *supra* note 530, at 219, *see also* PICTET, *supra* note 132, at 246.

[699] *See* Art. 49 GC III.

[700] *See* PICTET, *supra* note 530, at 232.

[701] *Id.* at 317.

Chaplains who fall into the hands of the enemy Power and who remain or are retained with a view to assisting POW, are allowed to minister to them and to exercise freely their ministry amongst prisoners of war of the same religion, in accordance with their religious conscience.[702] The limitation of ministry to POW of the same religion could be considered a significant restriction.[703] The formulation that chaplains may "remain" for the assistance of POW must be understood as a deliberate and voluntary decision of the chaplain himself to stay in captivity that then needs the consent of the Detaining Power.[704] It is the only exception to the otherwise absolute prohibition to renounce conventional rights.[705] The question arises whether chaplains who voluntarily remain in the hands of the adversary party after capture enjoy the same status as retained chaplains. Art. 33 GC III grants the preferential status of not being POW to "chaplains while retained". Art. 28 (2) GC I does the same for "personnel thus retained". The creation of two different classes of chaplains in captivity – those who remain voluntarily and those who are retained – with different levels of protection would contradict the concept of stability of religious personnel[706] because both retained and voluntarily remaining chaplains find themselves in the same situation and fulfill the same tasks.[707] The framers of the conventions had in mind primarily medical personnel[708] when they worded Art. 28 (2) GC I, Art. 33 GC III as these norms are equally applicable to them. The "remain" clause of Art. 35 GC III applies exclusively to chaplains. Furthermore, the norms of the GCs are not designed for the protection of the chaplain as such but for his service that should continue in captivity. Then it would be absurd to apply the special norm of Art. 35 GC III without applying the general norm of Art. 33 GC III on chaplains remaining voluntarily.[709] The chaplains' protection of the conventions is then applied in its entirety also on chaplains remaining voluntarily: They are not considered POW.[710]

Retained chaplains are to be allocated among the various camps and labor detachments containing prisoners of war belonging to the same forces, speaking the same language or practicing the same religion. This is to ensure an equal level of assistance for prisoners of war as World War II had shown difficulties in

---

[702] *See* Art. 35 GC III.

[703] *See* Rausch, *supra* note 139, at 39 n.51.

[704] *See* PICTET, *supra* note 530, at 231, Koerber, *supra* note 565, at 424, *but see also* Stadlmeier, *supra* note 155, at 528 n.32.

[705] *See infra* note 771.

[706] *See supra* at 83, *see also* Stadlmeier, *supra* note 155, at 527.

[707] *See* PICTET, *supra* note 530, at 231.

[708] *See* FEDERAL POLITICAL DEPARTMENT, *supra* note 218, at 287.

[709] *See also* Hiebel, *supra* note 180, at 14.

[710] *See* Stadlmeier, *supra* note 155, at 528.

this regard.[711] Retained chaplains are provided the necessary facilities. These facilities may also include prerogatives that prisoners' representatives enjoy such as libraries, reading rooms or the circulation of a newspaper that proves "most useful for chaplains".[712] Chaplains should also be given separate quarters so they may converse freely and frankly with prisoners.[713] They are free to correspond on matters concerning their religious duties with the ecclesiastical authorities in the country of detention and with international religious organizations.[714] This correspondence is considered additional to a possible quota on personal mail.[715] Instead, the number of these letters and cards must never be limited.[716] The correspondence remains, however, subject to censorship but will be reviewed with priority if censorship by the Detaining Power results in a backlog.[717] "The purpose of such censorship is presumably to ensure the non-combatant purpose of all letters".[718] With this requirement, confidential communications touching matters falling under professional secrecy are excluded from such correspondence.[719]

Art. 36 GC III grants a treatment similar to this of detained chaplains to prisoners of war who are ministers of religion, without having officiated as chaplains to their own forces. Regardless of their denomination, they enjoy the liberty to minister freely to the members of their community. For this purpose, they receive the same treatment as the chaplains retained by the Detaining Power and must not be obliged to do any other work. However, their status remains this of POW.[720] The Detaining Power may refuse to grant its necessary consent to the exercise of ministry by the POW minister of religion if there is no need for his assistance e.g. because there are no POW belonging to his faith.[721] Art. 36 GC III does not apply to ministers of religion who – as it is practice in many countries – are members of the medical corps without being chaplains.[722] They enjoy

---

[711] *See* JEAN S. PICTET, THE GENEVA CONVENTIONS OF 12 AUGUST 1949, COMMENTARY, IV GENEVA CONVENTION 406 (1958), Schollmeyer, *supra* note 547, at 63, Rabus, *supra* note 575, No. 832 at 373.

[712] PICTET, *supra* note 530, at 232.

[713] *See id.*

[714] *See also* U.S. ARMY, *supra* note 653, § 3-15 u (for U.S. regulations allowing also correspondence with authorities of the country on which the retained chaplain depends).

[715] *See* Art. 71 GC III.

[716] *See* PICTET, *supra* note 530, at 221-22.

[717] *See id.* at 232-33.

[718] Odom, *supra* note 7, at 38.

[719] *See* MARCHEGGIANO, *supra* note 107, at 108.

[720] *See* Rabus, *supra* note 575, No. 837 at 374, Rausch, *supra* note 139, at 32, *but see* Kussbach, *supra* note 144, at 390, *see also* Stadlmeier, *supra* note 155, at 525 (on a possible status of POW ministers of religion as protected persons).

[721] *See* PICTET, *supra* note 530, at 233.

[722] *See* Schlögel, *supra* note 38, at 273.

the status of detainees due to their medial personnel characteristic. For them, Art. 36 GC III can only be used as argument to allow them the exercise of religious ministry besides their medical duties.

Exercise of religious duties and of intellectual pursuits could also be combined for clergy in formation: A "seminary behind barbed wire" for German POW was run between August 1945 and June 1947 in Chartres. Established by the French *Direction générale des prisonniers de guerre* and supported by the local church and the Apostolic Nuntiature – then headed by GUISEPPE RONCALLI –, up to 440 seminarians received theological and spiritual formation.[723] A similar institution had shortly existed for French POW in German Moosburg for the winter semester 1940/41.[724]

Rather sensible in tone and stipulations, Art. 37 GC III takes into account the situation of POW who do not have the assistance of a retained chaplain or of a POW minister of their faith. Then, a minister belonging to the prisoners' or a similar denomination, or in his absence a qualified layman may be appointed to fill this office, at the request of the prisoners concerned. This may well be a chaplain or civilian minister of the Detaining Power.[725] Such a procedure is put under the premise that it is "feasible from a confessional point of view". The appointment is subject to the approval of the Detaining Power. If the Detaining Power refuses to approve the appointment of a minister of religion, it should inform the Protecting Power in a procedure similar to that of Art. 79 GC III when refusing the approval for a prisoners' representative.[726] In addition, appointment takes place with the agreement of the community of prisoners concerned and, wherever necessary, with the approval of the local religious authorities of the same faith. This is to preclude the possibility to place a propaganda agent by the Detaining Power.[727] The person thus appointed has to comply with all regulations established by the Detaining Power in the interests of discipline and military security. If the "minister" of the Art. 37 procedure is chosen from the POW community, his status of POW does not change.[728] The detaining authorities pay working pay to POW who are required to carry out spiritual duties on behalf of their comrades.[729] The procedure of Art. 37 GC III balances and

---

[723] *See* CHARTRES 1945 (Karl Heinz Kloidt ed. 1988).

[724] *See* Georg Werthmann, *Kurse zur Weiterbildung kriegsgefangener Theologiestudenten*, 1966 MILITÄRSEELSORGE 78, 79.

[725] *See* Schollmeyer, *supra* note 547, at 61; Rabus, *supra* note 575, No. 805 at 370, No. 838 at 374, *see also* U.S. MARINE CORPS, *supra* note 182, Appendix K (for the practical implementation of ministry to enemy POW).

[726] *See* PICTET, *supra* note 530, at 235.

[727] *See id.* at 235, *see also* FEDERAL POLITICAL DEPARTMENT, *supra* note 217, at 441-42.

[728] *See* Rabus, *supra* note 575, No. 840 at 375.

[729] *See* Art. 62 (2) GC III.

eases the restriction of detained chaplains to minister only to persons of their faith and is very open with regard to possible results.[730]

The German Manual sees detained chaplains not confined to their religious duties. They may furthermore perform the function of a personal advisor, take care of the last wishes of dying soldiers and provide material assistance.[731] In this reading, the position of chaplains is marked more by duties rather than by rights.[732]

Even though chaplains are detained, the Detaining Power is not relieved of its conventional obligations with regard to the spiritual welfare of POW. This responsibility is particularly not shifted to the retained personnel and exists even if no chaplains are detained.[733]

Chapter V of GC III then takes up religious activities in a POW camp. Such activities play an important part in the life of a POW camp as "inner life tends to grow in importance"[734] for persons who have lost their freedom – regardless of their religion. Art. 34 GC III stipulates very generally that prisoners of war enjoy complete latitude in the exercise of their religious duties, including attendance at the service of their faith. This right to exercise follows the formula of the Hague Regulations and is an important precondition for the mental well-being of POW.[735] It is conditioned by compliance with the disciplinary routine prescribed by the military authorities. Views on the disciplinary routine requirement are divided. While it is on the one hand seen as a serious restriction on the possibility of exercise religion, others consider it as an improvement compared to the requirement to "comply with the routine and police regulations" of the military authorities.[736] The 1949 Convention tries to establish a balance between the obligation of POW to comply with the disciplinary routine and the obligation of the Detaining Power to afford complete latitude to POW in the exercise of their religion.[737] On the one hand, the organization and administration of the camp must not be such as "to hinder the observance of religious rites".[738] The exercise

---

[730] *See* Schlögel, *supra* note 38, at 274.

[731] *See* Rabus, *supra* note 575, No. 806 at 370, *see also* PICTET, *supra* note 132, at 220 (for chaplains hearing wishes of the dying), MARCHEGGIANO, *supra* note 107, at 98-99 (for other "practical" assignments of chaplains).

[732] *See* Hiebel, *supra* note 180, at 23, HIEBEL, *supra* note 142, at 215-16.

[733] *See* Art. 28 (5) GC I, O'BRIEN, *supra* note 154, at R.3, Watson, *supra* note 7, at 45, Odom, *supra* note 7, at 37.

[734] PICTET, *supra* note 530, at 225, *see also* FEDERAL POLITICAL DEPARTMENT, *supra* note 217, at 260, KIMMINICH, *supra* note 297, at 129.

[735] *See* Horst Fischer, *Protection of Prisoners of War*, *in* THE HANDBOOK OF HUMANITARIAN LAW IN ARMED CONFLICTS 321, 352 (Dieter Fleck ed. 1995).

[736] Art. 16 Geneva Convention II of 1929.

[737] *See* PICTET, *supra* note 530, at 227.

[738] *Id.*

of religious duties – including attendance at services – is allowed "without special authorization as part of the normal system of administration, general timetable and other activities".[739] Yet, the exercise of religious duties must be compatible with this routine administration of the camp so that reservations must be made concerning the performance of certain rites if they conflict with the normal disciplinary routine of a POW camp.[740] Special challenges here are religious practices of a physical character, methods of preparing food, periods of fast or prayer or the wearing of ritual adornments.[741] Under no circumstances may the disciplinary routine render the practice of religion impossible or substantially impede it.[742] While freedom of religion remains inalienable,[743] the compliance with the disciplinary routine criterion is a limit to the complete latitude in the exercise of religious duties, but both are interrelated as for instance freedom of religion and the limitation of compliance with public order are interrelated in national constitutional law.

The limitation by the disciplinary routine for religious exercise in Art. 34 GC III also has effects on the interpretation of the limitations for chaplains' ministry by military laws and regulations in Art. 33 GC III. The more restrictive latter must be interpreted in the light of the first. Then, regulations of the Detaining Power for its own armed forces – that would be also civil and military laws – cannot limit the exercise of ministry in a POW camp.[744] This is why during the second Gulf War 1990/91, specific arrangements had to be taken as non-Islamic worship is forbidden in Saudi Arabia where POW captured by the Desert Storm alliance were detained. The application of such religious restrictions on POW would have been a breach of GC III.[745]

Implicit in the right of POW to attendance at religious services is the right of retained chaplains to conduct such services and to have access to adequate premises provided where religious services are held.[746] These premises do not need to be dedicated solely for religious services. Instead, it is sufficient if any necessary modifications can be made. Adequacy is assured if the premises are large, clean and so constructed as to provide adequate accommodation for those who attend the services. PICTET considers "a hut, a tent or a room in a building" to be "quite

---

[739] *Id.* at 228.
[740] *See id.* at 228.
[741] *See* PICTET, *supra* note 711, at 405.
[742] *See* Fischer, *supra* note 735, at 352.
[743] *See* Hiebel, *supra* note 180, at 8.
[744] *See* PICTET, *supra* note 530, at 231, *but see* PICTET, *supra* note 132, at 246 (same rules as for national staff are applicable).
[745] *See* MCCOUBREY/WHITE, *supra* note 619, at 271-72.
[746] *See* O'BRIEN, *supra* note 154, at R.5.

suitable".[747] In the U.S.A., joint services of enemy POW and U.S. military personnel are not permitted.[748]

Prisoners of war are allowed to receive parcels with articles of a religious character to meet their needs. This includes books or devotional articles[749] and possibly articles needed for religious services.[750] These materials have great importance when prisoners are undergoing long captivity.[751] Another form of spiritual assistance may come from representatives of religious organizations accredited with the Detaining Power who are entitled to receive from the Detaining Power all necessary facilities when visiting POW camps and distributing material for religious, educational or recreational purposes and when assisting POW in organizing their leisure time within the camps.[752] The explicit mention of religious relief organizations is a novelty of the 1949 GC III and takes into account that religious bodies in Word War II were able to carry out activities on the basis of the Article relative to relief societies and wished to have this point mentioned expressly.[753] It had been particularly in the interest of the Holy See to assure that the Red Cross Movement did not monopolize relief efforts for POW.[754] Nonetheless, the Detaining Power may limit the number of societies allowed to carry out their activities as long as adequate relief is ensured. This limitation opens the door to arbitrary action on the part of the Detaining Power.[755]

Furthermore, even a POW who serves a penal sentence is entitled to receive the spiritual assistance he desires.[756] The detaining authorities have to ensure that prisoners of war who have died in captivity are buried honorably and - if possible - according to the rites of their religion.[757]

These norms on exercise of religion in captivity are certainly not realizing a concept of comprehensive protection of freedom of religion, but compared to the provisions of GC I and GC II, they are still far from being "relatively poor".[758]

---

747 PICTET, *supra* note 530, at 228-29.

748 *See* U.S. MARINE CORPS, *supra* note 182, Appendix K.

749 *See* Art. 72 GC III.

750 *See* O'BRIEN, *supra* note 154, at R.5.

751 *See* Hiebel, *supra* note 180, at 9.

752 *See* Art. 125 GC III.

753 *See* PICTET, *supra* note 530, at 595, *see also* FEDERAL POLITICAL DEPARTMENT, *supra* note 217, at 301, 690.

754 *See* KÖCK, *supra* note 143, at 604 n.14.

755 *See* Hiebel, *supra* note 180, at 10 (also for the possibility for religious organizations to assume the responsibilities of a Protecting Power), *see also* FEDERAL POLITICAL DEPARTMENT, *supra* note 217, at 287.

756 *See* Art. 108 (3) GC III, *see also* PICTET, *supra* note 530, at 505.

757 *See* Art. 120 (4) GC III.

758 *But see* Schlögel, *supra* note 38, at 274, *see also* KIMMINICH, *supra* note 297, at 131 (norms do not comprehensively protect religious freedom).

The freedom granted to POW even extends to the observance of religious creeds that are prohibited to the civilian population of the Detaining Power.[759]

f. Naval warfare regulations in GC II

Art. 36 GC II speaks of "religious personnel" of hospital ships who are protected and respected. A specific chaplain characteristic is not explicitly demanded here,[760] though the norm is interpreted with parallels to GC I and requires the attachment to the navy or merchant marine.[761] Religious personnel may not be captured during the time they are in the service of a hospital ship, regardless of whether there are wounded and sick on board or not. They form an "integral part of the ship" without which the ship "would be merely a derelict".[762] They cannot be retained even if they leave the ship temporarily or land.[763] Religious personnel on hospital ships utilized by national Red Cross Societies, by officially recognized relief societies or by private persons enjoy the same protection if the party to the conflict on which they depend has given them an official commission and has notified their status to the parties to the conflict.[764]

Religious personnel at sea servicing other groups such as regular navy forces, militias and volunteer corps, civilian persons accompanying armed forces at sea, merchant marine crews and shipwrecked civil aircraft crews and the levée en masse are also respected and protected if they fall into the hands of the enemy. In accordance with Art. 37 GC II, they may continue to carry out their duties as long as this is "necessary for the care of the wounded and sick". The adaptation of this norm to medical personnel and a lack of consideration for religious personnel are evident. Religious personnel are to be sent back as soon as the responsible Commander-in-Chief considers it practicable. They may take with them their personal property when they leave the ship. This level of protection for personal property is "special and particularly favorable".[765] If it is necessary to retain some of this personnel owing to the spiritual needs of POW, everything possible has to be done for their earliest possible landing. On landing, retained personnel are subject to the provisions of GC I.[766] Norms to guarantee to retained chaplains at sea the same allowances and pay as chaplains of the own forces were included in the 1907 Red Cross Convention but dropped in GC II.[767]

---

[759] *See* PICTET, *supra* note 530, at 227.
[760] *See* Schollmeyer, *supra* note 547, at 61, Rabus, *supra* note 575, No. 802 at 370.
[761] *See* PICTET, *supra* note 559, at 199, 201.
[762] *Id.* at 204.
[763] *See id.*
[764] *See* Art. 24, 22 GC II.
[765] Hiebel, *supra* note 180, at 21.
[766] *See* Art. 37 (3) GC II.
[767] *See* PICTET, *supra* note 559, at 210.

Retention of chaplains attached to naval forces must be exercised with outmost restraints and the priority of repatriation over retention stressed. As chaplains who are specialized and accustomed to traveling by sea are few in number, they should, if somehow possible, be repatriated to service at sea.[768] Of relevance for chaplains is also Art. 20 (2) GC II: It stipulates that the provisions of GC I are also applicable if dead persons are landed.

The norms of GC II follow the outlines of GC I very closely but less detailed with regard to capture and return stipulations. This is not a significant disadvantage because GC I is applicable as soon as the vessel and its crew is landed.

g. Chaplains as protected persons

Chaplains may benefit by the activities of the Protecting Power, a neutral Power or the ICRC.[769] Chaplains may be invited by the Protecting Power to meetings of the belligerent parties initiated to settle disagreement regarding the application of conventional norms and thus contribute to a conciliation procedure between the parties.[770] The provisions of the GCs apply by analogy to the chaplains received or interned in neutral territory.[771]

In any circumstances, chaplains cannot partly or entirely renounce their conventional rights.[772] Though the conventions deal primarily with the ministers of religion and have only few stipulations on the recipient of religious ministry, it is these recipients' right to spiritual assistance and the respect for their religious convictions that provides the ratio for the protection of religious personnel.[773] It is then only consistent that chaplains cannot deliberately dispose of their protective rights. However, they may be deprived of the privileges exceeding the statutory minimum of protection provided to them by the GCs.[774]

Reprisals against chaplains as protected personnel are prohibited.[775] Any attack directed against chaplains and any infringement of their rights is considered a grave breach of the GCs and the PAs that has to be subject to criminal prosecution.[776] It must be conceded that the conflicts of the 1990s brought along an increasing number of violations of humanitarian law.[777] Of special importance for the prosecution of such violations will be the International Criminal Court

---

[768] *See id.*.

[769] *See* Art. 8-10 GC I.

[770] *See* Art. 11 (2) GC I, Art. 11 (2) GC II, *see also* O'BRIEN, *supra* note 154, at R.6.

[771] *See* Art. 4 GC I, Art. 5 GC II.

[772] *See* Art. 7 GC I, Art. 7 GC II.

[773] *See* Art. 34 GC III, Art. 27 GC IV, *see also* Rausch, *supra* note 139, at 32.

[774] *See* Rabus, *supra* note 575, No. 814 at 371.

[775] *See* Art. 46 GC I, Art. 47 GC II, Art. 20 PA I.

[776] *See* Rabus, *supra* note 575, No. 816 at 371, Kussbach, *supra* note 144, at 390, *see also* Art. 85 (2) PA I.

[777] *See* BLOCK-SCHLESIER, *supra* note 295, at 49.

that has penal jurisdiction over war crimes. Of particular significance for the security of religious personnel is Art. 8 b xxiv of the Rome Statute[778] that penalizes intentionally directing attacks against personnel using the distinctive emblem of the GCs in conformity with international law. The "comprehensive protection" includes civilian and military religious personnel.[779] The current ICC regime expressively protects religious personnel from being murdered, mutilated, treated cruelly, tortured, degraded, taken hostage and sentenced without due process.[780]

The parties to the GCs pledged to undertake efforts to disseminate knowledge about humanitarian law so that particularly chaplains know its principles.[781] Thus, the obligation of dissemination is primarily in the sphere of the states though religious authorities may play a part in this.[782] It is regrettable that BLOCK-SCHLESIER[783] intensively discusses the efforts of dissemination of IHL on both military and civilian levels in Germany but does not mention the activities of the military chaplaincy in the introductory classes for its personnel and also in the continuing training of its staff.

In Switzerland, "chaplains turn their attention also on the compliance with the Geneva Conventions ..., as well as the Hague Agreement ...".[784] In 1996, the role of the chaplain as "protector of human dignity, advocate of humanity, expert on international martial law, custodian of the Geneva Convention" was one of the topics of the Swiss Chaplain School Seminar.[785] Engagement for and knowledge about IHL is important for chaplains also because war crimes may be reported to them.

---

[778] *Rome Statute of the International Criminal Court*, United Nations Diplomatic Conference of Plenipotentiaries on the Establishment of an International Criminal Court, U.N. Doc. A/CONF.183/9 (July 17th, 1998), Version as corrected by procès-verbaux of November 10th, 1998, July 12th, 1999, November 30th, 1999, May 8th, 2000, January 17th, 2001 and January 16th, 2002 *available at* http://www.icc-cpi.int/library/basicdocuments/rome_statute(e).pdf.

[779] 1 THE ROME STATUTE OF THE INTERNATIONAL CRIMINAL COURT 410 (Antonio Cassese et al. eds. 2002).

[780] *See Elements of Crime*, Assembly of States Parties to the Rome Statute of the International Criminal Court, 1st Sess., New York, 3-10 September 2002, Official Records, U.N. Doc. ICC-ASP/1/3, *available at* http://www.icc-cpi.int/library/basicdocuments/elements(e).pdf.

[781] *See* Art. 47 GC I, 48 GC II, José Luis Fernandez-Flores, *The Dissemination of the Law of War*, 1989/90 INTERNATIONAL INSTITUTE OF HUMANITARIAN LAW, YEARBOOK 23-24 (1992), *see also* Art. 127 GC III, 144 GC IV, 83 (1) PA I, 19 PA II (for more general norms).

[782] *See* O'BRIEN, *supra* note 154, at D.1.

[783] *See* BLOCK-SCHLESIER, *supra* note 295, at 77-108.

[784] Règlement pour le service de l'aumônerie de l'armée, No. 26 (January 1st, 1997), *see also* Schubiger, *supra* note 145, at 2.

[785] *See* Christoph Stucki, *Swiss Chaplaincy 1996*, 7 EUROPEAN CHAPLAINCY YEARBOOK 122, 123 (1997), *see also* MARCHEGGIANO, *supra* note 107, at 13 (not granting to the military chaplaincy the role of a legal advisor to the commander in the application of humanitarian law in an Italian context).

The dissemination of IHL knowledge on the part of the catholic church even continues on the international level of the Holy See. During the 27th International Conference of the Red Cross and the Red Crescent, the Holy See stressed that religions could offer a valuable contribution to dissemination which should not only focus on teaching the norms of IHL but also on making its principles understood.[786] This is why the Holy See pledged at the same conference "[t]o take suitable initiatives in favor of instruction in international humanitarian law for religious personnel in the armed forces (Catholic military chaplains)".[787] One step to implement this pledge was an international course on IHL for catholic chaplains held in March 2003 at San Calisto Palace in Rome's quarter Trastevere. This course was a joint undertaking of the Pontifical Council for Justice and Peace and the Congregation for the Bishops[788] and offered an opportunity for the Holy See to ask the military ordinariates to contribute to the promotion of Humanitarian Law at their respective national levels according to possibilities and circumstances.[789] The course in addition was a prominent example that international humanitarian law can greatly benefit from cooperation with religious authorities.[790]

Chaplains under the GCs enjoy an international legal status that has been developed with rare consistency and continuity.[791] This development even continues as new situations in IHL evolve: The catalog of IHL applied by UN Forces states in Section 9.4 that these forces respect and protect religious personnel in all circumstances.[792] The protection of religious personnel is also still considered to belong to the core of the GCs. This is reflected e.g. in the mentioning of religious personnel in a communiqué distributed by the ICRC before the 2nd Golf War on December 14th, 1990.[793]

---

786 *See* GIUSEPPE BERTELLO, *supra* note 303.

787 Pledge No. P062, *available at* http://www.icrc.org/Applic/p127e.nsf/va_PBA/064EA4AD0ECB671CC1256ADA0038D977.

788 *See* JOHN PAUL II, *supra* note 261.

789 *See* Answer to the Questionnaire on the follow-up to the 27th International Conference received on 10 September 2003, *available at* http://www.icrc.org/APPLIC/P127e.nsf/va_IBP/E211EB4B22523319C1256DA4002B68BF, *see also* TOMASI, *supra* note 268, No. 4 (for the Holy See's willigness to continue such activities).

790 *See* Giorgio Filibeck, *Restoring a just order in post-conflict situations in the light of the social teachings of the Catholic Church*, 1998 INTERNATIONAL REVIEW OF THE RED CROSS 75, *available at* http://www.icrc.org/web/eng/siteeng0.nsf/iwpList166/B5105412999C5848C1256B66005B8C9C.

791 *See* Ipsen, *supra* note 586, at 89.

792 *See UN Secretary-General's Bulletin on Observance by United Nations Forces of International Humanitarian Law*, U. N. Secretariat, § 9.4 at 3, U.N. Doc. ST/SGB/1999/13 (August 6th, 1999).

793 Hans-Peter Gasser, *Die Aktivitäten des Internationalen Komitees vom Roten Kreuz im Golfkrieg*, *in* DAS HUMANITÄRE VÖLKERRECHT IM GOLFKRIEG UND ANDERE ROTKREUZ-FRAGEN 5, 25 (Wolfgang Voit ed. 1992).

2. Additional Protocol I of 1977

In February 1974, the Swiss government extended to the parties of the GCs an invitation for a diplomatic conference to discuss drafts for two protocols additional to the GCs. Four sessions of this conference took place from 1974 to 1977. An innovation at this conference was the input that the preparatory consultations received from religions. Taking into accounts the sway of western religions at that time, the 1949 Geneva Conventions had been determined by religious groups of the Jewish-Christian tradition.[794] Besides the religious organizations mentioned in the context of the GCs, Muslim representatives contributed actively and committed to the preparations for the 1977 additional protocols. Certainly, all world religions and many smaller religious groups in one way or another provide spiritual assistance to armed forces[795] and thus have an interest in the protection of their personnel. But given this commitment, SCHLÖGEL holds it legitimately to consider humanitarian law as such and as framed in both the GCs and the PAs to be supported by all the world's major religion and holds this support to be essential for efficiency of humanitarian law in case of war.[796] A very recent restatement even holds that religious leaders may provide solid motivations for complying with international humanitarian law.[797]

The nature of the additional protocols is another than that of the different and revised versions of the Red Cross Convention. Whereas a revised Red Cross Convention took the place of its predecessor, the additional protocols were designed to supplement the existing law with the Geneva Conventions of 1949 remaining in force. Dogmatically, the PAs merged Hague Law on means and methods of combat and Geneva Law on the protection of victims of war.

PA I for the first time defines protected religious personnel. The first draft of the PAs had religious personnel covered by the proposed definition for medical personnel.[798] On the initiative of the Holy See and some other countries, a definition of the expression "religious personnel" was inserted in Art. 8 PA I.[799]

---

794 *See* Hiebel, *supra* note 180, at 6.

795 *See* MARTIN BOCK, RELIGION WITHIN THE ARMED FORCES 368 (1998).

796 *See* Schlögel, *supra* note 38, at 276.

797 *See* § 328 of the Tentative text for the San Remo Manual on the protection of Victims of Non-International Armed Conflict, *cited in* DIETER FLECK, HUMANITARIAN PROTECTION OF THE CIVILIAN POPULATION IN ARMED CONFLICTS at 11 n.19 (Paper presented at the International Course for the formation of catholic military chaplains in humanitarian law, Rome, March 25th, 2003), *see also* Filibeck, *supra* note 142 (for the "fruitful synergies" of collaboration between humanitarian organizations and religious leaders), Michel Veuthey, *Remedies to Promote the Respect of Fundamental Human Values in Non-International Armed Conflicts*, *in* 30 ISRAELI YEARBOOK ON HUMAN RIGHTS 37 (2001) (on the role of religious leadership in the protection of victims of war).

798 *See* COMMENTARY ON THE ADDITIONAL PROTOCOLS, *supra* note 178, No. 360 at 127.

799 *See id.* No. 296 at 115-16.

The participation of more religions might also explain why the terminology of the PAs definitively shifts to the generic term "religious personnel" as this term is considered more neutral than the term "chaplain" with its Christian connotation.[800] Art. 8 d PA I defines religious personnel as military or civilian persons, who are exclusively engaged in the work of their ministry. Mentioning the exclusivity requirement explicitly in the definition is to prevent abuses. The positive definition of Art. 8 d PA I makes protection more effective by stating the conditions for protection and goes beyond the scope of the GC I understanding of chaplaincy.[801]

"Religious personnel" is now the term of art; the term "chaplain" is used by way of example. The definition knows the following types of attachment:

i. Attachment to the armed forces of a party to the conflict.

ii. Attachment to medical units or medical transports of a party to the conflict.

iii. Attachment to medical units or medical transports in accordance with Art. 9 § 2 PA I made available to a party to the conflict for humanitarian purposes:

  a) by a neutral or other state which is not a party to that conflict;

  b) by a recognized and authorized aid society of such a state. In this case, the society needs the consent of its own government and the authorization of the party to the conflict concerned (Art. 27 GC I).

  c) by an impartial international humanitarian organization

iv. Attachment to civil defense organizations of a party to the conflict.

The definition widens the field of application of protection. But it does not substantially change the criteria constitutive for protection: attachment and exclusivity. It is consistent with the earlier concept of chaplains and does not – as the shift in terminology to the term religious personnel that has no military connotation might indicate – grant a general protection for religious ministers.[802] The consistency of the definition of religious personnel with the notion of chaplaincy also becomes clear when PA I refers to chaplains under GC III in its stipulations on combatants.[803] It considers chaplains – though members of the armed forces – as non-combatants who do not have the right to participate directly in hostilities. The reference is limited to chaplains and Art. 33 GC III.

---

[800] *See* Rabus, *supra* note 575, at 369, COMMENTARY ON THE ADDITIONAL PROTOCOLS, *supra* note 178, No. 362 at 127, see also Thomas R. Elßner, *Bezeichnet der Begriff "Nicht-Kombattant" in jedem Falle eine zivile Person?*, 2003 MILITÄRSEELSORGE 259, 274 n. 48 (for the various terms in the German language).

[801] *See* MICHAEL BOTHE ET AL., NEW RULES FOR THE VICTIMS OF ARMED CONFLICTS 95 (1982).

[802] *See* HIEBEL, *supra* note 142, at 355.

[803] *See* Art. 43 (2) PA I.

The attachment of religious personnel may be either permanent (exclusive assignment for an indeterminate period[804]) or temporary (exclusive assignment for a limited period[805]). The level of protection is the same unless otherwise specified.[806] However, for temporary religious personnel, the protection does not exceed the time of the temporary assignment.[807] Furthermore, the assignment must be exclusive. Lay preachers are not covered by the definition.[808] However, it should be underlined that lay preachers in this context should be understood as persons who are not exclusively engaged in ministry, usually engaged in another full-time occupation and involved only part-time in religious ministry.[809] Lay people in an ecclesiastical sense are not excluded from the coverage of the definition.

None of the documents seeks in any way to judge the "thorny question"[810] of what is a religion. Difficulties surrounding this question are known from national constitutional law. Would witches who applied for recognition as faith group in the U.S.A. in 1999[811] qualify as endorsement agency for chaplains? The German Manual underlines that the content of GC I and PA I shows that "religious" has to be interpreted restrictively and only incorporates genuine religious personnel.[812] Without providing a positive definition, it excludes political officers from the scope of that definition. In some fields, namely in their concern for morale, families, free time and personal counsel, the political officers of the armies of communist countries – in spite of a number of differences - fulfilled functions that in another environment are fulfilled by chaplains.[813] These similarities are not taken into account. In any case, political officers are protected as non-combatants.[814] The order to kill Red Army Commissars by the *Wehrmacht* in World War II was clearly illegal.[815]

---

[804] *See* Art. 8 k PA I, MARCHEGGIANO, *supra* note 107, at 17.
[805] *See id.*
[806] *See also* Art. 8 k PA I.
[807] *See* Rabus, *supra* note 575, at 369.
[808] *See* Stadlmeier, *supra* note 155, at 531, GREEN, *supra* note 133, at 25-26, *but see* Kussbach, *supra* note 144, at 390, O'BRIEN, *supra* note 154, at D3.
[809] *See* BOTHE ET AL., *supra* note 801, at 99, *see also* MARCHEGGIANO, *supra* note 107, at 114 (for the exclusivity criterion and part-time ministry).
[810] O'BRIEN, *supra* note 154, at D1, *see also id.* D3.
[811] *See* HERSPRING, *supra* note 434, at 46.
[812] *See* Rabus, *supra* note 575, 369, *see also infra* at 152 (for recent developments in the protection of personnel fulfilling functions similar to these of religious personnel).
[813] *See* HERSPRING, *supra* note 434, at 216, 221.
[814] *See* FRIEDRICH BERBER, [2 Kriegsrecht] LEHRBUCH DES VÖLKERRECHTS 141 (2nd ed. 1969).
[815] *See* REGINA BUß, DER KOMBATTANTENSTATUS 188, LXVIII-LXIV (1992).

Civilian religious personnel must be respected and protected.[816] This norm is considered to eventually "reflect general practice as recognized as law".[817] Even though the term "religious personnel" itself does not refer to a specific military context, this context is established by the definition of Art. 8 d PA I.[818] Thus, unlike the civilian status of ministers of religion in Art. 58 GC IV, the civilian nature of religious personnel in PA I can only consist in the attachment as a civilian to the military or the attachment to a civil defense organization.[819] PA I cannot be interpreted as generally applying the protection of the GCs on civilian religious ministers as well. These civilian ministers remain covered by the general protection accorded to the population and all civilian persons.[820]

On the other hand, the norm does not grant protection to military religious personnel. The combination of protection under the GCs and the extended definition of PA I then raises the following rather particular but problematic question: What protection applies to military religious personnel servicing to civilian medical units or transports? As military personnel they are not protected under Art. 15 (5) PA I. Since they are mentioned in the definition of Art. 8 d PA I, they would only profit from the fundamental guarantees in Art. 75 PA I. As they are attached to a civilian installation it is questionable whether they are protected under the GCs that require the attachment to the armed forces. The extension of the protected group in the Art. 8 d PA I-definition, the protection of the GCs and the protection of civilian religious personnel in Art. 15 (5) PA I here leave a gap of protection that could not have been intended as PA I just wanted to apply a protection also for civilian medical units and transports. This has to be taken into account when Art. 15 (5) PA I is interpreted.[821] Then, the term "civilian" in this norm – though meant with regard to the quality of religious personnel – would have to be understood extensively in the light of the wide PA I definition in a way that the civilian nature of the unit or transport covers the original military quality of the attached religious personnel: The protection of Art. 15 (5) PA I could be applied. However, this result is dogmatically weak so that this consistency of PA I should be improved by eliminating the restriction on civilian personnel in Art. 15 (5) PA I in a possible revision.[822]

---

[816] *See* Art. 15 (5) PA I.

[817] THEODOR MERON, HUMAN RIGHTS AND HUMANITARIAN NORMS AS CUSTOMARY LAW 66 (1989).

[818] *See* COMMENTARY ON THE ADDITIONAL PROTOCOLS, *supra* note 178, No. 637 at 195.

[819] *See* Stadlmeier, *supra* note 155, at 531, Rößler, *supra* note 568, at 309, *but see* Rausch, *supra* note 139, at 40 n.74 (for the attachment to a civil defense organization).

[820] *See* COMMENTARY ON THE ADDITIONAL PROTOCOLS, *supra* note 178, No. 638 at 195, BOTHE ET AL., *supra* note 801, at 126, *but see* DETTER, *supra* note 78, at 326, Georg Bock, *Der Schutz sanitätsdienstlicher, ärztlicher und seelsorgerischer Aufgaben, in* DIE GENFER ZUSATZPROTOKOLLE 184, 191 (1993), KIMMINICH, *supra* note 297, at 129.

[821] *See* Stadlmeier, *supra* note 155, at 531-32.

[822] *See id.* at 532.

The provisions concerning the protection and identification of medical personnel also apply to civilian religious personnel.[823] Thus, religious personnel attached to a civil defense unit will also use the red cross/red crescent distinctive emblem instead of the distinctive emblem of civil defense organization.[824] In this, the protection of religious – and medical – personnel exceeds that of the other personnel of civil defense organizations. The reference in the stipulations on civil defense organizations to religious personnel[825] was added to ensure that religious personnel rendering spiritual assistance to the dying and wounded enjoy proper protection and that their presence alongside rescue, medical and first aid personnel is justified.[826] Note that the definition of Art. 8 d PA I does not consider as religious personnel ministers to civil defense organization of third parties operating in the territory of a party to the conflict under Art. 64 PA I.[827] These personnel would then make use of the distinctive emblem of civil defense organizations and may be issued the appropriate identity card.[828] PA I then also deals with the identification of civilian religious personnel. In Art. 18 (1) it calls the parties to ensure that all religious personnel are identifiable. In addition to the existing norms on identification of chaplains under the GCs, civilian religious personnel should furthermore be recognizable by the distinctive emblem and an identity card certifying their status in occupied territory and in areas where fighting is taking place or is likely to take place. The technical details of identity cards for civilian religious personnel are regulated in chapter I of Annex I to PA I as amended on November 30th, 1993. The card is of pocket size and as durable as practicable. It shows the distinctive emblem and mentions the name, the date of birth (or, if that date is not available, the age at the time of issue) and the identity number, if any, of the holder. It furthermore states in what capacity the bearer is entitled to the protection of the GCs and of PA I and the dates of issue and of expiry of the card. The amended version of 1993 also asks to indicate, whenever possible, the holder's blood group on the reverse side of the card. The wording is in the national or official language and, in addition and when appropriate, in the local language of the region concerned. The local language requirement was an innovation of the 1993 version of Annex I and subject to a reservation made by Jordan. The card bears the photograph of the holder together with his signature or his thumbprint - or both - and the stamp and signa-

[823] *See* Art. 15 (5) PA I.

[824] *See* BOTHE ET AL., *supra* note 801, at 395, *see also* COMMENTARY ON THE ADDITIONAL PROTOCOLS, *supra* note 178, No. 2699 at 789, *but see* O'BRIEN, *supra* note 154, at O2, *see also infra* Appendix I a (for a sample of the distinctive emblem of civil defense organization).

[825] *See also* Art. 61 f PA I (religious assistance).

[826] *See* COMMENTARY ON THE ADDITIONAL PROTOCOLS, *supra* note 178, No. 2374 at 725.

[827] *See also* BOTHE ET AL., *supra* note 801, at 99.

[828] *See infra* Appendix II d (for a sample).

ture of the competent authority. Annex I to PA I provides a model identity card[829] and demands the parties of a conflict at the outbreak of hostilities to transmit to each other a specimen of the model they are using if it differs from the model of the Annex. Art. 3 of Annex I demands similar identity cards for temporary civilian religious personnel. If this is not possible, they should be at least provided with a certificate signed by the competent authority certifying that the person to whom it is issued is assigned to duty as temporary religious personnel and stating, if possible, the duration of such assignment and his right to wear the distinctive emblem. The certificate should mention the holder's name and date of birth (or again if that is not available, his age at the time when the certificate was issued), his function and identity number, if any. It shall bear his signature or his thumbprint, or both. Finally, religious personnel carrying out their duties in the battle area should, as far as possible, wear headgear and clothing bearing the distinctive emblem.[830] This, however, is at the discretion of the competent authority.[831]

The problems with military religious personnel servicing to civilian medical units or transports concerning their protection as has been discussed can also be solved by taking into account the clause to ensure that all religious personnel are identifiable in Art. 18. This norm points out that the provisions on identification of civilian religious personnel in PA I can be applied also on this problematic group and support the approach followed above to broadly interpret the criterion of civilian in the protection clause of Art. 15 (5) PA I.

When PA I applies the protection that GC II provides for military hospital ships also for such vessels carrying civilians and for civilian medical ships, this takes effect also for the personnel of these vessels.[832] As religious personnel on these ships are members of the crew, they are inviolable and may not be captured.[833]

3. Religious personnel in non-international armed conflict

While the 16th and 17th century knew an "international civil war"[834] meaning a conflict between international entities with quasi civil character because all these entities were part of the same *populus christianus*, the 20th century could use a similar term but would then refer to a civil war with international implications. Non-international armed conflicts with serious regional implications have oc-

---

829 *See infra* Appendix II c (for this model identy card).

830 *See* Art. 4 No. 2 Annex I (to the Protocol I as of 6 June 1977), Art. 5 (4) Annex I (to the Protocol I as amended on 30 November 1993).

831 *See* O'BRIEN, *supra* note 154, at O2.

832 *See* Art. 22 (1) c PA I, Art. 23 (5) PA I.

833 *See supra* at 93.

834 *See* SCHMITT, *supra* note 62, at 123.

curred in an increased number in the 1990s. In many instances, these conflicts looked like religious conflicts with religion fueling the conflict. But this perception is based on a widespread prejudice and in-depth analysis reveals that the root cause of such conflicts is often the struggle for power that manipulates religious identity to give added strength to the reasons for fighting.[835] The fact, that a conflict is defined in fundamentalist religious terms does not mean that a conflict is due to the impact of religious fundamentalism.[836] Religion is an aspect "in addition to social, economic and political factors".[837]

Common Art. 3 of the GCs determines minimal provisions for non-international armed conflict. It prescribes a humane treatment of non-combatants without discrimination for reasons of faith or religion or outrages upon personal dignity. A respect-for-convictions-and-religious-practices clause is not found in common Art. 3. This concise norm cannot serve as a basis to claim active support for religious activities.[838] But the humane treatment requirement as the true *Leitmotiv*[839] of the GCs must be understood here in its broadest sense as applying to "all aspects of man's life".[840] Religious freedom that is stronger than any violence or injustice truly safeguards the dignity of the human person.[841] Then, common Art. 3 can be widely interpreted as not excluding spiritual rights[842] or even guaranteeing spiritual rights as an aspect of humane treatment.[843] However, its application is limited to non-combatants.[844]

Furthermore, human rights treaties establish a regime effective in non-international armed conflict and in cases not covered by common Art. 3 such as civil disturbances and political tension.[845] The Universal Declaration of Human Rights[846] provides in Art. 18 for a free exercise of religion and in Art. 19 for

---

[835] *See* FLECK, *supra* note 797, 11, Filibeck, *supra* note 790.

[836] *See* Istvan Pogany, *Religion, the Palestinian-Israeli Conflict and International Law, in* INTERNATIONAL LAW AND ARMED CONFLICT 93, 100 (A. G. D. Bradney ed. 1992).

[837] LAKSHMIKANTH RAO PENNA & STEPHEN P. MARKS, JURIDICAL APSECTS OF MORAL AND SPIRITUAL ASSISTANCE DURING ARMED CONFLICTS NOT OF AN INTERNATIONAL CHARACTER, INTERNAL DISTURBANCES AND SITUATION OF POLITICAL TENSION 3 (paper submitted to the Colloquium on spiritual and intellectual assistance in the time of armed conflicts and civil disturbances, Milan, September 21st-23rd, 1973).

[838] *See* Rausch, *supra* note 139, at 32, *see also* KIMMINICH, *supra* note 297, at 124-25 (the claim for active support cannot even be based on the norms of GC IV).

[839] *See* PICTET, *supra* note 711, at 204, PICTET, VICTIMS, *supra* note 132, at 123.

[840] PICTET, *supra* note 711, at 204, *see also* COMMENTARY ON THE ADDITIONAL PROTOCOLS, *supra* note 178, No. 4523 at 1370.

[841] *See* JOHN XXIII, *supra* note 244, No. 14.

[842] *See* Hiebel, *supra* note 180, at 4, HIEBEL, *supra* note 142, at 164.

[843] *See* PENNA/MARKS, *supra* note 837, at 12-13.

[844] *See id.* at 9.

[845] *See id.* at 25-26, 28, 31.

[846] *See Universal Declaration of Human Rights*, G.A. Res. 217 A (III), U. N. GAOR, U.N. Doc. A/810 (December 10th, 1948).

freedom of opinion. These rights are subject to such limitations as determined by law.[847] The International Covenant on Civil and Political Rights (ICCPR)[848] provides in Art. 18 that "everyone shall have the right to freedom of thought, conscience and religion". It also stipulates that this right includes the freedom to manifest religion or belief in worship, observance, practice and teaching. The norm is non-derogable even in times of armed conflict[849] but subject to such limitations as may be necessary in order to protect public order. Art. 19 ICCPR extends protection to non-religious views as it states that everyone has the right to hold opinions without interference. In that, the ICCPR supplements the GCs' protection of freedom of religion.[850] This aspect is particularly underlined in the preamble of PA II that recalls international instruments relating to human rights and the protection of the human person by the principles of humanity. Here, streams of humanitarian and human rights considerations meet.[851] However, it should be noted that the parties to the GCs and the parties to the ICCPR are not identical.[852]

The relevant document for non-international armed conflicts is PA II that supplements common Art. 3[853] as it provides specific rules for the protection of religious personnel. With regard to the protection of medical and religious personnel, PA II "could be regarded not as new rules, but as necessary development and completion of the principle contained in Article 3 of 1949" and as "measures of implementation".[854]

PA II mentions respect for "convictions and religious practices" of persons who do not take a direct part or who have ceased to take part in hostilities amongst its fundamental guarantees.[855] This right is an element of humane treatment.[856] The respect for convictions and religious practices includes the right to receive spiritual assistance from those performing religious functions.[857] Guaranteed is also religious education for children according to their parents' wishes.[858] Persons whose liberty has been restricted due to detention or internment are

---

[847] *Id.* Art. 29.

[848] *See International Covenant on Civil and Political Rights,* G.A. Res. 2200 A (XXI), U.N. GAOR, U.N. Doc A/6316 (December 16th, 1966).

[849] *See id.* Art. 4 (2). .

[850] *See* KIMMINICH, *supra* note 297, at 124

[851] *See* DRAPER, *supra* note 7, at 249.

[852] *See* Kussbach, *supra* note 144, at 388-89.

[853] *See* Bock, *supra* note 820, at 184.

[854] Bosko Jakovljevic, *Rules of combat limitation ratione personae: Protection of wounded, sick and medical personnel in non-international armed conflicts, in* 1989/90 INTERNATIONAL INSTITUTE OF HUMANITARIAN LAW, YEARBOOK 181, 186 (1992).

[855] *See* Art. 4 (1) PA II.

[856] *See* COMMENTARY ON THE ADDITIONAL PROTOCOLS, *supra* note 178, No. 4521 at 1370.

[857] *See* GREEN, *supra* note 133, at 327.

[858] *See* Art. 4 (3) a PA II.

allowed to practice their religion and, if requested and appropriate, to receive spiritual assistance from persons, such as chaplains, performing religious functions.[859] This guarantee is a novelty in the context of internal armed conflict.[860] Religious personnel are respected and protected and are to be granted all available help for the performance of their duties.[861] This protection applies throughout the duration of the personnel's mission, including times when such personnel do not carry out their duties temporarily.[862] Given the lack of a definition for chaplains and religious personnel, the terminology of PA I is applied.[863] This is also consistent with the views of the drafting Working Group.[864] The original draft of a definition for religious personnel in PA II also included religious personnel attached to medical units of relief societies authorized by a party to the conflict.[865] PA II underlines that religious personnel must not be compelled to carry out tasks which are not compatible with their humanitarian mission.[866] This stipulation goes rather far.[867] Spiritual assistance is again seen with the end of ministry. Religious personnel are entitled to display the distinctive emblem.[868] The level of protection established by PA II and is prohibition to attacks on religious personnel is identical with the level of Art. 14 of the Turku Declaration of Minimum Humanitarian Standards by IHL experts.[869]

However, the nature of non-international armed conflict with confusing frontlines and often the government being a party to the conflict on the one hand and the understanding of religious personnel with the required official act of attachment on the other hand are difficult to reconcile. The extraordinary cases in the conventions of militias and the levée en masse can be solved from the "normal" perspective of an attachment to regular armed forces.[870] Such a line of interpretation is, however, insufficient with regard to the situation of non-international armed conflict. Almost any conflict of this kind will have forces of parties who are incapable to perform the act of attachment. Then, protection of religious ministers will not necessarily come from a position privileged in law but from

---

[859] *See* Art. 5 No. 1 d PA II.
[860] *See* Kussbach, *supra* note 144, at 389.
[861] *See* Art. 9 No. 1 PA II.
[862] *See* COMMENTARY ON THE ADDITIONAL PROTOCOLS, *supra* note 178, No. 4675 at 1421.
[863] *See* HIEBEL, *supra* note 142, at 355, Stadlmeier, *supra* note 155, at 533 n.49, Rausch, *supra* note 139, at 40 n.78.
[864] *See* COMMENTARY ON THE ADDITIONAL PROTOCOLS, *supra* note 178, No. 4662 at 1418-19.
[865] *See id.* No. 4671 at 1421.
[866] *See* Art. 9 No. 1 PA II.
[867] *See* Schlögel, *supra* note 38, at 277.
[868] *See* Art. 12 PA II.
[869] *See Report of the Sub-Commission on Prevention of Discrimination and Protection of Minorities*, U.N. ESCOR, Commission on Human Rights, 52nd Sess., Annex, at 16, U.N. Doc. E/CN.4/1996/80 (November 28th, 1995), *see also* DAVID, *supra* note 662, No. 2.183 at 371..
[870] *See also infra* at 127 (for the attachment to the levée en masse in particular).

the protection of religious activities. The deficiencies in this regard have also been identified on the part of the chaplaincies and a supplementation of the existing legal norms has been expressed as a *desideratum*.[871] Nonetheless, the level of protection thus derived will have to take into account the role of religions and its leaders in facilitating negotiations between the parties to the conflict and in supporting post-conflict peace building.[872]

VII. The protection of civilian ministry

Historical protection for clergy under canon law did not differentiate into protection of civilian ministers and chaplains but established one uniform level of protection because the structured institution of military chaplaincy did not yet exist. The norms of the GCs and the PAs then took "refuge in the highly structured institution of the military chaplaincy".[873] It seems as if this was not so much due to "certain conservatism"[874] among the participants of the diplomatic conferences but more a question of feasibility and pragmatism in a universal legal instrument. The categories of chaplains and religious personnel with a special level of protection make a distinction easier and take into account a special exposure.[875] In this, military chaplaincy is the "stable nucleus"[876] of spiritual assistance in armed conflict. All the same, assistance may certainly develop in law and in fact to exceed the scope of this nucleus. Then, the need to recognize spiritual assistance "in its wider reality and especially in its dynamic aspect"[877] demands a review particularly of the protection for civilian ministry and its personnel.

1. Civilian ministry in armed conflicts

Important aids come from religions in a civilian context in times of armed conflict. Religions can contribute to eliminate cause of violence by spreading a clearer sense of the oneness of the human family.[878] They can contribute to the creation of substantial peace founded on disarmament of minds and "a reconciliation of hearts"[879] because peace takes root in a "renewal of moral and spiri-

---

[871] *See* Witte, *supra* note 593, at 3.
[872] *See also supra* note 797.
[873] Hiebel, *supra* note 180, at 25, *see also* HIEBEL, *supra* note 142, at 217.
[874] *See* Schubiger, *supra* note 145, at 7.
[875] *See* HIEBEL, *supra* note 142, at 219.
[876] *See* NICOLAS, *supra* note 16, at 311.
[877] Hiebel, *supra* note 180, at 27, *see* Schubiger, *supra* note 145, at 5.
[878] *See* John Paul II, *World Day of Peace Message 2002*, 94 AAS 132 (2002).
[879] WAYS OF PEACE 75 (Pontifical Commission „Iustitia et Pax" ed. 1987).

tual convictions".[880] The catholic church and all Christianity[881] in particular see their task in tackling the causes of armed conflict by restoring sensibility for the spiritual dimension of human existence in order to bring about peace.[882] As the dynamics of law alone in many cases cannot restore outrages of human dignity and disruptions of peace completely, Christian churches give significant input to just and in some cases non-judicial post-conflict resolution. A well-known example is the work in Truth and Reconciliation Commissions[883] where religious spirituality and even a sort of sacramental reconciliation are ancillary aspects. Forgiveness is promoted as a means to heal and rebuild troubled human relations from their foundations.[884] In such efforts, the seed of conscience is sowed that later may bear the fruit of normative structures. In conflicts with religious components, religions can provide platforms for trust building. After the conflict in former Yugoslavia, for instance, ecumenical efforts between the Croatian catholic church and the Serbian orthodox church such as meetings of members of the episcopate, academic conferences of theologians or joint services during the Week for the Unity of Christians were not limited in their inter-denominational effects but should also be seen as contributions for the reconciliation of the two countries.[885] The role of religion in post-conflict processes is also internationally recognized: In his Report on the protection of civilians in armed conflict, UN Secretary-General Kofi Annan challenges the civil society to contribute to a move "from vulnerability to security and from war to peace"[886] and mentions religious congregations as a reference point of civil society.[887]

But assistance is also provided in the heat of battle. In this, civilian ministry may also extend to military. HIEBEL's interpretation of Art. 18 GC I deserves to be mentioned: The norm lays down that "military authorities may appeal" to the inhabitants and "shall permit" them to collect and care for the wounded and the sick. HIEBEL considers such care by civilians to include spiritual assistance, as it is a form of relief. He criticizes that such an assistance in order to be protected has to take place under the authority of the military and military authorities

---

880 JOHN PAUL II AND THE FAMILY OF PEOPLES, *supra* note 250, at 155.

881 *See also* Konrad Raiser, *The Role of the World Council of Churches in the Solution of Conflicts in this World*, 4 EUROPEAN CHAPLAINCY YEARBOOK 190-201 (1994), HIEBEL, *supra* note 142, at 428-429 (for activities of the World Council of Churches).

882 *See* John Paul II, *Address to the 34th Session of the General Assembly of the United Nation* (October 2nd, 1979), *in* HUMAN RIGHTS IN THE TEACHING OF THE CHURCH, *supra* note 223, A.120.16 at 191.

883 *See* Filibeck, *supra* note 790, *see also* Filibeck, *supra* note 142 (for the example South Africa).

884 *See* John Paul II, *supra* note 878, at 133.

885 *See* Nediljko A. Ancic, *Den Krieg erleiden – Versöhnung fördern*, 2000 MILITÄRSEELSORGE 104, 115.

886 *Report of the Secretary-General to the Security Council on the protection of civilians in armed conflict*, U.N. GAOR, at 2, U.N. Doc. S/2001/331 (March 30th, 2001).

887 *See id.* at 13

become the administrators of humanitarian law and spiritual assistance as a form of relief.[888] However, as the norms of the conventional instruments are addressed to the state parties, it primarily defines their sphere of responsibility.

People in existential distress and situations of oppression, when other strategies fail, take refuge in religion.[889] In the case of the armed conflict in Croatia after its breaking off from the former Yugoslavia, pastors were amongst the refugees and expellees and also stayed with their communities in occupied territories.[890] Such a continuous ministry also bears the danger of being targeted during hostilities. In times of occupation, there is usually an interregnum between the exercise of power by the defeated and the victorious party. Religious institutions, however, remain and may exercise some authority.[891] ULRICH TILGNER, the correspondent of the German ZDF TV station, reported about Muslim ministers who tried to curb looting masses after the defeat of Iraq in the third Gulf War.[892]

Another example for such civilian wartime ministry in the setting of a non-international armed conflict is Colombia: With more than 90 % of the Colombian population claiming catholic faith, the church is a serious social actor – even though the situation is very diverse in the different parts of the country. During the past decades of armed conflict with various actors, namely the military, government-backed paramilitaries and leftist guerrillas, pastoral ministry to all parties to the conflict was criticized as a possible upgrade of the belligerents' status and prolonging armed hostilities but is meanwhile commonly accepted and earned the church high credibility and acceptance. Efforts are strong in order to not exclude any side from being ministered to. An agency to carry such activities is the *Pastoral Social*. The sign of its caritas provides a protection similar to that of the red cross in some parts of country. In other cases, bishops and priests are asked to act as mediators in cases of abduction or to negotiate humanitarian corridors in order to protect civilian population.[893] Besides such emergency interventions, the goal of the church remains to change in cooperation with the other players of civil society the political structures that currently foster violence.

On the background of this role, religious ministers had continuous access to San Vicente del Caguán. The municipality in the Department of Caquetá had

---

888 *See* Hiebel, *supra* note 180, at 6-7.
889 *See* Ancic, *supra* note 885, at 110.
890 *See id.* at 111, *see also* MARCHEGGIANO, *supra* note 107, at 187 (for religious ministers remaining with civilians during enemy occupation).
891 *See* MARCHEGGIANO, *supra* note 107, at 148.
892 *See* ANARCHIE IN BELGRAD (ZDF Newsreport April 11th, 2003), *available at* http://www.heute.t-online.de/ZDFheute/artikel/6/0,1367,POL-0-2041542,00.html.
893 *See* Anna Dirksmeier, *Kultur der Gewalt*, 57 HERDERKORRESPONDENZ 564, 566 (2003).

been part of a demilitarized zone and became the location for peace talks between the government and guerrillas in late 1998. After these negotiations had failed in February 2002, the region became site of fights between the groups with numerous casualties among the civilian population. In the unclear situation and in the presence of guerrilla and paramilitary checkpoints, access to most of the rural areas of San Vicente del Caguán was difficult except for catholic priests and some humanitarian organizations.[894] Especially in these rural areas, where the civilian population is exposed directly to the belligerents, it is often only clergy who have access to all parties to the conflict. In this situation, the national secretariat of *Pastoral Social* also took up the task of training ministers from conflict areas in IHL.[895]

Nonetheless, religious personnel are deliberately killed by the parties to the conflict.[896] On March 16th, 2002, the Archbishop of Cali, ISAÍAS DUARTE CANCINO became the 50th victim among Colombian clergy. The outspoken critic of drug traffickers and both guerrillas and paramilitary whose firm opposition to all types of violence and dedication to social action was praised by Pope JOHN PAUL II in a eulogy[897] was assassinated when leaving a church after officiating to marriage ceremonies. Another well-known example of religious personnel affected by the conflict was JORGE ENRIQUE JIMÉNEZ CARVAJAL. The bishop of the Columbian diocese of Zipaquirá and then President of the Latin American Episcopal Council (CELAM), was kidnapped on November 11th, 2002 along with a priest of his diocese on the way to a religious ceremony in the town of Pacho. The abduction of the two clergy drew worldwide publicity but is unfortunately only one among others in recent years. Appeals to release them were launched and expressed the solidarity of the Holy See and numerous bishops' conferences. Particularly remarkable is a statement issued by Cardinal PEDRO RUBIANO SAENZ on the same date as the kidnapping took place in which the Archbishop of Bogotá and President of the Colombian Bishops' Conference condemned all kidnappings as a violation of life, dignity and freedom of the human person. Pronouncing the abduction an offence to the church, to the bishops of Colombia and to the bishops of all Latin America, he warned the kidnappers that they

---

894 *See* AMNESTY INTERNATIONAL, SAN VICENTE DEL CAGUÁN AFTER THE BREAKDOWN OF THE PEACE TALKS, AMR 23/098/2002, at 7 (October 16th, 2002), *available at* http://web.amnesty.org/aidoc/aidoc_pdf.nsf/Index/AMR230982002ENGLISH/$File/AMR2309802.pdf.

895 *See* Roland Bigler, *Disseminating international humanitarian law in Colombia*, 1997 INTERNATIONAL REVIEW OF THE RED CROSS 421-432, *available at* http://www.icrc.org/web/eng/siteeng0.nsf/iwpList162/DEF661C2493E2B05C1256B66005AC80B.

896 *See* U.S. DEPARTMENT OF STATE, 1999 COUNTRY REPORTS ON HUMAN RIGHTS PRACTICES FOR COLOMBIA (February 25, 2000), *available at* http://www.state.gov/www/global/human_rights/1999_hrp_report/colombia.html.

897 *See* LE PAROLE DEL PAPA ALLA RECITA DELL'ANGELUS (March17th, 2002), *available at* http://www.vatican.va/news_services/bulletin/news/10418.php?index=10418.

risked serious canonical punishment.[898] Canon law in this case was mobilized to provide protection for the kidnapped clergymen. After four days of captivity, police and armed forces freed Bishop JIMÉNEZ and his companion.

Cases in other countries involve killing and disappearances of clergy and other religious ministers or threats against them on suspicion of supporting one political cause or the other. In addition, civilian ministers are specially exposed in armed insurgency for instance as human rights activists, political educators or humanitarian workers. To maintain the safety of civilian ministers even in situation of armed conflicts, an efficient protection of civilians, a "culture of protection for civilians in armed conflict"[899] seems to be the most appropriate tool.

2. Protection of civilian ministry in GC IV

The legal basis for the protection of civilians in international armed conflict and following occupation is GC IV, which in 1949 was a fundamental novelty. The Hague Regulations dealt with the protection of civilians only incompletely when referring to the authorities of the Occupying Power in times of war.[900] The attempt to formulate rules for a civilian society during times of occupation turned out to be just as difficult as manifold the activities of such a society are. In comparison, the command system that is characteristic for a military environment turns out to be helpful. This could be a reason why GC IV in its provisions on exercise of religion switches the perspective. Relevant stipulations in GC IV focus on the recipients of spiritual assistance: protected persons. The effects of these rules are more open and larger in scope as those focused on the ministers. GC IV does not use the term "chaplains" or "religious personnel" which both refer to ministry in a military context but instead speaks of "ministers".[901] On the other hand, GC IV does not grant protection to religious personnel falling under one of the first three GCs.[902]

Like the Hague Regulations earlier, Art. 27 GC IV states the principle that protected persons are entitled to respect for their religious convictions and practices. Protected persons are defined in the context of GC IV as persons in a conflict or during occupation who find themselves in the hands of a party to the conflict or Occupying Power of which they are not nationals.[903] Respect for religious convictions and practices must be seen in the context of freedom of thought, of conscience and of religion.[904] Then, protected persons in an occupied

---

[898] *See* BOLETÍN N° 14, El Catolicismo (November 12th, 2002), *available at* http://www.elcatolicismo.com.co/content.php?menu=7602&page_id=1396.
[899] *See* REPORT OF THE SECRETARY-GENERAL, *supra* note 886, at 2
[900] *See* Kimminich, *supra* note 172, at 165.
[901] *See* Art. 17, 38 (3), 58, 93 (2, 3) GC IV.
[902] *See* Art. 4 GC IV.
[903] *See id.*
[904] *See* PICTET, *supra* note 711, at 203.

territory must be able to practice their religion without restrictions other than those necessary for the maintenance of public order.

Aliens who are not repatriated are also allowed to practice their religion and to receive spiritual assistance from ministers of their faith.[905] This norm is the equivalent of Art. 27 GC III.[906] Facilitating the exercise of religion to orphans – namely by way of religious instructions – and children separated from their families is put into the responsibility of the parties to the conflict in times of war and succeeding occupation.[907] This seemingly insignificant stipulation is of enormous practical relevance. It precludes attempts to wean children from their known environment for instance for reasons of political propaganda.[908] The protection applies to children of the adversary party but also to children of the own population in armed conflict.[909] This is an exception to Art. 4 (1) GC IV that considers persons only protected if they are not nationals of the Occupying Power.[910] PA I extends the guarantees of GC IV and includes evacuated minors for whom religious education should be continued upon request of their parents.[911]

GC IV furthermore guarantees the free passage of objects necessary for religious worship intended for civilians of adversary parties.[912] The Occupying Power furthermore has to accept consignments of books and articles required for religious needs and to facilitate their distribution in occupied territory.[913] Protected persons cannot be transferred to another country where the level of protection by GC IV with regard to freedom of religion is not guaranteed.[914]

Persons interned according to Section IV of GC IV also enjoy latitude in the exercise of their religious duties, including attendance at the services of their faith.[915] This latitude is conditioned by compliance with the disciplinary routine prescribed by the detaining authorities. Norms on exercise of religion in internment are generally very similar to those of GC III: The Detaining Power provides premises suitable for the holding of religious services.[916] "Suitable" here

---

[905] *See* Art. 38 (3) GC IV.
[906] *See* PICTET, *supra* note 711, at 247-48.
[907] *See* Art. 24, 50 (3) GC IV.
[908] *See* PICTET, *supra* note 711, at 187.
[909] *See id.*, *see also* Schlögel, *supra* note 38, at 275.
[910] *See also* OLSEN, *supra* note 195, at 136 (for the lack of protection of own population by the Occupying Power).
[911] *See* Art. 78 No. 2 PA I.
[912] *See* Art. 23 GC IV, *see also* Art. 69 No. 1 PA I (for a similar norm ensuring the provision of objects necessary for religious worship).
[913] *See* Art. 58 (2) GC IV.
[914] *See* Art. 45 (4) GC IV, *see also* Rausch, *supra* note 139, at 33.
[915] *See* Art. 93 GC IV.
[916] *See* Art. 86 GC IV.

means the same as "adequate" in Art. 34 (2) GC III.[917] The access and distribution of religious materials by representatives of religious organizations is possible.[918] Mortal remains of deceased internees are to be buried honorably and – again only if possible – according to the rites of their religion.[919] Persons detained and accused or convicted have the right to receive any spiritual assistance that they may require.[920]

GC IV also deals with religious ministers during occupation. The Occupying Power has to permit ministers of religion to give spiritual assistance to the members of their religious communities.[921] If this provision is compared with the parallel provision regarding medical assistance that speaks of "the duty of ensuring and maintaining"[922] medical services, the less peremptory and therefore more equivocal character of norms on spiritual assistance becomes clear.[923] Civilian ministry may not be used as a pretext for political agitation against the Occupying Power.[924] Otherwise, the Occupying Power would be "entitled to take appropriate action".[925] Usually, the Occupying Power cannot impose ministers of religion of its own nationality. However, in exceptional cases, ministers of the Occupying Power's nationality, e.g. military chaplains of the Occupying Power, may serve the civilian population in occupied territories.[926] But the question for the nationality of a minister of religion is misleading because even foreign ministers can be attached as chaplains.[927]

A respect-and-protection clause as it exists for chaplains in GC I and GC II does not exist in GC IV for civilian religious ministers.[928] However, they are to be respected and protected if they are exclusively employed at a civilian hospital and care for sick and wounded civilians, for maternity cases or infirm.[929] The level of protection for these personnel is similar to that of chaplains attached to hospitals under the 1864 Red Cross Convention. The development that followed for chaplains could be a sign of the potential regarding possible developments in the protection for civilian ministers. The parties to the conflict are encouraged to

---

917 *See* PICTET, *supra* note 711, at 388, *see also supra* at 91.
918 *See* Art. 142 GC IV.
919 *See* Art. 130 (1) GC IV, *see also* PICTET, *supra* note 711, at 506.
920 *See* Art. 75 (3) GC IV.
921 *See* Art. 58 (1) GC IV.
922 Art. 56 GC IV.
923 *See* Hiebel, *supra* note 180, at 4.
924 *See* MARCHEGGIANO, *supra* note 107, at 149.
925 PICTET, *supra* note 711, at 318.
926 *See* Rabus, *supra* note 575, No. 805 at 370.
927 *See also* Beyer, *supra* note 350, at 251 (for the practical and canonical implications of serving in a foreign military ordinariate), Vatican Information Service Daily Bulletin of February 14th, 2004 (for the appointment of an Ecuadorian bishop as military ordinary of Peru).
928 *See* BOTHE ET AL., *supra* note 801, at 90.
929 *See* Art. 20 GC IV, MARCHEGGIANO, *supra* note 107, at 111.

conclude local agreements to allow passage of "ministers of all religions" to besieged or encircled areas.[930] These ministers may well be ministers of the besieging or the besieged Power's nationality.[931] The term "chaplain" in the original draft was substituted in the run of the diplomatic conference of 1949.[932] Ministers of religion who are interned are allowed to minister freely to the members of their community.[933] However, these interned ministers of religion do not have a privileged status like detained chaplains in POW camps, but are detainees like the other civilians in the camp.[934] Their free movement is more restricted than that of detained chaplains in POW camps.[935] The equitable allocation of ministers amongst the various places of internment in which there are internees speaking the same language and belonging to the same religion is to be assured. If the number of interned ministers is too small, the Detaining Power has to provide them with the necessary facilities to move from one place to another, including means of transportation. Ministers of religion should be authorized to visit internees who are in hospital. They are furthermore free to correspond on matters concerning their ministry with the religious authorities in the country of detention and, as far as possible, with international religious organizations of their faith. This correspondence does not fall under a possible quota for personal mail[936] but may be subject to censorship. These stipulations could work to the disadvantage of small religious groups who do not have an international structure.[937] In case of lack or shortage of suitable ministers of religion, a procedure similar to GC III is initiated: In agreement with the Detaining Power, the local religious authorities of the same faith may appoint a minister of the internees' faith or, if such a course is feasible from a denominational point of view, a minister of similar religion or a qualified layman. The agreement of the community of internees is not necessary for the appointment. As internment takes place in the country of the internees, the danger of abuse of the appointment procedure by the Detaining Power can be met by the intervention of local religious authorities.[938] The appointed minister enjoys the facilities granted to the ministry he has assumed. He has to comply with all regulations laid down by the Detaining Power in the interests of discipline and security. Similar to the stipulations in GC III, a ministry to persons not belonging to the own faith is the exception.

---

[930] Art. 17 GC IV (similar to Art. 15 GC I).
[931] *See* PICTET, *supra* note 711, at 140.
[932] *See* FEDERAL POLITICAL DEPARTMENT, *supra* note 217, at 700.
[933] *See* Art. 93 (2) GC IV.
[934] *See* O'BRIEN, *supra* note 154, at R.7.
[935] *See* Hiebel, *supra* note 180, at 19.
[936] *See* Art. 93, 107 GC IV.
[937] *See* O'BRIEN, *supra* note 154, at R4.
[938] *See* PICTET, *supra* note 711, at 407, *see also supra* at 89 (for the different procedure in GC III).

All these stipulations of GC IV form a high level of protection for freedom of religion but they can hardly constitute a claim for active support from the Occupying Power for religious activities but only a claim for non-interference on the part of the Occupying Power.[939]

3. Protection of Places of worship

A particular protection in IHL is granted to places of worship and even includes a protection for personnel. It seems interesting to examine whether this may result in a protection of civilian ministers.

Already Pharaoh RAMSES III in the 6th century B.C. had recognized a right of humanitarian asylum in religious temples. The Israelites knew six cities of asylum from the avenger of blood.[940] When the Goths conquered Rome in 410, their leader ALARIC considered the great basilicas to be inviolable places of refuge.[941] In spite of this, destruction of religious places and monuments aimed at the demoralization of the enemy and attempting to target his spiritual sphere occurred throughout history.[942]

Art. 27 of the Hague Regulations[943] demands that all necessary steps are taken in sieges and bombardments to spare as far as possible edifices devoted to religion provided that they are not used for military purposes at the same time. A similar norm was contained in Art. 5 of the Convention respecting bombardment by naval forces in time of war (Hague IX of October 18th, 1907).[944] These provisions constitute a rather low level of protection.[945] The "as far as possible" clause indicates that whatever protection is granted may be lifted for reasons of military necessity. Nonetheless, this weak protection seems to apply to all places of worship. Humanitarian reasons – churches are places where civilians gather – appear as motives[946] along with the intent to protect cultural patrimony.

Another relevant document is the Hague Convention for the Protection of Cultural Property in the Event of Armed Conflict of May 14th, 1954 (HC). This instrument protects cultural property as "cultural heritage of all mankind".[947] But it only protects property "of great importance to the cultural heritage of every peo-

---

[939] *See* KIMMINICH, *supra* note 297, at 124-25, Rausch, *supra* note 139, at 32, Rößler, *supra* note 568, at 313.

[940] *See Numbers* 35:9-15.

[941] *See* Liedermann, *supra* note 43, at 1, 2, *see also* HIEBEL, *supra* note 142, at 5-7 (for examples of protection of religious places in ancient times).

[942] *See* Matthias Herdegen, *Der Kulturgüterschutz im Kriegsvölkerrecht*, *in* RECHTSFRAGEN DES INTERNATIONALEN KULTURGÜTERSCHUTZES 161, 162 (Rudolf Dolzer et al. eds. 1994).

[943] *See* THE LAW OF WAR, *supra* note 36, at 319.

[944] *See id.* at 350.

[945] *See* Herdegen, *supra* note 942, at 164.

[946] *See* SCOTT, *supra* note 163, at 536, 597.

[947] Preamble para. 2 HC.

ple" - of both religious and secular nature.[948] Efforts to explicitly mention buildings of religion in an illustrative list of protected objects failed.[949] Unlike the Hague Regulations that included protection of religious places for humanitarian reasons, HC norms are aimed at the preservation of cultural heritage. The religious character of the edifice is not constitutive for the protection under the HC but only its possible extraordinary cultural value.[950] Religion appears as a form of culture; the protection granted deals not with living culture but with produced culture.[951] Accordingly, protection is not granted to ordinary places of worship that have only "some cultural importance".[952]

Protected objects may display the distinctive emblem of the convention.[953] They have to be safeguarded and respected in times of armed conflict and may not be used for purposes that expose them to destruction or damage. The parties furthermore pledge to refrain from any act of hostility against these objects.[954] This protection, however, can be derogated "where military necessity imperatively requires such a waiver".[955] It has been one of the aims of the 2nd Protocol to the HC of March 25th, 1999 to give a clear definition of such "military necessity" consistent with PA I.[956]

Aside from this general protection, the HC provides a special protection for cultural property of "very great importance"[957] that has been entered in the International Register of Cultural Property under Special Protection. From the time of entry, these objects enjoy immunity from any act of hostility. The whole of the Vatican City State, for instance, was registered in 1960 as a center containing monuments and is thus a specially protected object.[958] The 1999 2nd Additional Protocol furthermore established the third category of "enhanced protection" for objects of greatest importance.

---

948 Art. 1 a HC.

949 *See* JIŘÍ TOMAN, THE PROTECTION OF CULTURAL PROPERTY IN THE EVENT OF ARMED CONFLICT 47 (1996).

950 *See* Kussbach, *supra* note 144, at 386-37, MARCHEGGIANO, *supra* note 107, at 150, KIMMINICH, *supra* note 297, at 129.

951 *See* NICOLAS, *supra* note 16, at 102.

952 *But see* O'BRIEN, *supra* note 154, at W2.

953 *See* Art. 17 HC, *see also infra* Appendix I a (for the distinctive emblem of the HC).

954 *See* Art. 4 (1) HC.

955 Art. 4 (2) HC, *see also* Art. 11 (2) HC (for derogation when specially protected objects are concerned), U.S. AIR FORCE INTELLIGENCE TARGETING GUIDE, AIR FORCE PAMPHLET 14-210 INTELLIGENCE, Attachment 4, A4.5.2 (February 1st, 1998), *available at* http://www.fas.org/irp/doddir/usaf/afpam14-210/part17.htm (for military necessity regarding "religious monuments" in the highly relevant practice of aerial warfare).

956 *See* Art. 1 (f) Second Protocol to the Hague Convention of 1954 for the Protection of Cultural Property in the Event of Armed Conflict, The Hague (March 26th, 1999).

957 Art. 8 HC.

958 *See* TOMAN, *supra* note 949, at 108, BOTHE ET AL., *supra* note 801, at 330.

The protective scope of the HC is not limited to cultural property but also includes "personnel engaged in the protection of cultural property".[959] These personnel have to be respected and may continue to exercise their duties. But the respect for personnel is not absolute as they are respected only "as far as it is consistent with the interests of security". Here again, a military necessity aspect comes into play and makes the norm "markedly weaker"[960] than the comprehensive "respect and protection in all circumstances" clauses of the GC I-III. A state can practically evade the obligation to respect protected personnel "as it wishes".[961]

The definition of protected personnel is very general. TOMAN sees the assignment and the dedication to protection of cultural property constitutive for protection.[962] For him, the terminology of the HC covers unpaid volunteers as well as professional military and civilian staff engaged in protection.[963] Ministers of religion cannot generally be considered to be engaged in the protection of cultural property.[964] This question needs a case-by-case analysis. First, the nature of the place of worship in question will have to be determined: Its character as a property of great importance to the cultural heritage must be stated. The role of a place of worship as a monument of architecture, as a site of pieces of art or as a location of historical importance has to be taken into account. Furthermore, personnel that claim protection must be assigned for the protection of this cultural property. Not all ministers of religion meet this criterion; not every clergyman is responsible for every place of worship. But canon law knows the specific assignment of responsibility for a church building. The office of pastor of a parish, for instance, is associated with the canonical duty of care for the parochial church.[965] As many sanctuaries of special significance are not integrated into parish structures, they are assigned a *rector ecclesiae* according to can. 556 CIC, who must be a priest. Such a rector is entrusted with the preservation of the church building.[966] Even chapels and private chapels need a responsible person to take care of liturgy and maintenance.[967] Responsible are also custodians of a chapter church and superiors of a religious institute for their edifices. Notwithstanding the rights of clergy in liturgy, responsible for a place of worship could

---

[959] Art. 14 HC.

[960] TOMAN, *supra* note 949, at 174.

[961] *Id.* at 175.

[962] *Id.* at 174.

[963] *See id.* at 174, 186.

[964] *See* MARCHEGGIANO, *supra* note 107, at 155 (very general).

[965] *See* Hans Paarhammer, *Vor can. 556*, No. 1, *in* 3 MÜNSTERISCHER KOMMENTAR ZUM CODEX IURIS CANONICI (Klaus Lüdicke ed., 36th delivery December 2002).

[966] *See* can. 562 CIC.

[967] *See* Hans Paarhammer, *can. 556*, No. 5, *in* 3 MÜNSTERISCHER KOMMENTAR ZUM CODEX IURIS CANONICI (Klaus Lüdicke ed., 36th delivery December 2002).

also be laypeople such as the sacristan, the janitor or a member of the community entrusted with technical aspects of maintenance.[968] Since religious places of great cultural importance tend to be large buildings, there will usually be a number of persons responsible for the edifice - some of them even specialized for particular aspects. These responsibilities may serve as indicators whether a person is engaged in protection. Usually, persons entrusted by canon law or by their employment contract with care for a church building or its maintenance can be considered as engaged in protection. They are thus protected persons under the HC.

Naturally, these personnel are only protected as long as they abstain from any participation in acts of hostility. Under Art. 21 of the Regulations for the Execution of the Convention that "constitute an integral part" of the HC,[969] protected personnel may wear an armlet and an identity card[970] bearing the distinctive emblem of the convention. Both items have to be issued and stamped by the competent authorities. Details regarding the role and status of personnel and extended rights or protection may be regulated in special agreements among the parties of the convention in accordance with Art. 24 HC.[971]

The 1977 PAs also address the question of protection of places of worship and do so without prejudice to the HC. Art. 16 PA II prohibits committing any acts of hostility directed against places of worship that constitute the cultural or spiritual heritage of peoples. It is also prohibited to use these places in support of the military effort. PA I is similarly worded in Art. 53 and additionally formulates the prohibition to make a place of worship the object of reprisals. The protection in the PAs is "somewhat narrow"[972] because it is again conditioned by the cultural value of the religious establishment. For places of worship of cultural value, the PAs establish a protection stricter than that of the Hague Regulations or the HC: As long as these objects are not abused as military objects, no attack is permitted. On the other hand, if a protected religious establishment is used for military purposes – famous example in history is the monastery at Monte Cassino in 1944 – it looses its protection.[973]

While the HC dealt with property which is "of great importance to the cultural heritage", the PAs establish a wider protection for objects which "constitute the

---

[968] *See* Hans Paarhammer, *can. 562*, No. 5, *in* 3 MÜNSTERISCHER KOMMENTAR ZUM CODEX IURIS CANONICI (Klaus Lüdicke ed., 36th delivery December 2002), *see also* O'BRIEN, *supra* note 154, at W2.

[969] Art. 20 HC, *see* TOMAN, *supra* note 949, at 176, *see also* Art. 17 (2) c, d HC (on the display of the distinctive emblem by personnel engaged in protection).

[970] *See infra* Appendix II e (for a sample).

[971] *See* TOMAN, *supra* note 949, at 176, 272.

[972] GREEN, *supra* note 133, at 154.

[973] *See id.* at 155.

cultural or spiritual heritage". Though the basic idea is the same, the reference to the spiritual heritage clarifies the qualification of protected objects by introducing the criterion of spirituality.[974] A distinction between cultural and spiritual heritage will be difficult in practice, as religious monuments may be of value for a whole culture or a piece of secular art may have importance for religion. However, the spiritual heritage criterion constitutes a protection for "all objects of ... religious importance"[975] and also introduces an element of living culture. A special registration or marking is not necessary for protection under the PAs,[976] which furthermore is non-derogable.[977]

The diplomatic conference 1974-1977 discussed in length whether all places of worship were protected or merely those that form part of the cultural or spiritual heritage.[978] The notion to protect any and all places of worship was supported by religious reasons and traditions of immunity and asylum.[979] The fact that places of worship are refuges for civilian population in times of war has often been used as an argument for protection.[980] Other voices have called for a general protection of places of worship at least for certain times, e.g. Friday, Saturday or Sunday.[981] Examples from practice prove that the protection for such traditional shelters is still lacking efficiency: During fights between the leftist guerrillas and a paramilitary group in the Chocó district of north-western Colombia, a Mortar bomb exploded on May 2nd, 2002 in the church of the town of Bojaya. 119 persons were killed. Apparently, combatants had used the shelter-seeking crowd as a human shield and drew fire on the place of worship. The incident caused the United Nations High Commissioner for Human Rights Office in Colombia to issue a statement recalling the obligation of all parties to the conflict to respect the norms of IHL, particularly the prohibition to attack non-combatants and religious places.[982] Pope JOHN PAUL II denounced the lack of respect for people and sacred places in a message of condolences to the families

---

[974] *See* COMMENTARY ON THE ADDITIONAL PROTOCOLS, *supra* note 178, No. 2064 at 646.
[975] *Id.* No. 2066 at 646.
[976] *See* Herdegen, *supra* note 942, at 169, O'BRIEN, *supra* note 154, at W2.
[977] *See* COMMENTARY ON THE ADDITIONAL PROTOCOLS, *supra* note 178, note 28 at 647, *see* Herdegen, *supra* note 942, at 171.
[978] *See* TOMAN, *supra* note 949, at 382, COMMENTARY ON THE ADDITIONAL PROTOCOLS, *supra* note 178, No. 2042 at 640.
[979] *See* BOTHE ET AL., *supra* note 801, at 331.
[980] *See* JOACHIM BERNDT, INTERNATIONALER KULTURGÜTERSCHUTZ 37 (1998), SABINE VON SCHORLEMER, INTERNATIONALER KULTURGÜTERSCHUTZ 286 (1992).
[981] *See* Hiebel, *supra* note 496, at 25.
[982] *See* ONU EXIGE RESPETO A MISIÓN HUMANITARIA EN EL RÍO ATRATO (OACNUDH Comunicado de Prensa May 5th, 2002), *available at* http://www.hchr.org.co/publico/comunicados/2002/comunicados2002.php3?cod=13&cat=17.

of the victims.[983] Another even more recent example that underlines the shelter character of places of worship is the 2003 coalition campaign in Iraq when hundreds of civilians – both Christians and Muslims alike – sought refuge in Christian churches and were provided for by the Caritas.[984] At the same time, the third Iraq war may also be mentioned as an example for the abuse of places of religion: In early April, Iraqi troops fled into a the Shiite Ali shrine in Najaf. While U.S. officials accused them of firing at U.S. troops but declared to refrain from returning the fire, the Iraqi Information Minister Mohammed Saeed al-Sahaf accused the Americans of attacking places of worship.[985]

The understanding of a narrow scope of protection only for culturally valuable temples could be interpreted as contrary to the spirit of PA I.[986] However, it is not clear that this consideration was a motive for the explicit protection of places of worship. Those places are not protected as "storerooms for spiritual assistance"[987] or traditional shelters of civilians. Only HIEBEL constructed an indirect link to spiritual assistance considering cultural patrimony an instrument of such assistance.[988] Nonetheless, the protection as cultural patrimony seems to be the guiding aspect. As the question was discussed and the diplomatic conference opted for the formulation of Art. 53 PA I, the norm must be understood as granting protection only to places of a quality of sanctity that expresses "the conscience of the people" and not merely to places of "a local renown of sanctity which does not extend to the whole nation".[989] If on the other hand, a place of worship becomes site of a medical unit, a completely different regime governs, namely that of protected medical installations. Constitutive for this regime is then the actual use of a facility.

A willfully committed violation of Art. 53 PA I is considered a grave breach of the protocol under Art. 85 No. 4 d PA I

a) if the attack causes an extensive destruction of a clearly-recognized place of worship,

---

[983] *See* Fears grow for Colombian civilians (BBC Newsreport May 6th, 2002), *available at* http://news.bbc.co.uk/1/hi/world/americas/1970057.stm.

[984] *See* RADIOGIORNALE DELLA RADIO VATICANA (April 3rd, 2003), *available at* http://www.radiovaticana.com/radiogiornale/ore14/2003/aprile/03_04_03.htm#iraq_guerra.

[985] *See In der "roten Zone"*, FRANKFURTER ALLGEMEINE ZEITUNG, April 3rd, 2003, at 2, CENTCOM STATEMENT ON ALI MOSQUE (U.S. Central Command Press Release Number 03-04-16, April 2nd, 2003), *available at* http://www.centcom.mil/CENTCOMNews/News_Release.asp?NewsRelease=20030416.txt.

[986] *See* DETTER, *supra* note 78, at 295, *see also* BOTHE ET AL., *supra* note 801, at 332.

[987] *See* Schubiger, *supra* note 145, at 6.

[988] *See* HIEBEL, *supra* note 142, at 227.

[989] COMMENTARY ON THE ADDITIONAL PROTOCOLS, *supra* note 178, No. 2067 at 647, *see* TOMAN, *supra* note 949, at 388, SCHORLEMER, *supra* note 980, at 287-88, KIMMINICH, *supra* note 297, at 129-30, O'BRIEN, *supra* note 154, at W3.

b) if special protection has been given to the place of worship by special arrangement e.g. within the framework of a competent international organization,
c) if there was no evidence that the attacked place of worship has been used in support of the military effort
d) and if the place of worship was not located in the immediate proximity of military objectives.

It is clear that this norm overburdened with detail "is not a masterpiece of draftsmanship".[990]

The criterion of belonging to the cultural or spiritual heritage is also essential for protection of places of worship under Protocol II on Prohibitions or Restrictions on the Use of Mines, Booby-traps and Other Devices to the 1980 Convention on Conventional Weapons. Its Art. 6 (1) b prohibits to attach or associate booby-traps to such places of worship. Under the Statute of the ICC "buildings dedicated to religion" are protected regardless of their cultural value.[991]

Protection of places of cult may also come from the respect of religious convictions of civilian population. Ensuring this respect is also a task for the chaplain in his role as advisor to the commander.[992] For instance in Afghanistan, chaplains intervened when it was brought to their attention that office and sleeping areas for troops were set up in buildings reserved for Muslim worship.[993] The most significant protection for "ordinary" religious places – besides the weak protection of the Hague Regulations - then derives from another source: their civilian nature. As civilian objects, they are not to be made the object of attack or of reprisals according to Art. 52 PA I. The action taken by the armed forces of the parties of conflicts against a number of churches and mosques in the Balkans between 1991-95 constituted war crimes as their destruction was not justified by military necessity.[994] When a place of worship is used to make an effective contribution to military action, it becomes nonetheless a military object that can legitimately be attacked. In practice, places of worship often have strategic importance. The bell tower of a church or the minaret of a mosque can serve as excellent observation posts.[995] But since a place of worship

---

[990] BOTHE ET AL., *supra* note 801, at 519.
[991] *See* ICC Statute, *supra* note 778, Art. 8 e iv.
[992] *See* Merrifield, *supra* note 508.
[993] *See* Joseph A. Scordo, *A Chaplain in "The 'Stan'"*, THE NAVY CHAPLAINCY, October-December 2002, at 3.
[994] *See* DETTER, *supra* note 78, at 296, *see also* GREEN, *supra* note 133, at 325-326, ILIJA ZIVKOVIC, THE WOUNDED CHURCH IN CROATIA (1996), *see also* Monica Wallenfels, A Current Case: The Destruction of the Last Mosques in Banja Luka on 8 September 1993, 1993 HUMANITÄRES VÖLKERRECHT 217-20 (on the jurisdiction of the International Criminal Tribunal for the former Yugoslavia over such cases).
[995] *See* BOTHE ET AL., *supra* note 801, at 331.

is normally dedicated to civilian purposes, the presumption that the place of worship is not used for military purposes prevails in case of doubt about the actual use of a place of worship.[996]

The interrelationship between protection of personnel and places of cult as well as the difficulties evolving in an actual situation in this regard are well illustrated by the case of the Church of the Nativity in Bethlehem. In 1347, a friary had been erected in Bethlehem by the Franciscan Custody in the Holy Land. Ever since, attempts had occurred to violently expel the Franciscans from the site where the Prince of Peace is believed to be born.[997] In the wake of Operation Defensive Shield begun on March 29th, 2002, troops of the Israeli Defence Forces (IDF) entered the city of Bethlehem on April 2nd using tanks and armoured personnel carriers. Exchanges of fire occurred around the city on April 2nd and 3rd. IDF asserts that Palestinian militants fired on Israeli soldiers from churches, while the Palestinian National Authority accused IDF of attacking civilians and clerics on church premises.[998] 200 Palestinian men seeking sanctuary forced their way into the Church of the Nativity compound in Bethlehem. A report of the UN High Commissioner for Human Rights qualified the intruders as "combatants and civilians".[999] They carried about 90 weapons and barricaded themselves on the compound that consists of monastery buildings, a church and the basilica. The complex was immediately surrounded by IDF.

Friars appearing on windows of the besieged monastery caught IDF fire. In the morning of April 8th, 2002, as IDF fired on the compound, a building adjacent to the Basilica was hit by a grenade and a Palestinian trying to put off the resulting fire killed by IDF.[1000] Another Palestinian was shot the following day. Exchanges of fire continued to take place around the compound throughout the time of the siege. 8 persons were killed, 25 injured. As the IDF blocked any food supplies and cut off water, electricity and later also telephone lines, the Franciscans shared their food supplies with the 200 occupants. Only medicine for a diabetic Franciscan friar was delivered by the IDF on April 15th. Other friars were evacuated when their state of health got worse. With the inception of a

---

[996] *See* Art. 52 (3) PA I, *see also* BOTHE ET AL., *supra* note 801, at 327 (about the small likelihood of doubt).

[997] *See* THE FRANCISCAN EXPERIENCE, *available at* http://198.62.75.1/www1/ofm/sites/TSbtfran.html (on attacks on the fortified monastery by Turks in 1641 and 1817).

[998] *See Report of the Secretary-General prepared pursuant to General Assembly resolution ES-10/10*, G.A., U.N. GAOR, 10th Emergency Sess., Agenda Item 5, No. 74 at 15, U.N. Doc. A/ES-10/186 (July 30th, 2002).

[999] *Report of the United Nations High Commissioner for Human Rights and Follow-Up to the World Conference on Human Rights*, U.N. ESCOR, Commission on Human Rights, 58th Sess., Agenda Item 4, No. 52 at 10, U.N. Doc. E/CN.4/2002/184 (April 24th, 2002).

[1000] *See* ISRAELI ARMY INCURSION IN BETHLEHEM (OFM Press release April 4th, 2002), *available at* http://www.ofm.org/01eng/news/0408NeO92.html.

curfew regime, hundreds of families living around Manger Square were effected by the humanitarian emergency as well. The Franciscan friars compared themselves to voluntary hostages, as they could not leave Bethlehem in order to avoid a tragic massacre.[1001] Contrary to Israeli expectations to "cooperate and influence the terrorists in the church",[1002] they did not take party and considered themselves to be standing between the camps but appealed for a peaceful, dignified, honourable solution, which respected the life of all intruders regardless of the legality of their presence.[1003]

The IDF assessed that the Palestinians committed war crimes and grossly violated IHL when they penetrated the place of religion for the purpose of carrying out acts of hostility, mingled with civilians and held the friars as hostages to shield themselves from military attacks.[1004] The IDF campaign was therefore a "hostage rescue" operation. This view was repudiated by the Franciscans who stated that they were "in their own home, in the precise place where they should be in fidelity to their duty".[1005] The deliberate and voluntary character of the remaining brothers' decision became also clear in their chapter on April 13th when each friar confirmed the decision. The Custody tried to avoid the emergence of a pretext that could serve as a justification for an armed action inside the compound.

The standoff ended after more than five weeks on May 10th, 2002. 13 Palestinian occupants were sent into exile in the European Union while 26 returned to the Gaza strip and the others were set free. IDF troops eventually withdrew from Manger Square and the rest of the city. In conclusion, the Franciscans underlined their demand to "intensify even more the efforts to carry out an efficient international juridical protection of the Holy Places".[1006]

The crisis in Bethlehem was lined by heavy diplomatic efforts carried out by the Franciscan Curia General, the Holy See and the local churches. Pope JOHN PAUL II personally appealed to the parties of the conflict a number of times. All these efforts must be seen in the context of the Holy See's promotion of an

---

[1001] *See* WE FRANCISCANS CANNOT ABANDON, (OFM Press release April 5th, 2002), *available at* http://www.ofm.org/01eng/news/0405NeO90.html.

[1002] IDF NEWS AND INFORMATION, BRIEFING BY IDF COLONEL MIRI EISEN (April 14th, 2002), *available at* http://www.idf.il/english/announcements/2002/april/14.stm.

[1003] *See* INFORMATION FROM JERUSALEM-BETHLEHEM (OFM Press Release April 6th, 2002), *available at* http://www.ofm.org/01eng/news/0406NeO91.html.

[1004] *See* ISRAELI FOREIGN MINISTRY LEGAL ADVISOR, TERRORIST PENETRATION AND ARMED COMBAT IN HOLY PLACES - LEGAL PERSPECTIVES, (April 11th, 2002), *available at* http://www.mfa.gov.il/mfa/go.asp?MFAH0lj50, STATEMENT OF THE IRAELI REPRESENTATIVE LANCRY, 4525th meeting of the UN Security Council, S/PV.4525 (May 3rd, 2002).

[1005] 35 FRATERNITAS, No. 7, at 3-4.

[1006] A DEFINITIVE SOLUTION TO THE OCCUPATION-SIEGE OF THE NATIVITY IN BETHLEHEM (undated OFM News Release), *available at* http://www.ofm.org/01eng/news/0510Ne133.html.

internationally recognised status for Jerusalem. From the beginning, considerations of both the international community[1007] and the Holy See[1008] for such internationalization included the environs of Jerusalem and with it the municipality of Bethlehem south of Jerusalem. The siege also produced an audible response by the international community. The United Nations Commission on Human Rights (CHR) addressed the situation in a "special sitting" on the situation in the occupied Palestinian territories on April 5th, 2002.[1009] The CHR condemned "strongly ... the setting on fire of the church of the Nativity".[1010] Addressing the special sitting, the Holy See's representative Mons. DIARMUID MARTIN invoked "the right to demand scrupulous respect for human rights and humanitarian law in any conflict situation". Recalling the duty to respect and to safeguard the Holy Places, MARTIN also stressed the priority of returning to negotiations and of a political solution.[1011] MARTIN had in the same forum already referred to the HC and PA I when condemning disrespect for or misuse of religious sites in the Middle East as a violation of international norms.[1012] In the 4515th session of the UN Security Council, the French representative JEAN-DAVID LEVITTE expressed the concern of his country and the European Union about the "precarious plight" of the people inside the Church of the Nativity. He established the link to IHL when he stated that Israel had to take all necessary measures under the Geneva Conventions.[1013] The 10th emergency session of the UN General Assembly deplored Israeli military attacks on holy sites in the Occupied Palestinian Territory, including mosques and churches, and expressed its expectation "that the Israeli military siege on the Church of the Nativity in

---

[1007] *See* G.A. Res. 181 (II), Part III B, Annex B City of Jerusalem Boundaries proposed by the Ad Hoc Committee on the Palestinian Question with Map No. 104 (b) United Nations to the Plan of Partition with Economic Union (November 29th, 1947), *available at* http://domiNo.un.org/maps/m0103_1b.gif.

[1008] *See* Silvio Ferrari, *The Holy See and the Post-War Palestine issue*, 60 INTERNATIONAL AFFAIRS 261, 265, 267 (1984) (for the historic account) Silvio Ferrari, *La Santa Sede e la questione die Gerusalemme da Madrid a Camp David, in* GERUSALEMME - CHIAVE DELLA PACE 33, 33-34 (Nicola Bux et al. eds. 2002) (for the understanding in the pontificate of John Paul II).

[1009] *See* Press Release of the UN Department of Public Information, Geneva (April 5th, 2002).

[1010] Res. 2002/8, U.N. ESCOR, Commission on Human Rights, 58th Sess., U.N. Doc. E/CN.4/2002/200 (April 15th, 2002).

[1011] *See* Diarmuid Martin, *Respect Human Rights, Return To Negotiations*, L'OSSERVATORE ROMANO [english], April 17th, 2002, at 5, *available at* http://www.petersnet.net/research/retrieve.cfm?recnum=4227.

[1012] *See* Diarmuid Martin, *Respect The Rights Of Religious Minorities; Respect Holy Places*, L'OSSERVATORE ROMANO [english], April 24th, 2002, at 9, *available at* http://www.petersnet.net/research/retrieve.cfm?recnum=4262.

[1013] *See* Press Release of the UN Department of Public Information, New York, SC/7368 (April 19th, 2002).

Bethlehem would end immediately".[1014] The aspect of protecting cultural patrimony was underlined by participants of the UN International Meeting in Support of Middle East Peace held in Nicosia who expressed concerns "that the military operation could cause irreparable damage to the Church of the Nativity".[1015] Other voices in the international arena did not hold back from publicly expressing judgements. The Tunesian representative in the UN Security Council called the siege "an outrage that not even the war criminals of World War II dared commit".[1016] In the view of the Palestinian authorities, the siege constituted "a grave and gross violation of international norms, even religious norms".[1017] The Israeli government alleged the abuse of civilian objects because gunmen fired at IDF soldiers from the church. The unlawful use of holy sites to support a military attack constituted a war crime under international law, caused a loss of their protection as cultural objects and made them legitimate military targets.[1018]

This book cannot explore all legal questions raised by the case of the Church of the Nativity in detail. Many aspects come into play: the nature of the Middle East conflict and its possible qualification as internal or international armed conflict, the relationship of the occupants with the Palestinian National Authority and the liability of the latter for acts of the former, the truth in the statements of the various parties of interest... The matter also has a bilateral legal component: Both, the Fundamental Agreement between the Holy See and the State of Israel of December 30th, 1993[1019] and the Basic Agreement between the Holy See and the Palestine Liberation Organization of February 15th, 2000[1020] assure in their Art. 4 the maintenance and observance of, respectively the respect for the *status quo* in the Christian holy places where it applies. It seems then clear that these bilateral agreements was breached twice: when Palestinian combatants occupied the church and when IDF laid siege on the complex.[1021]

The Church of the Nativity certainly is part of the cultural heritage of all mankind according to the HC and a place of worship constituting the spiritual heritage of peoples under PA I and thus protected under IHL. Certainly not all of the Franciscan friars qualify as personnel entrusted with the protection of the nativity complex under the HC. All the same, the guardianship for the holy places

---

1014 G.A. Res. 10, U.N. GAOR, 10th Emergency Sess., at 1, U.N. Doc. A/RES/ES-10/10 (May 7th, 2002).

1015 Press Release UN Department of Public Information, New York, GA/PAL/886 (April 17th, 2002).

1016 U.N. SCOR, 4525th mtg. at 9, U.N. Doc. S/PV.4525 (May 3rd, 2002).

1017 U.N. SCOR, 4515th mtg. at 3, U.N. Doc. S/PV.4515 (April 18th, 2002).

1018 *Id.*

1019 86 AAS 716-29 (1994).

1020 92 AAS 853-61 (2000).

1021 Both acts undoubtedly impaired the sacred character of the church and thus violated Chapter 1, No. 3 of UN General Assembly Resolution 181 (II) of November 29th, 1947.

entrusted to them by Pope CLEMENT VI in 1342 created a bond that over the centuries made them an essential part of what is protected in armed conflict as spiritual heritage and strengthens their protection as civilians. The presence of the 23 Franciscan brothers, 6 sisters and other religious and their understanding as part of a living religious culture probably avoided a more significant loss of life and damage to property. They could not be expected to withdraw from the site and the principle of discrimination had to be applied diligently – by all parties.

4. Convergence of protection of religious personnel and civilian ministers

Some scholars call for a clearer regulation of civilian exercise of religion in international legal instruments since the *status quo* in GC IV lacked a protection clause.[1022] Particular emphasis here had to be laid on free movement of faithful in times of curfew when individual pastoral care and religious gatherings are impeded.[1023] From a practical perspective and taking into account the interests of the Occupying Power, privileges for religious ministers concerning exceptions from curfew seem to be more feasible than exceptions for the faithful in general – if at all. Such a comprehensive protection for actors is already reached in the medical field. Here, all those "carrying out medical activities"[1024] are protected without regard to whether they are civilians or attached to the military. Taking into account the fact that the presence of religious ministers in armed conflict is a demand of "the most elementary sentiments of humanity and respect for the individual",[1025] the application of such an integrated approach[1026] to spiritual assistance would merge military chaplaincy and civilian ministry in order to provide spiritual assistance in a joint endeavor by civilians and military personnel. However, a general protection comparable to that of medical activities is not contained in the PAs. Art. 58 GC IV, which permits ministers to give spiritual assistance is the furthest going norm.[1027] It should be noted further, that even though both protocols are in force, their stipulations are rather far ahead of legal reality and not yet commonly accepted. The extended scope of application (PA I e.g. for armed conflicts which peoples are fighting in the exercise of their right of self-determination[1028] – this would include some national liberation movements – and PA II for all non-international armed conflicts except internal

---

[1022] *See* Rausch, *supra* note 139, at 35, MARCHEGGIANO, *supra* note 107, at 186.

[1023] *See* Schlögel, *supra* note 38, at 278.

[1024] Art. 16 No. 1 PA I, similar formulations can be found in Art. 10 PA II, *see also* Schlögel, *supra* note 38, at 278 (for the desire of a similar status for religious personnel).

[1025] PICTET, *supra* note 132, at 157, PICTET, *supra* note 711, at 140.

[1026] *See also* Bock, *supra* note 820, at 186 (for the term).

[1027] *See id.* at 190.

[1028] *See* Art. 1 (4) PA I.

disturbances and tensions[1029]) is one of the reasons why the state parties reluctantly received the protocols. Those who without doubt legitimately call to push for an increased protection of religious ministers also in the civilian domain have to keep this in mind. And their call may not distract from the hope that the two PAs will become a subject of more attention and approval - in the interest of those religious personnel who risk their lives in the service of the troops entrusted to them, but more importantly in the interest of those who in the extreme circumstances of armed conflict are in need of spiritual assistance.[1030] In addition, it should again not be disregarded that the main source of protection of civilian ministry is its civilian character that assures respect. The basic rule of Art. 48 PA I ensuring "respect for and protection of the civilian population and civilian objects" by distinguishing between the civilian population and combatants must be considered a significant achievement: Civilian population and civilian religious ministers as part of it must not be the object of attack.[1031]

A comprehensive protection of ministry to civilians and military personnel may also come from another side. The right to spiritual assistance is attached to the recognition of freedom of religion.[1032] Spiritual assistance is a form of exercise of freedom of religion as protected in many international legal instruments since Art. 18 of the Universal Declaration of Human Rights.[1033] The moral imperative to protect fundamental rights like freedom of religion also in times of war reflects in international law, of which both IHL and human rights law are interrelated parts:[1034] When the PAs, for instance, are to be applied without distinction based upon "religion or belief",[1035] this criterion is taken from the prohibition of discrimination in common Art. 2 of the two UN Covenants of 1966.[1036] The past brought about frequent attempts to find a convergence of protection by humanitarian law and by human rights law – particularly in the case of non-international armed conflict where both fields of law supplement each other.[1037] Such an approach could also be followed with regard to the protection of religious personnel and civilian ministers because both their ministry to armed forces and civilian population derives from the same freedom of religion. The German national status of chaplains in the *Bundeswehr* has clearly

---

[1029] *See* Art. 1 PA II.
[1030] *See* Stadlmeier, *supra* note 155, at 534.
[1031] *See* Art. 51 (2) PA I.
[1032] *See* Hiebel, *supra* note 17, at 536.
[1033] *See supra* note 846.
[1034] *See* Kussbach, *supra* note 144, at 386.
[1035] Art. 9 (1), 75 (1) PA I, Art. 2 (1) PA II.
[1036] *International Covenant on Civil and Political Rights, International Covenant on Economic, Social and Cultural Rights*, G.A. Res. 2200 A (XXI), U.N. GAOR, U.N. Doc A/6316 (December 16th, 1966), *see* BOTHE ET AL., *supra* note 801, at 630.
[1037] *See supra* at 104.

shown how the institution of military chaplaincy is a result of maintaining freedom of religion in a military environment.[1038] The current legal regime takes convergence into account up to a certain degree for instance when ministers of religion who are POW receive a treatment similar to that of detained chaplains – conditioned by a functional need of ministers.[1039] Another example is the free passage of religious personnel – both civilian ministers and military chaplains – into besieged places.[1040] As a result, both military and civilian ministers could serve enclosed civilians and military personnel.[1041] Positive improvements also came with the 1977 PAs and the protection of civilian religious personnel attached to combatants, but also led to inconsistencies as the case of military religious personnel attached to civilian medical transports or units has shown.[1042]

a. The limits of the attachment criterion

An important argument for a comprehensive protection is the attachment criterion. It fails specially in cases where coherence is most needed. The issue of the attachment criterion in the case of conflicts where almost always one party is not able to perform the official act of attachment has been raised.[1043] The limiting effect of the attachment criterion also becomes evident in the case of the levée en masse. Levée en masse is defined in Art. 13 (6) GC I as inhabitants of a non-occupied territory, who on the approach of the enemy, spontaneously take up arms to resist the invading forces. The levée en masse did not have time to form themselves into regular armed units. Its members carry arms openly and respect the laws and customs of war. In the case of the levée en masse, civilians due to their conduct become combatants. It has been concluded[1044] that the legal concept of Art. 37, 13 GC II is tåken into account when interpreting the term "chaplains attached to the armed forces" so that chaplaincy attached to the groups listed in Art. 13 GC I is protected. That would mean that also chaplaincy attached to the levée en masse is protected.

KOERBER follows a rather strict approach here: He totally excludes a chaplaincy attached to the levée en masse. The argument of the legal concept in Art. 37, 13 GC II could not be raised as the levée en masse would "in fact be hardly possible" in naval warfare. The parties to the convention did not intend to develop a legal concept in this regard.[1045] Certainly, the case of mass levies has

---

[1038] *See supra* at 49.
[1039] *See supra* at 88.
[1040] *See* Art. 15 (3) GC I, Art. 17 GC IV.
[1041] *See* PICTET, *supra* note 711, at 140-41.
[1042] *See supra* at 100.
[1043] *See supra* at 105.
[1044] *See supra* at 75.
[1045] *See* Koerber, *supra* note 565, at 421, *see also* Ipsen, *supra* note 586, at 80 (for the decreased significance of the levee en masse in modern warfare).

become rarely in the practice of modern warfare.[1046] But the explicit reference to Art. 13 GC II in Art. 37 GC II and the mention of the levée en masse in Art. 13 GC II prove KOERBER wrong. The legal concept of the mentioned stipulations sees the levée en masse as a combatant category and excludes its chaplains since they are non-combatants. KOERBER is certainly right that there are difficulties in practice as it comes to the requirement of attachment and the use of the protective sign. However, these are problems inherent in the idea of the levée en masse. Unlike the other groups of combatants, the levée en masse does not have a responsible leadership[1047] and thus no authority to confer attachment. Nevertheless, this cannot result in a deprivation of legal protection that is commonly accepted also for chaplains ministering to the levée en masse.[1048] As a unilateral act cannot be sufficient to fulfill the attachment criterion,[1049] a bond has to pre-exist between the civilians who form the levée en masse and the religious minister who claims protection as its chaplain. It has to be sufficient that the protected minister was assigned to the spiritual care of the civilians, for example as their pastor.

b. Coherence from the facts in times of WMD

In many instances, assistance to civilians and to military personnel cannot be distinguished. The example of besieged locations and similar rights of passage for both religious personnel and civilian ministers has been mentioned.[1050] Such an "indiscriminate" spiritual assistance may also be stimulated by modern means of warfare.[1051] The issue of Weapons of Mass Destructions (WMD) in this context was raised by STOCKS:[1052] Assuming a consensus that WMD incidents will occur, she demands a contribution "to the design and implementation of an effective, multi-disciplinary and cohesive intervention strategy" on the part of religious personnel and civilian ministers to meet a realization of WMD threat. Before, during and in the aftermath of a WMD incident, the unique expertise of chaplaincy in providing crisis spiritual assessment would be needed also for civilian casualties. The tasks of chaplains would not be to discount faith, belief systems and personal values as motivators in keeping functional forces and general populace functioning but to represent the spiritual aspect in the dialogue, design and deployment of appropriate strategic interventions. As WMD would indiscriminately affect military personnel and civilians alike, such intervention mechanisms had to exist in both military and civilian communities. So if one

[1046] *See* PICTET, *supra* note 530, at 67.
[1047] *See* BERBER, *supra* note 814, at 145.
[1048] *See* FRIEDRICH AUGUST FREIHERR VON DER HEYDTE, 2 VÖLKERRECHT 352 (1960).
[1049] *See supra* at 76.
[1050] *See supra* at 127.
[1051] *See also* NICOLAS, *supra* note 16, at 311.
[1052] *See* Stocks, *supra* note 495.

follows STOCKS' reasoning and predictions, the mingling of military and civilian religious activities that has been tried to avoid in order to assure best possible protection might well be induced by a factual incident. Actually, this has already happed after September 11th, 2001: U.S. military chaplains did not only provide ministry at the crash site at the Pentagon, but 8 to 10 chaplains also formed a Chaplain Emergency Response Team until late October 2001 at what later became known as Ground Zero in New York City. They serviced to victims and to both civilian and military rescue personnel.[1053]

c. The option of a uniform level of protection

Developments in the near future will certainly not produce the mere application of the norms protecting military chaplaincy on civilian religious activities – for two reasons: Firstly, religious activities in a civilian environment are far more varied than these of chaplaincy, a specialized ministry in the military. The difficulties to distinguish protected and not-protected activities would then increase and become unmanageable. The appropriate field to discuss this question is that of freedom of religion in human rights law and to elaborate on the specific consequences of the relevant stipulations in the situation of armed conflict. The protection of civilian ministry may receive constructive impulses from this field. Secondly, the simple merger of protection of civilian and military ministry could lead to an erosion of the level of protection reached for military chaplaincy. In practice, the belligerents will very unlikely be willing to apply the same level of protection to both civilian and military religious ministers and if they agreed to a uniform level of protection consequently lower the level of protection. Military chaplaincy deserves a different level of protection with protection clauses because its ministry in a military environment is likely to be targeted in combat. The primary protection for civilian ministry comes from its civilian character. Thus, the two ministries depart from different points of departure. This does not exclude that both may eventually arrive at the same degree of protection, but certainly not by way of merger.

[1053] *See* Barry Crane, *Navy Chaplains and RPs Respond to the Attack on America*, THE NAVY CHAPLAINCY, Special Edition (December 2001), at 3, 4, Wilbur C. Douglass, *Chaplain Emergency Response Team (CERT) - World Trade Center*, THE NAVY CHAPLAINCY, Special Edition (December 2001), at 11-17 *passim*, *see also* COUNCELL, *supra* note 491, Appendix G (for possible constitutional restraints of ministry to civilians by military chaplains during Disaster Relief Operations in the USA).

VIII. Protection of religious personnel – some problems in the German context

1. The German national status of chaplains and protection in IHL

a. Compatibility of the German model with IHL

BOCK[1054] developed on the basis of a sociological empirical study – that considered legal aspects very strongly – the profile of a fictitious standard model of chaplaincy: Chaplaincy is admitted and structurally integrated in the armed forces with uniform and military rank for chaplains; it is organized by the state and religious personnel are subordinate to military superiors. Their specific religious mission is taken into consideration when incompatible assignments are excluded from their duties and autonomy in doctrinal matters is maintained on a statutory basis. The tasks of chaplains exceed the scope of individual pastoral care and also encompass the propagation of interdenominational socially integrative values. This "civil religion" dimension also reflects itself in ethical instructions taught by chaplains in an official military framework and as part of the soldiers' official duty roster. There is at least one chaplain on battalion level. Chaplaincy's service is uncontroversial in society. As has been discussed earlier, the German model differs in a number of points from this standard model.[1055] But the standard model makes it even clearer that chaplains are – in different forms – part of the armed forces. Is the German model with its strong civilian emphasis then at all compatible with the concept of chaplaincy under the GCs?

IHL cannot follow national peculiarities into its details. Instead, it establishes categories wide enough to cover the various forms that evolve around the world. One of them is the non-combatant class of military chaplains.[1056] HEYDTE names them members of the *passiver Kriegsstand* (passive military class)[1057]; LAUTERPACHT considers them "to belong indirectly to the Armed Forces".[1058] Besides these attempts of categorization, they are non-combatants and as chaplains subject to a further protection under international law.[1059] Unlike captured, wounded sick and shipwrecked soldiers who are combatants placed *hors de combat*, chaplains enjoy general immunity.[1060]

STADLMEIER argues that the 1906 and 1929 versions of the Red Cross Convention based on the assumption that chaplains were integrated in the military

---

[1054] *See* BOCK, *supra* note 795, at 306.
[1055] *See id.* at 314.
[1056] *But see* Elßner, *supra* note 800, at 266 (from a very German perspective holding that chaplains terminologically cannot be considered non-combatants but non-fighters).
[1057] *See* HEYDTE, *supra* note 1048, at 353.
[1058] HERSCH LAUTERPACHT, 2 INTERNATIONAL LAW 255 (7th ed. 1952).
[1059] *See also* Art. 43 (2) PA I.
[1060] *See also* GREEN, *supra* note 133, at 88.

structure as these documents spoke of chaplains' salaries according to rank.[1061]This argument can be refuted as the same documents speak about chaplains who do not have a military uniform.[1062] Moreover, as has been discussed earlier with the example of Bavaria, chaplaincies not integrated into the armed forces did exist at the time of the 1906 revision.[1063] STADLMEIER departing from an incorrect conclusion does not present the most convincing arguments for a broad understanding of chaplaincy without the restriction of a military national status:[1064] Art. 13 (4) GC I spoke of a service to civilians accompanying the armed forces and would speak against a narrow interpretation of chaplaincy. However, KOERBER presented the opposing argument with regard to the applicability of Art. 13 GC I on chaplaincy and also with regard to military chaplains servicing civilians of the entourage.[1065] STADLMEIER then continues and deduces a broad understanding of chaplaincy from Art. 36 GC III that grants prerogatives to POW ministers of religion who have not officiated as chaplains. The existence of a combatant class of religious ministers that enjoys privileges in captivity points out the origin of protection in freedom of religion but does not necessarily expose the understanding of chaplaincy that these norms base upon. In spite of these considerations, the strongest argument for a concept of chaplains notwithstanding their national status as civilians or military is the wording of Art. 24 GC I that speaks of "chaplains attached to the armed forces". Not the form of their integration into the armed forces but their exclusive engagement in religious duties and the attachment is the decisive distinction.[1066] Authorization to wear the armlet and the issuance of the identity card are exterior signs of their status but not constitutive.[1067]

RAUSCH interprets the German concept of cooperation between military commanders and chaplains in the *Bundeswehr* (*Zuordnung auf Zusammenarbeit*) as not fulfilling the internal disciplinary system that is a requirement for combatant status.[1068] Then, German chaplains would in any case be civilian non-combatants and protected accordingly. This idea is misleading because the hypothetical that chaplains could be considered combatants if they did not have their status under IHL does not play a role for the protection. Constitutive is only the attachment to the armed forces – regardless of the form of integration or form of disciplinary order.

[1061] *See* Stadlmeier, *supra* note 155, at 524.
[1062] *See supra* note 184.
[1063] *See supra* at 91.
[1064] *See* Stadlmeier, *supra* note 155, at 525.
[1065] *See supra* at 75.
[1066] *See* Rabus, *supra* note 575, 369.
[1067] *See* Bock, *supra* note 820, at 184, *see also* COMMENTARY ON THE ADDITIONAL PROTOCOLS, *supra* note 178, No. 4842 at 1440, *but see* O'BRIEN, *supra* note 154, at D2.
[1068] *See* Rausch, *supra* note 139, at 30.

The definitions of chaplains and religious personnel in contemporary international humanitarian law do not dictate a specific legal form for the national status of military chaplains.[1069] The nations have a freedom to develop different forms.[1070] Chaplains may be either military or civilian persons. This seems to be commonly accepted in legal discipline. The protection clause for civilian religious personnel in PA I[1071] is with regard to military chaplains who are not members of the military declaratory[1072] and constitutive only for personnel under the extended scope of the PA I definition. In consequence, the German model of civilian military chaplains is compatible with the concept of chaplains under IHL.

b. Attachment and exclusivity in national law – a public law relationship?

The two constitutive requirements of protection under the GCs – attachment and exclusivity – imply an immanent danger of interference in church affairs by the state because the exercise of a ministry – and its possible exclusivity – is an internal church matter. The attachment on the other hand can only be induced by a state act. But this danger does not necessarily have to materialize if both parts – church and state – succeed in creating a partnership[1073] for this matter. In such a dialogue relationship, religious communities must be willing to design their laws in a way that the exclusivity requirement can be met and the attachment practice of the state has to leave latitude to the religious communities in choosing personnel. Both sides have to contribute in designing rules that meet the necessities of that particular situation.

A former version of the *Bundeswehr* Joint Service Regulation on the status of chaplains in humanitarian law (ZDv 15/15) considered in its No. 12 the integration of chaplains into the armed forces to be based on national public law and the decision of the competent military authority constitutive for the status under IHL.[1074] It seems to have been a long-standing German policy that a public law legal relationship is constitutive for the protection of chaplains under IHL and that this public law relationship is based on the civil servant status of chap-

---

[1069] *See* COMMENTARY ON THE ADDITIONAL PROTOCOLS, *supra* note 178, No. 362 at 127, NICOLAS, *supra* note 16, at 104, Rausch, *supra* note 139, at 36, O'BRIEN, *supra* note 154, at D1, *see also* BOTHE ET AL., *supra* note 801, at 126 n.2 (religious personnel to be military as a rule), Ipsen, *supra* note 586, at 89 (religious personnel normally not members of the armed forces), Elßner, *supra* note 800, at 266 (not members of the armed forces).

[1070] *See* Witte, *supra* note 593, at 3.

[1071] *See supra* note 823.

[1072] *See* MARCHEGGIANO, *supra* note 107, at 119-120.

[1073] *See also* NICOLAS, *supra* note 16, at 314.

[1074] *See also* Schollmeyer, *supra* note 547, at 61.

lains.[1075] In a way, it seems clear that the attachment to the armed forces results in a form of public law relationship. However, it must be stressed in this context that German national law only known a *numerus clausus* of possible public law employments, civil servantship is amongst them. The question is whether a chaplain could be considered attached even though his employment is not governed by a form in this *numerus clausus*. It is helpful to emphasize here the character of the attachment as a sovereign act, an official state act.[1076] This may result in a public law relationship, on the other hand the national classification does not play a role as long as the attachment requirement is met.[1077] The public law foundation of chaplains' attachment was not repeated in service regulations that succeeded this Joint Service Regulation. This caused questions for legal basis of the public law relationship requirement in literature.[1078] Such statements should rather be seen in connection with the discussions on the nature of chaplains' status after the reunification in the protestant church branches of the acceding *Länder* of eastern Germany. These discussions were also rather illustrative with regard to possible forms of chaplains' employment without a public law relationship and stimulated most of the reflections in Germany on protection of religious personnel in the past decade.

Since there had been no military chaplaincy in the National People's Army of the German Democratic Republic,[1079] catholic chaplaincy applied the existing legal regime for its ministry in the five eastern *Länder* after reunification in 1990.[1080] The eastern branches of the protestant church, however, rejected to take over the Military Chaplaincy Agreement. Even though the German model of military chaplaincy is adjusted to a high level of independence, the structural organization of this independence was questioned. On the background of their pacific tradition and their experiences with a secular state, the eastern protestant church branches considered the existing regime for military chaplaincy to be too close to state activities and to endanger the freedom of religious teaching and pastoral care. The structure of chaplaincy would have to reflect that the armed

---

[1075] *See* PETER H. BLASCHKE & HARALD OBERHEM, BUNDESWEHR UND KIRCHEN 151 (1985), Schollmeyer, *supra* note 547, at 61, Heike Schmoll, *Zuviel Skepsis gegenüber dem Staat*, FRANKFURTER ALLGEMEINE ZEITUNG, July 20th, 1994, at 12, *see also* Reinhard Gramm, *Zur Lage der evangelischen Militärseesorge*, 23 ESSENER GESPRÄCHE ZUM THEMA STAAT UND KIRCHE 146, 148 (Heiner Marré & Johannes Stüting eds., 1989) (appearently taking this conclusion for granted).

[1076] *See supra* note 590, *see also* Koerber, *supra* note 565, at 418.

[1077] *See* Stadlmeier, *supra* note 155, at 525.

[1078] *See* Rausch, *supra* note 139, at 29, Ennuschat, *supra* note 421, at 427.

[1079] *See* BLEESE, *supra* note 39, at 394-409.

[1080] *See* Alfred E. Hierold, *Die Militärseelsorge in den neuen Bundesländern aus katholischer Sicht*, *in* KIRCHLICHER AUFTRAG UND POLITISCHE FRIEDENSGESTALTUNG 221, 221-227 (Alfred E. Hierold et al. eds. 1995).

forces are only the location of a special ministry but not its patrons.[1081] The first interim solution in 1991 was an unsatisfactory visitor status for chaplains set unilaterally by the Ministry of Defense: They had access to the barracks, but were not integrated in the infrastructure or the stream of information of the armed forces. They could not accompany troops on exercises or maneuvers.

Deliberations in the synod of the Evangelical Church in Germany (EKD) resulted in a decision to change the legal status of chaplains so that they would remain employees of their church instead of becoming civil servants. It was demanded to adapt the Military Chaplaincy Agreement accordingly. The German Federal Government then led by Chancellor HELMUT KOHL rejected this request for an adaptation in 1995 because the government believed that the existing legal regime provided optimal pastoral care to the soldiers and assured parity between catholic and protestant chaplaincy. The government, nonetheless, offered a temporary solution in the form of an administrative interim agreement that would not need the parliamentary ratification procedure. As a result of such an interim agreement concluded in June 1996 between the Evangelical Church in Germany (EKD) and the Ministry of Defense,[1082] chaplains of the eastern protestant churches were not civil servants like their western colleagues but employees of the Evangelical Church in Germany (EKD) that on its part got refunded by the federal budget but without a contribution to the chaplains' pensions. Chaplains under the interim agreement were admitted to *Bundeswehr* premises and could use its infrastructure.[1083] They had to be willing to accompany troops to military training areas and in deployment abroad.[1084] This obligation was a novelty of the interim agreement and had not been included in the prior legal regime.[1085] The discussions of the early 1990s subsided. The interim agreement expired in 2003. Since 2004, the Military Chaplaincy Agreement is applied in all parts of Germany. A joint memorandum of the protestant chaplaincy and the Ministry of Defense signed in June 2002 paved the way for this decision. That document clarifies the interpretation of the Military Chaplaincy Agreement in four points: (1) As a policy, more part-time chaplains will be assigned to military chaplaincy. They do not have a civil servant status but remain employees of the civilian churches. Pastoral care for military personnel only forms part of their duties. This form of chaplains' status so far has only been applied for smaller posts.[1086]

[1081] *See* Kruk, *supra* note 428, at 8.

[1082] *See* 1996 MINISTERIALBLATT DES BUNDESMINISTERIUMS DER VERTEIDIGUNG 281.

[1083] *See* Kruk, *supra* note 428, at 11-12.

[1084] *See* Art. 4 (2), 2nd sentence of the interim Agreement.

[1085] *See* Kruk, *supra* note 428, at 21.

[1086] *See* ZDv 66/1, *supra* note 385, No. 11 at 66, *but see* the very broad formulation in Military Chaplaincy Agreement, *supra* note 390, Art. 2 (2), *see also* Pontifical Statutes, *supra* note 394, Art. 18.

(2) Military chaplains may in exceptional cases be employees and not civil servants. (3) Senior positions in the military chaplaincy may be assigned temporarily and not solely to chaplains who as civil servants are appointed for life tenure. (4) The general dean as the head of the protestant church office - which is the equivalent of the military vicar general as the head of the catholic military bishop's office – does not have to be a theologian but may well be a lawyer.

The cosmetic nature of these changes is evident. Options *secundum legem* and *praeter legem* are formulated, and policy decisions, but not substantive changes, expressed. Besides, such substantive changes would have needed a parliamentary ratification procedure.[1087] This character is also underlined by an adaptation of the protestant church law on military chaplaincy – a merely religious law – that changed the terminology from "military chaplaincy" to "chaplaincy in the *Bundeswehr* ". Both acts are rather symbolic concessions to the pacific sensitivities in the eastern church branches, but mark the end of the dispute on military chaplaincy there as the independence of military chaplaincy under the legal regime of the Military Chaplaincy Agreement is recognized.

The dispute went through various stages. An emphasis on part-time chaplains stronger integrated into civilian church structures than into military structures and a status other than the public law status of civil servant were *desiderata* of the protestant church. Both aspects developed through the dispute and were taken into account by the joint memorandum. Along this process, possible solutions were always tested regarding their compatibility with protection under IHL. Along these tests, it became clear that a protection was granted regardless of a civil servant status because the attachment criterion could be met without the public law employment as civil servants.[1088]

c. Auxiliary religious personnel in Germany – the attachment criterion

The increasing shortage of clergy does not pass by the catholic military ordinariate. This reality coupled with structural reforms in the military that resulted in a reduced number of military posts. Now, the barracks belonging to one military parish are scattered around a larger territory. These developments attributed a growing importance to auxiliary religious personnel. Chaplaincy in Germany knows two sorts of auxiliary personnel: Parochial helpers (*Pfarrhelfer*) are mostly assigned administrative and supportive tasks. They are employees of the Federal Government (*Angestellte nach Bundesangestelltentarifvertrag*). They are of the same confession as the confession of the chaplaincy they are assigned. Usually, one parochial helper is assigned to each chaplain who is the superior of

---

[1087] *See also* INES-JACQUELINE WERKNER, SOLDATENSEELSORGE VERSUS MILITÄRSEELSORGE 134-38 (2001) (for the disputed question whether the framework agreement needed a ratification).

[1088] *See id.* at 237.

the parochial helper.[1089] RIEM compares parochial helpers with sacristans in civilian parishes.[1090] Canonically, the status of parochial helpers is considered a form of lay office in particular law according to can. 145, 228 § 1, 231 § 2 CIC.[1091] Pastoral assistants (*Pastoralreferenten*) as the second type of auxiliary personnel take particularly care of pastoral affairs. None of these auxiliary personnel is currently deployed on missions abroad. As support staff on missions, chaplains only have enlisted personnel as assigned drivers.

SEIBT mentions deacons as an example for auxiliary religious personnel. This is an incorrect example.[1092] Certainly, for deacons the aspect of service is underlined in their ministry. However, their ministry is original and not dependant. These are ecclesiological considerations.[1093] Decisive is again that deacons – at least those who do not have a full-time occupation outside of ministry – are devoted exclusively to the exercise of their ministry. Thus, also deacons may be attached as chaplains and then are fully protected.

The employment of pastoral assistants is governed by the norms of the German Bishops' Conference on pastoral assistants and was regulated 1987 for the catholic military chaplaincy in an agreement between the German Minister of Defense and the catholic military ordinary – with consent of the Holy See.[1094] In this document, the task of pastoral assistants is described as to stimulate within the parish "a Christian testimony in family, church and world." (Art. 2) They have a full university education in theology and furthermore passed a probation exam in a civilian German diocese.

The pastoral assistant is assigned to a military chaplain who is his superior. Like most chaplains, pastoral assistants serve in the military chaplaincy only temporary, usually for five to eight years. If a pastoral assistant were an employee of the Federal Government during this time, this would bring along legal difficulties under the current collective employment agreement (*Bundesangestelltentarifvertrag*) that tries to avoid long temporary employments. During

---

[1089] *See Richtlinien für die Pfarrhelfer in der Militärseelsorge*, Decree of the Federal Ministry of Defense, VR I 4 – Az. 36-25 (September 17th, 1973) in DOKUMENTATION ZUR KATHOLISCHEN UND EVANGELISCHEN MILITÄRSEELSORGE 86 (7th ed. 2002) (for the detailed description of the tasks of parochial helpers).

[1090] *See* RIEHM, *supra* note 432, at 3.

[1091] *See* Sabine Demel, *Pfarrhelfer*, *in* 8 LEXIKON FÜR THEOLOGIE UND KIRCHE col. 175 (Walter Kasper ed., 3rd ed. 1999).

[1092] *See* SEIBT, *supra* note 553, *see also* Kussbach, *supra* note 144, at 389-90 (for a correct interpretation), Diteweg, *supra* note 369, at 358 (for the difference in chaplain in the canonical sense and in common use).

[1093] *See also* Diteweg, *supra* note 369 (for permanent deacons in the practice of the U.S. Archdiocese for Military Service).

[1094] *See* 1987 MINISTERIALBLATT DES BUNDESMINISTERIUMS DER VERTEIDIGUNG 170-172, *see also* Pontifical Statutes, *supra* note 394, Art. 20 (confirming this practice).

the time of their assignment with military chaplaincy, pastoral assistants remain legally employed with the civilian diocese they came from. The diocese on its part is reimbursed from the budget of the Ministry of Defense. Agreements with the catholic military bishop's office regarding the specific duties of military chaplaincy are only additional and not original. Thus, there is no employment relationship between a pastoral assistant and the state.[1095] But in exercise of their functions, pastoral assistants have rights fairly similar to that of chaplains: They have access to military installations and use the offices and resources of the chaplaincy. The emphasis of their ministry is laid on pastoral care in military schools and academies as well as military hospitals. In practice, pastoral assistants are very much involved in the teaching of *Lebenskundlicher Unterricht.*[1096]

It is particularly KOERBER who – almost forty years ago – considers the difference between laypeople and persons authorized by an act of installation as a line of distinction in IHL protection.[1097] Then, pastoral assistants could never claim protection under IHL because in the ecclesiastical sense, they remain laypeople. But this point of view does not convince. KOERBER is too much focused on a clerical state and the sacramental act of creating it. Even contemporary commentators of the first Red Cross Convention in 1864 considered as chaplains everyone who is charged with religious assistance to soldiers, be it an ecclesiastic or a layman.[1098] Protection in armed conflict is not dependent on consecration, ordination, election, anointment or another ceremonial transfer of authority since the different religions have very different steps of initiation into a leadership class.[1099] Key criterion for protection is the exclusive dedication of the person to spiritual assistance and the attachment. RIEM holds that the GCs presuppose the qualifications of a professional theologian.[1100] This criterion is certainly met by pastoral assistants. However, some sort of faculty by a religious authority will in many cases be a prerequisite for the attachment in the particular setting of church and state but remains a merely internal religious affair. In some cases, Germany is amongst them, it may even be the religious authority that decides

---

[1095] *See* Rudolf Seiler, *§ 68 Seelsorge in Bundeswehr und Bundesgrenzschutz*, *in* 2 HANDBUCH DES STAATSKIRCHENRECHTS DER BUNDESREPUBLIK DEUTSCHLAND 961, 975 (Joseph Listl ed. 1995).

[1096] *See* Carlheinz Borchers, *Rechtliche Grundlagen der Militärseelsorge und ihre Bewährung in der Praxis*, *in* KIRCHLICHER AUFTRAG UND POLITISCHE FRIEDENSGESTALTUNG 201 (Alfred Hierold et al. eds. 1995).

[1097] *See* Koerber, *supra* note 565, at 418.

[1098] *See* NICOLAS, *supra* note 16, at 91, *see also* KIMMINICH, *supra* note 297, at 129 (for laypeople to be covered by the PA I definition of religious personnel).

[1099] *See* O'BRIEN, *supra* note 154, at D3, Stadlmeier, *supra* note 155, at 530, *see also* FEDERAL POLITICAL DEPARTMENT, *supra* note 217, at 439 (scope of conventions for not ordained ministers of religion), *but see* Elßner, *supra* note 800, at 275 n. 55 (still following a narrow interpretation presupposing an ordination).

[1100] *See* RIEHM, *supra* note 432, at 1.

who is presented for the attachment. But these are preliminary steps for the attachment that itself is solely decisive. Maybe the parallel to the medical personnel can be illustrative here: IHL does not determine what kind of education or license medical personnel must possess in order to be protected.

Undoubtedly, the employment of pastoral assistants is not based on genuine German public law as for instance the employment of chaplains as civil servants is. However, there is an indirect link to the domain of public law: The agreement between the Minister of Defense and the military ordinary, which is the basis for pastoral assistants' activities in the armed forces, is not a public law contract in the technical sense but an agreement between two juridical persons of public law and certainly itself of public law nature. It would be worth some reflections whether this agreement would be sufficient to consider pastoral assistants attached to the armed forces as required by IHL. The GCs do not dictate an attachment as public law relationship. For an official act constituting the attachment, it is sufficient that the state communicates in an official manner its intent to consider the personnel in question chaplains to its armed forces. Then, the attachment for civilian religious personnel must not necessarily be carried out in the form of the civil servant status as long as legal certainty is formally and officially assured.[1101] To assure this certainty, it would be favorable to supplement the existing agreement on pastoral assistants with an attachment clause. But generally speaking, the agreement could provide the attachment. Then, pastoral assistants could serve as chaplains and be protected under the GCs.[1102] Right now, their non-public law status is also seen as an obstacle for the deployment of pastoral assistants on missions abroad. Only ordained religious personnel are currently deployed abroad.

Auxiliary religious personnel in armed conflict according to the German Manual have the status of soldiers, are combatants and thus not protected by the GCs.[1103] This view was supported by the ICRC in a correspondence with the German government in 1963.[1104] Only parochial helpers were mentioned by way of example, as pastoral assistants were not yet employed for military chaplaincy when these norms were drafted. Auxiliary religious personnel are not entitled to wear the distinctive emblem.[1105] SCHLÖGEL criticizes this statement as illegitimate simplification since the changing terminology in the different conventions

---

1101 *See also* Witte, *supra* note 593 (the German Foreign Office comes to a similar result).

1102 *See also* Bernhard Pasche, *Reflections on the Swiss Army Chaplaincy in 1994*, 5 EUROPEAN CHAPLAINCY YEARBOOK 130, 131 (1995) (for the practice in Switzerland to have lay pastoral assistants in the rank of a captain amongst its militia chaplains.).

1103 *See* Rabus, *supra* note 575, No. 804 at 370.

1104 *See* RIEHM, *supra* note 432, at 1.

1105 *See* BLASCHKE/OBERHEM, *supra* note 1075, at 151.

also allows to cover auxiliary religious personnel.[1106] RAUSCH even goes as far as to say that the unclear terminology of the GCs has been helpful because it allowed to cover auxiliary religious personnel and the questions by the definition of religious personnel in PA I would have been avoided if the practice of the Geneva Conventions had been continued.[1107] WITTE very generally wants to examine the question further whether a rephrased job description could lead to the assumption to consider parochial helpers as chaplains.[1108] This is difficult as the GCs are reluctant to grant protection to categories of spiritual assistance personnel other than these mentioned.[1109] The reluctance of the German Humanitarian Law in Armed Conflicts Manual to state a broad scope of protection could be understood on the background of the intent to narrow the field of protection in order not to jeopardize it by a too extensive interpretation.[1110] The example of Israel, where the search for and burials of bodies are carried out by religious burial societies like the Jewish Chevra Kadisha who though certainly auxiliary in their nature could claim protection as religious personnel shows how far such claims could go. Effects of such a broad interpretation can be predicted by the comparison with auxiliary medical personnel and the development of its protection: They were also not protected in the first Red Cross Convention. Stretcher-bearers and ambulance drivers could only after the second revision in 1929 claim protection.[1111] In the 1949 revision, these auxiliary personnel again lost its preferential detainee status and are now POW. They may, however, be employed on their medical duties as far as the need arises.[1112] This reversal is caused by the understanding that auxiliary medical personnel are primarily combatant troops and only secondarily assigned to medical duties.[1113] But the mention of stretcher-bearers and ambulance drivers underlines that the parallelism of auxiliary medical personnel is only justified with regard to parochial helpers as the supportive aspect prevails with both groups and the combatant character is still strong. In addition, even for parochial helpers, protection is not entirely waived.[1114] It is uncontested that the chaplain cannot exercise his functions without a minimum of personnel and material aid.[1115] This is why it is consistent with

---

1106 *See* Schlögel, *supra* note 38, at 272 n.9.
1107 *See* Rausch, *supra* note 139, at 30.
1108 *See* Witte, *supra* note 593.
1109 *See* Hiebel, *supra* note 180, at 16.
1110 *See* RIEHM, *supra* note 432, at 2.
1111 *See* Watson, *supra* note 7, at 42.
1112 *See* Art. 29 GC I, *see also* Art. 32 GC III.
1113 *See* Watson, *supra* note 7, at 45.
1114 *But see* Rausch, *supra* note 139, at 35.
1115 *See* RIEHM, *supra* note 432, at 2.

the spirit of the GCs to grant parochial helpers as far as possible protection and respect.[1116]

Relevant regulations in the U.S. Armed Forces provide a combatant status for the enlisted chaplain assistant or religious program specialist and entrust him with the task to provide for the safety and security for the combat chaplain.[1117] As a matter of policy, the U.S. Archdiocese for Military Services as catholic endorsing agency only certifies ordained persons to the military chaplaincy.[1118]

d. Part-time religious personnel in Germany – the exclusivity criterion

The example of pastoral assistants may also serve to illustrate the exclusivity requirement. They are assigned for some years to military chaplaincy. IHL does not prohibit the temporary assignment of laymen for religious purposes.[1119] And pastoral assistants are exclusively devoted to ministry. This becomes clear in comparison with lay preachers who have a full-time occupation other than their ministry. Taking lay preachers as an example of a non-exclusive dedication for ministry, the diplomatic conference 1974-1977 did not consider them covered by the PA I definition of religious personnel.[1120]

Full time military chaplains with the *Bundeswehr* are civilian non-combatants according to the GCs. They do not become soldiers in the state of defense. They retain their double status of ministers and civil servants. Their status is without regard to the dress their wear and recognizable by the use of the distinctive emblem and the identity card. Part-time military chaplains with a private law relationship to the armed forces enjoy the protection of the GC IV only.[1121] They may for instance not be detained for pastoral care to their own forces. *Rausch* questions whether this interpretation reflects the present state of the law and thus the legitimacy of a distinction between part-time and full time chaplains as used by German military regulations.[1122] Underlining that PA I differentiates into permanent and temporary religious personnel and grants both the same protection,[1123] he argues furthermore that the requirement of exclusive engagement of medical staff in Art. 24 GC I in the same stipulation is not repeated as a characteristic for the attachment of chaplains.[1124] The ratio of the norm supports

---

[1116] *See supra* note 640.

[1117] *See* U.S. MARINE CORPS, *supra* note 182, No. 1006 c, HEADQUARTERS DEPARTMENT OF THE ARMY, FIELD MANUAL NO. 1-05, RELIGIOUS SUPPORT (April 18th, 2003) § 1-8, Odom, *supra* note 7, at 24-25.

[1118] *See* Diteweg, *supra* note 369, at 361.

[1119] *See* Art. 8 d PA I, *see also* COMMENTARY ON THE ADDITIONAL PROTOCOLS, *supra* note 178, No. 367 at 128.

[1120] *See supra* note 808.

[1121] *See* Rabus, *supra* note 575, No. 803 at 370, BLASCHKE/OBERHEM, *supra* note 1075, at 152.

[1122] *See* Rausch, *supra* note 139, at 30.

[1123] *See supra* at 99.

[1124] *See* Rausch, *supra* note 139, at 38-39 n.37.

RAUSCH in the sense that exclusivity for chaplains could only mean an exclusive devotion for the pastoral care and not an exclusive attachment. A delegate of the diplomatic conference 1974-1977 even expressed the opinion that the temporary assignment of religious personnel has no effect on the type of status of religious personnel that, by its very nature, is permanent.[1125] In a parallel case, the treatment of civilians in a military medical facility does not lead to a change in the level of protection of the facility.[1126] Even though military chaplaincy is part of a categorical pastoral care in the armed forces, its work is not exclusively aimed at soldiers but also at their family and persons associated with the military. On the other hand, an applicable criterion must exist to distinguish the different levels of protection for ministers of religion in the GCs: religious personnel attached to the armed forces, ministers of religion who are combatants or POW[1127] and merely civilian religious ministers. Thus, a difference exists between temporary exclusive attachment as chaplains that is protected and part-time non-exclusive attachment. The protestant approach of rooting military chaplaincy in the civilian churches with the means of part-time employment mixes – certainly on purpose – the civilian and military sphere but carries at least the potential to conflict with the concept of IHL that is based on the distinction of military and civilian ministry.

The International Law Department of the German Foreign Office proposed a solution that would take into account the problem of distinction. Part-time chaplains would be temporarily, but exclusively assigned to a unit in deployment on missions abroad or in a state of defense. To avoid a lack of clarity, the dedication of a non-permanent chaplain should not change during one and the same military operation.[1128] A similar approach is followed for reserve chaplains worldwide and in the chaplaincy of the Swiss Army. In its militia structure, persons who usually serve as civilian ministers become chaplains while on active duty during exercises and in case of armed conflict.

2. The use of arms by chaplains

Even though *Vaticanum II* expressed its admiration for those who forgo the use of violence to vindicate their rights,[1129] the scope of the question whether chaplains may use arms in armed conflict is not limited to the area of religious doctrine. Art. 22 GC I states that a medical unit or establishment is not deprived of its protection if its personnel are armed and use the arms to defend themselves

---

[1125] *See* COMMENTARY ON THE ADDITIONAL PROTOCOLS, *supra* note 178, No. 367 at 128.

[1126] *See* Art. 22 (5) GC I.

[1127] *See* Art. 36 GC III.

[1128] *See* Witte, *supra* note 593.

[1129] *See* PASTORAL CONSTITUTION ON THE CHURCH IN THE MODERN WORLD "GAUDIUM ET SPES", *supra* note 242, No. 78, *see* CATECHISM OF THE CATHOLIC CHURCH, *supra* note 243, No. 2306.

or the wounded and sick in their charge. A similar provision is found in Art. 35 GC II. It is important to note that the conventions neither prohibit nor permit the bearing of arms but for medical personnel leave this question to the discretion of the parties and only limit the use of arms to self-defense.[1130]

There is no specific mention on the use of arms by religious personnel. But the parallelism of protection for medical personnel and religious personnel is used as an argument that the possession of arms and their use in self-defense by chaplains does not deprive them of their status.[1131] It seems as if this is an example of a stipulation on medical personnel that is applicable for chaplains without special reference.[1132] SCHOLLMEYER deduces this conclusion from the generally recognized legal principle of self-defense and its notion that the rightful may resist against the wrongful that is also reflected in Art. 22 GC I.[1133] This reasoning is supported by Art. 35 GC II that allows arms for crews of hospital ships – this includes chaplains, too. It must be stressed that arms may only be used to repel attacks violating international law but not to prevent capture. The protection accorded to chaplains definitely ceases if they use the arms that they carry for any other purpose than that of self-defense or the defense of protected persons.[1134] As the type of weapon they may carry is not determined, this purpose has to be taken into account and will only allow to carry individual light weapons.[1135] If on the other hand a military authority requires religious personnel to bear arms that are consistent with non-combatant use, the legal instruments discussed are interpreted to not give the right to object to the order.[1136]

It should, nonetheless be mentioned that there are strong voices who hold that the regulations about arming and the right of self-defense applicable for medical personnel do not apply to religious personnel.[1137] This argument is supported by the practice of the Red Cross Conventions that since the 1906 revision granted the right to bear arms exclusively to medical and not to religious personnel. The right to bear arms in the present-day legal regime is regulated in chapter III GC I that deals with medical units and establishment whereas the protection of chaplains and medical personnel with its similarities is dealt with in chapter IV GC I

1130 *See* Watson, *supra* note 7, at 46.

1131 *See* U.S. MARINE CORPS, *supra* note 182, No. 1004 f, Hiebel, *supra* note 180, at 26, GREEN, *supra* note 133, at 105, Stadlmeier, *supra* note 155, at 529, BERBER, *supra* note 814, at 140, Koerber, *supra* note 565, at 425, Rabus, *supra* note 575, No. 817 at 372, BLASCHKE/OBERHEM, *supra* note 1075, at 151.

1132 *See supra* note 547.

1133 *See* Schollmeyer, *supra* note 547, at 62.

1134 *See* PICTET, *supra* note 132, at 203, Rabus, *supra* note 575, No. 818 at 372.

1135 *See* DRAPER, *supra* note 7, at 195, Schollmeyer, *supra* note 547, at 63.

1136 *See* O'BRIEN, *supra* note 154, at O4.

1137 *See* Ipsen, *supra* note 586, at 92, Rausch, *supra* note 139, at 31, Rausch, *supra* note 7, at 381 n.16.

on personnel. Simply taking the provision of one chapter from its context and applying it in the different context of another chapter would be unsystematic. A right of religious personnel to defend themselves against attacks that contravene international law could then only be based on the principle of self-defense – if the personnel are "willing and able to do so".[1138] In this result, both approaches agree.

The German Ministry of Defense allows in its General Administration Directive annexed to the Federal Arms Act[1139] to its civil servants to bear arms only in certain cases, e.g. if they are "endangered because of their official tasks" (§ 2 No. 4). In this case, they would need a special permission by the competent authority. This stipulation has so far not been applied to military chaplains. Their security is ensured by the troops. Accordingly, the manuals and the literature only note that "[i]n the Federal Republic of Germany chaplains may not be armed".[1140] In the practice of operation, this may turn into an identification of the chaplain from the distance by the fact that he is not armed[1141] or be a visible feature that distinguishes chaplains in battlefield environment.[1142] In historic instances, the fact of being unarmed became an alibi to cover taking over combat command in emergency situations that was violating non-combatant status.[1143] German chaplains, however, have a passive knowledge about arms and are for instance able to secure a weapon.

The German Humanitarian Law in Armed Conflicts Manual presupposes such a national authorization for the handling of firearms for chaplains to be allowed to bear and use small arms under international law.[1144] Then, a chaplain who bears an arm on duty that he is e.g. authorized to possess privately would not only be considered a dereliction of duty but also result in a loss of his status as non-combatant. IPSEN, the commentator of this manual passage, puts things straight as he considers the norms on the national level to implement the general authorization in international law.[1145] Thus, the right to bear arms for self-defense of chaplains in international law is not conditioned by the national authorization.

[1138] Ipsen, *supra* note 586, at 92, *see also* Odom, *supra* note 7, at 21.

[1139] *See* 1989 MINISTERIALBLATT DES BUNDESMINISTERIUMS DER VERTEIDIGUNG 174.

[1140] Rabus, *supra* note 575, No. 820 at 372, *see* Robrahn, *supra* 425, at 15, *see also* HEADQUARTERS DEPARTMENT OF THE ARMY, *supra* note 1117, § 1-7, *see* U.S. MARINE CORPS, *supra* note 182, No. 1004 f, Odom, *supra* note 7, at 19 (U.S. chaplains are not armed, too).

[1141] *See* Rausch, *supra* note 478, at 311.

[1142] *See* Odom, *supra* note 7, at 19.

[1143] *See* Wilkinson, *supra* note 309, at 253.

[1144] *See* Ipsen, *supra* note 586, at No. 315 at 90.

[1145] *See id.* at 91.

3. Chaplaincy to atheists?

So far, this monograph discussed issues of personnel of a religious creed. But in reality, many servicemen and -women do not claim a religious affiliation. These questions have become particularly topical after German reunification in 1990. German reunification had not only brought about a significant reduction of the number of German forces but also changed the social structure in the armed forces. Many of the young men and meanwhile also women who serve in the *Bundeswehr* come from the five eastern *Länder* (states) that acceded to the Federal Republic. They were raised in a country with a secular state ideology or lived in the largely secularized eastern *Länder*; for many of them the encounter with military chaplaincy is the first encounter with religious matters at all. This phenomenon grouped up with existing secular tendencies in the west and affected the armed forces as it affected other areas of society. HIEBEL regrets that atheists receive few guaranties in the convention documents and proves that freedom of religion in the GCs is understood in its positive aspect, as freedom of religious convictions and practices.[1146] SCHLÖGEL opposes this criticism strongly with "limits that cannot be exceeded". Though freedom of conviction was guaranteed in international law, applying the protection of spiritual assistance in armed conflict to atheists would be in contradiction to the unique nature of religion and pastoral care. It would amount to a paradox to apply the protection of spiritual assistance on opponents of religion.[1147] Now, this line of argumentation can be opposed from many points of views. As a Christian, one could argue with the Apostle PAUL that we are all sinners and all in need of redemption[1148] – anytime, anywhere. This is a good argument for mission, but cannot be sufficient to justify pastoral care to non-believers in international law. From another approach, it seems questionable at least from a present-day point of view to attribute to atheists a militancy against religion as SCHLÖGEL does in his argument. The attitude of contemporary non-believers seems more marked by indifferentism. A recent interview with a military chaplain was even headed "No atheists in the trench".[1149] But SCHLÖGEL's case fails yet at another point: Spiritual assistance is a form of relief.[1150] Every man reflects on himself on different levels of consciousness. Existential questions are raised especially in an environment of armed conflict.[1151] In this process of reflection, somebody might eventually conclude that there is no God or that he is unable to grasp him ration-

---

[1146] *See* Hiebel, *supra* note 180, at 7, HIEBEL, *supra* note 142, at 172.
[1147] *See* Schlögel, *supra* note 38, at 276, *see also* DRAPER, *supra* note 7, at 249.
[1148] *See Romans* 3:22-24.
[1149] *"Im Schützengraben gibt es keine Atheisten"*, RHEINISCHEN MERKUR, No. 13, March 27th, 2003, *available at* http://www.kmba.de/aktuell/internas/270303/270303.html.
[1150] *See* Hiebel, *supra* note 180, at 6, PICTET, *supra* note 530, at 595.
[1151] *See supra* at 61.

ally. Such a conclusion is legitimate and deserves respect. But this does not free himself from the need of company along the way to this conclusion and even thereafter when this conclusion is challenged as life goes on. Freedom of religion and conviction is here translated into a right of assistance.

The individual may still choose not to make use of assistance. The right to opt against, the freedom not to believe and not to practice a religion is also part of his right to freedom of religion. But this possibility cannot serve as a cause to bar from him spiritual assistance as such. The spiritual needs of atheists – maybe it is more appropriate to use HIEBEL's term of nontheists[1152] – have to be met in two aspects that are in the current state of law not yet properly dealt with: in guaranties for their negative freedom of religion and in the possibility of a positive assistance in their freedom of conviction. "Very meagre" guarantees for the latter sees HIEBEL in the obligation of the Detaining Power to encourage the practice of intellectual, educational and recreational pursuits of POW[1153] and of the Occupying Power to take into consideration the moral and ethical susceptibilities of the population of the occupied territory.[1154] Another helpful provision here is the principle of equal treatment without any adverse distinction based on religious belief enshrined in Art. 16 GC III.

The furthest going formulations are found in Art. 4 (1) PA II. Again, the issue was raised whether the norm provides for a protection of opinions and beliefs other than those of religious nature in non-international conflicts. The preliminary works of the diplomatic conference attributed some importance to this question.[1155] As a result, the formulation "religious convictions and practices" in Art. 27 GC IV was intentionally changed into "convictions and religious practices" in Art. 4 (1) PA II. Now, the religious character is only relevant with regard to practice and the protocol assures respect also for philosophical and political convictions.[1156] PICTET had already interpreted the respect-for-religious-convictions clause of Art. 27 GC IV to imply freedom to believe or not to believe, thus to imply negative freedom of religion.[1157]

Christian anthropology sees man as a religious being with the desire for god written in his heart,[1158] as a creature able to search for truth and enter into relationship with his creator. Religious freedom is then protected in order to

---

[1152] *See* Hiebel, *supra* note 180, at 7.
[1153] *See* Art. 38 (1) GC III.
[1154] *See* Art. 56 (3) GC IV.
[1155] *See* LINDSAY MOIR, THE LAW OF INTERNAL ARMED CONFLICT 213 (2002).
[1156] *See* COMMENTARY ON THE ADDITIONAL PROTOCOLS, *supra* note 178, No. 4522 at 1370, DRAPER, *supra* note 7, at 248, MOIR, *supra* note 1155, at 213.
[1157] *See* PICTET, *supra* note 711, at 203, PICTET, VICTIMS, *supra* note 132, at 123.
[1158] *See* CATECHISM OF THE CATHOLIC CHURCH, *supra* note 243, No. 27, 28, *available at* www.vatican.va/archive/ccc_css/archive/catechism/p1s1c1.htm.

safeguard the religious aspect in human nature. Religion can take many forms nowadays, everything from a sophisticated theological doctrine as a result of centuries of reflection passed on from one generation to another to a vague and often unexpressed religiosity in a rather personal scenery. From a religious perspective one could state that god is unknown to those who nevertheless search for him without knowing and to whom he has been close as to so many.[1159]

However, human reflections may not necessarily reach a religious level but lead to another level, the level of conscience, a level without reference to a superior being. The place of religion as a source to give meaning to life may be taken by a secular philosophy[1160] since individuals look for a moral code also outside of religion.[1161] But the path to this level of conscience departs from the same human nature and thus deserves to be protected. In practice, the issue may arise whether conscientious answers are sufficient to respond to the religious human nature – especially if one departs from a religious angle. But these practical reservations cannot justify setting up "limits that cannot be exceeded", withholding protection.

Another fact is interesting at this point: In a study of the Institute of Social Sciences of the *Bundeswehr*, 96 % of the soldiers asked in a German camp of the Bosnian SFOR mission agreed to the following statement: The chaplain should be there for every soldier, regardless of his denomination and regardless of whether he is religious at all.[1162] It is remarkable that soldiers wish that the chaplain was available even for those who are not associated with a religion. In addition, 88 % of the non-denominational soldiers welcome the presence of military chaplains on mission.[1163] On the other hand, the statutorily defined outreach of military chaplaincy is not limited to soldiers who are members of the respective military parish.[1164] In the same survey, only 2 % of the soldiers from the eastern *Länder* opposed the presence of chaplains in the camp.[1165] Nontheists and soldiers distant to their church did not feel encroached or occupied by the activities of military chaplaincy.[1166] This might come from the fact that chaplains serve without a missionary overzealousness but approach all soldiers deliberately without excluding someone because of his origin or confession.[1167] So, does an assistance with a religious background to non-religious serve the current spiri-

1159 *See* PAUL VI, *supra* note 233, No. 7.
1160 *See* NICOLAS, *supra* note 16, at 310.
1161 *See* COMMENTARY ON THE ADDITIONAL PROTOCOLS, *supra* note 178, No. 3034 at 871.
1162 *See* BOCK, *supra* note 501, at 73.
1163 *See id.* at 75.
1164 *See* Military Chaplaincy Agreement, *supra* note 390, Art. 9.
1165 *See* BOCK, *supra* note 501, at 81.
1166 *See id.* at 93.
1167 *See id.* at 92.

tual needs best? If the need for chaplains' ministry even to non-denominational soldiers is felt, it is not a huge step to see freedom of religion and freedom of conscience interwoven in providing the basis for chaplaincy and chaplains' protection. Then, underlining the spiritual needs of non-believers would even strengthen the position of the chaplain *de facto* and *de iure*.

However, it should be recalled that the German soldiers questioned could not take into account the hypothetical alternative of a non-religious chaplaincy to nontheists. The chaplain is perceived as somebody who is present and cares while he enjoys a privileged status. A chaplain even went as far as to state that soldiers approach a chaplain not because he is a religious pastor but because they need someone to talk to, a person they can trust.[1168] Specific religious peculiarities – confessional differences would be a typical example in Germany – are not highly valued. At least from the needs of the soldiers, it is then worth some reflection why that position of being present and caring of the chaplain could not be taken by a non-religious chaplain or whether then the religious basis would be missed. Also, from a religious angle it is difficult to see how spiritual assistance can be provided without religious groundings, to see the legitimacy of spiritual assistance without religious reference given the religious nature of man and – pragmatically – given the existing alternative of psychiatrists, psychologists, social workers and off duty time entertainment staff. And it is also hard to imagine where a non-religious spiritual assistant gets his spiritual aliments from and what may prevent his burn out as he lacks a religious spirituality. In any case, non-religious assistance would result in a loss of religion in society since military chaplaincy is a form of presence in societal everyday life.[1169] But these are pragmatic considerations.

On the national constitutional level, the question may be raised whether freedom of conviction could justify a non-religious chaplaincy providing company and assistance. The German Basic Law assures freedom for both religious confessions and philosophical convictions. Generally, these two are distinguished by the recurrence of the first to transcendent and of the latter to immanent phenomena.[1170] But this distinction is not sharp. It is then controversial whether the guarantee of access to the armed forces in Art. 141 Weimar Constitution incorporated by Art. 140 of the Basic Law[1171] is applicable for both religious and philosophical communities. Seen in the system of the Weimar Constitution, Art. 141 only mentions religious communities – unlike for instance Art. 137 on legal personality of religious communities that has an equivalency

---

[1168] *See* Löffler, *supra* note 441, at 53.

[1169] *See id.*

[1170] *See* Klaus Obermayer, *Art. 140*, *in* 13 KOMMENTAR ZUM BONNER GRUNDGESETZ, No. 42 at 42 (continued looseleaf collection as of 2003).

[1171] *See supra* at 48.

clause in paragraph VII for philosophical communities which is not applicable to Art. 141.[1172] In addition, Art. 141 uses specific religious terms such as divine service (*Gottesdienst*) and religious acts.[1173] However, this narrow interpretation cannot convince in the system of the current Basic Law.[1174] Instead, the guarantee of Art. 141 must be seen as complementary rights to religious and philosophical freedom as comprehensively regulated in Art. 4 paragraph 1 and 2 of the Basic Law[1175] The concept of Art. 4 that treats religious and philosophical creeds equally supersedes the system of the Weimar constitution and allows for an equal treatment of religious creed and philosophical confession also in the area of military chaplaincy.[1176]

On the other hand, there are differences with religion and conviction. In hierarchically structured religions where the chaplain is indispensable for the exercise of religion, the presence of a chaplain can easily be justified on grounds of freedom of religion. The essential role of the catholic chaplain can serve as an illustration: The presbytery in the catholic understanding does not only provide ordinary pastoral care but is necessary to provide specific assistance to enable the faithful to find holiness in the military environment and with the means of the sacraments to fully develop their mission in the world and in the church.[1177] As the state puts his military personnel in a special situation where these ministers are usually unavailable, freedom of religion demands from the state to create an environment in which the minister of cult can join the troops in order to administer his functions. The soldier cannot practice his religion without the minister, thus the minister is sent along as military chaplain. Does a comparable situation exist for the atheist? Could a positive protection of the freedom of conscience possibly result in a protected category of "ministers"? What is the role of leadership in atheism or is it by nature horizontally structured? The setting of interests seems at least different here. Practicing his atheism appears not to be essentially linked with a minister of cult. Company in extreme situations of life, a company that gives feedback, this has become an important aspect in military

---

[1172] *See* Ulfried Hemmrich, *Art. 140*, *in* INGO VON MÜNCH & PHILIP KUNIG, 3 GRUNDGESETZ-KOMMENTAR No. 44 at 1478 (5th ed. 2003), *but see* Dirk Ehlers, *Art. 140 – Art. 141 WRV*, *in* GRUNDGESETZ No. 5 at 2496 (Michael Sachs ed., 3rd ed. 2003) (applying Art. 137 VII on Art. 141).

[1173] *See* Hemmrich, *supra* note 1172, *see also* Stefan Korioth, *Art. 140 – Art. 141*, *in* 5 GRUNDGESETZ No. 6 at 308 (Theodor Maunz & Günter Dürig eds., continued looseleaf collection as of 2003) (for practical difficulties of exercising the right of access by philosophical communities).

[1174] *See* Axel v. Campenhausen, *Art. 141 WRV*, *in* 3 DAS BONNER GRUNDGESETZ No. 11 at 2986 (Christian Starck ed., 4th ed. 2001).

[1175] *See* Ulrich K. Preuß, *Art. 140*, *in* 3 KOMMENTAR ZUM GRUNDGESETZ FÜR DIE BUNDESREPUBLIK DEUTSCHLAND No. 70 at 67 (Erhard Denninger ed., 3rd ed., continued looseleaf collection as of 2003).

[1176] *See also* Ehlers, *supra* note 1172 (for the same result)

[1177] *See* Baura, *supra* note 335, at 104-05.

chaplaincy. But such company could also be provided without religious inspiration by military psychologists, off-duty time entertainment staff, councillors, political officers.[1178] Maybe personnel charged with such spiritual company could be given a status outside the chain of command as nowadays chaplains enjoy. An answer to the question whether such company justifies a privileged and protected status if it is not linked with a vertical religious approach must be referred to further examinations. These examinations would also have to consider protecting spiritual needs and the personnel servicing them in a broad sense – religious or non-religious, inspired by religion or conviction or whatever else – maybe only under the aspect of equal treatment.

The Dutch armed forces employ spiritual assistants from religions but also non-denominational humanistic councilors.[1179] The issue of spiritual assistance by non-religious personnel had already been addressed by the Dutch delegation at the diplomatic conference 1975 – and was met by opposition from the Holy See.[1180] Based on the constitutional freedom of religion and conviction, the service of the Dutch humanist spiritual assistance provides assistance for existential questions and in plight departing from a humanist approach to life.[1181] Their number even grew on the expense of traditional military chaplaincy. This development paired with structural reform in the Dutch armed forces and contributed to a professionalization of military chaplaincy as a whole.[1182] In the catholic church, these fairly unknown phenomenon of non-religious councilors was as early as in the year 1980 classified as "causing difficulties".[1183] In practice, however, the deployment of humanistic councilors in missions abroad turns out to be difficult as religious chaplains and councilors are not "interchangeable".[1184] It is difficult to specify this interchangeability criterion. Maybe a different perception of religious ministers and non-religious councilors by the soldiers is meant.

In Germany, a similar development as the one that took place in the Netherlands seems unrealistic – at least for the moment. Most humanist groups in the diverse scene of philosophical associations in Germany generally oppose military chaplaincy as such and incorrectly consider it illegal and unconstitu-

---

[1178] *See supra* at 99.

[1179] *See* BOCK, *supra* note 795, at 144.

[1180] *See* HIEBEL, *supra* note 142, at 359-361.

[1181] *See* MISSION STATEMENT DIENST HUMANISTISCHE GEESTELIJKE VERZORGING (HGV), *available at* http://www.dico.nl/dgv/organisatie/hgv/index.html.

[1182] *See* W.H. Louwerse, *The Royal Netherlands Air Force*, 1 EUROPEAN CHAPLAINCY YEARBOOK 71, 72 (1992).

[1183] *See* Beyer, *supra* note 350, at 272.

[1184] Frank Jansen, *Protestant Chaplaincy in the Dutch Armed Forces in 1996*, 7 EUROPEAN CHAPLAINCY YEARBOOK 106, 107 (1997).

tional.[1185] On this background, the initiative of two members of parliaments who then served on the national board of the Humanistic Association of Germany in 1993 for a state-funded spiritual assistance to non-religious service personnel by philosophical groups was exceptional and even met polemic opposition by other humanist groups.[1186] After almost a decade of abstinence on the topic also because of resistance amongst its own members, the Humanistic Association took it up again in 2003. Its central committee decided on January 18th, 2003 that the Humanistic Association would apply for the institution of humanistic counseling with the federal government. The Humanistic Association's federal convention supported this decision in a resolution passed on Sepember 20th, 2003 and expressed its wish to agressivly develop the concept of humanistic counseling in society. Even though the Humanistic Association seems to be willing to take the issue to court if necessary, a concept of overcoming the formal requirement of membership, namely a sufficient number of registered members amongst soldiers, appears to be lacking. The example illustrates that spiritual assistance to non-believers and to non-Christian faithful are issues of relevance but not yet widely received in societal debate. The Joint Service Regulation on military chaplaincy provides that upon request by a religious community, chaplaincies for confessions other than the catholic and protestant must be established.[1187]

In the early times of the Bundeswehr, many Jews were exempt from service therein if they met the qualifications of § 11 II No. 1 + 2 of the German Conscription Act: If all of the applicant's brothers – in absence of brothers, all his sisters – have died due to the effects of World War II or of National Socialist persecution or if one parent has died for similar cause and the applicant is the sole surviving son. For some Jews, who were collectively persecuted by National Socialist norms,[1188] these conditions applied, but not for all of them, not even for all Jewish descendants of victims of Nazi tyranny. This has been subject of criticism.[1189] The norm has become obsolete.[1190] Currently, the *Bundeswehr* considers itself incapable of providing kosher meals to Jewish service

---

[1185] *See* Stellungnahme der Fachtagung des Deutschen Freidenker-Verbandes und des Internationalen Bundes der Konfessionslosen und Atheisten am 26./27.1.2002 zum Thema "Militärseelsorge" (January 27th, 2002), *available at* http://www.ibka.org/artikel/ag02/erklaerung.html (for a recent joint statement of the International League of Non-Religious and Atheists and the Freethinkers association), *see also* Satzung des Bundes der Konfessionslosen § 2 VI No. 11, *available at* http://www.ibka.org/artikel/miz73/bdk.html (for the abolition of military chaplaincy being included as a goal in the statutes of the League of Non-Religious).

[1186] *See Das Kuckucksei*, MATERIALIEN UND INFORMATIONEN ZUR ZEIT 4/1993, *available at* http://www.ibka.org/artikel/miz93/kuckucksei.html.

[1187] *See* ZDv 66/1, *supra* note 385, No. 2.

[1188] *See* WALTER BRUNN ET AL., 1 DAS BUNDESENTSCHÄDIGUNGSGESETZ 21 (1981).

[1189] *See Art. 11*, *supra* note 453, No. 72 at 241.

[1190] *See* WOLFGANG STAUF, 3 WEHRRECHT No. 4 at 27 (2002), *Art. 11*, *supra* note 453, No. 41 at 231.

personnel and tries to serve requests of these personnel with provision from outside facilities or allowing lodging at home.[1191] There are no plans to establish a chaplaincy for the estimated 150 Jews in the *Bundeswehr* of whom most are commissioned officers. However, students from the Abraham Geiger Kolleg for Rabbis in Potsdam are regularly offered internships with the existing chaplaincies as part of their curriculum.

Institutionalized chaplaincy for Muslims does not yet exist in the *Bundeswehr*. The number of Muslims in the military was estimated as about 500 in 1999 so that Muslims do not qualify for the normal German ratio of 1500 soldiers on 1 chaplain.[1192] Right now, spiritual assistance to Muslims as for other members of religious communities currently not institutionalized in a chaplaincy is organized on a case by case basis by the military superior in order to assure compatibility of military service and exercise of religion.[1193] In addition, a suitable institution on the part of the Muslim community does not yet exist to take over responsibility in this regard.[1194] But the development of recognized partners for Islamic religious instructions in public schools hints to the creation of a partner also for military chaplaincy. This will also be influenced by the future of conscription in the German armed forces and the resulting social structure of the troops. The development of suitable partners for Islamic religious instructions in public schools hints to the creation of a partner also for military chaplaincy that is currently inexistent. But secularism is indifferent and simply not organized. An institution suited to provide ministry to non-believers does not seem in sight. The model of non-religious ethical instructions (LER) in the public schools of the *Land* Brandenburg exposed the dangers of attempts of the state to fill this lack of organizations after having identified existing needs.

The question for the protection of non-religious councilors is solved. During the diplomatic conference 1975, the Netherlands pushed for an aquivalency clause for such non-religious councilors. Efforts to apply the protection of religious personnel on "other persons performing similar functions" were meant to

---

[1191] *See* Baader, *supra* note 473, at 746.

[1192] *See* Tade Matthias Spranger, *Militärseelsorge für Moslems?*, 1999 BUNDESWEHRVERWALTUNG 174, ANTWORT DER BUNDESREGIERUNG – GROßE ANFRAGE „ISLAM IN DEUTSCHLAND", Drucksache 14/4530, at 47 (Deutscher Bundestag ed. November 8th, 2000), *available at* http://dip.bundestag.de/btd/14/045/1404530.pdf, *see also* Baader, *supra* note 473 (for the lack of experiences with Muslim spiritual assistance in the armed forces), *Multikulti im Schützengraben*, DER SPIEGEL, No. 27, June 29th, 1998, at 60 (for an overview on the issue), Greg Noakes, *Muslims in U.S.Military Make Advances*, 1994 WASHINGTON REPORT ON MIDDLE EAST AFFAIRS 55/85 (for early developments on Muslim chaplaincy in the U.S. Armed Forces).

[1193] *See Hamburg Administrative Court*, 1994 NEUE ZEITSCHRIFT FÜR VERWALTUNGSWISSENSCHAFTEN 816 (instructive for this practice and possible administrative appeal), *see also* ANTWORT DER BUNDESREGIERUNG – GROßE ANFRAGE „ISLAM IN DEUTSCHLAND", *supra* note 1192, at 19, 92-93 (for the views of the federal government).

[1194] *See* Spranger, *supra* note 1192, Baader, *supra* note 473.

include personnel of non-religious bodies who acted from humanitarian considerations.[1195] The delegation of the Netherlands put a particular emphasis to have its initiative for an equivalency clause retained in the run of the negotiations and framed them in a special amendment.[1196] It read: Persons attached to civilian medical units, who are giving not religious but other spiritual help, shall be protected and respected. The Holy See on the other hand wished to avoid any ambiguity on the notion of religious personnel or any extension of the scope of the drafted provisions that would jeopardize the protection of religious personnel.[1197] This opposition was supported for instance by Egypt and France. The final vote on the issue took place on February 13th, 1975 when the amendment of the Netherlands was rejected with 13 to 6 votes with the number of abstentions as ranking high as 29.[1198] With the Statute of the International Criminal Court, the international community decided to adopt another view, accept the notion of non-religious spiritual assistance and grant protection to its personnel. Its definition of protected "religious personnel" includes "those non-confessional non-combatant military personnel carrying out a similar function".[1199] It seems as if this clause appeared for the first time in a working paper by the Coordinator of the Working Group on Elements of Crimes[1200] who happened to be from the Netherlands. It was subsequently included in the draft of the elements of crimes as approved by the second session of the Preparatory Commission for the ICC.[1201]

[1195] *See Statement of Mr. Deddes, in* FEDERAL POLITICAL DEPARTMENT, 11 OFFICIAL RECORDS OF THE DIPLOMATIC CONFERENCE ON THE REAFFIRMATION AND DEVELOPMENT OF INTERNATIONAL HUMANITARIAN LAW APPLICABLE IN ARMED CONFLICT 52, Conference Doc. CDDH/II/SR.7 No. 19 (1978), *Statement of Mr. Deddes, id.* at 145, CDDH/II/SR.16 No. 15.

[1196] *See* Conference Doc. CDDH/II/216 *quoted in* FEDERAL POLITICAL DEPARTMENT, 13 OFFICIAL RECORDS OF THE DIPLOMATIC CONFERENCE ON THE REAFFIRMATION AND DEVELOPMENT OF INTERNATIONAL HUMANITARIAN LAW APPLICABLE IN ARMED CONFLICT 80, Conference Doc. CDDH/221/Rev. 1 No. 60 (1978).

[1197] *See Statement of Marie-Claude Chevallier-Buensod, in* FEDERAL POLITICAL DEPARTMENT, 8 OFFICIAL RECORDS OF THE DIPLOMATIC CONFERENCE ON THE REAFFIRMATION AND DEVELOPMENT OF INTERNATIONAL HUMANITARIAN LAW APPLICABLE IN ARMED CONFLICT 343, Conference Doc. CDDH/I/SR.33 No. 4 (1978), *Statement of Charles Klein, in* FEDERAL POLITICAL DEPARTMENT, *supra* note 1195, at 147, Conference Doc. CDDH/II/SR.16 No. 31.

[1198] *See* FEDERAL POLITICAL DEPARTMENT, *supra* note 1195, at 184, Conference Doc. CDDH/II/SR.19 No. 65, FEDERAL POLITICAL DEPARTMENT, *supra* note 1196, at 81, Conference Doc. CDDH/221/Rev. 1 No. 66 b, HIEBEL, *supra* note 142, at 361.

[1199] *Elements of Crime, supra* note 780, Part. II B at 145 n. 56.

[1200] *See Article 8 (2) (c)*, Discussion paper proposed by the Coordinator, Preparatory Commission for the ICC, 2nd Sess., Working Group on Elements of Crime, U.N. Doc. PCNICC/1999/WGEC/RT.5/Rev.1 (August 11th, 1999).

[1201] *See Proceedings of the Preparatory Commission*, Preparatory Commission for the International Criminal Court, 2nd Sess., at 68, U.N. Doc. PCNICC/1999/L.4/Rev.1 (August 18th, 1999), *see also Proceedings of the Preparatory Commission*, Preparatory Commission for the International Criminal Court, 1st Sess., (March 2nd, 1999), U.N. Doc. PCNICC/1999/L.3/Rev.1 (for the clause not yet being included).

This equivalency appears as the most fundamental legal modification since the 1974-1977 diplomatic conference. For many countries, this change will not be of relevance because their internal legal regime does consider non-confessional spiritual assistance. But for the Netherlands, where such an assistance is already in practice, or for Germany, where the legal set-up at least seems to not exclude it, this explicit statement of an equal level of protection introduces a new development.

IX. Spiritual assistance in the 21st century – Global challenges

1. Religious personnel as IHL violators

Under the current legal regime, chaplains must "abstain from all hostile acts".[1202] Apparently, the 1949 diplomatic conference did not consider the possibility of violent acts by ministers of religion. The same is true for the preliminary study commission that simply thought, "spiritual comfort ... should never be considered as offences".[1203] If religious personnel that would be entitled to protection under GC I–III participate in combat action or engage in conduct incompatible with their status they lose their protection in combat. A chaplain acting hostile violates IHL what may cause the liability of his state and his personal criminal prosecution.[1204] He may be subject to penal punishment in accordance with Art. 68 GC IV and becomes a lawful target in case he attacks enemy forces.[1205] If he continued to use the protection of the distinctive emblem he could furthermore commit perfidy. The perfidious use of the distinctive emblem could amount to a grave breach of the GCs.[1206] Nonetheless, the process of cessation of protection should only occur in a manner parallel to that applied to medical personnel, namely after a due warning has been given and after such warning has remained unheeded.[1207]

It would be furthermore improper for a commander to allow chaplains under his control to take a direct part in combat.[1208] It is, however, difficult to clearly determine acts that violate the non-combatant status of religious personnel. As

---

1202 PICTET, *supra* note 132, at 220, PICTET, *supra* note 559, at 201, *see* MARCHEGGIANO, *supra* note 107, at 149, HIEBEL, *supra* note 142, at 199, Elßner, *supra* note 800, at 266.

1203 *Cited in* Hiebel, *supra* note 180, at 26.

1204 *See* U.S. MARINE CORPS, *supra* note 182, No. 1004 e, HEYDTE, *supra* note 1048, at 353, Koerber, *supra* note 565, at 425, PICTET, VICTIMS, *supra* note 132, at 80, Hiebel, *supra* note 180, at 26, Rausch, *supra* note 7, at 381.

1205 *See* Odom, *supra* note 7, at 22.

1206 *See* Art. 38, 85 (3) f PA I.

1207 *See* Art. 21 GC I, *see also* PICTET, *supra* note 132, at 221, 215 (applying this norm also on chaplains).

1208 *See* GREEN, *supra* note 133, at 105.

they are devoted to ministry, they must not contribute to the direct warfare efforts. Thus, they must not operate arms and weapons systems in combat. Furthermore, they are not allowed to engage in supportive military efforts such as intelligence activities, observation and interception of communication, translation and interrogation or the assessment of civilian data for military purposes. Nonetheless, chaplains may engage in activities that do not derive exclusively from their spiritual mission as long as they are not harmful to the enemy.[1209] They may without prejudicing their special protection e.g. engage in social service activities to support combatants and their families and could be involved in the provision of recreation activities.[1210]

Especially prior to the first Red Cross Convention of 1864, numerous cases of chaplains becoming actively involved with combat activities were reported.[1211] RAUSCH mentions an example of incompatible military engagement of a military chaplain during the Falkland conflict 1982.[1212] A more recent example of an alleged IHL violation by a chaplain is that of Captain MARK SARGENT. The catholic chaplain with the Canadian Airborne Regiment Battle Group deployed in Somalia during UNOSOM II appeared on what was alleged to be a "trophy photo": On the photograph that was published by Radio Canada in July 1996, SARGENT stood behind five young Somali captives who were bound and blindfolded and wore signs that read "I am a thief." SARGENT stated later that the photo was misleading and that he actually was trying to defuse the situation. The case was also brought to the attention of the Somalia Inquiry Commission of the Canadian Department of National Defence. SARGENT was called upon to explain himself before this commission that investigated into events transpired during the deployment of Canadian troops in Somalia. These events included the shooting of Somali intruders at the Canadian compound, the beating to death of a 16-year-old Somali trespasser by two Canadian commandos and videotapes of "repugnant hazing activities" in 1993. SARGENT's case was not mentioned in the final report of the commission released in 1997, but reemerged in 2002. After retirement from the Canadian Forces, SARGENT was hired as part-time investigator by the Ombudsman for the Department of National Defence and the Canadian Forces. After critical news coverage, the Ombudsman issued a report on the role of Chaplain SARGENT.[1213] The document recounted the proceedings against SERGANT by military police and in the chain of command, which both cleared SARGENT of all charges. Another investigation led by the Chaplain General and assisted by the catholic military ordinary also found no fault on his part. The

---

[1209] *See* Hiebel, *supra* note 180, at 25.
[1210] *See* O'BRIEN, *supra* note 154, at O3 (also for functioning in messes, wardrooms and canteens).
[1211] *See* BUDD, *supra* note 511, at 21.
[1212] *See* Rausch, *supra* note 139, at 39 n.40.
[1213] *See* HIRING OF MARK SARGENT, REPORT OF THE DND/CF OMBUDSMAN (August 7th, 2002).

report confirmed SARGENT's statement that he was defusing the situation: Not visible in the photograph were a group of village elders who were setting about to beat the teenagers. "Mr. SARGENT intervened to defuse the situation by speaking to the elders via a translator while physically separating the elders from the teenagers." Chaplain SARGENT was issued a commendation by the Chief of Defence Staff because his initiative may have saved the captives from serious injury or death.

The most prominent case currently discussed of a military chaplain charged with crimes under international law is that of EMMANUEL RUKUNDO at the International Criminal Tribunal for Rwanda (ICTR). The ICTR was established by the UN Security Council[1214] acting under chapter VII of the UN-Charter. The tribunal can prosecute only a *numerus clausus* of crimes, namely genocide, crimes against humanity and violations of common Art. 3 of the GCs and of PA II,[1215] if they were committed in 1994 in Rwanda or by Rwandans in neighboring countries.[1216] RUKUNDO, born in 1959, is charged with genocide and crimes against humanity for murder and extermination. The Office of the Prosecutor sees the case as follows:[1217] Notwithstanding acts of hatred against fellow Tutsi seminarians during his time of formation, RUKUNDO was ordained to priesthood in July 1991 by the ordinary of Kabgayi diocese and became military chaplain of the Rwandan Armed Forces (FAR) thereafter. RUKUNDO is accused of mobilizing Hutu population against the Tutsi minority. He allegedly denounced to Rwandan government authorities a fellow priest as supporter of the Rwandan Patriotic Front (RPF), which is the Tutsi rebel army. This other priest was identified and eventually killed by soldiers of the Hutu dominated FAR. According to the prosecutor's indictment, he used his easy access to church facilities such as seminars, schools and convents where Tutsi had fled to search for Tutsi refugees and issued orders to attack them. Escorted by soldiers and Hutu militia and appearing in uniform and armed, he drew up lists of persons who later were killed or seriously injured by his escorts.

When reading these allegations, it surprises that RUKUNDO is not charged with war crimes. The requirement of an armed conflict could easily be asserted with the conflict between FAR and RPF. It is also obvious that RUKUNDO's victims were not taking part in the hostilities and not legitimate targets. It seems to be a strategy of the Office of the Prosecutor to focus charges on genocide because the third legal requirement for a war crime, a nexus between the alleged crimes and

---

1214 *See* SC Res. 955, U.N. SCOR, 3453th mtg., U.N. Doc. S/RES/955 (November 8th, 1994).

1215 *See* Art. 2-4 Statute of the International Criminal Tribunal for Rwanda as amended, *available at* http://www.ictr.org/ENGLISH/basicdocs/statute.html.

1216 *See id.* Art. 7.

1217 *See* The Prosecutor v. Emmanuel Rukundo, Case No. ICTR-2001-70-I (March 27th, 2003), *available at* http://www.ictr.org/ENGLISH/cases/Rukundo/indictment/rukundo.pdf.

the armed conflict, is a standard that turned out to be difficult to meet in trial. Given RUKUNDO's affiliation with the FAR, his orders to troops and his appearance in uniform, proof of the nexus seems very likely. War crime charges could be introduced by amending the indictment. But even if the nexus is established, other legal question arise: The tribunal held in May 2003 that LAURENT SEMANZA, the Bourgmestre of Bicumbi committed war crimes when he aided and abetted in the intentional murders of Tutsi civilians at a church. He was sentenced to 25 years in prison but not convicted of war crimes because the court held these charges to be in ideal concurrence with the crime of complicity in genocide he was convicted of.[1218] SEMANZA's case is pending on appeal.

RUKUNDO left Rwanda after the genocide and spent some time in Rome before he was arrested on July 12th, 2001 in Switzerland where he officiated as priest in a Geneva parish. He was transferred to the ICTR in Arusha in September the same year.[1219] In his initial appearance before the ICTR on September 26th, 2001, RUKUNDO pleaded not guilty.[1220] At the time of this being written, RUKUNDO is awaiting trial before Trial Chamber 3. A motion of his defense to fix a date for the commencement of his trial or provisional release was denied by the trial chamber.[1221] Given the current backlock of cases at the ICTR, his case is not expected to be tried before the year 2005. Among the more than 50 detainees at the United Nations Detention Facility in Arusha, there have been four other civilian clergymen:[1222] The catholic priest ATHANASE SEROMBA is charged with genocide and crimes against humanity. The indictment holds SEROMBA accountable for supervising the killing of Tutsi who had fled into his parish church.[1223] Another accused priest is HORMISDAS NSENGIMANA, former rector of the Catholic Christ-Roi College.[1224] Both, SEROMBA, who wears holy garments in court,

---

[1218] *See* The Prosecutor v. Laurent Semanza, Case No. ICTR-97-20-T, Judgment and Sentence (May 15th, 2003), *available at* http://www.ictr.org/ENGLISH/cases/Semanza/judgement/6.htm, § 535-536.

[1219] *See also* Collection des arrêts du Tribunal fédéral Suisse, 1A.129/2001 (September 3rd, 2001), *available at* http://www.polyreg.ch/bgeunpubliziert/Jahr_2001/Entscheide_1A_2001/1A.129__2001.html (for the decision to transfer Rukundo to the ICTR by the Swiss Federal Court).

[1220] *See* Minutes of Proceedings, Initial appearance, September 26th, 2001, *available at* http://www.ictr.org/ENGLISH/cases/Rukundo/minutes/2001/260901.pdf.

[1221] *See* The Prosecutor v. Emmanuel Rukundo, Case No. ICTR-2001-70-I, Decision on defence motion to fix a date for the commencement of the trial of father Emmanuel Rukundo or, in the alternative, to request his provisional release (August 18th, 2003), *available at* http://www.ictr.org/ENGLISH/cases/Rukundo/decisions/180803.htm.

[1222] *See also* Wambui Kimani, *Military chaplain on genocide charges*, WEST AFRICA, October 15th – 21st, 2001, at 23 (for a summary of clergy cases at the ICTR).

[1223] *See* The Prosecutor v. Athanase Seromba, Case No. ICTR-2001-66-I, Indictment (June 8th, 2001), *available at* http://www.ictr.org/ENGLISH/cases/Seromba/indictment/seromba.pdf.

[1224] *See* The Prosecutor v. Hormisdas Nsengimana, Case No. ICTR-2001-69-I, *available at* http://www.ictr.org/ENGLISH/cases/Nsengimana/indictment/index.pdf.

and NSENGIMANA, are awaiting trial. No canonical sanctions have become public against either one of the indicted three catholic clergymen. Seventh Day Adventist Church pastor ELIZAPHAN NTAKIRUTIMANA was acquitted of war crime charges but convicted of genocide and sentenced to 10 years imprisonment in February 2003.[1225] The case is pending on appeal. Proceedings against SAMUEL MUSABYIMANA, the former Anglican bishop of the Shyogwe diocese, were terminated after the death of the accused on January 24th, 2003.[1226]

2. Ministry to Guantanamo detainees

Following the events of September 11th, 2001, the military operations in Afghanistan and the ensuing captures of numerous Al Qaida and Taliban individuals, U.S. authorities made the decision to transfer a number of detainees to facilities on U.S. Naval Station Guantanamo Bay on the island of Cuba. The detainees were first accommodated in Camp X-Ray and in late April 2002 moved on to a permanent facility named Camp Delta. Responsibility for security and handling of the detainees is vested with a specially created Joint Task Force Guantanamo (JTF GTMO). The U.S. government does not consider Al Qaida or Taliban fighters to qualify as legal combatants but consider them illegal combatants.[1227] The only concession that has been made is to apply law of armed conflict during the hostilities against Taliban fighters.[1228] The detainees are not granted POW status of GC III that is applicable to combatants in international armed conflicts. This is not the place to discuss the status of the Guantanamo detainees,[1229] but even if they are not considered combatants in warfare and POW upon capture, the demand for humane treatment of common Art. 3 applies. This requirement and the access of chaplains to the detainees were also acknowledged by the U.S. government.[1230]

[1225] *See* The Prosecutor v. Elizaphan and Gérard Ntakirutimana, Cases No. ICTR-96-10 & ICTR-96-17-T, (February 21st, 2003), *available at* http://www.ictr.org/ENGLISH/cases/NtakirutimanaE/judgement/index.htm.

[1226] *See* The Prosecutor v. Samuel Musabyimana, Case No. ICTR-2001- 62 –I, Order Terminating the Proceedings against Samuel Musabyimana, (February 20th, 2003) (unpublished).

[1227] *See also supra* at 60 (for the German government's qualification of Al Qaida fighters as illegal combatants).

[1228] *See* DoD NEWS BRIEFING BY DEFENSE SECRETARY RUMSFELD AND GENERAL MYERS (February 8th, 2002), *available at* http://www.defenselink.mil/news/Feb2002/t02082002_t0208sd.html, THE WHITE HOUSE, FACT SHEET: STATUS OF DETAINEES AT GUANTANAMO (February 7th, 2002), *available at* http://www.whitehouse.gov/news/releases/2002/02/20020207-13.html.

[1229] *See also critially* HUMAN RIGHTS WATCH, LETTER TO DONALD RUMSFELD (May 29th, 2002), *available at* http://hrw.org/press/2002/05/pentagon-ltr.pdf.

[1230] *See* DoD NEWS BRIEFING, *supra* note 1228.

The detainment is based on a military order issued by President GEORGE W. BUSH on November 13th, 2001.[1231] The order in Sec. 3 (b) assures humane treatment without religious discrimination in a formulation parallel to common Art. 3. Detainees are "allowed the free exercise of religion consistent with the requirements of such detention".[1232]

Chaplains accompanied detention at all stages: The chaplain on board the naval vessel USS Bataan which processed detainees, for instance, visited them.[1233] A navy chaplain was a member of the Special Psychiatric Rapid Intervention Team requested to train the guarding personnel regarding stress management, suicide prevention and spiritual self-care in early 2002. The chaplain's responsibility was training in Spiritual Readiness/Self Care.[1234] Navy Chaplain Lieutenant ABUHENA MOHAMMAD SAIF UL ISLAM was sent to Guantanamo in January 2002. His role was twofold: "His primary responsibility"[1235] was to act as an advisor to the commander of the detaining unit in matters of religion. ODOM underlines the importance of the chaplain cooperating with other services like the staff judge advocate, the legal advisor, because the latter is the expert on the law while the chaplain is the expert in the spiritual needs of the detainees.[1236] The second task of the chaplain was to minister to the detainees. He visited them one on one and led them in prayer. According to chaplain SAIF UL ISLAM, he was present in the camp to the detainees and occasionally was asked theological questions by the detainees, such as clarifications on religious rulings and Koran readings. He described his task as establishing "a cordial relationship with anybody, whether they are a detainee or not". His role as a chaplain was to approach everybody as human beings.[1237] Chaplain SAIF UL ISLAM also held press briefings because he was considered to be in touch with the detainees.

The dual-hatted role of the chaplain as minister to the detainees and advisor to the commander of the Joint Task Force "can be complex"[1238] and is certainly not unproblematic. When a number of detainees went on hunger strike after an

---

[1231] Military Order of November 13, 2001, Detention, Treatment, and Trial of Certain Non-Citizens in the War Against Terrorism, 66 Federal Register 57.833 (November 16th, 2001), *available at* http://frwebgate.access.gpo.gov/cgi-bin/getdoc.cgi?dbname=2001_register&docid=01-28904-filed.pdf.

[1232] *Id.* Art. 3 (d).

[1233] *See* Ron Craddock, *From the Front: Ministry in a War Zone*, THE NAVY CHAPLAIN, No. 3/2003, at 9, 10.

[1234] *See* Kelvin C. James, *Guantanamo Bay Reflections: Spiritual Readiness and the New War*, THE NAVY CHAPLAIN, No. 3/2003, at 13.

[1235] Odom, *supra* note 7, at 50.

[1236] *See* Odom, *supra* note 7, at 41.

[1237] *See* STEPHEN KAUFMAN, EID AL-ADHA OBSERVED AT CAMP X-RAY (U.S. Department of State International Information Programs February 26th, 2002), *available at* http://usinfo.state.gov/topical/pol/terror/02022604.htm.

[1238] Odom, *supra* note 7, at 41.

inmate had been bared from wrapping his head while praying, SAIF UL ISLAM convinced them to resume taking meals with arguments based on Islamic scripture.[1239] Also, in the course of their captivity, detainees only have limited social contacts among themselves and to intelligence interrogators who are questioning them about their previous activities. When meeting the chaplain, they show emotions and open up to him.[1240] It is important to this relationship to remain one of spiritual assistance and not to be used for intelligence ends. It seems also very dangerous that communications between chaplains and detainees are not privileged. Instead, content of such communications is admissible at military commissions trials that some of the detainees will be facing.[1241] Very interesting is ODOM's approach who – given the vague language of U.S. Navy regulations on privileged communications – constructs a duty to refrain from disclosing content of communications with detainees from the non-combatant character of chaplains.[1242] At first sight, it looks like a remote link, but at second look, it appears as a very consistent interpretation of the non-combatant role of a chaplain that is worth to be noted.

Respect for communications between detainees and the chaplain may also be a dictate of the humane treatment requirement of common Art. 3. Privileges for the minister/faithful relationship serve to protect an absolute core of privacy, a sphere of intimacy. And this sphere of intimacy is an outflow of human dignity because every man needs some inviolable refuge that cannot be touched by the state, not even in cases of prosecution or situations of emergency. This is especially true for detainees. Under the circumstances of their confinement, they hardly have such an intimate sphere: Their social interactions among themselves are extremely restricted. The social contacts that remain are either that with JTF GTMO interrogators or with the chaplain. Emotionally opening up to the chaplain then seems to be a very human movement. It should, however, be recognized that in the actual circumstances, pressure on the chaplain to disclose content of communications either for formal proceedings or for intelligence gather-

---

[1239] *See* JIM GARAMONE, TENSION EASES AT GUANTANAMO HOLDING FACILITY (American Forces Press Service March 1st, 2002), *available at* http://www.dod.gov/news/Mar2002/n03012002_200203012.html, Odom, *supra* note 7, at 54.

[1240] *See* DETAINEES AT GUANTANAMO BAY OPEN UP TO MUSLIM CHAPLAIN (Transcript of a news item aired on CNN February 3rd, 2002), *available at* http://edition.cnn.com/TRANSCRIPTS/0202/03/sun.11.html.

[1241] *See* Odom, *supra* note 7, at 60, *see also* MICHAEL N. SCHMITT, TRIAL, DETENTION OR RELEASE? (May 17th, 2002), *available at* http://www.crimesofwar.org/expert/detain-schmitt.html (for the evidentiary standards of military commission proceedings in general).

[1242] *See* Odom, *supra* note 7, at 63 (Odom, however, contradicts himself. First he argues that the appointment of U.S. chaplains as substitute ministers in U.S. detention facilities did not follow the letter of the law. *see id.* at 52, but then tries to apply the law of armed conflict with regard to substitute ministers in order to construct a duty to protect communications through an obligation of compliance with professional ethics. *see id.* at 64.)

ing may be significant. ODOM mentions three hypothetical scenarios in this regard.[1243]

From the little that is know about the routine in Camp Delta in the media, some action has been taken with regard to the exercise of religion by the about 680 detainees of 40 nationalities who receive visits from the ICRC:[1244] The detention cells are equipped with signs that indicate the direction of Mecca so that Muslim prisoners know which way to face during prayer.[1245] The public-address system of the camp calls for prayer five times a day. The design of meals is sensitive to the halal rules.[1246] Detainees are issued a spare towel to use as prayer mat and are supplied with prayer caps, prayer oils and finger prayer beads.[1247] In addition, they were handed a copy of the Koran and have access to a selection of religious readings. Camp guards and other personnel were generally trained to be sensitive to the elements and culture of Islam.[1248] The small number of Christian detainees has been provided with bibles and is ministered to by a Christian chaplain.[1249]

In addition to Guantanamo, less prominent detention camps are located in Bagram Air Base, Afghanistan, and at the U.S. Navy Support Facility, located at Diego Garcia, a British Territory in the Indian Ocean.[1250] Conditions on exercise of religion in these facilities are fairly unknown.

Developments regarding spiritual assistance in Guantanamo took an unexpected turn when the Muslim military Chaplain Captain JAMES J. YEE was accused of smuggling classified material out of Cuba. YEE, a Chinese-American, is a 1990 graduate of the U.S. Military Academy West Point and subsequently served as an air defense artillery officer. After leaving active duty, he spent some time in Syria and returned to active duty in order to become a Muslim chaplain.

1243 *See id* at 65.

1244 *See* ICRC, GUANTANAMO BAY: THE WORK CONTINUES (Operational update July 18th, 2003), *available at* http://www.icrc.org/web/eng/siteeng0.nsf/iwpList124/5C867C1D85AA2BE541256C94006000EE.

1245 *See* Ted Conover, *In the Land of Guantánamo*, THE NEW YORK TIMES MAGAZINE, June 29th, 2003, at 40.

1246 *See* DETAINEES TREATED HUMANELY, OFFICIALS SAY (CNN news item January 23rd, 2002), *available at* http://edition.cnn.com/2002/US/01/21/xray.conditions/, GRIM LIFE AT GUANTANAMO (BBC news item February 7th, 2002), *available at* http://news.bbc.co.uk/1/hi/world/americas/1777033.stm.

1247 *See* Neil A. Lewis, *Fate of Prisoners From Afghan War Remains Uncertain*, THE NEW YORK TIMES, April 24th, 2003, at 1.

1248 *See* JOSHUA S. HIGGINS, RELIGION 101: MPS GET EDUCATION DURING DUTY (February 2002), *available at* http://www.defendamerica.mil/awt/feb2002/awt020702a.html.

1249 *See* KAUFMAN, *supra* note 1237.

1250 *See* Dan Priest & Barton Gellman, *U.S. Decries Abuse but Defends Interrogations*, THE WASHINGTON POST, December 26th, 2002, at A01, *available at* http://www.washingtonpost.com/ac2/wp-dyn/A37943-2002Dec25.

He completed the Army Chaplain's Officer Basic Course in April 2001. Prior to September 2003, he spent 10 months with JTF GTMO as its Muslim chaplain.[1251] During media statements, he repeatedly underscored the peaceful character of Islam.[1252]

Flying out from Guantanamo on rest and recuperation leave, YEE was arrested at Jacksonville Naval Air Station on September 10th, 2003 and then held in pre-trial confinement at the Naval Consolidated Brig at Charleston, SC. On September 15th, a military magistrate ruled that the military had sufficient reason to hold Chaplain YEE while it continued its investigation.[1253] Especially during these first weeks of the investigation without formal charges, speculations on possible espionage on the part of YEE circulated in the Media with references to unnamed military officials.[1254] YEE's arrest was the second of a series of three arrests of JTF GTMO personnel which caused a review of security procedures at Guantanamo.[1255] The U.S. Federal Bureau of Investigation considered these three cases – including that of Chaplain YEE - to be "potentially serious breaches of national security".[1256]

On October 10th, 2003, YEE was officially charged with two specifications of failing to obey a lawful general order by taking classified materials to his home and wrongfully transporting them without proper containers or covers which

---

1251 *See* Donna Miles, *Military Investigates Guantanamo Bay Cases*, AMERICAN FORCES INFORMATION SERVICE, September 24th, 2003, *available at* http://www.defenselink.mil/news/Sep2003/n09242003_200309245.html.

1252 *See* James J. Yee, *Chaplain's Corner*, THE WIRE, January 31st, 2003, at 3, 10, *available at* http://www.nsgtmo.navy.mil/jtfgtmo/wire/v03/i0/9/TheWire-v3-i09-31Jan03.pdf.

1253 *See* MILES, *supra* note 1251.

1254 *See* John Mintz & Susan Schmidt, *Muslim Army Chaplain Is Held in Investigation*, THE WASHINGTON POST, September 21st, 2003, at A16, Chris Plante, *U.S. Army Muslim chaplain arrested* (CNN News item, September 22nd, 2003), *available at* http://edition.cnn.com/2003/US/09/20/chaplain.arrest/index.html, *see also* Rowan Scarborough, *Islamic chaplain is charged as spy*, THE WASHINGTON TIMES, September 20th, 2003, *available at* http://www.washingtontimes.com/national/20030919-105619-9614r.htm (for the very first media report).

1255 *See* Donna Miles, *Third Suspect Eyed in Guantanamo Bay Case*, AMERICAN FORCES INFORMATION SERVICE, September 30th, 2003, *available at* http://www.defenselink.mil/news/Oct2003/n10012003_200309307.html, Steve Vogel & John Mintz, *Guantanamo Security Probe Widens*, THE WASHINGTON POST, September 25th, 2003, at A03, Eric Schmitt, *Ex-Chaplain With Detainees Is Charged*, THE NEW YORK TIMES, October 11th, 2003, at 10.

1256 *Terrorist Recruitment and Infiltration in the United States: Prisons and Military as an Operational Base: Hearing Before the Subcomm. on Terrorism, Technology, and Homeland Security of the S. Judiciary Committee*, 108th Cong. 4 (October 14th, 2003) (statement for the Record by John S. Pistole, FBI Assistant Dir., Counterterrorism Div.), *available at* http://kyl.senate.gov/legis_center/subdocs/101403_pistole.pdf.

constitute a violation of the U.S. Uniform Code of Military Justice (UCMJ).[1257] On November 25th, additional charges of false official statement,[1258] conduct unbecoming an officer[1259] and adultery were filed. Following an appeal of his lawyers to U.S. President George W. Bush,[1260] Chaplain YEE was released and assigned to Fort Benning, Ga. to face a preliminary investigation of the charges directed by the JTF GTMO commander in accordance with Art. 32 UCMJ.[1261] This pre-trial investigation would whether YEE had to stand court-martial and began on December 8th, 2003 but was suspended the following day in order to complete a classification review of documents used in the hearings. During the first day of the hearing, the investigating officer heard a U.S. customs special agent who had searched YEE's backpack at Jacksonville Naval Air Station and found therein a list of detainees and interrogators at JTF GTMO and several "suspicious" hand-written pages in small, green notebooks. The bag was not locked and the documents were not marked classified or in any way protected. In addition, a female Navy Lieutenant under a grant of immunity gave testimony of a sexual relationship with YEE during the time of their assignment to Guantanamo.[1262] Especially with emphasis on the adultery charges, media saw the spy charge against YEE falling apart[1263] - and should be right in the end. The pre-trial hearing against Yee was never resumed. It was delayed repeatedly before the military dismissed all charges citing national security concerns that would arise from the release of the evidence.[1264] This was made public on March 19th, a

---

1257 *See* CHARGES PREFERRED ON ARMY CAPTAIN JAMES YEE (U.S. Southern Command Media Statement), *available at* http://www.southcom.mil/pa/Media/Releases/PR031010.pdf, *see also* CHARGE SHEET FOR THE YEE CASE, *available at* http://news.findlaw.com/cnn/docs/dod/armyyee101003chrg.pdf.

1258 *See* 2ND CHARGE SHEET FOR THE YEE CASE, *available at* http://news.findlaw.com/hdocs/docs/dod/armyyee112503chrg.html (for the charge concerning the clearance of a Compact Disk for release to detainees).

1259 *See* John Mintz, *Chaplain's Release Comes With New Charges*, THE WASHINGTON POST, November 26th, 2003, at A05 (for the charge concerning pornographic material allegedly found on Yee's government computer).

1260 *See* John Mintz, *Lawyer Asks Bush to Free Chaplain*, THE WASHINGTON POST, November 25th, 2003, at A07.

1261 *See* YEE FACES ADDITIONAL CHARGES, ARTICLE 32 RELEASED FROM PRETRIAL CONFINEMENT (U.S. Southern Command Media Statement), *available at* http://www.southcom.mil/pa/Media/Releases/PR031125.pdf.

1262 *See* Kim Dooley, *Issues delay Yee hearing, Investigation held up by review*, U.S. ARMY TRAINING AND DOCTRINE COMMAND NEWS SERVICE, *available at* http://www-tradoc.army.mil/pao/TNSarchives/December03/121902.asp.

1263 *See Captain Yee's Ordeal*, THE NEW YORK TIMES, December 14th, 2003, at 10 (calling the prosecution "mean-spirited" and "incompetent"), Mark Miller, *A Very Curious Case*, NEWSWEEK [U.S. Edition], December 22nd, 2003, at 41.

1264 See CHARGES DISMISSED IN YEE CASE (U.S. Southern Command Media Statement), *available at* http://www.southcom.mil/pa/Media/Releases/PR040319Yee.pdf

Friday night in order to cause as few publicity as possible. On March 22nd, after an hour-long administrative hearing as part of a non-judicial proceeding in accordance with Art. 15 UCMJ, the JTF GTMO commander issued a reprimand against Yee for committing adultery and viewing pornography.[1265] The unprofessional management of the case was attributed to inexperienced reservist personnel deployed with the counter-intelligence of JTF GTMO. High public attention prevented to impose administrative disciplinary measures at an earlier stage.[1266]

The arrest of YEE coincided with arrest of ABDURAHMAN ALAMOUDI in late September 2003. The U.S. Muslim political activist who happened to be also active in the American Muslim Armed Forces and Veterans Affairs Council was charged with accepting money from Libya in violation of the U.S. embargo against the African country.[1267] The Council is the group that endorsed YEE for chaplaincy and came under review along with the other religious group recognized by the U.S. Department of Defense for the endorsement of military chaplains.[1268] Reviewed was also the Graduate School of Islamic and Social Sciences in Leesburg, Va. that trained a number of Muslim chaplains in the U.S. Armed Forces.[1269] The School certified the equivalence of YEE's qualifications with the academic requirements of its own Master program so that YEE could join military chaplaincy.[1270] An earlier federal investigation had focused on alleged financial ties of the School with al Quaeda sources.

Following the arrest of YEE and apparently not unrelated to it,[1271] the Subcommittee on Technology, Terrorism and Government Information of the U.S. Sen-

---

1265 *See Yee Guilty On Adultery, Porn Charges*, THE WASHINGTON POST, March 23rd, 2004, at A04.

1266 *See* Neil A. Lewis & Thom Shanker, *Missteps Seen in Muslim Chaplain's Spy Case*, THE NEW YORK TIMES, January 4th, 2004, at 1.

1267 *See* U.S. ALLEGES MUSLIM ACTIVIST HAS LIBYAN TIES (CNN News item, September 30th, 2003), *available at* http://edition.cnn.com/2003/LAW/09/29/muslim.arrest/, *see also Terrorist Recruitment and Infiltration in the United States: Prisons and Military as an Operational Base: Hearing Before the Subcomm. on Terrorism, Technology, and Homeland Security of the S. Judiciary Committee*, 108th Cong. (October 14th, 2003) (statement of J. Michael Waller, Annenberg Professor of International Communication, Inst. of World Politics), *available at* http://kyl.senate.gov/legis_center/subdocs/101403_wallerl.pdf (for a fairly comprehensive overview of media allegations against Alamoudi and his links to U.S. military chaplaincy).

1268 *See* Laurie Goodstein, *Pentagon says it will review Chaplain policy*, THE NEW YORK TIMES, September 28th, 2003, at 1.

1269 *See* Brian Ross, *Suspect School Ties* (ABC news item, September 29th, 2003), *available at* http://abcnews.go.com/sections/wnt/US/chaplain_school030929.html.

1270 *See* Letter of the GSISS executive dean to the chief of chaplains (April 18th, 2000), *available at* http://abcnews.go.com/sections/wnt/US/Ross_Statement4.html.

1271 *See Terrorist Recruitment and Infiltration in the United States: Prisons and Military as an Operational Base: Hearing Before the Subcomm. on Terrorism, Technology, and Homeland Security of the S. Judiciary Committee*, 108th Cong. 2 (October 14th, 2003) (Opening Statement of Sen. Jon Kyl, Chairman, Chairman, Subcommittee on Terrorism, Technology, and Homeland Security), *available at* http://kyl.senate.gov/legis_center/subdocs/101403_jkopen.pdf.

ate Judiciary Committee held a hearing about "Terrorist Recruitment and Infiltration in the United States: Prisons and Military as an Operational Base" on October 14th, 2003. In this hearing, a representative of the U.S. Department of Defense confirmed that his agency was seeking to find endorsement agencies for Muslim chaplains other the ones recognized.[1272] This committee hearing was supported additionally by political pressure built up by the senior Senator of the State of New York, CHARLES E. SCHUMER, himself a member of the Senate Judiciary Committee who used the arrest of YEE to renew his request to review the groups authorized to endorse Muslim chaplains for the armed services and underlined allegations against the American Muslim Armed Forces and Veterans Affairs Council.[1273] One of his press releases portrays SCHUMER as being baffled "that a chaplain who spent time in Syria ... and was trained by a group with ties to terrorism, would be allowed to serve as a cleric to a bunch of Taliban and al-Qaeda".[1274] He is quoted in the media criticizing that the military had chosen "a narrow, fundamentalist and extreme band of the spectrum ... [to] have a monopoly on who becomes an imam in the military".[1275] Asked about SCHUMER's initiative, U.S. Secretary of Defense Donald H. Rumsfeld conceded that "the services that handle the organizing and training and equipping of people in the military ought to reflect on that suggestion".[1276]

Compared to the early accusations of espionage, the charges that have actually been filed against YEE so far are relatively minor. In the end, the case which started off as a matter of national security appears more as coming down to personal misconduct by a chaplain – especially with the added charges of adultery.[1277] Even with a reprimand for personal shortcomings and individual missteps of Chaplain YEE who has publicly expressed gratitude to activists and

---

[1272] *See Groups Lose Sole Authority On Chaplains For Muslims*, THE NEW YORK TIMES, October 15th, 2003, at 15.

[1273] *See* Letter to the DoD Inspector General Joseph Schmitz (September 22nd, 2003), *available at* http://www.senate.gov/~schumer/SchumerWebsite/pressroom/special_reports/Imam%20Inspector%20General%20DoD%209.22.03.pdf, NEW REVELATION: CAPTAIN YEE WAS TRAINED AND SELECTED TO BE A MUSLIM CHAPLAIN BY GROUP BEING INVESTIGATED FOR TERRORISM (U.S. Senator Charles E. Schumer Press Release, September 23rd, 2003), *available at* http://www.senate.gov/~schumer/SchumerWebsite/pressroom/press_releases/PR02043.html.

[1274] *See* WITH GUANTANAMO ARRESTS SUGGESTING MAJOR MILITARY SECURITY PROBLEM, SCHUMER URGES TOP-TO-BOTTOM REVIEW OF MOST SENSITIVE BASES (U.S. Senator Charles E. Schumer Press Release, September 24th, 2003), *available at* http://www.senate.gov/~schumer/SchumerWebsite/pressroom/press_releases/PR02044.html.

[1275] *See* Goodstein, *supra* note 1268.

[1276] Secretary Rumsfeld Interview with Morris Jones, Sinclair Broadcasting (September 25th, 2003), *available at* http://www.defenselink.mil/transcripts/2003/tr20030925-secdef0708.html.

[1277] *See also* John Mintz, *Ex-Muslim Cleric at Guantanamo Faces Minor Charges*, THE WASHINGTON POST, October 11th, 2003, at A06 (quoting experts qualifying the case to be "relatively insignificant"). Neil A. Lewis, *Hearing Starts for Muslim Army Chaplain*, THE NEW YORK TIMES, December 9th, 2003, at 20 (for the effects on Yee's family).

supporters for calling public attention to his case[1278], the presumption of his innocence prevails. One thing, however, is already clear: On the losing side are the detainees at Guantanamo. With the legal status of their detention being unresolved, they do not know their future fate nor may dispose of means of recourse through any legal mechanism. These conditions cause the psychological health of many detainees to deteriorate.[1279] In this situation which is specially burdensome because of its open-endedness, the detainees do not have the assistance of religious personnel of their faith. Since the arrest of Chaplain YEE, no Muslim imam have been allowed to minister to the detainees and media learnt that there were no plans to provide a new chaplain in the future. The Army chaplain who was assigned in December 2003 to JTF GTMO only serves as religious advisor to the JTF commander and ministers to Muslims amongst service personnel.[1280] This reduction of the chaplain's role certainly solves the conflict of interests with the dual role of advisor to the commander and spiritual assistant to the detainees addressed earlier. Even with the disputed statuts of the detainees, the lack of any qualified spiritual assistance to them infringes upon their right to spiritual assistance. Disregarding even the requirements of the presidential order, Guantanamo is far from being a place of humane treatment and free exercise of religion. The dignity of the detainees and its religious aspect are disregarded.

3. Religious ministers as instigators

In the context of the aftermath of September 11th, 2001, western leaders did not fail to underline that their "war against terrorism" is not a conflict with the Muslim religion. However, the fact that extremists fuel the conflict with religious rhetoric and seemingly religious arguments demands a closer look at the circumstances.

Generally speaking, military chaplaincy is not unfamiliar in a Muslim environment. In history, a Muslim military chaplaincy existed e.g. in the Austrian royal and imperial army from 1882 until the end of World War I.[1281] Of course, contemporary Muslim military chaplaincy has its peculiarities, for instance in

---

[1278] *See* STARS AND STRIPES, December 5th, 2003, at 3, *available at* http://www.slite.afis.osd.mil/stripes/Dec2003/20031205.pdf.

[1279] *See* Neil A. Lewis, *Red Cross Criticizes Indefinite Detention In Guantánamo Bay*, THE NEW YORK TIMES, October 10th, 2003, at 1, GUANTANAMO BAY: OVERVIEW OF THE ICRC'S WORK FOR INTERNEES (ICRC Operational update, November 6th, 2003), *available at* http://www.icrc.org/web/eng/siteeng0.nsf/html/5QRC5V.

[1280] *See* Barbara Starr, *Pentagon official: No Muslim clerics for detainees* (CNN News item, January 6th, 2004), *available at* http://edition.cnn.com/2004/US/01/06/gitmo/index.html.

[1281] *See* Claudia Ham, *Von den Anfängen der Militärseelsorge bis zur Liquidierung des Apostolischen Feldvikariates im Jahr 1918*, *in* MILITÄRSEELSORGE IN ÖSTERREICH 66 (Roman-Hans Gröger ed. 2001) (four military imams in the rank of a captain and a military mufti in the rank of a major served Muslims enlisted from Bosnia-Herzegovina).

Iran where practice of religion is compulsory and enforceable by coercive means and closely associated with Shiite Islam as state doctrine. In Pakistan and Bangladesh, nearly all state institutions including military barracks have their own mosques and an associated religious official (*maulana*).[1282] Nothing is known about religious ministers amongst Taliban and Al Qaida fighters. However, even if they existed, current state practice of not attributing combatant quality to these groups would bare them from attaching protected chaplains to their ranks. Moreover, protection of religious ministers is not unknown amongst Muslims. Already the first caliph ABU BAKR (573-634) told his army that they would encounter pious people who lived in monasteries to serve god in seclusion. He ordered to leave them in peace, not to kill them and not to destroy their monasteries.[1283] His orders, however, were only too often disregarded. Religious personnel is also nowadays protected under Muslim law.[1284]

It is important to underline that religious ministers on all sides must not turn into instigators of the conflict – without regard whether they are civilian ministers or qualify as religious personnel. In the past years, self-defense against non-state actors was invoked and civilian terrorism repulsed with military campaigns. With categories converging, it seems attractive to consult another time period for sources that dealt with ministers when the distinction between military chaplains and civilian ministers did not yet exist: GENTILI expressed a differentiated view on the protection of clergy already in 1612. He elaborated that force did not consist merely in inflicting wounds. If religious men aided their countrymen by words or encouraged them against the enemy in speeches, during expeditions or amid the toils of war, their protected status ceased. Citing the Italian lawyer ANDREA ALCIATI'S *Emblemata*, he argued that the inciter is equally culpable with the committer of the sin. The horn-blower in AESOP'S fable, who excuses himself on the ground that he was not active in arms and wounded no one's body with the cruel sword, committed a greater sin since he roused other to arms.[1285] GENTILI conceded that religious instigators might be punished more mildly than soldiers, as their infliction was a contributing cause unless the doer of the deed would otherwise not have done it. This seems to be a helpful criterion also with regard to the distinction of legitimate support of and assistance to individuals in warfare by religious personnel and illegitimate fomentation of hostilities. Thus, the contribution of ministers of religion to a conflict must be examined very

---

[1282] *See* BOCK, *supra* note 795, at 250-251.

[1283] *See* NICOLAS, *supra* note 16, at 80, Liedermann, *supra* note 43, at 3, DEUTSCHES ROTES KREUZ, DIE GENFER ROTKREUZ-ABKOMMEN 4 (7th ed. 1980).

[1284] *See* AMEUR ZEMMALI, COMBATTANTS ET PRISONNIERS DE GUERRE EN DROIT ISLAMIQUE ET EN DROIT INTERNTIONAL HUMANITAIRE 449 (1997).

[1285] *See* GENTILI, *supra* note 128, at 262.

carefully in each case and the nature, origin and causes of the particular conflict have to be taken into account.

VATTEL later saw clergy as persons "who are often ready to fan the flame of discord and to provoke bloody wars".[1286] He positively defines the group of protected clergy as those "who are engaged in teaching religion, in governing the church and in celebrating public worship".[1287] In his view, ministers of the altar do not necessarily as a result of their vocation have "any character of inviolability".[1288] Instead, he considers refraining from the use of force as constitutive for protection. So, "they do not resist the enemy by force or violence, they give the enemy no right to use it towards them".

"Any form of participation – even indirect – in hostile acts"[1289] may jeopardize the protection of religious personnel. NICOLAS goes as far as to assert that activities solely designed to support the morale of the troops on the part of the chaplain jeopardize his protection under the GCs.[1290] A look into history reveals that judgment here is not as easy. Drawing a feasible line of distinction is difficult especially in cases where church and state are not separated but interwoven and engagement for belligerent cause have a religious dimension. Clergy in Spain, Italy, Austria and Germany played an active role in inciting the population in occupied countries and organizing resistance against Napoleonian France.[1291] A popular song in World War II was named "Praise the Lord and pass the ammunition". Words and lyrics by FRANK LOESSER describe a chaplain manning a gun during the December 7th, 1941 Japanese air raid on Pearl Harbor.[1292] The actual incident is historically not proven but would certainly have been a violation of status. An understanding of chaplaincy as a means to strengthen military discipline and the efficiency of the fighting force by way of strengthening the role of religion in the military existed in modern western armies still in the late 1960s. Making troops "more faithful to the flag" was seen as a responsibility of the chaplain.[1293] Meanwhile, the emphasis of chaplaincy as an institution to maintain freedom of religion prevailed.[1294] However, questions remain: What then is direct support for a military operation? What about advocating values that happen to be functional to soldierly performance and de-

---

[1286] VATTEL, *supra* note 120, bk. III, ch. 2, § 10 at 238.
[1287] *Id.*
[1288] *Id.* bk. III, ch. 2, § 146 at 283.
[1289] PICTET, *supra* note 132, at 221, *see also supra* note 1202.
[1290] *See* NICOLAS, *supra* note 16, at 309.
[1291] *See* KARMA NABULSI, TRADITIONS OF WAR 58-59 (1999) (with illustrative examples).
[1292] *See* Walt East, *Chaplain Inspires Ammo Handlers at Pearl Harbor*, THE NAVY CHAPLAIN, July/ August 2001, at 15.
[1293] Paul. J.Weber, *The first amendment and the military chaplaincy*, 22 Journal of church and state 459, 465 (1980).
[1294] *See id.* at 465.

emphasizing values that are potentially dysfunctional?[1295] The commentators of the San Remo Manual of naval warfare expressively excluded from protected vessels on religious missions cases in which the use of force for religious ends is advocated.[1296] Where does such advocacy start; and where does it end? So what is the distinction between admissible and inadmissible activities of chaplaincy? When does such activity turn hostile? Serving the spiritual needs of soldiers indirectly also serves to uphold their combativity, their capacity to engage in warfare and military efficiency. In order to preserve its status, chaplaincy will have to firmly grasp the notion of serving religion as an aspect of human dignity instead of serving the military effort. They have to remain neutral to the belligerent enterprise. The same is true for ministers to the civilian population.

HIEBEL in his attempt to define spiritual assistance points out the nature of chaplaincy as presence and aid.[1297] This may serve as a line of orientation but must be seen in the context of the presence for and aid to the individual and not to the common military endeavor. The comparison with the Red Cross Red Crescent medical personnel whose activities are governed by the principles of neutrality, impartiality and independence emphasize the difficulties of this distinction. Religion tries do remain independent, but is far from being impartial and neutral as it sides with the poor, the weak and the oppressed and publicly expresses political and moral views. The Commission for the Revision of the CIC in 1980 even went as far as to delete the prohibition for clergy to participate in civil war and internal disturbances from canon law because it felt that clerics could not remain indifferent in these cases.[1298] Religions in many cases – even some aspects of the Christian religion – are revolutionary in nature. The term revolutionary is used here intentionally because its implications in humanitarian law hint to the difficulties it causes in the context of protection of religious personnel.

Examples for a strong dedication to abstain from incompatible activities that may be interpreted as hostile are found with the U.S. Navy. U.S. Navy Regulations are very clear in their Article 1063 that provides: "While assigned to a combat area during a period of armed conflict, members of … Chaplain … Corps … shall be detailed or permitted to perform only such duties as are related to … religious service and the administration of … religious units and establishments".[1299] The U.S. Navy not even a month after September 11th, 2001

[1295] *See* HERSPRING, *supra* note 434, at 47

[1296] *See supra* note 170.

[1297] *See* Hiebel, *supra* note 17, at 540.

[1298] *See supra* note 339.

[1299] DEPARTMENT OF THE NAVY, U.S. NAVY REGULATIONS, Art. 1063 at 89 (1990) *available at* http://neds.nebt.daps.mil/Directives/regs/ch-10.pdf.

issued a policy letter addressed to all Navy chaplains[1300] that very strictly stated the restrictions on chaplains' conduct: Non-combatant status required to "do more than simply refrain from carrying or using weapons; it requires a non-combatant state-of-mind." This meant to "never participate in any activity that compromises non-combatant status." The examples of such prohibited conduct in the policy letter included: "participating in the planning of military actions", "carrying or conveying military intelligence" and "transporting weapons or ammunition from one location to another". It seems as if this policy does not "raise the bar above the standards established under international law",[1301] but merely interprets the norms of international law in a correct manner. Interesting here is a self-defense scenario that ODOM mentions: If a chaplain and his auxiliary personnel catch fire by a sniper in a combat environment, the chaplain is not permitted to order his subordinated auxiliary personnel to fire back even though he usually is superior in rank. The issuance of orders to return fire by the chaplain could be considered a hostile act and turn the chaplain into a lawful target.[1302]

X. Conclusions

Protection of ministers of religion has already been known to ancient cultures. For Christianity, their protection was associated with the prohibition to engage in warfare. This dualism is firmly rooted in a variety of sources from the classical period of canon law that also established a context to just war doctrine. Protection takes another form in the legal instruments of the *Treuga Dei.* A historical evaluation of this protection in canon law is difficult since a lot of aspects come into play - and none of them seem seems to have appeared in a pure form: temporary protection of civilian population paired with the aim of the church to protect its own goods and personnel,[1303] periods of peace as well as wars waged under ecclesiastical command to enforce a *Treuga Dei* – with clergymen carrying war banners into the battle field. The issue of ambiguity in motives and the question about the ethics of peace-creating military missions are apparently not only nowadays subjects of dispute. It seems, however, legitimate to conclude that the church approached war and that it did so in a dual sense; it engaged actively in warfare and at the same time tried to reduce the effects of wars that were not in its primary interest. Given this practice, church doctrine

---

1300 *See* DEPARTMENT OF THE NAVY, OFFICE OF CHIEF OF NAVAL OPERATIONS, CHIEF OF CHAPLAINS, CHAPLAIN OF THE MARINE CORPS AND DEPUTY CHIEF OF CHAPLAINS FOR TOTAL FORCE, POLICY LETTER 1730 Ser N097/01301 (November 8th, 2001) *cited in* Odom, *supra* note 7, at 20-21.

1301 *But see* Odom, *supra* note 7, at 21.

1302 *See id.* at 24-26.

1303 *See* DICKMANN, *supra* note 25, at 105.

was not convincingly clear. But the exemption of certain categories of persons from being targeted in warfare can be considered an achievement.

Modern times brought about a merger of protection under the chivalric custom and canon law. The new single doctrine took into account humanitarian considerations and formed a basis on which the contemporary legal category of non-combatants with the principles of discrimination and proportionality could be built.[1304] After the emergence of the modern state in Europe and the development of classical international law, the protection of clergy was taken away from the domain of religious law and was covered by inter-state law of war often in the form of individual agreements. Protection for ministers of religion in wartime was subsequently not reasoned by their sacred character but their function as providers of spiritual assistance and thus humanitarian considerations.

After the emergence of the Red Cross Movement in the second half of the 19th century, norms on respect and protection in legal conventions dealt with safeguards for the security of military chaplains. These norms saw a number of variations in the revisions of the following decades. The question of retention of chaplains after capture or their return to own forces is an illustrative example for such change. The Holy See as representation of catholic leadership in the international domain followed these developments after some hesitation with increasing interest. By the mid 20th century, the Holy See had recognized the functional protection provided by the revised Red Cross Conventions and had become an important contributor to the expanding body of IHL. The teachings of the catholic church nowadays go very thoroughly into the details of IHL, call unequivocally for its respect and development in the context of its peace doctrine and particularly underline the transcendent references of IHL. Acknowledgement of IHL as an instrument to curb the savagery of warfare appears to be legitimate and argumentatively well-founded. Parallely, the protected realm, military chaplaincy within the catholic church, has developed into a specialized ministry in a military environment on land and at sea with a number of peculiarities. After constructive experiences in the practice of various countries and concise policy statements of the Second Vatican Council in this regard, the search for a suitable place of military chaplaincy in catholic ecclesiology and canon law has significantly progressed in the passed decades.

German history has seen various models of military chaplaincy with different levels of integration into the armed forces. The impressions of two world wars produced a civilly organized chaplaincy in the Federal Republic of Germany on the basis of constitutionally guaranteed freedom of religion and a number of agreements between the state and the churches. Cooperation with military structures without integration assures a ministry near to the soldiers and at the

---

[1304] *See* JOHNSON, *supra* note 76, at 166.

same time independent from the state. A specific, though not undisputed feature of the German domestic legal system, which turns out to have protective value for religious ministers in armed conflict, is the incorporation of the *privilegium immunitatis* of the 1917 CIC: Ministers are exempt from military service.

German military chaplains have been deployed on missions abroad since the early 1990s. Even though none of these operations has been qualified as an armed conflict, operations in the aftermath of September 11th, 2001 pose a new quality of conflict and an increased level of threat to German troops and their chaplains. Company to soldiers on missions has become an important aspect of religious ministry in the armed forces. The extraordinary environment of foreign deployment and the conditions of camp life confront chaplains with special challenges in the pastoral care for soldiers. Their assistance in many cases happens on the basic level of existential questions about human existence and suggests answers without going into the details of religious doctrine. Specific practical tasks are assigned to chaplains as advisors in religious affairs during peacekeeping and humanitarian operations.

The Geneva Conventions of 1949 are the most significant source of legal protection for military chaplains that is similar to that of medical personnel. While sometimes unclear in their terminology, the GCs assure respect and protection. The activities of a chaplain in the exercise of his functions are protected through the possibility to exercise these functions and to provide best possible conditions therefor.[1305] The two requirements of protection for chaplains are their attachment to the armed forces as official state act and exclusivity of their ministry. Respect for chaplains is assured by the use of the distinctive emblem of the GCs on protective means for chaplains like armlet and identity card. As a consequence of their protection, chaplains may only be retained upon capture if the spiritual needs of POW demand so and otherwise have to be returned to their party. In captivity, they enjoy a privileged detainee status with the rules on POW treatment as a bottom line. Retained chaplains and chaplains remaining voluntarily with POW enjoy a number of facilities. When framing the norms concerning these facilities, the international legislator was guided by a balance between assurances for an effective exercise of religious ministry among POW and the security needs in the setting of a POW camp. The status of chaplains at sea is similar to that of chaplains on land even though chaplains of hospital ships may not be retained. The groups of combatants to which chaplains may be attached was clarified and enlarged by the definition of PA I. This definition also opted definitively for the term religious personnel but understands it as only applying to ministers serving in a military environment.

[1305] *See* PICTET, *supra* note 530, at 218.

In non-international armed conflict, religious personnel is protected on different levels that have not been equally well received by the states. Common Art. 3 assures humane treatment to non-combatants and is supplemented by international human rights instruments, specially those on the subject of freedom of religion. This protection is spelled out in detail in PA II. An issue of special concern is the execution of the attachment of chaplains by non-official actors in a non-international conflict.

Spiritual assistance to armed forces by religious personnel is a subject not systematically but comprehensively protected in the GCs and PAs.[1306] A lot has been achieved during the past in protection of religious personnel.[1307] Without doubt, it gained in precision and force within the past five decades.[1308]

The protection of religious ministers as carriers of pastoral care to civilian population during times of armed conflict and occupation is yet another topic. Even though religions give significant input to conflict resolution and post-conflict rebuilding, the practice shows a picture of ministers often targeted in warfare and exposes an urgent need for effective protection. Compared to the first three conventions, the approach of GC IV to protection of ministry in a civilian context is different in substance and in methodology: There is no protection-and-respect clause for civilian ministers but a focus on safeguarding the exercise of religion. Ministers' activities enjoy only very limited prerogatives. Beyond these prerogatives, they are protected by their civilian character and the respect for religious convictions and practices. Right now, an explicit protection for places of cults is only granted to protect cultural patrimony. The norms of the HC granting respect to personnel that is responsible for the protection of culturally valuable place of worship may also affect religious ministers. Other than that, religious places are protected as civilian objects.

The protection of ministry and ministers in international law is not an end in itself but must be seen associated with the exercise of religion based on freedom of religion as an aspect of the common and equal dignity of every person that is the basis of humanitarian law.[1309] Thus, protection is not a triumph of the "church as an institution"[1310] but a gesture of respect for the human nature. With this being said, the notion of a comprehensive protection of religious ministers in a civilian or military environment comes into reach. The current legal regime on protection follows such an approach only in very specific instances. Instead, it underlines the distinction between religious personnel and civilian ministers of religion but reaches limits in certain types of conflict. On the other hand, a con-

---

[1306] *See* Hiebel, *supra* note 180, at 14, Rausch, *supra* note 139, at 35.
[1307] *See* Kussbach, *supra* note 144, at 390, Schlögel, *supra* note 38, at 278.
[1308] *See* Hiebel, *supra* note 180, at 27.
[1309] *See* BERTELLO, *supra* note 303.
[1310] *See* Schubiger, *supra* note 145, at 5, HIEBEL, *supra* note 142, at 220.

cept integrating civilian and military ministry may be favored by a dogmatic convergence of protection under IHL and human rights law and by a practical convergence of spiritual needs after WMD incidents. However, for reasons of practical and policy considerations, a uniform level of protection by way of simply applying the existing regime of protection for religious personnel on civilian ministers does not appear desirable.

The atypical structure of military chaplaincy in Germany does not conflict with the concept of chaplaincy in IHL that does not prescribe a specific national status as long as the two requirements of attachment and exclusivity are fulfilled. Attachment does not necessarily have to be translated into the public law relationship of civil servantship in German domestic law. Pastoral assistants of the catholic military chaplaincy may well qualify as chaplains under IHL. Although laypeople in ecclesiastical terms, they are exclusively devoted to their ministry. Their attachment may be executed by way of a framework agreement of the state and the church because the manifestation of the intent of a state therein is sufficient for the official act of attachment. With parochial helpers, however, the supportive aspect dominates. As auxiliary religious personnel, they fail to meet the requirements of religious personnel character and are not covered by protection. Part-time chaplains are not to be considered protected religious personnel unless they are devoted exclusively to military chaplaincy for some time as temporary religious personnel.

The legality of the use of arms by chaplains in self-defense cannot be simply assumed from the parallelism to legality of the use by medical personnel as it is commonly done. Convincing systematic and historic arguments oppose such an assumption but cannot remove the legal principle of legitimacy of self-defense. Under no circumstances may a national rule on the legitimacy of carrying a weapon have an effect on legality under IHL.

Given the tendencies of secularization in German society, the option of a non-religious assistance to non-believers, e.g. by humanistic councilors, brings up the issue of a protection of these personnel in international law. The question arises whether such an assistance falls under the scope of freedom of religion and convictions in the same way as a religious chaplaincy. Viewing recent developments in international criminal law, the international legislator appears willing to grant the same protection its grants to religious personnel to non-confessional non-combatant military personnel carrying out a similar function.

Examples of violators of IHL among military chaplains and civilian minister are few and are even sometimes utilized to discredit a clergyman – but they do exist. Given the frail and imperfect human nature, this is not surprising. However, IHL violators in the ranks of religious ministry challenge religions to not hinder legal procedures following due process of law and to not connive equivocally a culture of impunity.

With new type of conflicts, new types of missions emerge for military chaplains. Ministry to so called illegal combatants detained on Cuba is one of them. The double function of the chaplain as minister to detainees of his creed and advisor to the commander of the detention unit bears the potential of conflicting interests. A policy that excludes any access of religious ministers to provide spiritual assistance to detainees is not compatible with the humane treatment requirement of IHL, disregards the religious aspect in the detainees' dignity and is therefore unacceptable. An observation of future developments with regard to exercise of religion and the role of the chaplain will certainly be worth the efforts. When many conflicts of this 21st century have a component that exploits religion for ends disassociated from religion and when these conflicts run the risk of making use of WMD, it is more than ever important to underline the duty of religious ministers to refrain from words and deeds that could stir the conflict. Drawing the line of distinction between permissible and impermissible conduct is difficult. As categories converge, the orientation of both civilian ministers and religious personnel towards a non-combatant state of mind seems required.

So, can protection of religious personnel have a place in a legal order that has to stand *etsi deus non daretur*? The answer in the affirmative seems appropriate and is also given by the international legislator who grants far reaching protection to religious personnel. Nonetheless, life and limb of religious personnel remains menaced by a factual cause termed military necessity. In the end, the decision whether collateral damage involving religious personnel is proportional is a case-by-case judgment.

Contemporary man is very much on the search for himself and his authentic nature and often close to loosing himself in the war theaters of this world that are manmade. Human laws designed to regulate human behavior on an interpersonal, on a societal or on an international level are inscribed in man's nature.[1311] If this is where they are found, human laws will have to be designed as tools to protect that very nature. Spiritual needs are an integral part of human existence.[1312] As it provides meaning and orientation, religion must not be excluded from the public domain, including a war scenery. And since no other way is lifelike, human laws provide protection in warfare. If taken seriously and not made instrumental to serve a hidden agenda, religion can hardly serve as a legitimate justification for war but helps to find the path for lasting peace. The "equation between true Peace and the dignity of Life"[1313] demands a comprehensive protection of human dignity – including its religious aspect – in order to reach true peace. This is done by protecting religious personnel.

[1311] *See* JOHN XXIII, *supra* note 244, No. 6.
[1312] *See* NICOLAS, *supra* note 16, at 311.
[1313] WAYS OF PEACE, *supra* note 879, at 101.

Appendix

I. Means of Protection

a. Distinctive Emblems

The shapes of the red cross, the red crescent or the red lion and sun (not used since 1980) for the distinctive emblem are recognized in Art. 38 GC I, Art. 41 GC II. The models are in accordance with Art. 3 (1) Annex I to PA I (as amended on November 30th, 1993).

Latest proposal for an additional distinctive emblem as published on the ICRC webpage. The final choice of the name and graphic design of the new emblem is subject to further consideration.

The international distinctive sign of civil defense according to Art. 66 (4) PA I and as referred to in Art. 15 (1) Annex I to PA I (as amended on November 30th, 1993).

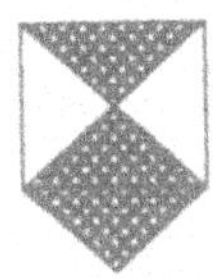

The Distinctive Emblem of the Convention for the Protection of Cultural Property in the Event of Armed Conflict according to Art. 16 HC.

b. Armlet of German Military chaplains

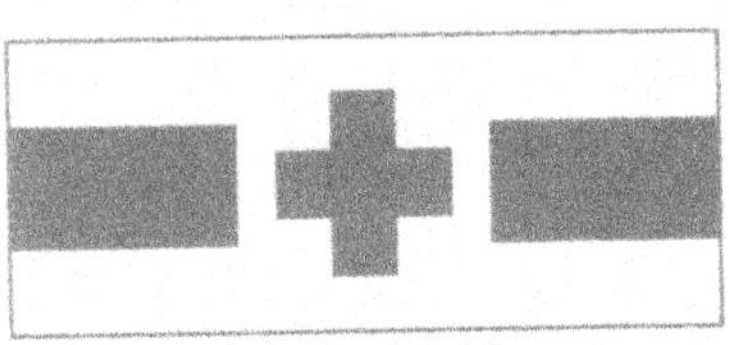

ordinary side

extraordinary side

II. Identity Cards
(reduced in size)

Front | Reverse Side

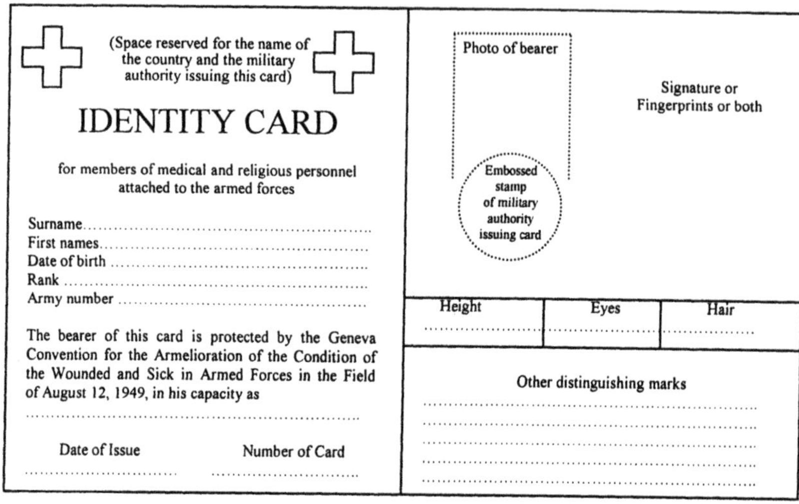
(Space reserved for the name of the country and the military authority issuing this card)

IDENTITY CARD

for members of medical and religious personnel attached to the armed forces

Surname........

First names........

Date of birth........

Rank........

Army number........

The bearer of this card is protected by the Geneva Convention for the Amelioration of the Condition of the Wounded and Sick in Armed Forces in the Field of August 12, 1949, in his capacity as

....

Date of Issue .... Number of Card ....

Photo of bearer

Embossed stamp of military authority issuing card

Signature or Fingerprints or both

Height	Eyes	Hair
....	....	....

Other distinguishing marks

....

a. Model Identity Card for Members of Medical and Religious Personnel attached to the Armed Forces referred to in Art. 40 (3) GC I and shown in Annex II to GC I

Front | Reverse Side

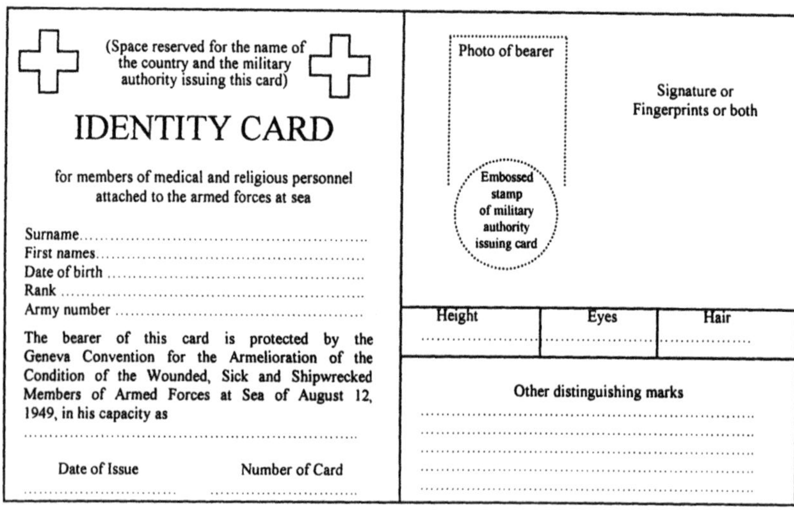
(Space reserved for the name of the country and the military authority issuing this card)

IDENTITY CARD

for members of medical and religious personnel attached to the armed forces at sea

Surname........

First names........

Date of birth........

Rank........

Army number........

The bearer of this card is protected by the Geneva Convention for the Amelioration of the Condition of the Wounded, Sick and Shipwrecked Members of Armed Forces at Sea of August 12, 1949, in his capacity as

....

Date of Issue .... Number of Card ....

Photo of bearer

Embossed stamp of military authority issuing card

Signature or Fingerprints or both

Height	Eyes	Hair
....	....	....

Other distinguishing marks

....

b. Model Identity Card for Members of Medical and Religious Personnel attached to the Armed Forces at Sea referred to in Art. 42 (3) GC II and shown in the Annex to GC II

FRONT

(space reserved for the name of the country and authority issuing this card)

IDENTITY CARD

for PERMANENT / TEMPORARY civilian medical / religious personnel

Name ....

Date of birth (or age) ....
Identity No. (if any) ....

The holder of this card is protected by the Geneva Conventions of 12 August 1949 and by the Protocol Aditional to the Geneva Conventions of 12 August 1949, and relating to the Protection of Victims of International Armed Conflicts (Protocol I) in his capacity as ....

Date of issue .... No. of card ....

Signature of issuing Autority

Date of expiry ....

REVERSE SIDE

Heihgt	Eyes	Hair ....

Other distinguishing marks or information

PHOTO OF HOLDER

Stamp	Signature of holder or thumbprint or both

c. Model of Identity card for permanent civilian medical and religious personnel (74 mm x 105 mm) according to Art. 1 (2) Annex I to PA I (as of 6 June 1977). The amended version of Annex I of 30 November 1993 also asks for the indication of the holder's blood group on the reverse side.

FRONT

(space reserved for the name of the country and authority issuing this card)

IDENTITY CARD
for civil defence personnel

Name ....

Date of birth (or age) ....
Identity No. (if any) ....

The holder of this card is protected by the Geneva Conventions of 12 August 1949 and by the Protocol Aditional to the Geneva Conventions of 12 August 1949, and relating to the Protection of Victims of International Armed Conflicts (Protocol I) in his capacity as ....

Date of issue .... No. of card ....

Signature of issuing Autority

Date of expiry ....

REVERSE SIDE

Height	Eyes	Hair ....

Other distinguishing marks or information:

Weapons ....

PHOTO OF HOLDER

Stamp	Signature of holder or thumbprint or both

d. Model Identity card for civil defense personnel (format: 74 mm x 105 mm) as referred to in Art. 15 (2) of Annex I to PA I (as amended on November 30th, 1993).

Front

Reverse Side

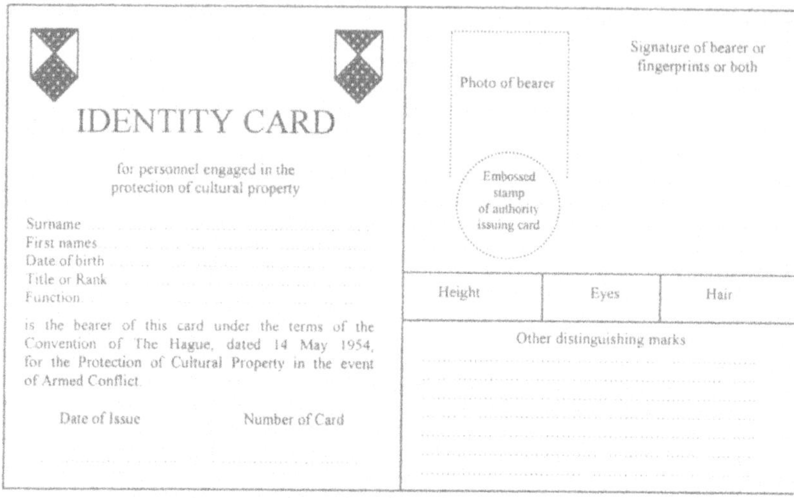

IDENTITY CARD

for personnel engaged in the protection of cultural property

Surname ....
First names ....
Date of birth ....
Title or Rank ....
Function ....

is the bearer of this card under the terms of the Convention of The Hague, dated 14 May 1954, for the Protection of Cultural Property in the event of Armed Conflict.

Date of Issue — Number of Card

Photo of bearer

Signature of bearer or fingerprints or both

Embossed stamp of authority issuing card

Height	Eyes	Hair

Other distinguishing marks

e. Identity Card of the Convention for the Protection of Cultural Property in the Event of Armed Conflict according to Art. 17 (1) d HC, Art. 21 Regulations for the Execution of the Convention for the Protection of Cultural Property in Event of Armed Conflict.

III. Shoulder boards used by Bundeswehr chaplaincy

By protestant chaplaincy

By catholic chaplaincy

Bibliography

Ackermann, Dirck	*Einsatz – Auf der Suche nach der Religion?, in* FÜR RUHE IN DER SEELE SORGEN 51 (2003).
Ackermann, Dirck	*Das deutsche evangelische Militärseelsorgemodell im internationalen Praxistest, in* FÜR RUHE IN DER SEELE SORGEN 116 (2003).
Alvarez, David	*The Holy See and the first Hague Peace Conference (1899),* 26 ARCHIVUM HISTORIAE PONTIFICIAE 431 (1988).
Amnesty International	SAN VICENTE DEL CAGUÁN AFTER THE BREAKDOWN OF THE PEACE TALKS, AMR 23/098/2002 (October 16th, 2002), *available at* http://web.amnesty.org/aidoc/aidoc_pdf.nsf/Index/AMR230982002ENGLISH/$File/AMR2309802.pdf.
Ancic, Nediljko A.	*Den Krieg erleiden – Versöhnung fördern,* 2000 MILITÄRSEELSORGE 104.
Assenmacher, Günter	DIE WEHRPFLICHTBEFREIUNG DER GEISTLICHEN (1987).
Baader, Peter	*Schutz religiöser Freiheitsrechte in den Streitkräften,* 2000 TRUPPENPRAXIS/WEHRAUSBILDUNG 744.
Ball, Albert	DIE ERRICHTUNG VON BUNDESOBERBEHÖRDEN (1964).
Bartmann, Reinhold	DIE RECHTLICHEN GRUNDLAGEN DER KATHOLISCHEN SEELSORGE IN DER BUNDESWEHR (unpublished „Diplom" thesis, University of Regensburg produced after 1986).
Baura, Eduardo	LEGISLAZIONE SUGLI ORDINARIATI CASTRENSI (1992).
Baura, Eduardo	*The Military Ordinariates from the perspective "Communio Ecclesiarum",* 1996 DIECI ANNI DOPO 55.

Baura, Eduardo	*The Episcopal Title of the Military Ordinary,* 1997 PASTORALIS MILITUM CURA No. 2, at 13.
Beal, John P. / Coriden, James A. / Green, Thomas J.	NEW COMMENTARY OF THE CODE OF CANON LAW (2000).
Berber, Friedrich	[2 Kriegsrecht] LEHRBUCH DES VÖLKERRECHTS (2nd ed. 1969).
Berndt, Joachim	INTERNATIONALER KULTURGÜTERSCHUTZ (1998).
Bertello, Giuseppe	INTERVENTION OF THE HOLY SEE AT THE 27TH INTERNATIONAL CONFERENCE OF THE RED CROSS AND RED CRESCENT SOCIETIES (November 2nd, 1999), *available at* http://www.vatican.va/roman_curia/secretariat_state/documents/rc_seg-st_doc_19991102_croix-rouge_fr.html.
Bettenson, Henry (ed.)	DOCUMENTS OF THE CHRISTIAN CHURCH (2nd ed. 1963).
Beyer, Jean	*Die Apostolische Konstitution Spirituali Militum Curae über die Militärordinariate,* 1990 MILITÄRSEELSORGE 235.
Bigler, Roland	*Disseminating international humanitarian law in Colombia,* 1997 INTERNATIONAL REVIEW OF THE RED CROSS 421-432, *available at* http://www.icrc.org/web/eng/siteeng0.nsf/iwpList162/DEF661C2493E2B05C1256B66005AC80B.
Blaschke, Peter H. & Oberhem, Harald	BUNDESWEHR UND KIRCHEN (1985).
Bleese, Jörn	DIE MILITÄRSEELSORGE UND DIE TRENNUNG VON STAAT UND KIRCHE (1969).
Block-Schlesier, Andreas von	DIE FRAGE DER AKZEPTANZ DES HUMANITÄREN VÖLKERRECHTS AM ENDE DES 20. JAHRHUNDERTS (1999).
Bock, Georg	*Der Schutz sanitätsdienstlicher, ärztlicher und seelsorgerischer Aufgaben, in* DIE GENFER ZUSATZPROTOKOLLE 184 (1993).

Bock, Martin	RELIGION WITHIN THE ARMED FORCES (1998).
Bock, Martin	DIE EINSTELLUNG ZUR MILITÄRSEELSORGE IN DER BEVÖLKERUNG UND BEI SOLDATEN IM BOSNIENEINSATZ DER BUNDESWEHR (2001).
Böckenförde, Ernst-Wolfgang & Spaemann, Robert	*Christliche Moral und atomare Kampfmittel,* 1960/61 MILITÄRSEELSORGE 267.
Boehm-Tettelbach, Wolfgang (ed.)	WEHRPLICHTGESETZ (3rd ed., continued looseleaf collection as of 2003).
Bogs, Harald	*Probleme des Geistlichenprivilegs im Wehrrecht,* 9 DER STAAT 43 (1970).
Böhm, A. H.	HET RECHT VAN KOLONISATIE (1936).
Bonhoeffer, Dietrich	LETTERS AND PAPERS FROM PRISON (1971).
Borchers, Carlheinz	*Rechtliche Grundlagen der Militärseelsorge und ihre Bewährung in der Praxis, in* KIRCHLICHER AUFTRAG UND POLITISCHE FRIEDENSGESTALTUNG 201 (Alfred Hierold et al. eds. 1995).
Bothe, Michael et al.	NEW RULES FOR THE VICTIMS OF ARMED CONFLICTS (1982).
Brunn, Walter et al.	1 DAS BUNDESENTSCHÄDIGUNGSGESETZ (1981).
Budd, Richard M.	SERVING TWO MASTERS: THE DEVELOPMENT OF AMERICAN MILITARY CHAPLAINCY (2002).
Bullard, Andrew J.	THE ROLE OF ARMY CHAPLAINS IN HUMANITARIAN RELIEF OPERATIONS (unpublished Directed Study, U.S. Army War College 2001).
Buß, Regina	DER KOMBATTANTENSTATUS (1992).
Butler, Carl Hubertus von & Walter, Jürgen	*Schritte auf dem Weg des Friedens, in* FÜR RUHE IN DER SEELE SORGEN 25 (2003).
Campenhausen, Axel v.	*Art. 141 WRV, in* 3 DAS BONNER GRUNDGESETZ (Christian Starck ed., 4th ed. 2001).
Cassese, Antonio et al. (eds.)	1 THE ROME STATUTE OF THE INTERNATIONAL CRIMINAL COURT (2002).

Catechism	CATECHISM OF THE CATHOLIC CHURCH (October 11th, 1992), *available at* http://www.vatican.va/ archive/ccc_css/archive/catechism/ccc_toc.htm.
Christus Dominus	DECREE CONCERNING THE PASTORAL OFFICE OF BISHOPS IN THE CHURCH "CHRISTUS DOMINUS" (October 28th, 1965), *available at* http://www.vatican.va/archive/hist_councils/ii_vatican_council/documents/vat-ii_decree_19651028_christus-dominus_en.html.
Conover, Ted	*In the Land of Guantánamo,* THE NEW YORK TIMES MAGAZINE, June 29th, 2003, at 40.
Councell, Gary R.	CHAPLAIN ROLES IN HUMANITARIAN AND CIVIC ASSISTANCE OPERATIONS (unpublished Directed Study, U.S. Army War College 1994).
Craddock, Ron	*From the Front: Ministry in a War Zone,* THE NAVY CHAPLAIN, No. 3/2003, at 9.
Crane, Barry	*Navy Chaplains and RPs Respond to the Attack on America,* THE NAVY CHAPLAINCY, Special Edition (December 2001), at 3.
David, Eric	PRINCIPES DE DROIT DES CONFLITS ARMÉS (2nd ed. 1999).
De Nó Louis Magalhaes, Eduardo	*Los acuerdos-tipo sobre retención y relevo del personal sanitario y religiosio,* 1958 REVISTA ESPAÑOLA DE DERECHO MILITAR, No. 5, at 135.
De Ram, Pierre-François-Xavier	RECHERCHES SUR L'HISTOIRE DES COMTES DE LOUVAIN ET SUR LEURS SÉPULTURES A NIVELLES (976-1096) (1851).
Demel, Sabine	*Pfarrhelfer, in* 8 LEXIKON FÜR THEOLOGIE UND KIRCHE col. 175 (Walter Kasper ed., 3rd ed. 1999).
Department of Defense	DOD NEWS BRIEFING BY DEFENSE SECRETARY RUMSFELD AND GENERAL MYERS (February 8th, 2002), *available at* http://www.defenselink.mil/ news/Feb2002/t02082002_t0208sd.html.
Department of the Army	THE LAW OF LAND WARFARE (1956).
Detter, Ingrid	THE LAW OF WAR (2nd ed. 2000).

Deutsches Rotes Kreuz	DIE GENFER ROTKREUZ-ABKOMMEN (7th ed. 1980).
Dickmann, Fritz	FRIEDENSRECHT UND FRIEDENSSICHERUNG (1971).
Dignitatis Humanae	DECLARATION ON RELIGIOUS FREEDOM "DIGNITATIS HUMANAE" ON THE RIGHT OF THE PERSON AND OF COMMUNITIES TO SOCIAL AND CIVIL FREEDOM IN MATTERS RELIGIOUS (December 7th, 1965), *available at* http://www.vatican.va/ archive/hist_councils/ii_vatican_council/documents /vat-ii_decl_19651207_dignitatis-humanae_en.html.
Dirksmeier, Anna	*Kultur der Gewalt,* 57 HERDERKORRESPONDENZ 564 (2003).
Direzione dell'Annuario Pontificio presso la Segreteria di Stato (ed.)	ANNUARIO PONTIFICIO PER L'ANNO 2003 (2003)
Diteweg, William T.	*The permanent deacon as military chaplain,* 51 THE JURIST 340 (1991).
DND/CF Ombudsman	HIRING OF MARK SARGENT, REPORT OF THE DND/CF OMBUDSMAN (August 7th, 2002).
Dolzer, Rudolf et. al. (eds.)	7, 13 KOMMENTAR ZUM BONNER GRUNDGESETZ (continued looseleaf collection as of 2003).
Döpfner, Julius	*Die Friedensfunktion der Kirche,* 1971 MILITÄRSEELSORGE 4.
Douglass, Wilbur C.	*Chaplain Emergency Response Team (CERT) - World Trade Center,* THE NAVY CHAPLAINCY, Special Edition (December 2001), at 11.
Draper, Gerald I.	REFLECTIONS ON LAW AND ARMED CONFLICTS (1998).
Dubost, Michel	*Spirituali Militum Curae and evangelium vitae,* 1996 DIECI ANNI DOPO 161.
Dunant, Henry	EINE ERINNERUNG AN SOLFERINO (1979).
East, Walt	*Chaplain Inspires Ammo Handlers at Pearl Harbor,* in THE NAVY CHAPLAIN, July/August 2001, at 15.

Edwards, Jim	*Lesson from the dirt*, THE NAVY CHAPLAIN, No. 4, Fall 2003, at 8.
Einig, Regina	*Die Achse der Unzufriedenheit,* DIE TAGESPOST, April 5th, 2003, at 3.
Ehlers, Dirk	*Art. 140 – Art. 141 WRV*, *in* GRUNDGESETZ (Michael Sachs ed., 3rd ed. 2003).
Elßner, Thomas R.	*Bezeichnet der Begriff "Nicht-Kombattant" in jedem Falle eine zivile Person?*, 2003 MILITÄRSEELSORGE 259.
Ennuschat, Jörg	*Sollen Militärgeistliche Staats- oder Kirchenbeamte sein? : Verfassungs-, völker- und beamtenrechtliche Aspekte,* 1996 ZEITSCHRIFT FÜR EVANGELISCHES KIRCHENRECHT 419.
Erdmann, Carl	DIE ENTSTEHUNG DES KREUZZUGSGEDANKENS (1974).
Falk, Bruno	*Militärseelsorge: Rechtliche Stellung und Verhältnis zur militärischen Führung*, 1973 TRUPPENPRAXIS 818.
Federal Political Department	2-A, 2-B FINAL RECORD OF THE DIPLOMATIC CONFERENCE FOR THE ESTABLISHMENT OF INTENATIONAL CONVENTIONS FOR THE PROTECTION OF WAR VICTIMS AND HELD AT GENEVA ON APRIL 21ST, TO AUGUST 12TH, 1949 (1950).
Federal Political Department	11, 13 OFFICIAL RECORDS OF THE DIPLOMATIC CONFERENCE ON THE REAFFIRMATION AND DEVELOPMENT OF INTERNATIONAL HUMANITARIAN LAW APPLICABLE IN ARMED CONFLICT (1978).
Fernandez-Flores, José Luis	*The Dissemination of the Law of War,* 1989/90 INTERNATIONAL INSTITUTE OF HUMANITARIAN LAW, YEARBOOK 3 (1992).
Ferrari, Silvio	*The Holy See and the Post-War Palestine issue,* 60 INTERNATIONAL AFFAIRS 261 (1984).
Ferrari, Silvio	*La Santa Sede e la questione die Gerusalemme da Madrid a Camp David, in* GERUSALEMME - CHIAVE DELLA PACE 33, 33-34 (Nicola Bux et al. eds. 2002).

Filibeck, Giorgio (ed.)	HUMAN RIGHTS IN THE TEACHING OF THE CHURCH (1994).
Filibeck, Giorgio	*Restoring a just order in post-conflict situations in the light of the social teachings of the Catholic Church,* 1998 INTERNATIONAL REVIEW OF THE RED CROSS 75, *available at* http://www.icrc.org/web/eng/siteeng0.nsf/iwpList166/B5105412999C5848C1256B66005B8C9C.
Filibeck, Giorgio	*The Force of Law Against the Law of Force,* L'OSSERVATORE ROMANO [english], August 11th/18th, 1999, at 6, *available at* http://www.petersnet.net/research/retrieve.cfm?recnum=1190.
Filibeck, Giorgio (ed.)	I DIRITTI DELL'UOMO NELL'INSEGNAMENTO DELLA CHIESA (2001).
Filibeck, Giorgio	LA CHIESA E IL DIRITTO UMANITARIO (unpublished paper presented at the International Course for the formation of catholic military chaplains in humanitarian law, Rome, March 25th, 2003).
Fischer, Heinz-Joachim	*Der Vatikan entdeckt die gerechte internationale Ordnung,* FRANKFURTER ALLGEMEINE ZEITUNG, February 26th, 2003, at 5.
Fischer, Heinz-Joachim	*Erziehung zum Frieden*, FRANKFURTER ALLGEMEINE ZEITUNG, December 16th, 2003, at 5.
Fischer, Horst	*Protection of Prisoners of War, in* THE HANDBOOK OF HUMANITARIAN LAW IN ARMED CONFLICTS 321 (Dieter Fleck ed. 1995).
Fischer, Horst	*Humanitäre Hilfe im Ausland*, 1996 HUMANITÄRES VÖLKERRECHT 198.
Fleck, Dieter	HUMANITARIAN PROTECTION OF THE CIVILIAN POPULATION IN ARMED CONFLICTS at 11 n.19 (Paper presented at the International Course for the formation of catholic military chaplains in humanitarian law, Rome, March 25th, 2003).

Friedberg, Emil (rev.)	1, 2 CORPUS IURIS CANONICI (photo. Reprint Lawbook Exchange 2000) (Aemilius Ludwig Richter ed. 1879).
Friedman, Leon (ed.)	1 THE LAW OF WAR (1972).
Friedrichsen, Gisela	*Krieg ist nicht human,* DER SPIEGEL No. 23, March 3rd, 2002, at 58.
Frohnhofen, Herbert	*Zwischen Pazifismus und Heiligem Krieg,* 116 STIMMEN DER ZEIT 831 (1991).
Gantin, Bernadin	*Discorso di apertura, in* DIECI ANNI DOPO 7 (1996).
Gardam, Judith Gail	NON-COMBATANT IMMUNITY AS A NORM OF INTERNATIONAL HUMANITARIAN LAW (1993).
Gasser, Hans-Peter	*Die Aktivitäten des Internationalen Komitees vom Roten Kreuz im Golfkrieg, in* DAS HUMANITÄRE VÖLKERRECHT IM GOLFKRIEG UND ANDERE ROTKREUZ-FRAGEN 5 (Wolfgang Voit ed. 1992).
Gasser, Hans-Peter	EINFÜHRUNG IN DAS HUMANITÄRE VÖLKERRECHT (1995).
Gasser, Hans Peter	PERSUADING STATES TO ACCEPT HUMANITARIAN TREATIES, *available at* http://www.icrc.org/ Web/eng/siteeng0.nsf/iwpList74/49849BB8753552 BCC1256B66005B05D1.
Gaudium et Spes	PASTORAL CONSTITUTION ON THE CHURCH IN THE MODERN WORLD "GAUDIUM ET SPES" (December 7th, 1965), *available at* http://www.vatican.va/ archive/hist_councils/ii_vatican_council/documents /vat-ii_cons_19651207_gaudium-et-spes_en.html.
Gentili, Alberico	1, 2 DE IURE BELLI LIBRI TRES (photo. reprint 1995) (Oxford ed. 1933).
Gilner, Matthias	BARTOLOMÉ DE LAS CASAS UND DIE EROBERUNG DES INDIANISCHEN KONTINENTS (1997).
Giovanni Paolo II	DISCORSO AL COMITATO INTERNAZIONALE DELLA CROCE ROSSA (June 15th, 1982), available at http://www.vaticanradio.org/ArchivioViaggi/Organ jsmiInternazionali/CRI15_06_82.htm.

Giovanni Paulo II	LA VITA CHRISTIANA COME CAMMINO VERSO LA PIENA COMUNIONE CON DIO (General Audience August 11th, 1999), *available at* http://www.vatican.va/holy_father/john_paul_ii/audiences/1999/documents/hf_jp-ii_aud_11081999_it.html.
Goodstein, Laurie	*Pentagon says it will review Chaplain policy,* THE NEW YORK TIMES, September 28th, 2003, at 1.
Görris, Gerhard Carl Wilhelm	DE DENKBEELDEN OVER OORLOG EN DE BEMOEIINGEN VOOR VREDE IN DE ELFDE EEUW (1912).
Gramm, Reinhard	*Zur Lage der evangelischen Militärseesorge*, 23 ESSENER GESPRÄCHE ZUM THEMA STAAT UND KIRCHE 146 (Heiner Marré & Johannes Stüting eds., 1989).
Gramm, Reinhard	*Den Standort geistig bestimmen,* 1990 INFORMATIONEN FÜR DIE TRUPPE 78.
Green, Leslie C.	THE CONTEMPORARY LAW OF ARMED CONFLICT (2nd ed. 2000).
Grewe, Wilhelm G. (ed.)	1 FONTES HISTORIAE IURIS GENTIUM (1995).
Grewe, Wilhelm G.	THE EPOCHS OF INTERNATIONAL LAW (Michael Byers trans. 2000).
Gronbach, Alfred	*Auf Leben und Tod, in* FÜR RUHE IN DER SEELE SORGEN 102 (2002).
Grotius, Hugo	DE JURE BELLI AC PACIS, THE TRANSLATION (photo. reprint Hein 1995) (1925).
Gurlt, Ernst Julius	ZUR GESCHICHTE DER INTERNATIONALEN UND FREIWILLIGEN KRANKENPFLEGE IM KRIEGE (photo. reprint 1972) (1873).
Hallek, Henry Wager	ELEMENTS OF INTERNATIONAL LAW AND LAWS OF WAR (1866).
Ham, Claudia	*Von den Anfängen der Militärseelsorge bis zur Liquidierung des Apostolischen Feldvikariates im Jahr 1918, in* MILITÄRSEELSORGE IN ÖSTERREICH 66 (Roman-Hans Gröger ed. 2001).

Harnack, Adolf	MILITIA CHRISTI (1981).
Hausmann, Paulus A.	*Die Spuren der treuga dei im Völkerrecht oder Vom Wandel des Friedensverständnisses, in* FRIEDEN UND VÖLKERRECHT 235 (Georg Picht et al. eds. 1973).
Hay, Gilbert	1 THE BUKE OF THE LAW OF ARMYS (1901).
Headquarters Department of the Army	HEADQUARTERS DEPARTMENT OF THE ARMY, FIELD MANUAL NO. 1-05, RELIGIOUS SUPPORT (April 18th, 2003).
Heinz Zahrnt	*Einführungs-Essay,* in 37 CHRISTLICHER GLAUBE IN MODERNER GESELLSCHAFT 15 (Franz Böckle et al. eds. 1984).
Hemmrich, Ulfried	*Art. 140, in* INGO VON MÜNCH & PHILIP KUNIG, 3 GRUNDGESETZ-KOMMENTAR (5th ed. 2003).
Henn, Petra	*Im Kontext der Neuevangelisierung – Theologische, pastorale und praktische Überlegungen zur „neuen" Bischöflichen Ordnung für die Fort-, Aus- und Weiterbildung der hauptamtlichen katholischen Militärgeistlichen und Pastoralreferenten,* 2002 MILITÄRSEELSORGE 96.
Herdegen, Matthias	*Der Kulturgüterschutz im Kriegsvölkerrecht, in* RECHTSFRAGEN DES INTERNATIONALEN KULTURGÜTERSCHUTZES 161 (Rudolf Dolzer et al. eds. 1994).
Herspring, Dale R.	SOLDIERS, COMMISSARS AND CHAPLAINS (2001).
Heydte, Friedrich August Freiherr von der	2 VÖLKERRECHT (1960).
Hiebel, Jean-Luc	CONTENU DE L'ASSISTANCE SPIRITUELLE POUR LES DIFFERENTS CROUANTS RELIGIEUX (paper submitted to the Colloquium on spiritual and intellectual assistance in the time of armed conflicts and civil disturbances, Milan, September 21st-23rd, 1973).
Hiebel, Jean-Luc	*Droit de l'Aumônerie, Droit de l'Assistance spirituelle,* 1 ANNUAIRE FRANÇAIS DES DROITS DE L'HOMME 531 (1974).

Hiebel, Jean-Luc	ASSISTANCE SPIRITUELLE ET CONFLITS ARMÉS (1980).
Hiebel, Jean-Luc	*Human rights relating to spiritual assistance as embodied in the Geneva Conventions of 1949,* 1980 INTERNATIONAL REVIEW OF THE RED CROSS 3. Also published in German: *Seelsorge als Menschenrecht in den Genfer Abkommen von 1949,* 1981 MILITÄRSEELSORGE 105. And also published in French: *Les droits humains de l'assistance spirituelle dans les Conventions de Genève de 1949,* 1980 REVUE INTERNATIONALE DE LA CROIX-ROUGE 3.
Hierold, Alfred E.	*Die Statuten für den Jurisdiktionsbereich des Katholischen Militärbischofs für die Deutsche Bundeswehr,* 1990 ARCHIV FÜR KATHOLISCHES KIRCHENRECHT 94.
Hierold, Alfred E.	*Die Militärseelsorge in den neuen Bundesländern aus katholischer Sicht, in* KIRCHLICHER AUFTRAG UND POLITISCHE FRIEDENSGESTALTUNG 221 (Alfred E. Hierold et al. eds. 1995)
Hierold, Alfred E.	*§ 54 Militärseelsorge, in* HANDBUCH DES KATHOLISCHEN KIRCHENRECHTS 555 (Joseph Listl et al. eds., 2nd ed. 1999).
Hörisch, Jochen	*Gegenfragen an Gretchen,* DER TAGESSPIEGEL, April 20th/21st, 2003, at 25.
Hörmann, Karl	*Krieg (ethisch), in* KATHOLISCHES SOZIALLEXIKON 1556 (2nd ed. 1980).
Huber, Max	DAS VÖLKERRECHT UND DER MENSCH (1952)
Human Rights Watch	LETTER TO DONALD RUMSFELD (May 29th, 2002), *available at* http://hrw.org/press/2002/05/pentagon-ltr.pdf.
ICRC	GUANTANAMO BAY: THE WORK CONTINUES (Operational update July 18th, 2003), *available at* http://www.icrc.org/web/eng/siteeng0.nsf/iwpList124/5C867C1D85AA2BE541256C94006000EE.

International Institute of Humanitarian Law (ed.)	POPE JOHN PAUL II TO THE INTERNATIONAL INSTITUTE OF HUMANITARIAN LAW (1982).
International Institute of Humanitarian Law	SAN REMO MANUAL ON INTERNATIONAL LAW APPLICABLE TO ARMED CONFLICTS AT SEA (1995).
Ipsen, Knut	*Combatants and Non-Combatants, in* THE HANDBOOK OF HUMANITARIAN LAW IN ARMED CONFLICTS 65 (Dieter Fleck ed. 1995).
Jahresbericht	UNTERRICHTUNG DURCH DEN WEHRBEAUFTRAGTEN - JAHRESBERICHT 2002 (44. BERICHT), Drucksache 15/500 (Deutscher Bundestag ed. November 3rd, 2003).
Jakovljevic, Bosko	*Rules of combat limitation ratione personae: Protection of wounded, sick and medical personnel in non-international armed conflicts,* 1989/90 INTERNATIONAL INSTITUTE OF HUMANITARIAN LAW YEARBOOK 181 (1992).
James, Kelvin C.	*Guantanamo Bay Reflections: Spiritual Readiness and the New War,* THE NAVY CHAPLAIN, No. 3/2003, at 13.
Jansen, Frank	*Protestant Chaplaincy in the Dutch Armed Forces in 1996,* 7 EUROPEAN CHAPLAINCY YEARBOOK 106 (1997) (the volume contains also French and German language versions of this article).
Joblin, Joseph	*Le Saint-Siège et la Vie Internationale Contemporaine,* 31 ARCHIVUM HISTORIAE PONTIFICIAE 225 (1993).
Joblin, Joseph	*At the Origins of Humanitarian Law: the Attitude of the Holy See*, L'OSSERVATORE ROMANO [english], August 11th/18th, 1999, at 3, 6, *available at* http://www.petersnet.net/research/retrieve.cfm?recnum=1187.

John Paul II	ADDRESS TO THE THIRD INTERNATIONAL AND INTERDENOMINATIONAL CONFERENCE OF CHIEF MILITARY CHAPLAINS OF EUROPE AND NORTH AMERICA (February 6th, 1992), *available at* http://www.vatican.va/holy_father/john_paul_ii/speeches/1992/documents/hf_jp-ii_spe_19920206_military-chaplains_en.html.
John Paul II	*Witnesses to Christ in Military Life,* L'OSSERVATORE ROMANO [english], June 2nd, 1999, at 4 *available at* http://www.petersnet.net/research/retrieve.cfm?RecNum=1081.
John Paul II	*World Day of Peace Message 2002,* 94 AAS 132 (2002).
John Paul II	MESSAGE TO THE MILITARY CHAPLAINS (March 24th, 2003), *available at* http://www.vatican.va/holy_father/john_paul_ii/speeches/2003/march/documents/hf_jp-ii_spe_20030325_cappellani-militari_en.html.
John XXIII	PACEM IN TERRIS (April 11th, 1963) *available at* http://www.vatican.va/holy_father/john_xxiii/encyclicals/documents/hf_j-xxiii_enc_11041963_pacem_en.html.
Johnson, James Turner	JUST WAR TRADITION AND THE RESTRAINT OF WAR (1981).
Johnson, James Turner	CAN MODERN WAR BE JUST? (1984).
Johnson, James Turner	*Historical Roots and Sources of the Just War Tradition in Western Culture, in* Just War and Jihad 3, 20 (John Kelsay et al. 1991).
Jone, Heribert	1 GESETZBUCH DER LATEINISCHEN KIRCHE (1950).
Journet, Charles	1 L'ÉGLISE DU VERBE INCARNÉ (1941).
Justenhoven, Heinz-Gerhard	FRANCISCO DE VITORIA ZU KRIEG UND FRIEDEN (1991).
Kalshoven, Frits	*The Undertaking to Respect and Ensure Respect in All Circumstances,* 2 YEARBOOK OF INTERNATIONAL HUMANITARIAN LAW 3 (1999).

Karst, Heinz	*Stellungnahme eines Soldaten,* 1961/62 MILITÄRSEELSORGE 126.
Kerstiens, Thomas G. J.	*Philosophy and practical possibilities of church organizations, in* ASSISTING THE VICTIMS OF ARMED CONFLICT AND OTHER DISASTERS 61 (Frits Kalshoven ed, 1989).
Kestel, Georg & Theis, Walter	*Pastorale Gegebenheiten und Schwerpunkte der katholischen Militärseelsorge,* 2001 MILITÄRSEELSORGE 50.
Kimminich, Otto	SCHUTZ DER MENSCHEN IN BEWAFFNETEN KONFLIKTEN (1979).
Kimminich, Otto	RELIGIONSFREIHEIT ALS MENSCHENRECHT (1990).
Kimminich, Otto	*Der völkerrechtliche Gehalt der Enzyklika Pacem in Terris, in* ALFRED KLOSE, FRIEDEN UND GESELLSCHAFTSORDNUNG 67 (1988).
Kimminich, Otto	*Die friedenstiftende Kraft des Völkerrechts, in* 17 DOKUMENTATION ZUR KATHOLISCHEN MILITÄRSEELSORGE 115 (Katholisches Militärbischofsamt ed. 1991).
Kimminich, Otto	*Theologie und Völkerrecht,* 1992 MILITÄRSEELSORGE 99.
Kloidt, Karl Heinz (ed.)	CHARTRES 1945 (1988).
Köck, Heribert Franz	DIE VÖLKERRECHTLICHE STELLUNG DES HEILIGEN STUHLS (1975).
Koerber, H.E.	*Probleme der Bestimmungen über die Militärgeistlichen in den Genfer Abkommen vom 12. August 1949,* 1966 REVUE DE DROIT PÉNAL MILITAIRE ET DE DROIT DE LA GUERRE 417.
Kötting, Bernhard	*Die Stellung der frühen Kirche zum Militärdienst,* 1981 MILITÄRSEELSORGE 183.
Korioth, Stefan	*Art. 140 – Art. 141, in* 5 GRUNDGESETZ (Theodor Maunz & Günter Dürig eds., continued looseleaf collection as of 2003).

Kredel, Elmar Maria	*Anprache bei der Übergabe des Apostolischen Breves, in* PÄPSTLICHE DOKUMENTE FÜR DIE MILITÄRSEELSORGE IN DER DEUTSCHEN BUNDESWEHR 42 (1990).
Kreutzer, Rudolf	*Der Begriff des Geistlichen im Wehrpflichtgesetz,* 11 DIE ÖFFENTLICHE VERWALTUNG 151 (1958).
Kruk, Volkmar	*Die rechtlichen Probleme der Militärseelsorge,* 1997 NEUE ZEITSCHRIFT FÜR WEHRRECHT 1.
Kunz, Josef L.	*The Status of the Holy See in International Law,* 46 AMERICAN JOURNAL OF INTERNATIONAL LAW 312 (1952).
Kussbach, Erich	*Schutz der Religionsfreiheit und des geistlichen Beistands in bewaffneten Konflikten,* 21 ÖSTERREICHISCHE MILITÄRISCHE ZEITSCHRIFT 385 (1983).
Lauterpacht, Hersch	2 INTERNATIONAL LAW (7th ed. 1952).
Lays, Charles	ÉTUDE CRITIQUE SUR LA VITA BALDERICI EPISCOPI LEODIENSIS (1948)
Lewis, Neil A.	*Hearing Starts for Muslim Army Chaplain,* THE NEW YORK TIMES, December 9th, 2003, at 20
Lewis, Neil A.	*Red Cross Criticizes Indefinite Detention In Guantánamo Bay,* THE NEW YORK TIMES, October 10th, 2003, at 1.
Lewis, Neil A. & Shanker, Thom	*Missteps Seen in Muslim Chaplain's Spy Case,* THE NEW YORK TIMES, January 4th, 2004, at 1.
Lewis, Neil A.	*Fate of Prisoners From Afghan War Remains Uncertain,* THE NEW YORK TIMES, April 24th, 2003, at 1.
Liedermann, Helmut	*Das humanitäre Völkerrecht: von den Anfängen bis zur Gegenwart,* 1999 WIENER BLÄTTER ZUR FRIEDENSFORSCHUNG 1.
Loest, Udo	*"Unabhängig von staatlicher Weisung", in* FÜR RUHE IN DER SEELE SORGEN 48 (2003).

Löffler, Roland	*Seelsorge im Ernstfall,* ZEITZEICHEN 11/2000, at 54.
Louwerse, W.H.	*The Royal Netherlands Air Force,* 1 EUROPEAN CHAPLAINCY YEARBOOK 71 (1992) (the volume contains also French and German language versions of this article).
Lüdicke, Klaus (ed.)	MÜNSTERISCHER KOMMENTAR ZUM CODEX IURIS CANONICI (36th delivery December 2002).
Lunze, Stefan	*Der Apostolische Stuhl reformiert die Ausbildung im kanonischen Recht,* 2003 JURISTISCHE SCHULUNG 725.
Marcheggiano, Arturo	DIRITTI E DOVERI DEL CAPPELLANO MILITARE IN TEMPO DI GUERRA (Rivista Militare ed. 1992).
Martin, Diarmuid	*Respect Human Rights, Return To Negotiations,* L'OSSERVATORE ROMANO [english], April 17th, 2002, at 5, *available at* http://www.petersnet.net/research/retrieve.cfm?recnum=4227.
Martin, Diarmuid	*Respect The Rights Of Religious Minorities; Respect Holy Places,* L'OSSERVATORE ROMANO [english], April 24th, 2002, at 9, *available at* http://www.petersnet.net/research/retrieve.cfm?recnum=4262. *also available at* http://www.vatican.va/roman_curia/secretariat_state/documents/rc_seg-st_doc_20020412_martin-human-rights_en.html.
Martin, Diarmuid	INTERVENTION AT THE MEETING OF THE CCW GROUP OF GOVERNMENTAL EXPERTS (July 23rd, 2002), *available at* http://www.vatican.va/roman_curia/secretariat_state/documents/rc_seg-st_doc_20020723_martin-geneve_en.html.

Martin, Michael	ENTEHUNG, GLIEDERUNG UND RECHTSLAGE DEUTSCHER SPEZIALEINHEITEN AM BEISPIEL DER EINSATZEINHEITEN DES KOMMANDO SPEZIALKRÄFTE UND DER GRENZSCHUTZGRUPPE 9 (unpublished seminar paper, University of the Armed Forces, February 17th, 2000),
McCoubrey, Hilaire & White, Nigel D.	INTERNATIONAL LAW AND ARMED CONFLICT (1992).
Meron, Theodor	HUMAN RIGHTS AND HUMANITARIAN NORMS AS CUSTOMARY LAW (1989)
Merrifield, William	*The Unit Ministry Team in Military Operations Other Than War,* THE ARMY CHAPLAINCY, Summer-Fall 1997, *available at* http://www.usachcs.army.mil/TACarchive/ACTNG /merrifield.htm.
Michaelis, Peter	*Die Militärseelsorge im Auslandseinsatz, in* BEITRÄGE ZUR EVANGELISCHEN MILITÄRSEELSORGE, I/97, 60.
Michaelis, Peter & Theis, Walter	*Seelsorgerische Begleitung bei Auslandseinsätzen deutscher Soldaten,* 2001 MILITÄRSEELSORGE 67. *Also published* 1999 TRUPPENPRAXIS/WEHRAUSBILDUNG 505.
Michaelis, Peter	*Unabhängig und solidarisch zugleich, in* FÜR RUHE IN DER SEELE SORGEN, 156 (2003).
Miller, Mark	*A Very Curious Case,* NEWSWEEK [U.S. Edition], December 22nd, 2003, at 41.
Mintz, John	*Chaplain's Release Comes With New Charges,* THE WASHINGTON POST, November 26th, 2003, at A05.
Mintz, John	*Lawyer Asks Bush to Free Chaplain,* THE WASHINGTON POST, November 25th, 2003, at A07.
Mintz, John	*Ex-Muslim Cleric at Guantanamo Faces Minor Charges,* THE WASHINGTON POST, October 11th, 2003, at A06.

Mintz, John & Schmidt, Susan	*Muslim Army Chaplain Is Held in Investigation,* THE WASHINGTON POST, September 21st, 2003, at A16.
Mintz, John & Vogel, Steve	*Guantanamo Security Probe Widens,* THE WASHINGTON POST, September 25th, 2003, at A03
Moir, Lindsay	THE LAW OF INTERNAL ARMED CONFLICT (2002).
Moser, Georg	*Friedensbemühungen der Päpste in unserem Jahrhundert,* 1973 MILITÄRSEELSORGE 161.
Müller-Kent, Jens	MILITÄRSEELSORGE IM SPANNUNGSFELD ZWISCHEN KIRCHLICHEM AUFTRAG UND MILITÄRISCHER EINBINDUNG (1990).
Nabulsi, Karma	TRADITIONS OF WAR (1999).
Nagel, Ernst Josef	DIE FRIEDENSLEHRE DER KATHOLISCHEN KIRCHE (1997).
Nicolas, Claude	L'ASSISTANCE SPRITUELLE DANS LE DROIT DE LA GUERRE (1991).
O'Brien, Roderick	A MANUAL OF INTERNATIONAL HUMANITARIAN LAW FOR RELIGIOUS PERSONNEL (1993).
O'Brien, William	THE CONDUCT OF JUST AND LIMITED WAR (1981).
Ochoa, Javier & Diez, Aloisio (eds.)	*Summa de poenitentia, in* 1 B UNIVERSA BIBLIOTHECA IURIS (1976).
Odom, Jonathan G.	*Beyond Arm Bands and Arms Banned, Chaplains, Armed Conflict, and the Law,* 49 NAVAL LAW REVIEW 1 (2002), *available at* http://www.chaplain.navy.mil/Attachments/ Chaplains_in_Armed_Conflict.pdf.
Olsen, Dorbjørn	DIE NATUR DES MILITÄRORDINARIATS (1998).
Ottaviani, Alfredo	1 INSTITUTIONES IURIS PUBLICI ECCLESIASTICI (3rd ed. 1947).
Pasche, Bernhard	*Reflections on the Swiss Army Chaplaincy in 1994,* 5 EUROPEAN CHAPLAINCY YEARBOOK 130 (1995).
Pastoral Guidelines	*Pastorale Leitlinien der Katholischen Militärseelsorge,* 2001 MILITÄRSEELSORGE 5.

Patberg, Gotthold	*Nicht jeder Tag ist Mittwoch, in* FÜR RUHE IN DER SEELE SORGEN 81 (2003).
Paul IV	DISCOURS À L'ORGANISATION DES NATION UNIES À L'OCCASION DU 20ÈME ANNIVERSAIRE DE L'ORGANISATION No. 1 (October 4th, 1965), *available at* www.vatican.va/holy_father/paul_vi/speeches/1965/documents/hf_p-vi_spe_19651004_united-nations_fr.html.
Penna, Lakshmikanth Rao & Marks, Stephen P.	JURIDICAL APSECTS OF MORAL AND SPIRITUAL ASSISTANCE DURING ARMED CONFLICTS NOT OF AN INTERNATIONAL CHARACTER, INTERNAL DISTURBANCES AND SITUATION OF POLITICAL TENSION (paper submitted to the Colloquium on spiritual and intellectual assistance in the time of armed conflicts and civil disturbances, Milan, September 21st-23rd, 1973).
Pertz, Georg Heinrich (ed.)	1 MONUMENTA GERMANIAE HISTORICA SRCIPTORES (1835).
Pertz, Georg Heinrich (ed.)	4 MONUMENTA GERMANIAE HISTORICA SRCIPTORES (1841).
Phillipson, Coleman	2 THE INTERNATIONAL LAW AND CUSTOM OF ANCIENT GREECE AND ROME (1911).
Pictet, Jean S.	THE GENEVA CONVENTIONS OF 12 AUGUST 1949, COMMENTARY, I GENEVA CONVENTION (1952).
Pictet, Jean S.	THE GENEVA CONVENTIONS OF 12 AUGUST 1949, COMMENTARY, II GENEVA CONVENTION (1960).
Pictet, Jean S.	THE GENEVA CONVENTIONS OF 12 AUGUST 1949, COMMENTARY, III GENEVA CONVENTION (1960).
Pictet, Jean S.	THE GENEVA CONVENTIONS OF 12 AUGUST 1949, COMMENTARY, IV GENEVA CONVENTION (1958).
Pictet, Jean S.	*The Principles of International Humanitarian Law,* 1966 INTERNATIONAL REVIEW OF THE RED CROSS 455.
Pictet, Jean S.	HUMANITARIAN LAW AND THE PROTECTION OF WAR VICTIMS (1975) [cited as: PICTET, VICTIMS].

Pictet, Jean S.	DEVELOPMENT AND PRINCIPLES OF INTERNATIONAL HUMANITARIAN LAW (1985).
Pirson, Dietrich	*§ 64 Das Dienstrecht der Geistlichen und Kirchenbeamten, in* 2 HANDBUCH DES STAATSKIRCHENRECHTS DER BUNDESREPUBLIK DEUTSCHLAND 845 (Joseph Listl ed. 1995).
Plan of Action	*Plan of Action for the years 2000-2003*, 1990 INTERNATIONAL REVIEW OF THE RED CROSS 880, *available at* http://www.icrc.org/Web/eng/siteeng0.nsf/iwpList188/E5749851E7D0231BC1256B66005DE9C1.
Pogany, Istvan	*Religion, the Palestinian-Israeli Conflict and International Law, in* INTERNATIONAL LAW AND ARMED CONFLICT 93 (A. G. D. Bradney ed. 1992).
Ponifical Council for Justice and Peace (ed.)	JOHN PAUL II AND THE FAMILY OF PEOPLES (2002).
Pontifical Commission „Iustitia et Pax“	WAYS OF PEACE (1987).
Preuß, Ulrich K.	*Art. 140, in* 3 KOMMENTAR ZUM GRUNDGESETZ FÜR DIE BUNDESREPUBLIK DEUTSCHLAND (Erhard Denninger ed., 3rd ed., continued looseleaf collection as of 2003).
Priest, Dan & Gellman, Barton	*U.S. Decries Abuse but Defends Interrogations*, THE WASHINGTON POST, December 26th, 2002, at A01, *available at* http://www.washingtonpost.com/ac2/wp-dyn/A37943-2002Dec25.
Rabus, Walter	*Religious personnel, in* THE HANDBOOK OF HUMANITARIAN LAW IN ARMED CONFLICTS 369 (Dieter Fleck ed. 1995).
Raiser, Konrad	*The Role of the World Council of Churches in the Solution of Conflicts in this World,* 4 EUROPEAN CHAPLAINCY YEARBOOK 190 (1994).
Rausch, Wolf Werner	*Seelsorge im humanitären Völkerrecht,* BEITRÄGE AUS DER EV. MILITÄRSEELSORGE 4/1992, at 24.
Rausch, Wolf Werner	*Seelsorge – ganz konkret,* 1994 WEHRAUSBILDUNG 310.

Rausch, Wolf Werner	*Kirchliche Begleitung – wohin auch immer, Militärseelsorge im nationalen und internationalen Recht*, 1995 TRUPPENPRAXIS/WEHRAUSBILDUNG 379.
Richtlinien	*Richtlinien für die Pfarrhelfer in der Militärseelsorge, Decree of the Federal Ministry of Defense,* VR I 4 – Az. 36-25 (September 17th, 1973) in DOKUMENTATION ZUR KATHOLISCHEN UND EVANGELISCHEN MILITÄRSEELSORGE 86 (7th ed. 2002).
Riehm, Gustav Adolf	LES PROBLÈMES D'UNE PROTECTION PARTICULIÈRE DU PERSONNEL AUXILIAIRE ET DU MATÉRIEL DES AUMÔNIERS MILITAIRES ET DES MINISTRES CIVILS D'UN CULTE 2 (paper submitted to the Colloquium on spiritual and intellectual assistance in the time of armed conflicts and civil disturbances, Milan, September 21st-23rd, 1973).
Robrahn, Joachim	*Der Militärpfarrer im Auslandseinsatz,* 2003 MILITÄRSEELSORGE 12.
Rößler, Peter	*Rechtsstellung der Geistlichen nach dem IV. Genfer Abkommen und den Zusatzprotokollen,* 1989 MILITÄRSEELSORGE 304.
Rousseau, Jean-Jacques	GESELLSCHAFTSVERTRAG (Alexander Heine ed. 1977).
Russell, Frederick H.	THE JUST WAR IN THE MIDDLE AGES (1975).
Sandoz, Yves	*This Is Not a Celebration But a Reflection on Common Values,* L'OSSERVATORE ROMANO[english], August 11th/18th, 1999, at 5, *available at* http://www.petersnet.net/research/retrieve.cfm?recnum=1189.
Sandoz, Yves et al. (eds.)	COMMENTARY ON THE ADDITIONAL PROTOCOLS (1978).
Schlögel, Anton	*Schutz der Seelsorge im humanitären Völkerrecht, in* VÖLKERRECHT IM DIENSTE DES MENSCHEN 259 (Yvo Hangartner ed. 1996) *Also published* 1989 MILITÄRSEELSORGE 116.

Schmidt, Wolfram	*Helfen und wieder loslassen, in* FÜR RUHE IN DER SEELE SORGEN 174 (2003).
Schmitt, Eric	*Ex-Chaplain With Detainees Is Charged,* THE NEW YORK TIMES, October 11th, 2003, at 10.
Schmitt, Carl	DER NOMOS DER ERDE IM VÖLKERRECHT DES JUS PUBLICUM EUROPAEUM (4th ed. 1997).
Schmoll, Heike	*Zuviel Skepsis gegenüber dem Staat*, FRANKFURTER ALLGEMEINE ZEITUNG, July 20th, 1994, at 12.
Schollmeyer, Karl-Josef	*Die völkerrechtliche Stellung des Militärgeistlichen,* 1966 NEUE ZEITSCHRIFT FÜR WEHRRECHT 59.
Schorlemer, Sabine von	INTERNATIONALER KULTURGÜTERSCHUTZ (1992).
Schubiger, Maurice	*Die geistige Betreuung gestern, heute und morgen in den Genfer Abkommen,* DER FELDPREDIGER No. 71 (August 1991), at 2. [DER FELDPREDIGER : Mitteilungsblatt der Gesellschaft der Feldprediger der Schweizerischen Armee] And published in French: L'assistance spirituelle hier, aujourd'hui et demain dans les Conventions de Genève, in L'AUMÔNIER MILITAIR : bulletin de la société des aumôniers de l'Armee suisse, n° 71, (August 1991), at 204-207.
Schwendenwein, Hugo	*Der Schutz der religiösen Sphäre in den Genfer Konventionen vom Roten Kreuz, in* PAX ET IUSTITIA 509 (Hans Walter Kaluza et al. eds. 1990).
Scordo, Joseph A.	*A Chaplain in "The 'Stan'",* THE NAVY CHAPLAINCY, October-December 2002, at 3.
Scott, James Brown	[1 Conferences], [2 Documents] THE HAGUE PEACE CONFERENCES OF 1899 AND 1907 (1909).
Scott, James Brown	THE SPANISH ORIGIN OF INTERNATIONAL LAW (1934).
Seibt, Horst	COMPENDIUM OF CASE STUDIES OF INTERNATIONAL HUMANITARIAN LAW (1994).

Seiler, Rudolf	*§ 68 Seelsorge in Bundeswehr und Bundesgrenzschutz, in* 2 HANDBUCH DES STAATSKIRCHENRECHTS DER BUNDESREPUBLIK DEUTSCHLAND 961, (Joseph Listl ed. 1995).
Sekretariat der Deutschen Bischofskonferenz (ed.)	GERECHTER FRIEDE (2000).
Selby, Peter	*Christianity in a World Come of Age, in* THE CAMBRIDGE COMPANION TO DIETRICH BONHOEFFER 226 (John W. de Gruchy ed. 1999).
Simon, Erwin	DIE KATHOLISCHE MILITÄRSEELSORGE NACH DEM CODEX IURIS CANONICI UND DEN DAZU ERGANGENEN SONDERBSTIMMUNGEN UNTER BERÜCKSICHTIGUNG DER MILITÄRSEELSORGE IN DER BUNDESWEHR (1962).
Simon, Joachim	*Achterbahn der Emotionen,* AUFTRAG No. 250, at 32 (2003).
Sinderhauf, Monica	HISTORISCHE ENTWICKLUNG DER MILITÄRSEELSORGE (unpublished paper dated February 13th, 2003).
Spranger, Tade Matthias	*Militärseelsorge für Moslems?*, 1999 BUNDESWEHRVERWALTUNG 174.
Stadlmeier, Sigmar	*Die Stellung des Militärseelsorgers im humanitären Völkerrecht, in* PAX ET IUSTITIA 521 (Hans Walter Kaluza et al. eds 1990).
Stadtmüller, Georg	1 GESCHICHTE DES VÖLKERRECHTS (1951).
Stauf, Wolfgang	3 WEHRRECHT (2002).
Stocks, Karen H.	*Understanding The Chaplain's Role in an Age of Weapons of Mass Destruction,* 166 MILITARY MEDICINE Suppl. 2, at 55 (2001).
Stooss, Andreas	*Die Armeeseelsorge gestern – heute – morgen,* TRUPPENINFORMATIONSDIENST, Bulletin 4/99, at 11.
Stucki, Christoph	*Swiss Chaplaincy 1996,* 7 EUROPEAN CHAPLAINCY YEARBOOK 122 (1997).

Stucki, Christoph	*Die Armeeseelsorge vor neuen Herausforderungen,* 166 ALLGEMEINE SCHWEIZERISCHE MILITÄRZEITSCHRIFT 23 (5/2000).
Tammler, Ulrich	*Die Stellung der Ordensleute im Wehrrecht der Bundesrepublik Deutschland,* 1983 MILITÄRSEELSORGE 165.
Tammler, Ulrich	*Das Katholische Militärbischofsamt als selbständige Bundesoberbehörde,* 1988 NEUE ZEITSCHRIFT FÜR WEHRRECHT 106.
Tanner, Norman P.	1 DECREES OF THE ECUMENICAL COUNCILS (1990).
The White House	FACT SHEET: STATUS OF DETAINEES AT GUANTANAMO (February 7th, 2002), *available at* http://www.whitehouse.gov/news/releases/2002/02/20020207-13.html.
Tierney, Brian	[1 Souces of Medieval History] THE MIDDLE AGES (4th ed. 1983).
Toman, Jiří	THE PROTECTION OF CULTURAL PROPERTY IN THE EVENT OF ARMED CONFLICT (1996).
Tomasi, Silvano M.	INTERVENTION BY THE HOLY SEE AT THE 28TH INTERNATIONAL CONFERENCE OF THE RED CROSS AND RED CRESCENT SOCIETIES (December 2003), *available at* http://www.vatican.va/roman_curia/secretariat_state/2003/documents/rc_seg-st_20031209_red-cross_en.html.
Tomuschat, Christian	*Völkerrecht, in* 10 LEXIKON FÜR THEOLOGIE UND KIRCHE col. 854 (Walter Kasper ed., 3rd ed. 2001).
U.S. ARMY	ARMY REGULATION 190–8, ENEMY PRISONERS OF WAR, RETAINED PERSONNEL, CIVILIAN INTERNEES AND OTHER DETAINEES (October 1st, 1997), http://www.au.af.mil/au/awc/awcgate/law/ar190-8.pdf.
U.S. Department of State	1999 COUNTRY REPORTS ON HUMAN RIGHTS PRACTICES FOR COLOMBIA (February 25, 2000), *available at* http://www.state.gov/www/global/human_rights/1999_hrp_report/colombia.html.

U.S. Marine Corps	FLEET MARINE FORCE MANUAL (FMFM) 3-61, MINISTRY IN COMBAT (June 22nd, 1992) *available at* http://www.chaplain.navy.mil/ Attachments/FMFM%203-61.pdf.
U.S. Senate	SPECIAL REPORT OF THE SELECT COMMITTEE ON INTELLIGENCE, JANUARY 4, 1995 TO OCTOBER 3, 1996 (January 22nd, 1997).
Vattel, Emer de	3 THE LAW OF NATIONS OR THE PRINCIPLES OF NATURAL LAW (photo. reprint 1995) (Charles G. Fenwick trans. 1916).
Verri, Pietro	DICTIONARY OF THE INTERNATIONAL LAW OF ARMED CONFLICT (1992).
Veuthey, Michel	*Remedies to Promote the Respect of Fundamental Human Values in Non-International Armed Conflicts,* 30 ISRAELI YEARBOOK ON HUMAN RIGHTS 37 (2001).
Veuthey, Michel	*International Humanitarian Law and Spirituality,* 21 REFUGEE SURVEY QUARTERLY No. 3, at 45 (2002).
Vitoria, Francisco de	2 VORLESUNGEN (Ulrich Horst et al. eds. 1997).
Vogt, Arnold	*Militärseelsorge in den königlich bayerischen Streitkräften bis 1918,* 1986 MILITÄRSEELSORGE 126.
Wallenfels, Monica	A Current Case: The Destruction of the Last Mosques in Banja Luka on 8 September 1993, 1993 HUMANITÄRES VÖLKERRECHT 217-20.
Walter, Jürgen	*Als Seelsorger in Afghanistan, in* FÜR RUHE IN DER SEELE SORGEN 68 (2003).
Walz, Dieter	Wehrpflichtgesetz (2002).
Watson, Liselotte B.	*Status of medical and religious personnel in international law,* JAG JOURNAL Sep-Oct-Nov 1965, at 41.
Weber, Paul. J.	*The first amendment and the military chaplaincy,* 22 Journal of church and state 459 (1980).

Weeramantry, Christopher G.	*Foreword* to RELIGION AND INTERNATIONAL LAW vii (Mark W. Janis & Carolyn Evans eds. 1999).
Werkner, Ines-Jacqueline	SOLDATENSEELSORGE VERSUS MILITÄRSEELSORGE (2001).
Werminghoff, Albert (ed.)	[Legum Sectio III, Concilia, Vol. II part. I : Concilia aevi Karolini, Vol. 1-1] MONUMENTA GERMANIAE HISTORICA (1904).
Werthmann, Georg	*Kurse zur Weiterbildung kriegsgefangener Theologiestudenten,* 1966 MILITÄRSEELSORGE 78.
Wilkinson, Alan	*The paradox of the military chaplain,* 84 THEOLOGY 249 (1981).
Witte, Barthold C.	*Völkerrechtliche Aspekte der Militärseelsorge, in* EKD-INFORMATIONEN MILITÄRSEELSORGE doc. 12 (Kirchenamt der Evangelischen Kirche in Deutschland ed. 1993).
Wyller, Trygve	GLAUBE UND AUTONOME WELT (1998).
Zahrnt, Heinz	*Einführungs-Essay,* in 37 CHRISTLICHER GLAUBE IN MODERNER GESELLSCHAFT 15 (Franz Böckle et al. eds. 1984)
Zemmali, Ameur	COMBATTANTS ET PRISONNIERS DE GUERRE EN DROIT ISLAMIQUE ET EN DROIT INTERNTIONAL HUMANITAIRE (1997).
Ziegler, Karl Heinz	VÖLKERRECHTSGESCHICHTE (1994).
Zivkovic, Ilija	THE WOUNDED CHURCH IN CROATIA (1996).

Abstracts

The protection of religious personnel in armed conflict

This monograph undertakes to determine the protected status of religious personnel in armed conflict, to recall the evolutions that led to this status and to identify possible problems. In addition, the ontological reasons of spiritual assistance in armed conflict and its protection are discussed.

Clergy was protected in warfare since ancient times. Protection in classical canon law shifted to the domain of secular law after the emergence of the modern states in Europe. In the wake of the Red Cross Movement, military chaplains' security was safeguarded by international conventions from the 19th century onwards. The catholic church, which operates military chaplaincy in various countries worldwide, followed the developments in the succeeding decades with increasing interest. In Germany, for instance, chaplains of a civilly structured military ordinariate accompany troops also during deployment abroad and provide spiritual assistance to them.

Present-day international humanitarian law provides a set of norms that protect and respect chaplains exclusively attached to the military in international and non-international armed conflict in a stable manner. Civilian ministry and its personnel are also protected by their civilian nature and the respect for religious convictions and practices. Both domains approach each other by legal and factual convergence. In the context of German chaplaincy, protection of groups other than chaplains, the use of arms by chaplains and spiritual assistance to non-believers are matters of interest. Problematic issues in the international arena are violations of international humanitarian law by ministers of religion, ministry to detained "illegal combatants" and the role of ministers as instigators of conflicts.

De tutela clericorum castrensium in contentionibus armis gessis

Ea disputatione conditionem protectam hominum in cura pastorali laborantium in contentionibus armis gessis et res ad eas ducentes et pericula, quae fieri possunt explicare studetur. Praeterea de causis auxilii spiritualis eiusque tutela dicitur.

Clerici ab antiquis temporibus in bellis protegebantur. Post exordium novae rei publicae tutela veteris canonici iuris ad ius civile tradita est. Commozione crucis rubrae incolumitas clericorum castrensium ab undevicesimo saeculo internationalibus conventionibus protecta est. Ecclesia catholica, quae diversis in rebus publicis animarum curam castrensem habet, eo progressus crescente studio observabat. Exempli causa: In Germania clerici ordinariatus castrensis civili modo dispositi copiis in alienis terris agentibus adsunt.

Hodierno ad humanos sensus propenso iure gentium clerici castrenses, qui cum copiis coniuncti sunt perpetuo in nationalibus interntionalibusque contentionibus armis gessis temperantia tutelaque instructi sunt. Cura quoque animarum civilis et pro ea laborantes etiam sua natura civili reverentiaque fidei et caerimoniarum protecti sunt. Utraque res convergentia iuridica realique appropinquat altera alteram. Tutela earum tumarum, cuius membra clerici castrenses non sunt, usus armorum a clercicis castrensibus, cura pastoralis pro infidelibus, ea omnia quaestiones graves sunt, quae ad curam pastoralem Germanicam pertinent. Multae quaestiones in rebus internationalibus inveniri possunt, quae fiunt ex noxiis iuris gentium ad humanos sensus propensi, per clericos castrenses, ex cura pastorali pro captivis illegalibus pugnatoribus, denique a clericis castrensibus, qui discrepantias fecerunt.

La protection du personnel religieux en conflit armé

Cette thèse essaie de déterminer l`état protégé du personnel en conflits armés, de rappeler les évolution qui ont mené à cet état et d`identifier de possibles problèmes. En plus, seront discutées les raisons ontologiques de l`assistance spirituelle et de sa protection.

Le clergé a été protégé en guerre depuis les temps anciens. Après l´apparition de l´État moderne en Europe, la protection par le droit canonique classique s'est retrouvée dans le domaine du droit séculaire. A partir du 19ième siècle, à l´aube du mouvement de la Croix Rouge, la sécurité des aumôniers militaires a été assurée par des conventions internationales. L´église catholique, qui opère des aumôneries militaires dans différents pays dans le monde entier, a poursuivi les développements dans les décennies suivantes avec un intérêt croissant. En Allemagne, par exemple, des aumôniers appartenant à un ordinariat militaire organisé d'une manière civile accompagnent les troupes également en action à l'étranger et offrent une assistance spirituelle.

Le droit international humanitaire de nos jours offre un conjoint de normes protégeant et respectant d'une manière stable les aumôniers attachés exclusivement aux forces armées en conflit armé international et non-international. L'assistance spirituelle civile et son personnel sont protégés aussi par sa nature civile et par le respect de convictions et pratiques religieuses. Les deux domaines s'approchent l'un de l'autre par une convergence légale et effective. Dans le contexte de l'aumônerie en Allemagne, la protection de groupes autres que les aumôniers ainsi que l' usage des armes par les aumôniers et assistance spirituelle à des non-croyants sont d'intérêt. Sujets problématiques dans l'arène internationale sont les violations du droit humanitaire par des ministres religieux, ministère aux «combattant illégaux» détenus et le rôle de ministres comme instigateurs de conflits.

La protezione del personale religioso in situazioni di conflitto armato
Scopo del presente lavoro è quello di identificare lo status protetto del personale religioso in situazioni di conflitto armato, di ricostruirne l'evoluzione e di individuare possibili aree problematiche. Inoltre, le ragioni ontologiche collegate all'assistenza spirituale ed alla protezione in situazioni di conflitto sono altresì oggetto di esame.

Il clero ha, sin dall'antichità, ricevuto protezione in guerra. Con l'emergere degli Stati-nazione in Europa, tale protezione, codificata nel diritto canonico classico, si ritrova altresì nel diritto secolare. Con la creazione del Movimento della Croce Rossa, la sicurezza dei cappellani militari viene salvaguardata da convenzioni internazionali codificate a partire dal XIX secolo. La Chiesa Cattolica, i cui cappellani militari operano in diversi paesi del mondo, ha, durante gli anni, seguito con crescente interesse tali sviluppi normativi. In Germania, ad esempio, i cappellani, che appartengono ad un ordinariato militare strutturato in maniera civile, accompagnano le truppe anche durante il loro impiego all'estero e forniscono loro assistenza spirituale.

Il diritto internazionale umanitario attuale prevede una serie di norme poste a protezione e rispetto dei cappellani destinati esclusivamente alle forze armate in situazioni di conflitto armato internazionale e non. Inoltre, il ministro ed il suo personale, in quanto civili, sono protetti dalle norme a tutela della popolazione civile e per il rispetto delle convinzioni e pratiche religiose. Entrambi i livelli di protezione si ricongiungono attraverso una convergenza di tipo fattuale e legale. Nel contesto della cura spirituale dei militari in Germania, la protezione di gruppi diversi dai cappellani, l'utilizzo delle armi da parte dei cappellani, l'assistenza spirituale ai non credenti sono argomenti di interesse. Aspetti controversi nell'arena internazionale sono le violazioni del diritto internazionale umanitario da parte dei ministri della religione, il ministero a "combattenti illegali" detenuti ed il ruolo dei sacerdoti come istigatori di conflitti.

Der Schutz von Seelsorgepersonal in bewaffneten Konflikten
Diese Arbeit unternimmt es, die geschützte Position von Seelsorgepersonal in bewaffneten Konflikten zu bestimmen, die Entwicklungen, die dahin führten, in Erinnerung zu rufen und mögliche Probleme zu benennen. Darüber hinaus werden die Gründe für geistlichen Beistand und seinen Schutz besprochen.

Kleriker waren seit dem Altertum im Krieg geschützt. Der Schutz durch das klassische kanonische Recht verlagerte sich nach der Bildung des modernen Staates in Europa auf das Gebiet des weltlichen Rechts. Im Zuge der Rotkreuz-Bewegung wurde die Sicherheit von Militärseelsorgern ab dem 19. Jahrhundert durch internationale Konventionen geschützt. Die katholische Kirche, die in verschiedenen Staaten der Welt Militärseelsorge unterhält, verfolgte die Entwicklungen der folgenden Jahrzehnte mit wachsendem Interesse. Beispielsweise in Deutschland begleiten Seelsorger eines zivil organisierten Militärordinariats Truppen auf Auslandseinsätzen und leisten geistigen Beistand.

Das heutige humanitäre Völkerrecht schont und schützt Feldgeistliche, die den Streitkräften zugeteilt sind, dauerhaft in internationalen und nicht-internationalen bewaffneten Konflikten. Zivile Seelsorge und ihr Personal sind auch durch ihre zivile Natur und die Achtung für religiöse Überzeugungen und Gepflogenheiten geschützt. Die beiden Bereiche bewegen sich durch eine rechtliche und tatsächliche Konvergenz aufeinander zu. Im Zusammenhang der deutschen Militärseelsorge sind der Schutz von anderen Gruppen als die der Militärseelsorger, der Waffengebrauch durch Militärseelsorger und geistlicher Beistand für Nichtgläubige interessante Angelegenheiten. Problembereich auf dem internationalen Gebiet sind Verletzungen des humanitären Völkerrechts durch Seelsorger, Seelsorge zu internierten illegalen Kombattanten und die Rolle von Seelsorgern als Anstifter von Konflikten.

La protección de personal religioso durante conflictos bélicos

Esta tesis tiene como objetivo determinar el grado de protección que tiene el personal religioso durante conflictos bélicos, analizar el proceso de desarrollo que llevo a alcanzar este status e identificar los posibles problemas que se presentan. Adicionalmente se discute los motivos para la asistencia espiritual y protección del personal religioso durante conflictos armados.

Desde la antigüedad, los clérigos han gozado de protección en las guerras. La protección ofrecida a través de derecho canónico clásico fue asumida por el derecho secular tras la formación de los estados modernos en Europa. A partir del siglo XIX, el movimiento iniciado por la Cruz Roja logró la protección de clérigos, por medio de convenios internacionales. La iglesia católica que, durante conflictos bélicos, opera mediante misiones de la pastoral militar alrededor del mundo, siguió con mucho interés el proceso de desarollo en este campo. En Alemania, por ejemplo, capellanes militares organizados de civiles acompaniaron a tropas militares durante sus operaciones militares el exterior, con el fin de ofrecer asistencia espiritual.

El derecho internacional humanitario moderno provee una serie de normas que protejen a los capellanes agregados a las fuerzas armadas durante conflictos bélicos, tanto durante conflictos bélicos nacional y internacional. Los clérigos y su personal a cargo son protegidos y respetados debido a su calidad de civiles, así como por sus convicciones y prácticas religiosas. Ambos niveles de protección se complementan a través de su convergencia de facto y de derecho. En cuanto a clérigos alemanes, son temas de interés: la protección de grupos que no son religiosos, el uso de armas por parte de capellanes y la asistencia espirirtual a no creyentes. Aspectos controversiales en el ámbito internacional constituyen, por ejemplo, la violación del derecho humanitario internacional por parte de clérigos, asistencia espiritual a los detenido definidos como "combatientes ilegales" y el papel de religiosos como fuente de conflictos.

De bescherming van religieus personeel in gewapende conflicten

In dit boek wordt getracht om de beschermde status van religieus personeel in gewapende conflicten te bepalen, de ontwikkelingen te beschrijven die leidden tot deze status, en om mogelijke problemen te identificeren. In dit onderzoek wordt ook ingegaan op de discussie inzake de ontologische redenen van spirituele bijstand en de bescherming van religieus personeel in gewapende conflicten.

De geestelijkheid werd reeds beschermd tijdens oorlogen sinds de oudheid. Bescherming door het klassiek kerkelijk recht maakte plaats voor het domein van het wereldlijk recht, na de opkomst van de moderne staat in Europa. Vanaf de 19e eeuw, met het ontstaan van de Rode Kruis beweging, werd de veiligheid van militaire aalmoezeniers beschermd door internationale conventies. De katholieke kerk stond in voor geestelijke verzorging bij de krijgsmachten in verschillende landen over de hele wereld, en volgde de ontwikkelingen in voorbije decennia met toenemende interesse. In Duitsland bijvoorbeeld, vergezellen de geestelijken van een burgerlijk militair ordinariaat de troepen tijdens buitenlandse missies om hen spirituele bijstand te bieden.

Het huidige internationale humanitaire recht voorziet in een aantal normen die een stabiele bescherming en respect bieden aan de aan de strijdkrachten verbonden geestelijken in internationale en non-internationale gewapende conflicten. Burgerlijke zielzorg en hun personeel worden beschermd omwille van hun burgerlijke status en het respect voor godsdienstige overtuiging en de waarneming van godsdienstplichten. Beide domeinen groeien naar elkaar toe, zowel op feitelijk als op juridisch vlak. In het geval van de Duitse geestelijkheid, wordt hier aandacht besteed aan de bescherming van andere religieuze groepen die niet onder de geestelijkheid vallen, het gebruik van wapens door aalmoezeniers en de religieuze bijstand voor niet gelovigen. Problematische aspecten in de internationale context zijn overtredingen van de internationale humanitaire regels door geestelijken, illegale strijders en de rol van zielzorgers als aanstichters van conflicten.

Охрана духовных лиц во вооруженных конфликтах

Эта работа намерена на определение охраненного положения военных священников во вооруженных конфликтах, она должна напоминать о ведших к этой ситуации развитиях, а также показать возможные проблемы. Более того, речь идет о причинах духовной поддержки и ее охраны.

Со времен древности, священники были охраненными во время войны. Эта охрана сначала классическим каноническим правом, а после возникновения современных государств в Европе заменялась светским правом. В связи с движением Красного Креста охрана военных священников с девятнадцатого века осуществлялась международными конвенциями. Римско-католическая церковь, которая в разных странах мира имеет военные священники, с большим интересом следила за развитиями следующих десятилетий. В Германии, например, военные священники одного по-гражданскому организованного ординариата сопровождают войскам на миссиях за границу и оказывают духовную поддержку.

Настоящее международное гуманитарное право прочно оберегает и охраняет полковых священников, прикрепленных к вооруженным силам, в международных и внутренних конфликтах. Гражданское духовенство является охраненным благодаря своему гражданскому положению и вследствие уважения религиозных убеждений и обычаев. Обе области приближаются друг к другу путем правовой как и фактической конвергенций. В связи с немецкими военными священниками интересны охрана других групп, не принадлежащих военным священникам, применение оружий военными священниками, а также моральная поддержка со стороны священника для неверующих. Что касается международный уровень, то нарушения международного гуманитарного права полковыми священниками, забота о спасении душ интернированных нелегальных комбатантов, и роль духовников как подстрекатели конфликтов являются проблематичными.

Index and Norms

Issues that are covered by a whole sub-section are not indexed. *Italic* numbers refer to references in footnotes. Names are given in CAPITAL letters.

1864 Red Cross Convention
  Art. II....................................36
  Art. III *37*
  Art. IV *37*
  Art. VII..................................*37*
1906 Red Cross Convention
  Art. IX 39
  Art. XII..................................40
  Art. XX..................................*40*
1929 Red Cross Convention I
  Art. XII..................................41
1929 Red Cross Convention II
  Art. XVI 41, *113*
AC Pastor Bonus
  Art. 76 62
Afghanistan.................79, 145, 185
  ISAF.....................................88
armed forces
  term 95
armlet........37, 41, 66, 99, 157, 200
  of HC..................................142
  practical difficulties.............101
  responsibility of the state........99
  state responsability.......101, 102
  use in Germany 102
  use in U.S. Navy..................*102*
auxiliary religious personnel......*see religious personnel, auxiliary*
Basic Law
  Art. 4 67
  Art. 87 b *70*
  Art. 96 (4).............................*70*
  Art. 140 ....67, 175
battle of Hoegaerde 25
besieged areas 92, 98, 137, 152, 154
Brussels declaration (1874)
  Art. 38 39
Canada..................................... 182
canon law..................17, 18, 26, 41
  as means to protect clergy 17, 26, 28, 29, 32, 65, 134
  classical period 33, 198
  responsibility for church building.......................... 141
cartels 32
Central Office for pastoral coordination of the military ordinariates 63
chaplains.....*see religious personnel*
chivalric custom 27, 29, 198
Christian image of man 19, 54, 173, 204
Church of the Nativity (Bethlehem) 146
Codes Iuris Canonici
  can. 3..................................... 60
  can. 213................................. 61
  can. 285................................. *77*
  can. 285 § 1........................... 61
  can. 285 § 3........................... 71
  can. 287 § 1........................... 61
  can. 289........................... 61, *77*
  can. 517 § 2........................... 64
  can. 556............................... 141
  can. 562............................... *141*
  can. 564................................. *64*
  can. 566................................. 64
  can. 569........................... 60, 62
  can. 672................................. *77*
Codes Iuris Canonici /1917
  can. 72................................... *60*
  can. 121........................... 59, *77*
  can. 123................................. *60*
  can. 141 § 1........................... *60*

CIC/1917 (continued)
can. 141 § 2 .... *60*
can. 188 No. 6 .... *60*
can. 451 § 3 59
can. 614 .... *77*
can. 680 .... *77*
can. 987 No. 5 .... *60*
can. 2334 No. 1 .... *59*
civilian ministry 201
civilian character .. 151, 155, 201
in times of war 77, 131
protection 130
protection by human rights ... 155
protection like military chaplaincy 155
civilian-military-cooperation 88
clergy
as instigators of conflicts 194, 203
as mediators in conflict .. 43, 132
carrying weapons 61
civil war and internal disturbances 60, 197
formation in POW camps 111
immunity from warfare ... 25, 26, 29, 32, 130, 195, 198
impartiality in warfare 57, 197
military service 57, 61, 75
non-combatants 29, 33
religious spirituality 83
returning from war 60
warfare prohibition 21, 24, 26, 198
Cold War 66
Colombia 132, 143
Concordat with Italy (1929)
Art. 24 45
conflict prevention 55
Congregation for the Bishops 63, 69
Conscription Act
§ 11 .... 75, 77
§ 12 (2) 77
Conscription Act (continued)
§ 48 [2] Nr. 4 .... *77*
Conventional Weapons Convention 145
Council
Lateran II 25, 27
Lateran III 28
Lateran IV 23
Vatican II .49, 52, 53, 58, 61, 62, 168, 199
cultural heritage 139, 201
and spiritual heritage 142
of very great importance 140
DEFREGGER, MATTHIAS 57
development of IHL 52, 54, 119, 199
distinctive emblem 35, 99, 125
abuse 181
display 129
marking chaplains' vehicles . 102
of civil defense organization 124
of HC 140
on headgear and clothing 125
DUNANT, HENRY 34
early Christianity 19, 20
era of discoveries 28
European Union 74
Evangelical Church in Germany 68, 160
Federal Administrative Court 75, 76
Federal Civil Servants Act
§ 4 .... *71*
Federal Constitutional Court 76
feud 26
formation of the conscience. 52, 53, 54, 131
Framework Act on Civil Servantship
§ 2 71
freedom of religion 201
and armed forces 199
and military chaplaincy 196

freedom of religion (continued)
basis for spiritual assistance ..92, 152
in the armed forces ...59, 67, 152
negative 172, 173
protection by the state 58, 59, 176
GC I
Art. 4 ....*92*, *117*
Art. 6 ....*92*, *98*
Art. 7 ....*92*, *117*
Art. 8 ....*116*
Art. 9 ....*92*, *116*
Art. 10 ....*116*
Art. 11 (2)............................*117*
Art. 13 ....96, 97, 101, 153
Art. 13 (4)............................157
Art. 13 (6)............................153
Art. 15 ....92, *137*
Art. 15 (3).......................98, *152*
Art. 17 (1)..............................*99*
Art. 18 131
Art. 18 (4)..............................98
Art. 21 ....*181*
Art. 22 ....168, 169
Art. 22 (5)............................*168*
Art. 24 ......94, 96, *103*, 157, 167
Art. 24 (1)..............................*93*
Art. 27 ....*107*
Art. 28 ....103, *104*, 107
Art. 28 (2)....................*106*, 109
Art. 28 (5)............................*112*
Art. 29 ....*166*
Art. 30 107
Art. 31 ....*107*
Art. 32 107
Art. 38 99
Art. 40 ....99, *102*
Art. 46 ....*117*
Art. 47 ....*118*
GC II
Art. 5.................................. *117*
Art. 7.................................. *117*
Art. 11 (2).......................... *117*
Art. 13..................... 95, 96, 153
Art. 20.................................. *99*
Art. 22................................ *116*
Art. 24................................ *116*
Art. 35................................ 169
Art. 36.......................... *93*, 115
Art. 37.............95, 96, 116, 153
Art. 37 (3).......................... *116*
Art. 40 (2).......................... *100*
Art. 40 (3).......................... *101*
Art. 42.......................... 99, *102*
Art. 47................................ *117*
Art. 48................................ *118*
GC III
Art. 4 c............................... *108*
Art. 5 (2)............................ 104
Art. 16................................ 172
Art. 27................................ 135
Art. 32................................ *166*
Art. 33....*93*, *104*, *105*, 108, 109, 113, 122
Art. 34..........*105*, 112, 113, *117*
Art. 34 (2).......................... 136
Art. 35.......................... *93*, 109
Art. 36.....97, 110, 111, 157, 168
Art. 37........................ 111, 112
Art. 38 (1).......................... 172
Art. 49................................ *108*
Art. 62 (2).................. 109, *112*
Art. 71................................ 110
Art. 72................................ *114*
Art. 79................................ 111
Art. 108 (3)........................ *115*
Art. 118 (1)........................ *105*
Art. 120 (4)........................ *115*
Art. 125.............................. *114*
Art. 127.............................. *118*

GC IV
Art. 4 .... *135*
Art. 17 .... 98, *135*, *137*, *152*
Art. 20 .... *137*
Art. 23 .... *103*, *136*
Art. 24 .... *135*
Art. 27 .... *117*, 135, 172, 173
Art. 38 (3)............................. *135*
Art. 38 No. 3............................ *94*
Art. 45 (4)............................. *136*
Art. 50 (3)............................. *135*
Art. 56 .... *136*
Art. 56 (3)............................. *172*
Art. 58 .... 123, *135*, 151
Art. 58 (1)........................ *94*, *136*
Art. 58 (2)............................. *136*
Art. 68 181
Art. 86 .... *136*
Art. 93 .... *135*, *136*, *138*
Art. 93 (2)............................. *137*
Art. 107 .... *138*
Art. 130 (1)........................... *136*
Art. 142 .... *136*
Art. 144 .... *118*
GCs
common Art. 3 ...... *91*, 126, 127, 128, 183, 185, 186, 187, 200
preamble................................ 90
German Bishops' Conference..... 49, 53, 74, 163
goals of IHL.......................... 17, 55
Greek temples and priests 19
GROTIUS, HUGO 16, 32
Gulf War
II 78, 114
III 50, 79, 132
Hague Convention III (1899)
Art. VII.................................. 37
Hague Convention IX (1907)
Art. 5 139
Hague Convention X (1907)
Art. X 37
Hague Covention XI (1907)
Art. 4...................................... 38
Hague Regulations...................... 38
Art. 3...................................... 39
Art. 17.................................... *39*
Art. 27.................................... 139
Art. 46.................................... *39*
Art. 56.................................... *39*
HC
Art. 1 a.................................. *139*
Art. 4 (1)............................... *140*
Art. 4 (2)............................... *140*
Art. 8..................................... *140*
Art. 11 (2).............................. *140*
Art. 17................................... *140*
Art. 17 (2).............................. *142*
Art. 20................................... *142*
Art. 24................................... 142
hedging of war............... 31, 32, 47
Holy See 42, 108, 114, 148, 199
and the 1864 diplomatic conferenece 42
and the 1949 diplomatic conference......45, 46, 90, 100
and the diplomatic conference 1974-1977................ 46, 120
and the Hague Conferences ... 43
financial contributions to ICRC 47
pledge with ratification of PAs 55
holy war idea 23, 30
hospital ships 115, 126, 169, 200
human dignity.....36, 51, 52, 54, 55, 58, 90, 127, 187, 196, 201, 204
and military chaplaincy.. 59, 118
outrages upon.............. 126, 131
human rights...35, 52, 90, 127, 155, 200
and humanitarian law.... 54, 128, 148, 152, 202

humane treatment. 53, 54, 126, 127, 128, 185, 187, 200
ICRC 35, 44, 45, 46, 47, 52, 100, 107, 116, 119, 165, 188
identity card ... 40, 41, 99, 100, 125, 157, 200
  use in Germany 102
Imperial Constitution
  Art. 61 66
International Covenant on Civil and Political Rights
  Art. 2 152
  Art. 4 (2)................................ *127*
  Art. 18 127
  Art. 19 127
International Criminal Court48, 118
Iraq 132, 144
Jehovah's witnesses 76
Jewish priests 19
just international order 49, 55
just war idea 21, 26, 31, 47
levée en masse..... 96, 116, 129, 153
  chaplaincy attached to the 153
Lieber-Code
  Art. 53 34
medical personnel 33, 91, 101, 102, 106, 108, 109, 116, 120, 124, 150, 164, 167, 181, 200
  auxiliary................................ 166
  use of arms 168, 202
Military Chaplaincy Act.............. 68
  Art. 2 .... *71*
Military Chaplaincy Agreement. 68, 160, 161
  Art. 2 (1)................................. 70
  Art. 2 (2)............................... *161*
  Art. 9 .... *174*
  Art. 14 .... *72*
  Art. 19 .... *71*
  Art. 23 .... *71*
  Art. 27 .... *73*
military chaplaincy in Germany 18, 41, 199
  and armed conflict 80, 199
  Bavarian model 66, 157
  church among soldiers 69
  church and state relations....... 73
  civil servant status..71, 159, 161, 164, 167, 202
  cooperation with military73, 157
  Defense Commissioner 74
  deployment abroad.. 78, 80, 160, 199
  discussions in the 1990s. 74, 160
  disintegrated and civilian status 67, 74, 84, 158, 167, 174
  divine services 81
  ecumenism 81, 88
  Lebenskundlicher Unterricht 73, 163
  military vicar general 69, 72
  national authorization to handle arms......................... 170, 202
  non-Christian chaplaincy 178
  parochial helpers...162, 165, 202
  part-time chaplains....... 167, 202
  pastoral assistants..162, 163, 202
  protective gear 72
  Prussian model........................ 65
  religious teams 84
  unusual model........ 74, 156, 202
military ordinariate 58, 62
  ecclesiological nature....... 60, 62
military ordinary
  in Germany 70
  jurisdiction 63, 69
military personnel...58, 61, 63, 151, 152, 154, 174
  without religious affiliation .. 82, 85, 171, 174
Military Service Act
  § 36 67

ministers of religion .. 123, 134, 201
distinction to religious personnel . 130, 154, 157, 168, 194, 202
during occupation 136
employed in hospitals 137
engaged in the protection of cultural property 141, 201
improved protection 150
in captivity 110, 137
in the medical corps........ 77, 111
substitute 111, 138
Ministry of Defense 67, 72, 80, 102, 160, 163, 164, 170
modern state 26, 30, 32, 47
NATO 67, 75
out of area missions 78
Netherlands
humanistic councilors........... 176
non-international armed conflict 126, 127, 128, 129, 132, 152, 153, 200, 201
Operation Enduring Freedom 79, 80
Operation Iraqi Liberty *see Gulf War, III*
PA I
Art. 1 (4)............................. *151*
Art. 8 .... *102*
Art. 8 d 121, 123, 124, *167*
Art. 8 d iii *107*
Art. 8 k *122*
Art. 9 .... *91*
Art. 9 (1)............................. *152*
Art. 15 (5)............ 123, 124, 126
Art. 16 No. 1........................ *150*
Art. 18 125
Art. 18 (1)........................... 124
Art. 20 .... *117*
Art. 22 (1) c *126*
Art. 23 (5)........................... *126*
Art. 38 .... *181*
Art. 43 (2).................... *121*, *156*
Art. 48 151
PA I (continued)
Art. 51 (2) *151*
Art. 52 145
Art. 52 (3) *146*
Art. 53 .... 142, 144, 145
Art. 61 f *124*
Art. 64 124
Art. 69 No. 1 .... *103*, *136*
Art. 75 .... *91*, 123
Art. 75 (1) *152*
Art. 78 No. 2 .... *135*
Art. 83 (1) *118*
Art. 85 (2) *117*
Art. 85 (3) f......................... *181*
Art. 85 No. 4 d 145
PA II
Art. 1 .... *151*
Art. 2 .... *91*
Art. 2 (1) *152*
Art. 4 (1) *128*, 172
Art. 4 (3) a *128*
Art. 5 No. 1 d *128*
Art. 9 No. 1 .... *129*
Art. 10 .... *150*
Art. 12 .... *129*
Art. 19 .... *118*
Art. 24 142
PAs
legal nature 120
reception 151, 200
scope of application 151
penitentials................................ 20
place of worship 19, 53, 139, 201
and the ICC 145
as medical installation.......... 144
as spiritual heritage 142
as traditional refuge 143, 184
civilian nature 145
military necessity .. 139, 140, 146
personnel engaged in the protection 140

Pontifical Statutes 68
Art. 2 70
Art. 3 ....*69*
Art. 6 ....*69*, *72*
Art. 7 ....*69*
Art. 10 ....*69*
Art. 13 ....*71*
Art. 14 ....*72*
Art. 15 ....*71*
Art. 16 ....*71*
Art. 17 ....*70*
Art. 18 ....*161*
Art. 20 ....*163*
Art. 23 ....*69*
Art. 27 ....*69*
Art. 32 ....*63*
principle of discrimination ... 33, 50, 150, 198
prisoners of war...............32, 38, 44
chaplains.................................34
religious activities 112
responsability of the Detaining Power.......................105, 112
privilegium immunitatis 59, 75, 199
in 1983 code 61
prohibition to engage in warfare *see clergy, warfare prohibition*
Protecting Power.......................116
public international law.. 16, 17, 18, 19, 31, 32, 33, 35, 49, 50, 117, 152, 171, 183, 198
Red Cross Movement... 35, 44, 100, 115, 199
Red Cross Red Crescent medical personnel 196
Red Cross Societies.......44, 45, 115
Reformation 30
Reichskonkordat 66, 68, 77
Art. 6 75
Art. 27 ....68, 71
relief organizations........46, 89, 114
religion
and conflict resolution . 130, 201
and secular philosophy 173
hierarchical structure 176
refuge in times of war .. 132, 183
support for IHL................... 120
religious burial........... 99, 115, 136
religious conflicts 126
religious education............ 128, 135
religious personnel.................... 130
abstention from hostile acts 181, 195
attachment......95, 121, 122, 129, 153, 158, 164, 200
auxiliary...37, 92, 101, 165, 197, 202
civil defense organization ... 123, 124
civilian . 123, 124, 125, 153, 158, 165
deacons 21, 64, 162
definition..............120, 129, 167
desertion.............................. 108
dissemination of IHL knowledge 118
exclusivity..92, 95, 98, 121, 122, 158, 167, 200, 202
facilities in POW camps 106, 108, 110, 200
from a neutral country 107
IHL violators................ 183, 203
in captivity ...36, 37, 40, 41, 103, 116, 200
intelligence use 86, 181, 188, 197
medical assistance.................. 97
no IHL dictate of legal form 158, 165, 202
non-combatant status 33, 34, 57, 110, 122, 156, 169, 170, 181, 187, 197
non-religious chaplains 176

religious personnel (continued)
personal privileges.....37, 85, 95, 129, 157
protected and respected...36, 39, 94, 115, 116, 119, 123, 128, 137, 180, 199, 200
remaining in retention..........109
reprisals...............................117
right to POW ministry..109, 114
stability........................105, 109
targeted 16, 26, 40, 94, 132, 133, 155, 181, 198, 201
term..92, 98, 115, 121, 123, 200
transportation.......................102
use of arms..................168, 202
renunciation of conventional rights
.....................................109, 117
repatriation of chaplains............*see religious personnel, in captivity*
respect for convictions and religious practices..39, 117, 126, 128, 135, 145, 172, 201
return of captured chaplains.......*see religious personnel, in captivity*
Roman priests.......................19, 20
Roman question....................43, 45
Rome Statute of the ICC
Art. 8 b xxiv........................117
Art. 8 e iv.............................*145*
RUKUNDO, EMMANUEL............183
SARGENT, MARK......................182
Scientology Church....................76
SFOR mission (Bosnia)......88, 173
societal pluralism.......................75
Soldatengesetz *see Military Service Act*
spiritual assistance....36, 42, 58, 67, 82, 93, 95, 129, 187
and chaplaincy......................130
and freedom of conscience....92, 176, 203
spiritual assistance (continued)
and freedom of conviction.. 171, 172, 175
and freedom of conviction... 177
as presence of chaplains.. 81, 82, 88, 174, 186, 196
by civilians.......................... 132
by world religions............... 120
cultural context........... 103, 144
for third persons............ 87, 168
from religious organizations 114
integrated approach..... 151, 154, 201
material help.......................... 88
materials...................... 103, 136
ministry and reception........... 92
needs of atheists....172, 174, 202
post-trauma counseling......... 83
privileged communications.. 187
study group........................... 89
term...................................... 94
to enemy armed forces.......... 98
to protected persons............ 134
Switzerland.....35, 42, 99, 100, 118, 119
Theology........17, 18, 22, 30, 31, 32
transcendent roots of IHL.......... 54
Treuga Dei......................... 27, 198
Turku Declaration.................... 129
U.S. Uniform Code of Military Justice
Art. 32 hearing.................... 190
U.S.A.. 36
armlet in U.S. Navy............ *102*
auxiliary religious personnel 166
chaplaincy after 9/11.... 155, 197
detention of "illegal combatants"
.... 185, 203
joint services of POW and military personnel.......... 114
POW-retained chaplains ratio
.... 104

U.S.A. (continued)
Senate Intelligence Committee 86
Senate Judiciary Committee . 192
unarmed chaplains *170*
use of distinctive emblem on chaplains' vehicles 103
witches as endorsement agency 122
UN-Charter
Art. 51 .... *48*, 79
chapter VII 48, 183
United Nations 47
General Assembly 149
Commission on Human Rights 148
Convention on the Safety of UN and associated Personnel ... 89
International Criminal Tribunal for Rwanda 183
Middle East Peace 149
Security Council 149, 183
UN Forces 119
UNHCHR 143, 146
Universal Declaration of Human Rights
Art. 18 .... 127, 152
Art. 19 127
Art. 29 .... *127*
UNOSOM II (Somalia) 86, 182
Vaticanum II *see Council, Vatican II*
violations of IHL . 53, 117, 149, 181
volunteer chaplains 97
warfare against infidels 23
warfare at sea 31, 37
landing 116
ministry to militias 96
religious missions 38
weapons of mass destruction 44, 47, 49, 55, 154, 202, 203
World War 47
I 40, 44, 60, 66, 194
II 41, 57, 66, 89, 110, 123, 195
Yugoslavia 131
Zuordnung auf Zusammenarbeit .... *see military chaplaincy in Germany, cooperation with military*

Adnotationes in Ius Canonicum

Herausgegeben von Elmar Güthoff und Karl-Heinz Selge

Band 1 Anton Morhard: Die gerichtliche Berufung im kanonischen Recht. Eine Analyse des klassischen remedium iuris. 1995.

Band 2 Elmar Güthoff (Hrsg.): Der Schutz des geistigen Eigentums in den Schriften von Winfried Schulz. Festgabe für Theodor Schmitz zur Vollendung des 80. Lebensjahres. 1997.

Band 3 Richard Puza/Andreas Weiß (Hrsg.): Iustitia in caritate. Festgabe für Ernst Rößler zum 25jährigen Dienstjubiläum als Offizial der Diözese Rottenburg-Stuttgart. 1997.

Band 4 Ernst Freiherr von Castell: Alkoholismus in der Rechtsprechung der Rota Romana. 1997.

Band 5 Burghard Pimmer-Jüsten: Facultas vel licentia imponendi tributa sacerdotibus. Partikularrechtliche Untersuchung zu den diözesanen "Pflichtabgaben" der Kleriker. 1997.

Band 6 Jürgen Olschewski: Das Recht auf Sakramentenempfang. Zur Entwicklung eines Fundamentalrechtes der Gläubigen vom Konzil von Trient bis zur Gegenwart. 1998.

Band 7 Martin Grichting: Die Umschreibung der Diözesen. Die Kriterien des II. Vatikanischen Konzils für die kirchliche Zirkumskriptionspraxis. 1998.

Band 8 Cesare Mirabelli/Giorgio Feliciani/Carl Gerold Fürst/Helmuth Pree (Hrsg.): Winfried Schulz in memoriam. Schriften aus Kanonistik und Staatskirchenrecht. 1999.

Band 9 Christoph Kühn: Die Rechtsbeziehungen des Heiligen Stuhls zum Europarat. 1999.

Band 10 Peter Stockmann: Außerordentliche Gemeindeleitung. Historischer Befund – Dogmatische Grundlegung – Kirchenrechtliche Analyse – Offene Positionen. 1999.

Band 11 Jürgen Cleve: Inkompatibilität und Kumulationsverbot. Eine Untersuchung zu c. 152 CIC/1983. 1999.

Band 12 Karl-Heinz Selge: Ehe als Lebensbund. Die Unauflöslichkeit der Ehe als Herausforderung für den Dialog zwischen katholischer und evangelisch-lutherischer Theologie. 1999.

Band 13 Elmar Güthoff / Karl-Heinz Selge (Hrsg.): Der Staat der Vatikanstadt, der Heilige Stuhl und die Römische Kurie in den Schriften von Winfried Schulz. Città del Vaticano, Santa Sede e Curia Romana negli Scritti di Winfried Schulz. Franz X. Walter zur Vollendung des 70. Lebensjahres. 1999.

Band 14 Hermann Kahler: Absentia consensus. Der fehlende Mindestwille zur Ehe als Ehenichtigkeitsgrund. 1999.

Band 15 Nikolaus Schöch: Die kirchenrechtliche Interpretation der Grundprinzipien der christlichen Anthropologie als Voraussetzung für die eheprozessrechtliche Beurteilung der psychischen Ehekonsensunfähigkeit. Eine kanonistische Studie unter besonderer Berücksichtigung der päpstlichen Allokutionen und der Judikatur der Römischen Rota. 1999.

Band 16 Michael Landau: Amtsenthebung und Versetzung von Pfarrern. Eine Untersuchung des geltenden Rechts unter besonderer Berücksichtigung der Rechtsprechung der Zweiten Sektion des Höchsten Gerichts der Apostolischen Signatur. 1999.

Band 17 Paul Weibel: Das Selbstbestimmungsrecht der römisch-katholischen Kirche. Eine staatskirchenrechtliche Studie am Beispiel des Kantons Schwyz. 2003.

Band 18 Stefan Korta: Der katholische Kirchenvertrag Sachsen. 2001.

Band 19 Jürgen Wätjer: Das katholische Domkapitel zu Hamburg von den Anfängen bis zur Reformation und seine Wiedererrichtung 1996. Eine kanonistische Untersuchung. 2001.

Band 20 Bernd Matecki: Der Traktat *In primis hominibus*. Eine theologie- und kirchenrechtsgeschichtliche Untersuchung zu einem Ehetext der Schule von Laon aus dem 12. Jahrhundert. Anhang: Edition des Traktates *In primis hominibus*. 2001.

Band 21 Stefan Gatzhammer: Der Souveränitätsanspruch des Apostolischen Stuhles in päpstlichen Lehraussagen und in der Kanonistik von 1846 bis 1978. 2001.

Band 22 Andreas Franitza: Das Domkapitel zu Hildesheim in der Zeit zwischen Preußenkonkordat (1929) und Niedersachsenkonkordat (1965) und seine Statuten von 1984. 2001.

Band 23 Péter Erdö: Die Quellen des Kirchenrechts. Eine geschichtliche Einführung. 2002.

Band 24 Rüdiger Althaus / Rosel Oehmen-Vieregge / Jürgen Olschewski (Hrsg.): Aktuelle Beiträge zum Kirchenrecht. Festgabe für Heinrich J. F. Reinhardt zum 60. Geburtstag. 2002.

Band 25 Hartmut Zapp / Andreas Weiß / Stefan Korta (Hrsg.): Ius Canonicum in Oriente et Occidente. Festschrift für Carl Gerold Fürst zum 70. Geburtstag. 2003.

Band 26 Johnson Michael Kallidukil: The Canonical Significance of the Synod of Bishops of 1994 on Consecrated Life. From the *Lineamenta* to the *Vita consecrata*. 2003.

Band 27 Hubert Schiepek: Der Sonntag und kirchlich gebotene Feiertage nach kirchlichem und weltlichem Recht. Eine rechtshistorische Untersuchung. 2003.

Band 28 Andreas Weiß / Stefan Ihli (Hrsg.): Flexibilitas Iuris Canonici. Festschrift für Richard Puza zum 60. Geburtstag. 2003.

Band 29 Benita von Beyme: Die Baulast für das Freiburger Münster. 2003.

Band 30 Nikolaus Schöch: Festlegung, Änderung und Konformität von Klagegründen im kanonischen Eheprozess. 2003.

Band 31 Andreas Weiß / Stefan Ihli (Hrsg.): Kulturgutschutz und Kirche, Bibel und Kirchenrecht. Symposion und Festakt anlässlich des 60. Geburtstags von Professor Dr. Richard Puza. 2004.

Band 32 Stefan Lunze: The Protection of Religious Personnel in Armed Conflict. 2004.

www.peterlang.de

www.ingramcontent.com/pod-product-compliance
Ingram Content Group UK Ltd.
Pitfield, Milton Keynes, MK11 3LW, UK
UKHW021842100926
8556IPUK00019B/1005

9 783631 522721